Go-betweens and the Colonization of Brazil

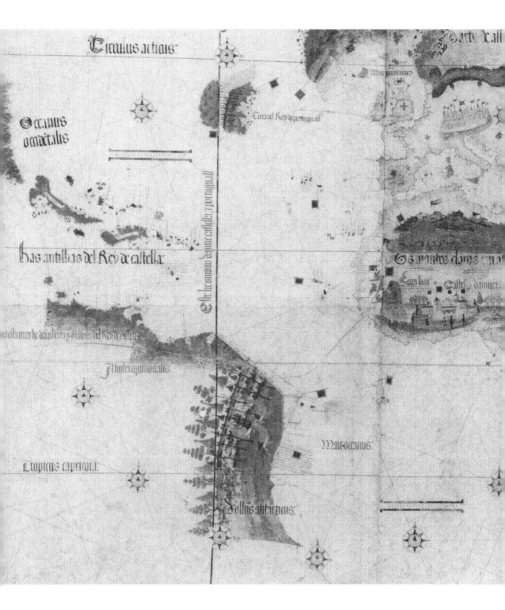

UNIVERSITY OF TEXAS PRESS   AUSTIN

ALIDA C. METCALF

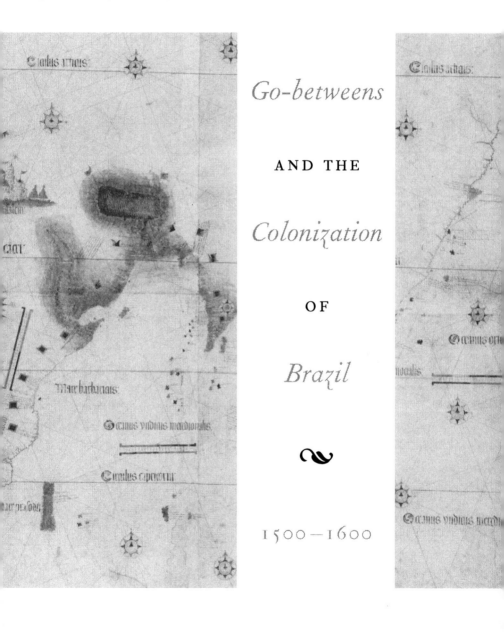

Go-betweens

AND THE

Colonization

OF

Brazil

෪

1500 — 1600

Requests for permission to reproduce
material from this work should be sent to:

Permissions

University of Texas Press

P.O. Box 7819

Austin, TX 78713-7819

www.utexas.edu/utpress/about/bpermission.html

♾ The paper used in this book meets
the minimum requirements of
ANSI/NISO Z39.48-1992 (R1997)
(Permanence of Paper).

Library of Congress Cataloging-in-Publication Data
Metcalf, Alida C., 1954 –
    Go-betweens and the colonization of Brazil, 1500 – 1600 / Alida C. Metcalf. — 1st ed.
        p.   cm.
    Includes bibliographical references and index.
    ISBN 978-0-292-71276-8
    1. Brazil—Colonization.   2. Brazil—History—16th century.   3. Indians of South
America—Brazil—First contact with Europeans.   4. Conquerors—Portugal—History—
16th century.   5. Conquerors—Brazil—History—16th century.   I. Title.
F2526.M48   2005
981'.032 — dc22
                                                                                    2005020020

For Daniel, Matthew, and Benjamin Rigney

Contents

A Note on Spelling and Citation

MANY OF THE sources on which this book is based are written in archaic Portuguese. Following the custom adopted by Brazilian historians, I have modernized the spelling of most places, names, and words in the text, preserving the original Portuguese only in the titles of publications. I have also modernized the few English, French, and Spanish quotations in the text. The sources for direct quotations, information, and the work of scholars generally appear in combined endnotes at the end of each paragraph. When possible, for the convenience of interested readers, published documents are cited rather than the originals in archives.

Acknowledgments

THIS BOOK BEGAN in the archives of the Portuguese Inquisition when I read for the first time the confession of a half-Portuguese, half-Indian man who made his living moving back and forth between the Indian and Portuguese worlds of sixteenth-century Brazil. Preserved within the formulaic language used by the Lisbon Inquisition lay the vivid details of a life so compelling and so remote that it seemed I was reading fiction. This story reminded me of a novel I had once read, *The Go-Between*, which begins with the unforgettable statement: "The past is a foreign country, they do things differently there." Novelist L. P. Hartley then employs his main character, a go-between, to re-create a lost time for his readers. As I thought about the life revealed in the confession, I began to see that go-betweens held keys to understanding certain historical processes, such as the formation of colonial societies. In this book I use go-betweens as a lens through which the sixteenth-century Portuguese colonization of Brazil can be understood.

I am most grateful to many colleagues and friends who encouraged me in my initial ventures into a new field; without their support I would never have been able to write this book. Four colloquia on colonial Brazilian history, hosted by Professor Maria Beatriz Nizza da Silva in Lisbon, were crucial to the early years of my research. To Maria Beatriz, and to all my colloquia colleagues, I am more grateful than I can fully express. Leila Agranti, Ângela Domingues, Márcia Graf, Richard Graham, Donald Higgs, Mary Karasch, Sandra Lauderdale Graham, Laura de Mello e Sousa, Lúcia Maria Bastos P. Neves, Guilherme Pereira das Neves, Donald Ramos, John Russell-Wood, Barbara Sommer,

James Wadsworth, and many others were kind enough to listen to my papers and to suggest directions for this work.

In addition to the Lisbon colloquia, I am grateful to many colleagues in Latin American and Brazilian history who organized sessions at professional meetings that provided me with a forum to develop the ideas expressed in this book. Among these, I especially thank Eni de Mesquita Samara, Laura Graham, Mary Karasch, Barbara Sommer, Hal Langfur, Judy Bieber, Barbara Ganson, John Russell-Wood, and John Monteiro. Tom McCoog, S.J., encouraged my research into the sixteenth-century Jesuits. My research into the Santidade de Jaguaripe religious movement appeared as part of an AHR Forum on the Millennium in the *American Historical Review* in 1999; I am most grateful to the anonymous reviewers for their comments.

Very early in my research Robert Rowland allowed me to consult the unpublished Gulbenkian Inquisition Database (1987) of the sixteenth-century trials of the Lisbon Inquisition, which gave this project life. Ronaldo Vainfas has also been a most generous colleague who has helped me to understand the Santidade de Jaguaripe millenarian movement. Sandra Lauderdale and Richard Graham copied a crucial letter for me from the Biblioteca Nacional in Rio de Janeiro when it was impossible for me to travel there. Donald Higgs and Ernst Pijning obtained for me a microfilm copy of the trial of Fernão Cabral de Taíde from the Arquivo Nacional da Torre do Tombo in Lisbon. Stuart Schwartz steered me to the Monumenta Brasiliae collection of Jesuit letters early in my research and invited me to present a preliminary version of my go-between typology at a conference in memory of Charles Boxer at Yale University. On a memorable afternoon, Mary Ann Mahoney took me to the sixteenth-century church of Santana in Ilhéus, which vividly re-created for me the distant world I was so intensely studying.

At Trinity University I am fortunate to have the wisdom of extraordinary colleagues in many fields who have given me insights, directions, and ideas to explore. At a faculty research dinner hosted by Francisco García Treto in 1997, I benefited enormously from comments by Frank García, Gary Kates, Pablo Martínez, Meredith McGuire, Richard Reed, Linda Salvucci, Sussan Siavoshi, Carolyn Valone, and Colin Wells. At a second dinner, hosted by Sarah Burke in 2002, Sussan Siavoshi, Larry Kimmel, Arturo Madrid, John Martin, and Richard Reed again provided many insights that helped me to clarify my ideas. John Martin suggested important texts that have informed my work, and Joan Burton's enthusiastic comments on go-betweens in literature were exhilarating.

I owe a special debt to Colin Wells, to whom I turned for help with Latin texts, and whose comprehensive knowledge of the Mediterranean world I frequently challenged with obscure but important questions. Eve Duffy encouraged me to think more systematically about go-betweens and empire, and my colleague at St. Mary's University, Antonia Castañeda, helped me to understand the complex roles played by those who translate.

Students, particularly at Trinity University, have also helped me work through the ideas that underlie this book. I taught two first-year seminars to Trinity students on the topic of go-betweens in literature; these discussions were a fascinating foray into characters who played roles as cultural brokers, intermediaries, and translators. I thank my colleague Thomas Sebastian for suggesting novels that feature go-betweens, many of which I read with my students. Over the past year, students in my classes have read chapters of the book, and their comments have been very helpful. Graduate students at the University of Texas at Austin invited me to present a preliminary version of this book in the fall of 2001; their comments in particular helped me to conceptualize the fifth chapter, in which I explore go-betweens and biology.

Research trips funded by the Faculty Development Committee and by the Joullian Fund at Trinity University allowed me to work in archives in Lisbon, Rome, Vatican City, Rio de Janeiro, and Salvador, as well as in major libraries in the United States. Thomas Cohen welcomed me to the Oliveira Lima Library in Washington, D.C.; the John Carter Brown Library in Providence provided the most exquisite collection of sixteenth-century editions of crucial texts that I have ever had the pleasure to read. The Newberry Library in Chicago provided a jump start for my discussion of mapmaking in the first chapter. I thank all the libraries and museums that granted me permission to reproduce the images that appear throughout the book.

This book took its final shape during an academic leave from Trinity University in 2001–2002, funded by Trinity's Faculty Leave Program and the National Endowment for the Humanities. This full year away from teaching allowed me to conceptualize this book in its present form. The chair of the History Department at Trinity University, John Martin, as well as former chairs Char Miller, Gary Kates, Allan Kownslar, and Terry Smart, facilitated many requests for travel and research expenses, and the Associate Vice President for Academic Affairs, Fred Loxsom, generously agreed to underwrite the permissions and photography for the illustrations. David Stinchcomb advised me as I drew the maps. The librarians at Trinity, especially Craig Likeness, Carl Hanson, Chris

Nolan, Mary Cervantes Clark, and Maria McWilliams, all enriched this book in countless ways. In the History Department, I thank Eunice Herrington for her assistance with travel, reimbursements, and scanning, and Rosa Salinas for photocopying, entering data, and keeping track of interlibrary loans. A very talented Trinity student, Elizabeth Farfán, provided outstanding assistance in three languages in proofreading the bibliography and footnotes.

Theresa May has been a delight to work with at the University of Texas Press; I thank also Lynne Chapman, Nancy Bryan, Allison Faust, and especially Nancy Warrington for the care they have taken with the manuscript. I am especially grateful to my two anonymous outside readers, whose careful and painstaking reads of the first draft of this book allowed me to correct errors and to develop my ideas more fully.

Sometime in the writing of this book, I realized that my fascination with go-betweens emerges from my own childhood, when, as the daughter of a naval officer, I was uprooted and moved every two to three years. In particular, our life in Lima, Peru, in the late 1960s sparked my interest in Latin America. I thank my mother for making those years abroad rich with cultural experiences. I thank my father for introducing me to the world of sailing, the sea, and navigation. My sister and brothers shared with me the complexities of living in and moving between cultures. My sister Mary Clare's experience in the Ivory Coast as a Peace Corps Volunteer, and my two trips to visit her there, sparked my long-standing interest in West Africa.

It is a special pleasure to thank Daniel Rigney, who provided many sociological insights to this dyed-in-the-wool historian. It is to Dan, my companion in marriage, and to our two sons, Matthew and Benjamin, that this book is affectionately dedicated.

Go-betweens and the Colonization of Brazil

1. Go-betweens

... her master asked her if she would be the third party ...

A question posed to an Aimoré woman, 1609

In the first years of the seventeenth century, the French Jesuit historian Pierre du Jarric introduces an Indian woman living in Brazil in his history of the "most memorable things" in the lands "discovered by the Portuguese." Leaving her unnamed, Jarric identifies her as a member of the Aimoré, an indigenous group greatly feared by colonists living in Salvador, Brazil's capital. Jarric explains that she no longer lived with the Aimoré but on the estate of a prominent colonist who lived outside of Salvador, where the woman had become "domesticated" in the ways of the Portuguese and had learned their language and customs. Her master believed that she might be able to persuade the Aimoré to accept peace with the Portuguese. He sent her with Portuguese "accoutrements" (clothes), food, and "various iron tools" such as knives and hatchets, and through her native language, she convinced a group of Aimoré to accept the gifts and the peace offered by the Portuguese. Some of the Aimoré came to her master's estate on the outskirts of the sugar plantation zone that surrounded the capital, and eventually an Aimoré chief met the governor of Brazil. He agreed that his people would live on an island in the Bay of All Saints, where the Jesuits would teach them Christianity. Jarric writes that a joyous procession was held in the capital to celebrate the peace.[1]

A Jesuit report of their mission in Brazil in the first years of the seventeenth century, on which Jarric bases much of his account, reveals that the woman's master asked her "if she would be the third party" and help to bring about a peace with the Aimoré. Because of her language, her mobility, and her understanding of two opposing cultures, this woman became the go-between who made possible peaceful encounters between two previously hostile groups. Her agency had enormous and far-reaching significance. The lives of the Aimoré whom she had persuaded to accept the Portuguese overtures for peace would never be the same, and the peace that she brought opened up opportunities for many in the Portuguese colony. But she was hardly unique. During the previous century, hundreds of similar encounters had already taken place, and certain ways of interaction between the Indian and the Portuguese worlds had already taken root in Brazil. She was part of a much larger process wherein go-betweens typically were present at meetings between Indian and Portuguese peoples. Many more go-betweens would facilitate future encounters in the succeeding centuries.

It has often been assumed that the contact between Europe and America was a dyadic relationship between two very different cultural groups, Europeans and Native Americans. But in these dealings, third parties, such as the Aimoré woman, invariably were present. Certainly, conceptualizing the Portuguese and Indian worlds as a dyadic relationship is key to understanding the conflict between two very different ways of life that competed for Brazil after 1500. But go-betweens, as third parties, influenced the relationship that emerged in fundamental ways. As sociologist Georg Simmel explains, "the triad is a structure completely different from the dyad," and "[i]t is sociologically very significant that isolated elements are unified by their common relation to a phenomenon which lives outside of them." [2] The Indian woman, speaking in the Aimoré language and giving presents of European clothes, food, and tools, was such a phenomenon. Through her, a very different relationship replaced the previously violent meetings that had characterized Portuguese and Aimoré interactions for at least fifty years. As go-between, she made possible a new kind of relationship between the Portuguese and the Aimoré, whether for better or for worse.

Go-betweens influenced the power dynamics at play in the relations between the Indian and European worlds. Simmel distinguishes between the mediator, who "guides the process of coming to terms," and the arbitrator, who "ends up by taking sides." For Simmel, mediators allow the two parties to determine the outcome of their conflict, whereas when the two sides choose an arbitrator, their "will to conciliation" is "personified in the arbitrator." The arbitrator thereby gains "a special impressiveness and power over the antagonistic forces." In historical settings, go-betweens can be neutral mediators, but in fact they rarely are. As a rule, they tend to become what Simmel calls arbitrators. In an encounter, the side that possesses the loyalty, or pays for (and retains) the allegiance, of the go-between gains an important advantage. There is a further dimension of power, however. Go-betweens may exploit their positions for their own benefit. Simmel labels this position the *tertius gaudens* (the third who rejoices). The tertius gaudens is an "egoistic exploiter of the situation" who enjoys many advantages because he (or she) is indifferent to the outcome.[3]

The complexities of go-betweens have fascinated novelists, who use fiction to explore the social tensions, the psychological dramas, and the power shifts that surround them. In fiction, go-betweens are individuals of in-between social status who are mobile, able to function in very different worlds, frequently fluent in several languages, sometimes dabblers in magic, and oftentimes involved in intense, sexually charged situations. Not surprisingly, go-betweens in fiction frequently encounter tragedy. Celestina, the wily matchmaker in the Spanish novel *La Celestina*, pays the price of death for facilitating love, and Leo, the young carrier of messages in L. P. Hartley's novel *The Go-Between*, suffers an emotional breakdown. Through the character of the hard-bitten spy Leamas, John Le Carré explores the complexities of manipulation, both by and of go-betweens, in *The Spy Who Came in from the Cold*, as does African novelist Amadou Hampaté Bâ. Bâ's character Wangrin brilliantly and craftily manipulates his role as translator to outwit the French colonial administrators in the novel *The Fortunes of Wangrin*. The go-between as agent of empire also emerges in J. M. Coetzee's brooding novel *Waiting for the Barbarians*, which probes the power and the moral compass of the government official at the edge of the empire. Resistance to authority emerges in Jurek Becker's character Jakob, who creates lies to bring hope to Jews in the ghetto controlled by the Nazis in *Jakob the Liar*. In all of these novels, go-betweens inhabit an "in-between" space, which gives them mobility, information, and power, but the stakes for them are always high. Go-betweens link groups or individuals who cannot communicate with each other, but the facilitation of that communication and contact inevitably leads to death, destruction, or madness.

Nearly all of these novels are set in recognizable historical periods that were times of conflict, contact, and change. Historians, too, have been fascinated by the go-betweens they have found in sources from the past. Some go-betweens have achieved near-mythical status in national and regional histories. Pocahontas, who lived at the same time as the unnamed Aimoré woman, is credited with bringing about peace between the English colony at Jamestown and the surrounding Powhatan people. Sacagawea (also spelled Sacajawea), a Shoshone woman who lived two hundred years later, is another individual go-between whose role as interpreter and guide is celebrated because she enabled Lewis and

Clark to explore the American Northwest. In the far west of nineteenth-century Brazil, Mary Karasch describes the life of a daughter of a prominent Caiapó chief who became the "Indian heroine of [the state of] Goiás." Damiana da Cunha was baptized into Christianity, lived as a hostage in the household of the governor of Goiás to guarantee peace, and undertook multiple expeditions to the Caiapó to bring them into the Portuguese colonial world.[4]

Perhaps the most famous individual go-between is Malintzin, also known as Doña Marina or La Malinche, Hernán Cortés' interpreter and mistress during the conquest of Mexico. Doña Marina was not the first interpreter to serve Cortés or the earlier captains who had sailed along the coast of the Yucatán, nor was she the last, but she is considered to be the most important. Baptized Indians, Indians captured in battle and freed on the condition that they carry messages, and even Spaniards who had gone "native" all served as translators for Cortés. Cortés immediately took advantage of Jerónimo de Aguilar, a Spaniard who had been shipwrecked among the Maya and who spoke Spanish and Mayan, and of Malintzin, later baptized as Marina, because she spoke Mayan and Nahuatl. As Doña Marina and Aguilar became experienced translators, they transformed the actual words of Cortés, which had limited power in Mexico because only Spaniards could understand them, into words and concepts that could be understood by Mayan and Nahuatl speakers. So ubiquitous was Doña Marina that Cortés, according to the Spanish foot soldier Bernal Díaz del Castillo, actually became known throughout Mexico as "Malinche," or Marina's captain. For Díaz, who wrote his memoirs of the conquest late in his life, Doña Marina was a crucial part of the Spaniards' success. He dedicates one chapter in his enormous account to her, stating at the end of the chapter, "I have wanted to declare this because without Doña Marina going with us, we could not understand the language of New Spain and Mexico."[5]

Many visual representations of Doña Marina as interpreter are preserved in accounts of the conquest compiled from the perspective of Aztec survivors. A black-and-white line drawing of the encounter between Moctezuma Xocoyotzin, the ruler of the Aztecs, and Spanish conquistadors appears in the *Codex Florentino*, a source written by the Franciscan priest Bernardino de Sahagún. Based on the memories of Nahua informants whom Sahagún and his Indian students interviewed following the conquest of Mexico, the *Codex Florentino* emphasizes the role of Doña Marina in its drawings and in its Spanish and Nahuatl texts. This particular image shows Doña Marina standing between the Spanish and the Indian sides. She is drawn in the center, listening to the words of

Figure 1.1. Doña Marina interprets for Moctezuma and Cortés. Bernardino de Sahagún, *História general de las cosas de Nueva España Códice florentino [Codex Florentino]*. Biblioteca Medicea Laurenziana, Florence.

Moctezuma. Her feet are bare and her hands are folded across her stomach. She wears a woven *huipil* (tunic) and skirt. She is shown looking directly at Moctezuma, whose right hand is raised with the index finger pointing. Speech glyphs float from his mouth to Doña Marina. The pictograph clearly conveys that this encounter was not exclusively a dyadic relationship between the Spaniards and Moctezuma, but one facilitated by a third party, Doña Marina, through whom words passed (Fig. 1.1).[6]

Most go-betweens, however, have not become mythical figures in national histories, mainly because they have been overlooked or forgotten. When Spanish conquistador Francisco Pizarro met the Inca Atahualpa at Cajamarca, Indian translators were present. Nevertheless, this meeting in 1532 is frequently presented as a dyadic "clash of empires," and the role of the interpreter is ignored.

Jared Diamond argues, for example, that not only does the meeting between Pizarro and Atahualpa mark "a decisive moment in the greatest collision of modern history," but that "the factors that resulted in Pizarro's seizing Atahualpa were essentially the same ones that determined the outcome of many similar collisions between colonizers and native peoples elsewhere in the modern world."[7]

Yet, as historian James Lockhart notes, the Spaniards had excellent interpreters when they met Atahualpa; not only had they acquired the interpreters before they entered the Inca Empire, but their interpreters "had traversed most of the Hispanic world and had lived among Spaniards for some years of their adolescence." Pedro Pizarro describes these interpreters as Indian boys, given to or captured by Pizarro and his partner Diego de Almagro on their previous reconnoitering expedition to the north coast of Peru. Two of the Indians were then taken to Spain before they accompanied Pizarro and Almagro to Peru.[8]

A remarkable history written by Felipe Guaman Poma de Ayala [Waman Puma], an Andean Indian of the seventeenth century, includes a visual representation of the meeting between Pizarro and Atahualpa that shows the presence of the interpreter. Guaman Poma places the interpreter in an intermediate space between Atahualpa and the conquistadors Diego de Almagro (who was not actually present), Francisco Pizarro, and the Franciscan priest, Fray Vicente. Atahualpa occupies the center and dominates the privileged upper position. Also in the upper position, to his right and left, are the Inca lords. Below him are the Spaniards.[9] Almagro and Pizarro kneel, as does Fray Vicente, who holds a cross and a prayer book. To Vicente's right, Atahualpa's left, stands an interpreter with his index finger extended. Each of the conquistadors is so labeled, as is the interpreter: "Felipe *yn⁰* [*indio*, Indian] *lingua* [tongue]" (Fig. 1.2). The interpreter, Felipe, occupies an intermediate space between the Indian and the Spanish worlds.[10]

Guaman Poma's visual rendering of the encounter between Pizarro and Atahualpa has its own logic, its own interpretation of events that had taken place many years before, and its own distortions. It is not my intent to read the image as a photograph of the meeting or to argue that it reflects exactly what transpired, but simply to note that it includes the presence of a third party, the interpreter.

Unlike the highly symbolic meetings at Cajamarca or at Tenochtitlan, most contacts between Europeans and Native Americans typically took place repeatedly over long periods of time, not only in frontier zones but in the daily encounters between Indians and European colonists. Modern historians of the

Figure 1.2. An interpreter (standing on right) translates for Atahualpa (center) and Pizarro (kneeling on left) at Cajamarca. Guaman Poma, *El primer nueva corónica y buen gobierno* [1615], 386. The Royal Library, Copenhagen. Digitized version online at: http://www.kb.dk/elib/mss/poma.

Americas now recognize whole classes of intermediaries. Nancy Hagedorn, for example, identifies more than one hundred interpreters who served in the British territories north of Virginia between 1740 and 1770. These men and women were skilled translators and cultural brokers who were central to the formal diplomatic meetings between the Iroquois and British government officials. Janaína Amado and Timothy Coates emphasize the importance of the *degredado*, the penal exile, in the Portuguese Empire. Amado argues that Portugal, a small, lightly populated Christian kingdom, could only achieve its ambitious overseas objectives by obsessively collecting information through all possible means. The Portuguese Crown therefore encouraged the creation of translators and intermediaries by sending condemned prisoners to live in exile in Africa, Asia, and Brazil. In Spanish America, mestizos, who inhabited the space between the Spanish and the Indian worlds, are frequently portrayed as important intermediaries. Berta Ares Queija sees the mestizos of sixteenth-century Peru as "condemned" to live between worlds, participating in both but belonging to neither. Their mobility, their ability to conduct themselves in two languages, and their skill at translating one symbolic universe to another were unique. Daniel Richter argues that Indian war captives, who were adopted into the Five Nation Iroquois villages in the seventeenth century, shaped the reception later received by Jesuit missionaries.[11]

Go-betweens often inhabit what American historian Richard White terms a "middle ground." White defines the middle ground as "in between cultures, peoples, and in between empires and the nonstate world of villages." This middle ground, he argues, is the periphery of the world system; it is "the area between the historical foreground of European invasion and occupation and the background of Indian defeat and retreat." What is particularly compelling is White's contention that in the middle ground, "minor agents, allies, and even subjects at the periphery often guide the course of empires."[12]

Operating in a middle ground where the influence of the empire is weak, go-betweens were often used to arbitrate relations in ways that over time benefited the interests of the European rather than the Indian world. An American historian grappling with the question of how the English "won" North America reflects that "[t]o understand how the Indians lost America and the English won it, we must look past the grand events—warfare, epidemics, the frontier's advance—to examine the less celebrated but no less important meetings between peoples." This "real (and still largely untold) story," he argues, lies in interactions between Indians and colonists, a history difficult to write because "[t]hese long-forgotten encounters lie in scraps of evidence, mere snatches of conversations."[13]

In such snatches of conversation go-betweens clearly took center stage, for they were the means of communication in the middle grounds of encounters. Who became go-betweens and who was served by the go-betweens were not inconsequential factors, and they often determined the outcome of meetings, encounters, negotiations, and conversations. As American historian James

Merrell emphasizes, go-betweens were perceived as fundamental to the negotiations between colonial officials and Indians, even if historians have not always perceived their importance.[14]

The literary scholar Stephen Greenblatt opens up many of the directions taken in this book. In *Marvelous Possessions*, Greenblatt is interested in the "representational practices" that Europeans carried with them and used to describe the Americas. For Greenblatt, those who wrote about America and Native Americans for European audiences created a "flood of textual representations, along with a much smaller production of visual images," that "delivered" the New World to the Old. Greenblatt's go-betweens tend to be the writers of texts and the sculptors of images, but he also recognizes the importance of go-betweens who, through their movement, linked Europe with America. He writes that "European adventurers not only depended upon go-betweens, but were themselves go-betweens." Of particular interest to Greenblatt are the translators who were essential to many encounters between Europeans and Americans. Reflecting on Doña Marina, Greenblatt represents her as "the figure in whom all communication between the two opposed cultures was concentrated." "She was," he writes, Cortés' "principal access to language—at once his tongue and ears—and hence the key to his hope for survival and success." Greenblatt even goes so far as to characterize her as "the supreme instance of the go-between in the New World" because she was the figure through whom all communication between the Aztec and Spanish worlds passed.[15]

Building on Greenblatt's observations, it is possible to see that go-betweens play multiple roles and that it is useful to distinguish between them. If we unpack and refine Greenblatt's generic "go-between," three major types of go-betweens emerge. At the most basic level is the physical go-between. The men, women, and children who crossed the Atlantic Ocean, thereby linking not only Europe and America, but Europe and Africa, and Africa and America, were all physical go-betweens. Though Greenblatt would argue that every physical go-between carried his or her "representational practices" and was part and parcel of the "representation" of America, I believe they are most significant as biological go-betweens. Biological go-betweens carried disease, introduced European domestic animals, and transplanted American flora and fauna to Europe and Africa. European sailors, sea captains, crews, colonists, and passengers all were physical and biological go-betweens, as were the Africans who traversed the Atlantic as slaves and the Indians who traveled to Europe as slaves, free servants, and exotic people from a new world.

A second type of go-between, the transactional, is the most immediately recognizable. Transactional go-betweens were translators, negotiators, and cultural brokers. Some are famous as individuals, such as Doña Marina or Sacagawea, while others remain nameless but are part of groups that were nevertheless influential, such as the mestizos of colonial Spanish America or the penal exiles of the Portuguese world. Transactional go-betweens possessed complex and shifting loyalties that are difficult for modern historians to reconstruct. Guaman Poma, for example, served as a transactional go-between in Peru following the conquest because of his fluency in Spanish and Quechua; he worked as an interpreter and an informer for Spanish colonial officials. Some of the most interesting of the transactional go-betweens were Indian women, but most still remain invisible in the written historical record.

Europeans as well as Indians perceived the power of the transactional go-between. The visual depictions of Doña Marina and Felipe at Cajamarca appear in documents influenced by Aztec and Andean Indians, who in hindsight saw the power that interpreters had given to the European side during the conquest. Many indigenous groups sought and acquired their own transactional go-betweens. For example, in North America, Hagedorn's work reveals that Iroquois chiefs hired their own interpreters for council fire meetings with English officials, and in Mexico, Indian litigants sought their own scribes, interpreters, and lawyers to pursue their cases before the Spanish courts.[16]

The third, and most powerful, type of go-betweens were those who, to use Greenblatt's term, "represented" America and Native Americans for Europeans, or Europeans to Native Americans. Whereas Greenblatt would see all go-betweens as representational, I draw a distinction between them that is largely based on power and influence. I term representational go-betweens those who, through writings, drawings, mapmaking, and the oral tradition, shaped on a large scale how Europeans and Native Americans viewed each other. Representational go-betweens were the cartographers, letter writers, and chroniclers—most but not all of whom were European. Bernal Díaz del Castillo, who described the role of Doña Marina in his history of the conquest of Mexico, is an example of a representational go-between. He interprets the conquest of Mexico, arguing that the Spanish were justified in what they did. Similarly, the Jesuits were powerful representational go-betweens for sixteenth-century Brazil; much of our knowledge of the crucial first century of Brazilian history is filtered through their words.

Although representational go-betweens on the Indian side are far more elusive to modern historians than their counterparts on the European side, it is important to remember that they most certainly existed. One of the most compelling is Guaman Poma, whose twelve-hundred-page book with nearly four hundred illustrations intended to inform King Philip III of the situation in Peru, and in particular of the poor treatment Indians received from Spaniards. His book, *El primer nueva corónica y buen gobierno* [1615], is today invaluable because it preserves the history of Peru before, during, and after the conquest from the Andean point of view. Similarly, the *lienzos* from colonial Mexico are another kind of representation—a visual picture of landscapes, land and water rights, sacred places, and genealogies—that reflects how the indigenous peoples of Mexico perceived their changing world. Reconstructing the depictions of Europeans from the Indian side in Brazil is more difficult, but the work of anthropologists is very insightful. Anthropologist Laura Graham illustrates how Warodi, a Xavante elder in central Brazil, interpreted past encounters through dreams, and how these images were shared through expressive performances. These portrayals of the past, Graham argues, influenced modern Xavante strategies for interacting with Brazilian government officials. Similarly, fieldwork by anthropologists in modern Amazonia reveals complex renderings of *o branco* ("the whites" or "the white man"). Comparable kinds of processes undoubtedly existed in the past that historians may be able to recover from written records and the oral tradition.[17]

Among the representational go-betweens are historians who, positioning themselves between the past and the present, interpret past cultures and represent them for modern readers. I, too, am a representational go-between as I shape an understanding of sixteenth-century Brazil. Like other present-day historians, I see multiple stories in the past, and by choosing to focus on some but not all of the possible themes, groups, series of events, or sets of documents, I construct a narrative of the sixteenth century that reflects what I deem important.

The three kinds of go-betweens that constitute the conceptual framework of this study are summarized in Table 1.1.

This book weaves physical, transactional, and representational go-betweens into a chronological narrative of the first hundred years of Brazilian history. The sixteenth century brought enormous change to indigenous peoples living in what was first called by the Portuguese the Land of the Holy Cross, to the

Table 1.1. Three kinds of go-betweens

Physical/Biological	Those who create material links between worlds; carriers of plants, animals, and disease; bearers of children of mixed race
Transactional	Those who facilitate social interaction between worlds; translators, cultural brokers, negotiators
Representational	Those who write, draw maps, and represent the "other" culture through texts, words, or images; historians

landscape itself, and to the peoples from Europe and Africa who came to live there. In this formative one hundred years, a time when the colony's future was indeterminate and in flux, patterns of interactions were established that would shape Brazil for centuries to come. Yet unlike the sixteenth century in Mexican, Peruvian, or Caribbean history, the sixteenth century in Brazilian history still remains poorly understood. By rewinding the narrative of Brazilian history back to the sixteenth century, and by looking for the go-betweens and listening to their voices, the formation of Brazil comes into focus.

In the sixteenth century are rooted many of the most important themes of Brazilian history: the discovery, exploration, and mapping of the land; the history of indigenous groups; the origins of slavery; the development of commercial agriculture; the influence of the Jesuits; the formation of religious identity; the ecological destruction of the tropical forests. Each of these themes can be developed into a rich narrative spanning the entire century, but it is my intention to tell one story: how the Portuguese won Brazil through the agency of go-betweens. In telling this story, I dip into many of the thematic narratives of the sixteenth century, and in referencing them I hope to provide a synthetic picture of the sixteenth century in Brazil.

This book ends in 1600, not because the story ends there, but because by that time the Portuguese had "won" the battle for key regions along the coast of Brazil. Increasingly during the sixteenth century, the arbitration provided by go-betweens granted the advantage to the Portuguese in their struggle with the Indians over which culture would dominate. With their colonies firmly established along the coast by the end of the sixteenth century, the Portuguese colonists were then able to extend their influence to new regions, where many of the same patterns of interaction would be replicated. Just as go-betweens had been indispensable in the "winning" of coastal Brazil in the sixteenth century, so, too, would they be crucial in tilting new frontiers toward Portugal in the seventeenth and eighteenth centuries, and in fostering the emergence of modern Brazil in the nineteenth and twentieth centuries.

Paradoxically, as the power and influence of the Portuguese increased in Brazil in the sixteenth century, the kingdom of Portugal was losing its influence in Europe. The extensive Portuguese maritime empire that kings of the Portuguese House of Avis had developed systematically from the early fifteenth century began to crack in the last quarter of the sixteenth. In 1578, the death of young King Sebastião in an ill-conceived, medieval-like crusade against Muslims in North Africa plunged Portugal into a dynastic crisis. King Philip II of Spain manipulated Portugal's weakness and imposed his claim to the throne in 1580, thereby bringing to an end the dynasty of the House of Avis. Although the administration of Portugal and Brazil remained separate from that of Spain, Portugal and Brazil immediately felt the effects of the Spanish succession. Philip impressed Portugal's fine merchant fleet into the armada that he sent against Queen Elizabeth in 1588. Its destruction dealt a severe blow to Portuguese mercantile trade. Portuguese possessions in Africa, America, and India fell under increasing attack by Spain's enemies, most notably the Dutch. Appended to Spain, Portugal, the once proud leader of maritime exploration, was destroyed politically, financially, and morally.[18] Yet, despite Portugal's declining power in the sixteenth century, it increasingly "won" Brazil. How was this possible? And when during the long sixteenth century did Portugal "win" Brazil? The answers to these questions lie with the go-betweens who are the subject of this book.

Seeking to understand these go-betweens and their power, I begin this book with the premise that in the encounters of the sixteenth century, hundreds of go-betweens were present—some named, but most not. I then retell the history of the sixteenth century in order to make the roles of these go-betweens visible. By examining the three kinds of go-betweens—physical, transactional, and representational—it is possible to see how go-betweens shaped the birth and evolution of the relationship between Portugal and Brazil. The Portuguese gained significant advantage in Brazil not by controlling all of the go-betweens, but by ensuring that the majority of them arbitrated for the Portuguese side. But the world that the Portuguese won through these go-betweens was not a reproduction of Portugal, nor did the "won" colony take the form that the kings of Portugal had once imagined. By 1600, the landscape and the peoples of Brazil differed markedly from those of Portugal. And even if Portugal could claim Brazil as a colony, that did not mean that Portuguese authority reigned supreme. Go-betweens had their own interests and exercised their own power, and conflicts erupted between them, even between those go-betweens who mediated for

Figure 1.3. A go-between in sixteenth-century Brazil. Vallard Atlas, 1547. This item is reproduced by permission of The Huntington Library, San Marino, California.

the Portuguese world. The interests of go-betweens also cast long shadows over the subsequent formation of Brazil.

I have found no visual representations of go-betweens mediating encounters in Brazil that are comparable to the sketches of Doña Marina in the *Codex Florentino* or those of Felipillo in Guaman Poma's *Primer nueva corónica*. But in a sixteenth-century atlas drawn in the French style known as the Dieppe School, several scenes of encounters appear as illustrations drawn over the interior of Brazil. One detail that portrays a European man engaged in trade with Indian men and women is particularly suggestive of the go-between. The European looks out from Brazil, as if across the Atlantic Ocean. With his index finger, he points to the brazilwood logs that Indian men have assembled. By his side is a basket of trading goods. The nameless European man portrayed in this carto-graphic detail is clearly a physical go-between who had crossed the ocean and entered Brazil. Although the artist does not reveal how, it is clear that this man is in charge of the exchange between the European world and Brazil, thus playing the role of the transactional go-between. And the fact that the artist chose to use him to represent Brazil illustrates the artist's recognition of his importance in the Brazilian trade (Fig. 1.3).[19]

As we shall see, the simple words, exchanges, and interactions hinted at in this drawing carried great and far-reaching consequences. For this nameless man (who is drawn significantly larger and in more detail than the indigenous men with whom he trades) clearly serves the European side. He stands above a care-fully drawn coastline that is labeled with names familiar even to this day, and his feet intersect with the radii of the compass rose that the cartographer has drawn just offshore. This man finds himself in Brazil because of the navigational exper-tise of European mariners, and he uses his skill to acquire the riches of Brazil. Such encounters and the patterns of interaction they began had occurred before and would be repeated over and over again. As this detail suggests, and as this book shows, go-betweens were central to the colonization of Brazil.

2. *Encounter*

. . . he spoke their language and gave information on everything.

Besicken Letter, 1505

It is tempting to see a single day, 23 April 1500, when the Portuguese admiral Pedro Álvares Cabral anchored his fleet of twelve ships off the coast of Brazil, as the beginning. Because his destination was India, Cabral remained in Brazil for only ten days, yet those few days in April and May marked the official Portuguese discovery of Brazil. Every recorded event and observation, therefore, is important and worthy of the attention of historians. But on closer inspection, what stands out in the surviving accounts is the calculated and restrained behavior of the Portuguese. Not only were they not particularly surprised by the situation at hand, but they understood the need to proceed with care. With the exception of the physical descriptions of the landscape and its inhabitants, the very ordinariness of Cabral's days in Brazil emerges in the long letter written by Pero Vaz de Caminha, a nobleman in the fleet. There is little in Cabral's behavior, or in that of his captains and crew, that Caminha finds particularly remarkable. This tone is even more pronounced in two other surviving sources: an account written by an anonymous Portuguese pilot or scribe, and a letter from Mestre (Master) João, a highly educated cosmographer, astronomer, and physician. Indeed, the comportment of the Portuguese, as revealed in these accounts, unfolds as if from a script, one that had been written from the experiences of hundreds of mariners before them. Those mariners had sailed, observed, charted, and mapped the entire west coast of Africa; they had hailed ports in East Africa and India; they had traded with kings; and they had contacted many previously unknown and unfamiliar peoples. Everything Cabral did in Brazil was informed by what the Portuguese had learned from their experience in Africa. And one of the things the Portuguese well understood was the danger of an encounter without go-betweens.[1]

Go-betweens at all three levels—physical, transactional, and representational—laid the foundation for Cabral's voyage, which did not linger in Brazil but continued on to India. In the fifteenth century, go-betweens facilitated the burst of Portuguese exploration and trade in Africa. *Homens do mar* (men of the sea) became physical go-betweens who connected diverse worlds, long isolated from each other. Among the key lessons mastered by Portuguese sea captains in the African trade was the crucial importance of transactional go-betweens— the translators and intermediaries—many of whom were not Portuguese, but Africans and increasingly Afro-Portuguese. Representational go-betweens drew the maps that guided captains and merchants and that with time dramatically recast how Europeans understood the wider world.

Whether their landing in Brazil in 1500 was accidental or not, Cabral and his men certainly planned to tie this new land henceforth into the world of Portugal, India, and Africa. The men on the twelve ships were each physical go-betweens. Some collected data, such as shooting their latitude where they made landfall, which would be transferred onto the charts carried by Cabral's captains.[2] On its return to Portugal, this information became crucial to the first depictions of Brazil on charts, maps, and especially the official map kept by the Crown. Other men certainly hoped to profit in some way from the information they could pass on to potential patrons, such as merchants, when they returned to Lisbon. But the expedition did not have any transactional go-betweens suitable for Brazil. Although Cabral's armada possessed many interpreters, none was able to communicate verbally with the peoples they met in Brazil. This fact made Cabral's ten days in Brazil potentially a very dangerous time.

Stephen Greenblatt characterizes an encounter without an interpreter as "a complete blank, a brute clash of bodies in which the invaders, hopelessly outnumbered, would certainly be destroyed."[3] Such was nearly the case when Vicente Yáñez Pinzón led four ships to the northern coast of Brazil in 1500 just a few months before Cabral. Pinzón, a Spanish captain who had sailed with Columbus in 1492, found out firsthand the danger of not having translators on board. As related in one of the earliest published accounts of the sixteenth century, written by Pietro Martire d'Anghiera, Pinzón anchored along the northeastern coast of Brazil and sent twenty-five armed men ashore to reconnoiter at night. Silently observing a well-populated village, the men withdrew. But when

Pinzón sent forty armed men ashore the next morning, they soon found themselves surrounded by "big men with grim faces of cruel aspect" who did not cease
threatening the Spaniards. Later, sailing along the coast still south of the mouth of
the Amazon, Pinzón and his men met "an infinite number of naked people, who
showed with gestures and acts that they greatly desired commerce with our men,"
but when four boats of Spaniards did attempt to land, the Indians captured one
of the boats and its captain, and eight Spaniards died before the rest managed to
escape.[4] These two encounters lacked translators, and without them, Pinzón and
his men could choose either to withdraw or to fight.

Without translators, captains such as Pinzón could not always meet their
most basic needs for food and water, nor satisfy their larger desires for trade and
information. Yet, three months later, when Cabral landed farther south along
the coast of Brazil and likewise possessed no translators, the initial encounter
was certainly successful from the Portuguese point of view. That success rested
in part on the Portuguese understanding of the importance of transactional
go-betweens and their past experience in such situations.

Given the absence of translators, one might think that the success of Cabral's
landing had everything to do with chance. Indeed, according to an account written by the anonymous pilot or scribe on Cabral's expedition, there was little communication, through either language or signs, during Cabral's time in Brazil.[5]
One might easily surmise, then, that these ten days were a long pantomime in
which the Portuguese and the Tupi-speaking peoples they met there attempted
to communicate through signs. But Caminha judged that much communication
had been possible. In his letter, he emphasizes the importance of gestures, good
manners, successful exchanges, and even music. Caminha describes how Cabral
allowed Indians to board his ship, where he served them food and drink and permitted them to spend the night. He notes how one of the Portuguese captains lis-
tened patiently to an Indian elder speak even "without anyone ever being able to
understand him or he us." Later he relates how one of the pilots, an experienced
mariner by the name of Diogo Dias, danced and laughed and played with the
people on shore to the music piped by a piper from the fleet; and on another day,
Caminha includes the fact that the Indians danced to the sound of a Portuguese
drum. Although lacking in verbal communication, these interactions convinced
Caminha that the Indians were "our friends."[6]

The sixteenth-century historian of the Portuguese discoveries, João de Barros,
later provided more details of the first language encounter. His account makes
clear that he understood the Portuguese trading practices in Africa to be the model

for the first contact with Brazil. Barros writes that Cabral sent a boat ashore with a black sailor as an interpreter. This sailor, who may have been a slave and was most likely an African, tried to speak with the peoples of Brazil in a language of West Africa. When he failed to communicate, other interpreters who knew Arabic and other languages also tried to make themselves understood. Only when all were "tired of waiting for a sign of understanding" did the men return to the ships.[7]

Cabral recognized that communication without language did not serve Portuguese interests and called a meeting of his captains to address the problem. According to Caminha, Cabral "asked his captains whether it would be well to take by force a pair of these [Indian] men to send to Your Highness, leaving behind, in their place, a pair of male criminal exiles." Cabral had brought nearly two dozen *degredados* (criminal exiles) on his expedition with the intention of leaving them behind in situations such as the one he found in Brazil. The two young men he proposed to leave in Brazil had been condemned to death for crimes committed in Portugal but had had their sentences commuted to banishment. According to Caminha, the captains agreed to leave the two degredados when the armada set sail, but counseled against taking anybody from Brazil. Caminha states that the captains were of the opinion that persons taken by force did not generally give accurate information, whereas the degredados would. Although this act of leaving behind the two men did not help Cabral, it laid the foundation for the creation of translators, necessary for future interaction with Brazil.[8]

The crucial roles that transactional go-betweens would play in Africa in the fifteenth century, and later in Asia and Brazil in the sixteenth, were not initially perceived, nor was there at the outset a conscious Portuguese strategy for creating them. Instead, the importance of go-betweens came into focus only gradually as the Portuguese experimented with trade in Africa. Initially, the Portuguese operated from a very different model of cultural interaction, one that was shaped by medieval traditions of chivalry and crusade. Well after the end of the Portuguese Reconquest, that tradition, which promoted war rather than diplomacy, lingered as the preferred means to deal with enemies or to encounter new peoples.

The Portuguese Reconquest, a century-long war between Christians and Muslims, ended in 1249 with the defeat of the last Muslim kingdom in southern Portugal. As in Spain, the Portuguese Reconquest took on the overtones of a medieval crusade in which Portuguese Christians, their ranks often bolstered with crusaders from northern Europe, saw themselves as justified in attacking

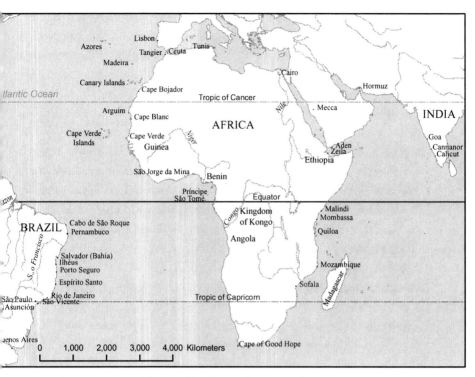

Map 2.1. The Portuguese maritime world in Africa, India, and Brazil

Muslims. After successful campaigns, battle lords received lands and booty taken from Muslim Iberians, as well as titles of nobility from the Portuguese king. By the end of the thirteenth century, Christian kings of Castile and Aragon in Iberia already envisioned extending the Reconquest south into Muslim North Africa to reclaim what had once been the Christian Visigothic province of Mauretania Tingitana, which had been ruled from Toledo. Similarly, religious and economic motivations, wrapped in the traditional language of chivalry and crusade, led Portugal to Africa. With the end of the Reconquest in Portugal, and with it the chances for obtaining honor through service to God and the king in battle, the Portuguese kings and nobles looked to Africa as a place where crusading might continue.[9]

This medieval crusading mentality resulted in the planning of a highly secret Portuguese assault on the Muslim city of Ceuta, an attack that historians cite as the beginning of the Portuguese exploration of Africa. Ceuta lay just across the Strait of Gibraltar in Morocco, and like other cities in northern Africa, it served as a Mediterranean terminus for the overland Saharan trade. The highly developed trans-Saharan trade linked the western African kingdoms of Ghana, Mali, and Songhai to the Mediterranean Sea and the Middle East; over its routes merchants carried gold, slaves, ivory, kola nuts, and salt out of the sub-Saharan African kingdoms and imported into them textiles, slaves, horses, and wheat. Much of the gold that entered Western Europe came across the Sahara in such caravans. As one modern scholar writes, there had always been "a golden thread linking the Iberian Peninsula through the western Maghrib with the sub-Saharan regions of Africa." Literate Iberians knew something of sub-Saharan Africa through the stories told by a Spanish Franciscan monk in a book titled *El libro del conoscimiento,* and Abraham Cresques' Atlas of 1375 identified several of the African cities, such as Timbuktu, on the trail across the Sahara. From the *Rihla,* or book of travels, which recounts the experiences of Abu 'Abdallah ibn Battuta, a Muslim from Tangier, and which was well known throughout the Islamic world of the fourteenth and fifteenth centuries, Iberians likely knew about the salt and gold mines of Mali.[10]

More than one hundred ships with 19,000 men under arms sailed from a plague-infested Lisbon in 1415, their destination unknown to all but a few. Armed with a papal bull that declared the attack a crusade against Islam, King João I (1385–1433) of Portugal, along with his sons, led the assault against Ceuta, a city also weakened by the plague. The city fell in just thirteen hours. After looting the city and consecrating the mosques to Christian use, King João knighted his sons, who in turn knighted others in their retinues. The invasion and sacking of Ceuta symbolized the extension of the Reconquest into North Africa and reflected how deeply steeped in its medieval traditions of chivalry and crusade Portugal remained in the fifteenth century. This same crusading mentality led Portugal to besiege other North African cities, such as Tangier, but with far less success.[11]

The Portuguese advances in Africa, however, proved not to be through the capture of the North African port cities, such as Ceuta, nor was it due to their Reconquest mentality. Rather, their success lay in the extension of sea travel and trade along the coasts of West Africa. Portuguese mariners under the patronage of the Portuguese royal family explored the coast of Africa, established a maritime link to the trans-Saharan trade, and colonized the islands of the Atlantic. These strategies succeeded because the Portuguese quickly learned how to use intermediaries in situations where they were at a disadvantage. Translators and bilingual brokers facilitated Portuguese interaction and trade with new peoples along the coast of Africa.[12]

Historians have long pointed to the patronage and vision of the Infante Dom Henrique (d. 1460), the third son of King João I, and his English wife, Philippa of Lancaster. Known in English as Prince Henry the Navigator and to his subjects as Dom Henrique or O Infante (the prince), Prince Henry is credited by historians with financing expeditions, promoting the caravel (a small ship rigged with triangular sails easily handled in coastal rivers and estuaries), demanding new standards in the drawing of maps, and supporting refinements in the art of navigation—all of which facilitated Portuguese ventures into the Atlantic Ocean. During Prince Henry's lifetime, Portuguese sea captains discovered Atlantic archipelagoes—Madeira, the Azores, and Cape Verde—and after his death, São Tomé and Príncipe. Prince Henry supported the work of cartographers, who mapped the coast of West Africa, thus establishing the foundation for a sea route to India as well as a new cartographic tradition that would revolutionize how Europeans understood the world. Yet, a modern biographer of Prince Henry argues that although these accomplishments have led historians to see Prince Henry as having a tremendous scientific legacy, in fact he was very much a medieval man who lived by a code of chivalry, believed fully in the morality of crusades against Islam, and trusted in the power of visionary dreams.[13]

A caravel, its sails emblazoned with a red cross, was the visual emblem of Prince Henry's campaign of exploration. The red cross symbolized the Order of Christ, a religious military order founded in 1319 to defend the Christian faith in Portugal, and the caravel was a ship well suited to coastal exploration and trade. After Prince Henry became administrator general of the order in 1420, its treasury helped to finance the voyages of exploration. In return, Prince Henry earmarked levies on goods from the African trade for the Order of Christ.[14]

In 1419, two young noblemen in the service of Prince Henry "officially" discovered the island of Porto Santo in the archipelago of Madeira. When it and the other islands in the group were found to be uninhabited, the Portuguese king made their colonization his personal project. In 1427, a Portuguese pilot discovered another Atlantic archipelago, the Azores, one thousand miles from Portugal. Because these islands were so distant from Africa, their colonization proceeded more slowly, and they remained on the periphery of the Portuguese

Atlantic world of the fifteenth century. During the last years of Prince Henry's life, in 1455–1456, sea captains under his patronage discovered the Cape Verde Islands. Given the proximity of these islands to the coast of Guinea, colonization began almost immediately. After Prince Henry's death in 1460, sea captains discovered yet another archipelago of islands, the two most important being São Tomé and Príncipe. These islands would also figure largely in the Portuguese maritime commerce with West Africa.[15]

The Portuguese Crown began modest colonization initiatives on the Atlantic islands, all of which were uninhabited, by turning to degredados, the very same sort of criminal exiles that Cabral would leave behind in Brazil some eighty years later. As a form of punishment, exile to frontier regions had deep roots in the Portuguese legal tradition, but with the development of overseas interests, the Portuguese Crown found a new use for prisoners deemed dangerous. In theory, penal exile was a privilege reserved for the nobility; commoners in a similar situation were to be exiled to the rowing galleys. In practice, however, exile became a regular punishment for commoners, both male and female, once Portugal had lands that needed settlers. When the exiles arrived at their place of banishment, they were allowed to live normal lives: they could move freely, they could work, they could marry and establish families. Thus, exiles became colonists, and as "forced colonists," they were ideally suited to the needs of a Crown bent on colonizing remote outposts.[16]

Portuguese colonists brought sugarcane to Madeira and imported large groups of African slaves to tend the plantations, creating the first Atlantic sugar economy. São Tomé and Príncipe, settled by Portuguese colonists, degredados, Jewish children forcibly taken from their parents, and slaves, followed the pattern established in Madeira. All of the Atlantic islands became important ports of call for Portuguese ships traveling along the coast of West Africa and would continue to play that role in the transatlantic voyages, initiated after 1500.[17]

Along the west coast of Africa, the Portuguese developed a maritime trade that competed with the overland trans-Saharan trade, long dominated by Arabic-speaking Muslim merchants. Individual Portuguese captains could initially obtain valuable cargoes by looting and attacking coastal villages, but to establish a more viable trade, the Portuguese had to make contact with African peoples and come to agreements with African chiefs. Modern African historian George Brooks emphasizes that it was the Europeans who "were obliged to adapt to African trading patterns and modes of social intercourse." This required that the Portuguese abandon their medieval crusade and conquest mentality and rely on transactional go-betweens to negotiate their interests.[18]

According to contemporary chroniclers, Prince Henry recognized the importance of translators and other intermediaries and took care to cultivate them. A Portuguese chronicler of the fifteenth century, Gomes Eanes de Zurara, writes that as early as 1436 a Portuguese captain, Alfonso Gonçalves Baldaia, carried orders from Prince Henry "to go as far as you can" and "to work to have an interpreter of these people." Baldaia sailed along the coast of modern-day Morocco and Moroccan Sahara past Cape Bojador, crossed the Tropic of Cancer, and almost reached Cape Blanc. Although Baldaia returned to Portugal having traveled farther than any previous voyage, and with a cargo of five thousand sea lion skins, he brought back no interpreter, leaving the Portuguese still unable to communicate with the non-Arabic-speaking peoples of Africa.[19]

From Zurara's account, it is clear that the very first translators along the coast of Africa did not willingly adopt this role and that the Portuguese used their conquest mentality to obtain their first interpreters. Antão Gonçalves and Nuno Tristão, whom Zurara cites as the first captains to bring potential interpreters back to Prince Henry, seized them by force from Berber peoples living in what is today Mauritania. First Gonçalves and his men plotted the capture of a "man or a woman" whom they could bring back to Prince Henry. Then Tristão brazenly advocated the seizure of many more. Following Tristão's plan, three groups of armed Portuguese secretly approached and attacked two villages at night. Drawing on Reconquest traditions, the men yelled "Portugal!" and "Santiago!" (St. James) before storming in. At least ten men, women, and boys were captured. One of the captives, a nobleman named Adahu, could make himself understood with an interpreter on Tristão's ship. For Zurara, the return of these two ships with their captives marked a turning point in Prince Henry's exploration of Africa. Although the Portuguese could not yet communicate easily with most of their African captives, Prince Henry was able to learn a great deal from Adahu. With Antão Gonçalves, Adahu later returned to his homeland, where his people delivered a ransom of slaves in return for his freedom. Tristão also returned to West Africa and found it easy to acquire more captives than his boats could carry.[20]

One hundred years later, Portuguese chronicler João de Barros similarly cites the importance of interpreters on the early voyages to Africa. For example, Barros writes that what Prince Henry most wanted was "an interpreter of this land because his intention in these discoveries was not the end of commerce, but to find people of that land, so remote from the church, and to bring them to baptism, and afterwards, to have communication and commerce with them for the benefit of the kingdom [of Portugal]."[21]

Zurara and Barros not only emphasize the importance of the communication provided by interpreters, but they recognize that the loyalty of the go-between was not certain and that go-betweens could equally well serve Africans. In their description of the voyage of Gonçalo de Sintra, for example, they reveal how the captain lost a key interpreter. The voyage occurred after the Portuguese had become aware that the Senegal River divided West Africa geographically and ethnically: to the north of the river lived "brown, slim, and short" peoples in an arid land, whereas south of the river lived "very black, tall, big, and well shaped" peoples in a fertile land of great trees and many kinds of fruits.[22] Captain Sintra deviated from the orders given by Prince Henry to sail south of the Senegal River directly to Guinea, which the Portuguese now called "the land of the blacks," and stopped first at the island of Arguim to see if he could obtain Berber captives. Sintra had with him one of Prince Henry's best Berber interpreters, a boy who "already knew the greater part of our language," Zurara writes, but because Sintra did not take sufficient care, the boy deserted one night. The intended interpreter for the Portuguese then gave the Berbers on the island information about the Portuguese. Sintra, determined to salvage his honor and his expedition, selected twelve of his best men to go ashore at midnight, but trapped by the tide, they were easily overwhelmed. Eight men, including Sintra, lost their lives. Zurara saw Sintra's death as teaching many lessons, two of which directly applied to go-betweens. Zurara believed that interpreters must be closely guarded in foreign lands. Moreover, he recommended that when "our enemies" have their own interpreters and information on "our power and our desires[,] . . . we must take great care when entering their lands." In other words, when the Africans had transactional go-betweens, the Portuguese were at an even greater disadvantage.[23]

Zurara and Barros were particularly impressed with a new kind of transactional go-between: a Portuguese man who went native among the Berbers. Both write about a João Fernandes who lived among the Berbers for seven months. Zurara describes João Fernandes as wishing "by his own will" to remain behind "to see things" and to "bring information" to Prince Henry when he returned to Portugal. Barros describes Fernandes as someone who intended to see for himself the lands of the Berbers, and to provide Prince Henry with information about them, because "he had confidence in their language, which he knew." Fernandes apparently had lived as a captive among Muslims in northern Africa and knew Arabic. Left by Antão Gonçalves in 1444, when Gonçalves returned, Fernandes immediately facilitated trade between Gonçalves and a Muslim merchant named Ahude. Zurara's account reveals that considerable preparations were made before any trade took place. Ahude and Gonçalves exchanged men, two on each side, to be held as surety. For Zurara, the pains taken were richly rewarded, for Gonçalves traded "things of little value" for nine slaves and a little gold dust. Barros recounts how Fernandes returned "healthy and safe" to Portugal, where he became a great source of information on the Muslim Berber peoples of West Africa.[24]

As the Portuguese sought new trading opportunities farther south, translators continued to be part of their unfolding strategy. References to the presence of interpreters on Portuguese ships invariably appear in the sources when sea captains could no longer communicate with Africans, which meant that they had reached the limits of the region where they could successfully trade. The Portuguese knew that they faced great danger when they initiated contact in a new region. As a result, sea captains tended to avoid prolonged contact with peoples for whom they had no interpreter. The Venetian merchant and navigator Alvise Cadamosto (also spelled Ca'da Mosto), who sailed on two Portuguese expeditions to the Guinea coast, in 1455 and 1456, often referred to the *trucimani* (intermediaries) and *lenguaʒi* (translators) on board. He expressed dismay when, on the second voyage, the interpreters could not parlay with Africans in two large canoes that had come out to meet his ship. The expedition resolved to turn back because, as they were "traveling in new lands," nothing could be done without new interpreters. Similarly, another Italian merchant, Antoniotto Usodimare, who entered the Portuguese-sponsored African trade to Guinea when he found himself heavily in debt, reckoned that he reached a place "where no Christian had ever arrived." There African fishermen showered his ship with arrows, "judging that we were enemies," he wrote to his brothers. "And I," he continued, "seeing that they did not wish to receive us, saw myself obliged to return."[25]

After Usodimare retreated from where he had been attacked, he met "a noble black lord" who traded forty slaves, a few elephant teeth, parrots, and musk (*almíscar*) for his cloth. Because Usodimare thought that this chief understood his desire for further trade, he agreed to take an emissary of the chief with him back to Portugal. Usodimare writes that the chief "sent with me to the king of Portugal one of his secretaries with a few slaves." [26] This emissary suggests that the Africans well understood the importance of having their own go-betweens; perhaps he had been given the task of negotiating peace and trade between this chief and the king of Portugal.

After Prince Henry's death, the Portuguese Crown took over his role. When Pedro de Sintra first reached Sierra Leone in 1462, he detained a man to comply with an order given by King Afonso (1438–1481) that he return with a new interpreter. The king had ordered that when Sintra judged that he had reached the farthest point of his voyage, if his interpreters could not be understood, he was to try to bring back to Portugal "several blacks of that land" so that they could try to communicate with the many African interpreters resident in Portugal. Similarly, when Diogo Cão first reached the Congo River, the language spoken was not one understood by the several interpreters that he already had with him. Accordingly, Portuguese chronicler Rui de Pina writes, Cão returned to Portugal with several Africans so that "later, after having learned the language customs, and intent of the king, and of the kingdom of Portugal, they would return to their lands and be the means through which the things from one side and the other could be well communicated." By 1494, when the German physician Jerome Münzer visited Portugal, he found that a number of black youths from Africa were being educated so that they might be sent back to Africa as missionaries, interpreters, and emissaries of the king.[27]

Although the trade with Africa enriched Portugal with gold and slaves, the Portuguese never lost sight of a possible sea route to Asia. If such a route could be opened, it would allow the Portuguese direct access to the spices of the Orient, then controlled by Muslim merchants in the Middle East. These middlemen sold Asian spices to Venetian merchants in Egypt, who then marketed the spices in Europe. A sea route to Asia would eliminate both the Middle Eastern and the Venetian middlemen and hence promised great profits for Portuguese merchants. Establishing a sea route to India required information, which the Portuguese obtained through spies and other agents. Just as go-betweens had been instrumental in the Portuguese exploration, trade, and colonization of West Africa, so, too, would they be in East Africa and Asia.

Vasco da Gama's successful voyage to India in 1498 rested not only on decades of Portuguese experience in sailing, navigation, and mapmaking, but also on Portuguese familiarity with encountering new peoples and exploiting the opportunities for trade. Interpreters, ambassadors, spies, and cultural brokers of various kinds were vital. In 1487, King João II (1481–1495) instructed Bartolomeu Dias to round the Cape of Good Hope, which he did with three caravels the following year. At the same time, the king entrusted a highly secret mission to two go-betweens who served as spies. One of the men, Pêro da Covilhã, was fluent in Arabic. The two men traveled to Cairo via Naples and Rhodes. From Cairo, they joined a caravan headed to Arabia. At Aden, the men separated: Covilhã headed to India while his companion, Afonso de Paiva, set out for Ethiopia. Covilhã visited the major commercial centers of western India: Calicut, Cannanore (today Kannur), and Goa, and after assessing the spice trade in these cities, he visited two cities of the east coast of Africa, Zeila (in present-day Somaliland) and Sofala (in present-day Mozambique). On returning to Cairo, he met up with two more emissaries sent by the Portuguese king, a Jewish rabbi from the Portuguese town of Beja and a Jewish shoemaker from the Portuguese town of Lamengo, who instructed him to write up a report to send back to the king, and then to continue to Ethiopia. Such missions led historian A. J. R. Russell-Wood to argue that to assess only the maritime successes of the Portuguese is to miss the great importance of "terrestrial initiatives," that is, the information the Portuguese acquired through "diplomatic, commercial, and religious initiatives." The information that Covilhã provided, for example, clearly influenced the strategy used to prepare for Vasco da Gama's voyage, even though King João II died before the voyage began.[28]

King João's successor, Manuel I (1495–1521), chose Vasco da Gama to lead the expedition to India. Leaving Lisbon in July of 1497 with four ships, one of which carried only supplies, da Gama sailed to the Cape Verde Islands and then directly for the Cape of Good Hope. His was not a large expedition, and therefore when da Gama arrived at the Cape, he relied on strategies that the Portuguese had perfected to avoid unnecessary violence and loss of life. Many details of these strategies for contacting Africans, both at the Cape of Good Hope and in East Africa, emerge in a journal written by one of the men on his expedition. The sailor's journal relates that when the Portuguese first made landfall just north of the Cape of Good Hope, they took an African captive, brought him on board da Gama's ship, and sat him at a table where "he ate of all we ate." The next morning, after spending the night on the ship, the captive was sent ashore in new clothes. Over the next few days, trade began, not so much because the Portuguese wanted to acquire things of value, but to ascertain what kinds of goods the land possessed. Care was taken to keep the atmosphere from turning violent. When the Africans played their musical instruments, for example, da Gama "ordered the trumpets to be sounded," and the sailor reports that "we, in the boats, danced, and the captain-major did so likewise." When da Gama feared his interpreter was in danger, he ordered a display of crossbows and lances, but not one that would result in overt conflict, for in the words of the seaman, "we had no desire to employ them." Da Gama also ordered the beach shelled by the bombard guns "to prove that we were able, although unwilling to hurt them." Later, after they rounded the Cape of Good Hope, da Gama continued to send his interpreters ashore, to present gifts of clothing to African chiefs, to trade, to invite individuals aboard, and to listen to music.[29]

Contacts and encounters became more complicated when the Portuguese sailed into waters in East Africa long dominated by Muslim merchants. The seaman's journal describes the lords of the land south of Mozambique as "very haughty" and notes that they "valued nothing which we gave them." But when da Gama reached Mozambique, his interpreters who spoke Arabic acquired detailed information from four Muslim merchants who had vessels in port laden with gold, silver, cloves, pepper, ginger, and pearls. This information made da Gama's men "so happy that we cried with joy, and prayed God to grant us health, so that we might behold what we so much desired." Da Gama negotiated for two Muslim pilots for the journey up the coast of East Africa. Such interactions, historian Jeremy Prestholdt claims, mean that the Portuguese did not immediately dismiss the Muslims they met all along the coast of East Africa as enemies, but rather recognized them as "familiar" and "known." The Portuguese sought Swahili-speaking Muslims to become their pilots, interpreters, and cultural brokers.[30]

Still, in all encounters, danger was present. Open conflict broke out when the Portuguese were prevented from drawing water north of Mozambique. When da Gama reached Mombassa, he mistrusted overtures from that country's king. After receiving a gift from the king of Mombassa, da Gama sent two degredados ashore "to confirm these peaceful assurances." The great Portuguese poet of the sixteenth century, Luís de Camões, includes this detail in his epic poem *The Lusiads:*

> Even so, from among those prisoners
> On board, sentenced for gross crimes

> So their lives would be hazarded
> In predicaments such as these,
> He sent two of the cleverest, trained
> To spy on the city and defences
> Of the resourceful Muslims
> (2.7)

Da Gama remained wary, so he resorted to torture to extract information from his Muslim pilots, on whom he depended but whom he did not trust.[31]

In Malindi, da Gama obtained an expert pilot who guided him to Calicut, India.[32] Once anchored at Calicut, da Gama sent ashore one of his degredados, who was astonished to meet two North Africans from Tunis who spoke Castilian and Genoese. According to the journal written by one of the men in da Gama's expedition, the first greeting the degredado received from these Castilian-speaking Muslims was: "May the devil take thee! What brought you hither?" Later, when the degredado returned to his ship with one of the Muslims, the author of the journal recorded that the Muslim declared: "A lucky venture, a lucky venture! Plenty of rubies, plenty of emeralds! You owe great thanks to God for having brought you to a country holding such riches!"[33] The poet Camões celebrates the importance of the meeting and of this man, whom he names Monsayeed:

> Among those who came running to see him
> Was a Mohammedan born in Barbary . . .
> Catching sight of the envoy, he exclaimed
> In delight, and in fluent Castilian
> —"Who brought you to this other world
> So far from your native Portugal?"
> (7.24—25)

Camões portrays Monsayeed as a great boon to da Gama, despite the fact that he was Muslim. In Camões' poem, Monsayeed was welcomed aboard the Portuguese ships, where da Gama embraced him and "plied him with questions/About India and all its ways" (7.29).[34]

India and all of its ways nearly proved to be the undoing of da Gama. When he and thirteen men disembarked to meet the *zamorin,* the ruler of Calicut, the small band of Portuguese men soon found themselves overwhelmed by the size of the crowds and the authority of the zamorin. Da Gama presented himself as an ambassador from the king of Portugal, and requested and received a private audience. Two days later, however, the zamorin kept da Gama waiting for four hours. Da Gama had prepared a gift of cloth, hoods and hats, strings of coral, hand-washing basins, sugar, oil, and honey for the zamorin, but the zamorin's factor and governor laughed when they saw it, saying that "the poorest merchant from Mecca, or any other part of India, gave more, and that if he [da Gama] wanted to make a present it should be in gold, as the king would not accept such things." Da Gama decided to forego the gift and simply present himself as an ambassador; he gave two letters, written in Portuguese and Arabic, to the zamorin from King Manuel. Again da Gama felt at a disadvantage, because he could not understand the letter written in Arabic. He asked the zamorin for a Christian interpreter who spoke Arabic. The interpreter, however, could not read Arabic, and da Gama soon found himself listening, but unable to understand, the translation of the letter from King Manuel given to the zamorin by four Muslim interpreters.[35]

Da Gama continued to exchange letters and messages—as well as threats, hostages, and prisoners—with the zamorin and his officials while he remained in India. Some trading occurred, but it proved to be disadvantageous to the Portuguese, for their trading goods, highly valued in Africa, were not deemed as desirable in India. Moreover, they competed directly with Muslim merchants, who did not welcome them. Translators and informants protected the safety of the Portuguese expedition by enabling the Portuguese to "parlay" rather than attack their way in and around Calicut. The information obtained was often imprecise, but it nevertheless enabled the Portuguese to gain a foothold. When da Gama left Calicut in August 1498, he carried away with him several men from India and took one more off Angediva Island, a man who spoke fluent Venetian and claimed to be a Christian forced into Islam. Later the Portuguese learned that this man, Gaspar da Gama, was a Jew and very knowledgeable about India.[36]

After a difficult journey, two of da Gama's ships, carrying just over half of the original crew, returned to Lisbon.[37] In addition to the information supplied by da Gama and his men, Gaspar da Gama provided detailed information in Lisbon about the spice trade, Muslim navigation techniques, trading commodities, and religious customs of India. King Manuel I quickly prepared a second expedition to India. João de Barros, the great Portuguese historian of the six-teenth century, vividly describes a Sunday, 8 March in 1500, when King Manuel and his entire court traveled to the mouth of the Tagus River to bid Pedro Álvares Cabral, the admiral of this second expedition, good-bye. At the church of Nossa Senhora de Belém (Our Lady of Bethlehem), they heard mass said by the bishop of Ceuta, the city in Africa whose capture in 1415 had marked the beginning of the Portuguese exploration of Africa. A flag of the Order of Christ adorned the altar, and the bishop blessed it before the king gave it to Cabral. The flag, con-sidered by Barros to be a symbol of Portuguese temporal and spiritual victories, was then carried as part of a procession of crosses and holy relics to the beach, where Cabral kissed the king's hand and bade him farewell. Nearly the whole city of Lisbon had gathered to watch the spectacle — many crowded onto the beach, others stood in the nearby fields, and still others boarded small boats for the best view. The music of horns, flutes, and drums filled the air as the men of the sea who were about to embark on such a long voyage sought to quell the "sadness of the sea." "The hearts of all were between pleasure and tears," Barros writes, "because this was the most beautiful and powerful armada that had ever left the kingdom for lands so far away." [38]

Cabral commanded thirteen ships and between 1,200 and 1,500 men, among whom were captains, pilots, and clerks who had sailed with da Gama; sailors, priests, and interpreters (including the men from India whom Vasco da Gama had picked up on the first expedition to India, such as Gaspar da Gama); and twenty degredados. [39] Cabral carried letters from King Manuel to the East Afri-can kings of Sofala, Quíloa (today Tanzania), and Melinde (today Malindi, Kenya) and to the zamorin of Calicut. [40] The fleet sailed the next day.

Cabral's every act in Brazil several weeks later makes clear sense when seen against the backdrop of how the Portuguese operated when faced with new peo-ples and new lands. Cabral's captains were not only highly experienced sailors; they understood the dangers in contacting new and unfamiliar peoples. Cabral searched for a common language, using the translators in the armada for the first contact with the peoples he met in Brazil. When a common language did not emerge, he and his captains carefully avoided potentially dangerous behav-iors and used music, singing, and humor as a means of communication. From Caminha's letter, it is clear that Cabral entrusted contact to his most experienced captains: Nicolau Coelho (who earlier had captained one of the ships led by da Gama); Bartolomeu Dias (the discoverer of the Cape of Good Hope); and Dias' brother, Diogo Dias (who had been a clerk on da Gama's voyage). Coelho was the first sent ashore with interpreters to make contact, and he and Bartolomeu Dias are cited by Caminha as leaders of subsequent interactions. Dias' brother, Diogo, was the man sent ashore to dance and sing.

Cabral intended to use his degredados not only to protect his own expedition but to facilitate future contact. Caminha writes that Cabral's intention was simply to leave two men behind to learn the customs of the Indians. But Caminha's choice of words—*amansar* (to domesticate) and *apaziguar* (to pacify)—reveals that the Portuguese had long-term interests that required the cooperation of the peoples they encountered. Cabral introduced the men slowly, at first taking them to the Indians with gifts and then leaving them ashore while the rest of the Portuguese retired to the ships. Later he ordered the men to spend the night at the nearby Indian village. However, the Indians did not want these Portuguese young men to remain with them and several times forced the men to return to the ships. Despite these clear indications that the men were not welcome, Cabral left two degredados behind anyway. When Cabral's ships prepared to sail, the two men on the shore began to cry, perhaps revealing that they were not apprised of (or resigned to) their fate. The anonymous pilot or scribe wrote that the men of Brazil "comforted them and showed that they had pity for them." But they were not alone. According to Caminha, the night before Cabral weighed anchor, two seamen stole a skiff, left the ship, and were not seen again.[41]

Cabral immediately sent his supply ship back to Lisbon with the news of the discovery while he continued onward to India. He lost four ships after leaving Brazil when the armada had a very difficult time rounding the Cape of Good Hope. One more ship sank off the east coast of Africa. In spite of these setbacks, Cabral successfully negotiated with the king of Malindi in East Africa "through interpreters," and before sailing for Calicut, he left behind two more degredados. Cabral took with him an important political figure from Malindi, who was being sent to Lisbon by the ruler of a prosperous town along the Swahili coast to establish an amicable relationship with the king of Portugal. In Calicut, Cabral had the assistance of five South Asian interpreters whom Vasco da Gama had brought back to Portugal and who "spoke Portuguese well" by the time Cabral disembarked. But four of the South Asian interpreters brought by the Portuguese were of such low status that they could not approach the zamorin; the Portuguese had to rely instead on one interpreter who spoke Arabic. Since the language of communication was Arabic, the Portuguese again had to approach the zamorin through Muslim go-betweens, whom they mistrusted. In Cabral's presence, the zamorin wrote two letters to King Manuel—one, an official document encased in a silver cover encrusted with a golden seal; the other, written on paper made from palm fronds.[42]

The presence of transactional go-betweens masked conflicts that might surface during initial encounters. But the exchange of letters and ambassadors did not preclude the use of force, nor did it mean that the Portuguese always intended to trade peacefully. The Portuguese aspired to monopolize the spice trade to Europe, and that required the building of forts, the arming of ships, and the patrolling of sea-lanes. Cabral seized a Muslim ship and shelled Calicut when Muslim merchants impeded his attempts to trade. The Portuguese later would violently attack seaports, such as Goa in 1510, Malacca in 1511, and Hormuz in 1515. Eventually, the Portuguese built fifty forts in East Africa, India, and the Moluccas, and manned a fleet of one hundred ships to patrol the waters. The Portuguese seagoing ships (*naus*), armed with cannons and other artillery, gave the Portuguese a critical advantage over the existing traders. Interpreters played crucial roles in the early stages of contact, but the Portuguese did not rely solely on these transactional go-betweens to maintain their commercial interests in Africa and India.[43]

The supply ship sent back from Brazil with letters from Cabral, his captains, and others reached Lisbon in 1501. In a private letter, Alberto Cantino, a Venetian living in Lisbon and an agent of a powerful Italian family, immediately wrote about the ship's return. He apparently had learned of the two degredados left behind in Brazil. In his letter to the Duke of Ferrara, Ercole d'Este, he comments that the Portuguese king hoped to encourage settlement in his new overseas possession by sending his degredados there. In his view, the "delectable airs" and "sweet fruits" of the newly discovered land known as Santa Cruz were such that few degredados would want to refuse.[44]

Almost immediately King Manuel sent a small expedition to explore Brazil. There is persuasive evidence that these Portuguese mariners found the degredados who had been left behind by Cabral in 1500 and that at least one was able to serve as their interpreter. On this reconnoitering mission was Amerigo Vespucci, who supplied information to his patrons, Lorenzo di Pierfrancesco de' Medici and Piero di Tommaso Soderini, both powerful men in Florence, in detailed letters. One of Vespucci's letters, known as the *Lettera*, distinguishes between two very different encounters. The first meeting, which occurred just as the expedition arrived in Brazil after an exhausting crossing in very stormy weather, was not successful due to the European crew's misreading of signs. Since there is no evidence that native peoples from Brazil returned to Portugal following Cabral's initial voyage, this first encounter occurred, as did Pinzón's and Cabral's in 1500, without an interpreter. The lack of an interpreter proved dangerous to the Portuguese.[45]

This first meeting took place in northeastern Brazil, along the beach in present-day Rio Grande do Norte.[46] After sighting land, anchoring, and coming ashore, the men spotted a group of men and women watching them from a mountain vantage. Vespucci writes, "And although we took great pains with them that they might come and speak with us, we could never reassure them, for they did not trust us." Since the sailors badly needed water, firewood, and provisions, they left bells and mirrors on the ground where the Indians could find them and returned to their ships. Only when they were "far out at sea" did the Indians come down to the shore and take the goods. The next day, seeing smoke signals rising from the land, the sailors, "thinking that they were calling to us," went ashore. The Indians "made signs" that they should go inland, and Vespucci relates that two men volunteered to go with them "to see what kind of people they were and whether they had any wealth either of spices or of drugs." The men took trading goods and promised to return in five days. Seven days later, the two men had still not returned. A third man went ashore and, according to Vespucci, in full view of the men on the ships, was killed, dragged away, cooked, and eaten. Vespucci believed this to have been the fate of the two men who had left the expedition earlier.[47]

The vivid story of a young man eaten in front of his companions may have been an embellishment added by Vespucci, or an editor, to achieve greater effect.[48] Nonetheless, the story underscores an important point: without interpreters, the Portuguese could not count on achieving even simple objectives. Whereas Cabral's armada had successfully landed, drawn water, and traded, the first encounter on the second Portuguese expedition had not. A French expedition that reached Brazil three years later, in 1504, likewise had a difficult time establishing contact in northern Brazil. Sailing a single French ship navigated by two Portuguese sailors, the French captain Binot Paulmier de Gonneville landed on the coast of northeastern Brazil and found, according to a memoir of his voyage, Indians "naked as they emerged from the womb" with bodies painted black and pierced lips with "polished green stones" in the holes. These Indians had already met Europeans, for they held European artifacts in their possession, and "although they showed no surprise at seeing the ship, they did show fear of the artillery." At the first anchorage, when several unarmed men went ashore to get water, the Indians attacked, taking two captive, killing a third, and wounding four others. Paulmier de Gonneville did make a second landing 100 French leagues (approximately 445 kilometers) farther along the coast, where he was able to provision the ship and trade.[49]

The crew of Vespucci's expedition wanted to go ashore and avenge the deaths of their companions, but their captain prevented them and ordered the ships to sail. As the expedition hugged the northeastern shore, Vespucci writes, "we made many stops and never found people who wanted to parley with us." Farther south, however, they made successful contact, which might have been facilitated by one of the degredados or sailors from the 1500 expedition. Vespucci reports that the expedition stayed five days with native people, and "although it took much effort to tame them, we nevertheless made them our friends and traded with them." Vespucci does not mention where he "lived among the Indians for twenty-seven days," as described in one letter. Instead, he says only that "we departed from this harbor sailing always to the southwest within sight of land, continually making many stops and speaking with countless people." Possibly the harbor was the Bay of All Saints, which in one letter Vespucci claims was named during this expedition. It seems highly likely that wherever the expedition remained for a month, they had a degredado interpreter with them.[50]

Amerigo Vespucci's letters do not mention the degredados whom the expedition supposedly met, nor does he reference any translator. Yet the detail of his letters suggests that the expedition did find at least one degredado who had become skilled enough in the indigenous language to serve as interpreter. One wonders if Vespucci thought the presence of a translator so obvious that it did not need to be mentioned—in other words, that his readers would assume that they had a translator with them.[51] In one letter he states that "we landed on several occasions and conversed in friendly fashion with the people" and that we "were warmly received by them, and sometimes stayed with them fifteen or twenty days at a time, always in a very friendly and hospitable way." Yet Vespucci provides no explanation of how he was able to communicate. Or, he writes about how much he "learned" from the peoples of Brazil, without revealing how he could have understood them. For example, in his letter from 1502, he declares, "I strove hard to understand their life and customs, since I ate and slept among them for twenty-seven days." He then offers his reader a description of their houses, social structure, food, marriage and childbirth customs, warfare, and the presentation of their bodies—all in considerable detail. Many of these things he could have simply observed, but he also tells his reader that an old man "explained to him" or that "we strongly reproached them" or that the Indians "promised us," suggesting that some form of verbal communication did take place.[52]

Other sources do confirm that this second expedition to Brazil did find at least one degredado who served as an interpreter. The king's notary stated in an official document that "two years after [1500], another fleet of the same Christian King [Manuel, of Portugal], with this as its goal, followed the coast of that land [Brazil] for almost 760 leagues [approximately 5,000 kilometers] and found amongst the people an interpreter and baptized countless numbers of them." The notary attested in 1503 that the information that he had collected in a book had come from "the accounts of two old men of the said land [of Brazil]," with whom he communicated through interpreters—the degredados who had returned to Portugal from Brazil. A letter printed in Italy in 1505, purporting to be a copy of a letter sent by King Manuel of Portugal to the king of Castile, refers directly to the degredados left behind by Cabral in Brazil. This document, known as the "Besicken Letter," states that the captain (Cabral) carried twenty condemned men, two of whom were left in Brazil, and that on another armada sent to Brazil by the king of Portugal one of the men returned, and "he spoke their language and gave information on everything." The historian João de Barros likewise believed that one of the degredados returned to Lisbon; he wrote in his brief account of Cabral's discovery of Brazil that "one of the two [degredados] later returned to this kingdom [of Portugal] and served as interpreter."[53]

While interpreters—the transactional go-betweens—facilitated contact, the first chroniclers of Brazil became influential representational go-betweens because they possessed a powerful new form of information, highly valuable to kings and merchants in Europe. Pero Vaz de Caminha became a representational go-between when he wrote his letter directly to the king. Clearly recognizing that he had seen things of particular interest to the king, and cognizant of the value of the information he passed on, he deemed it appropriate to ask, at the end of his letter, for a royal pardon for his son-in-law, who had been sent as a degredado to the island of São Tomé.[54]

Caminha wrote to the king of Portugal, but others passed or sold their information to powerful figures outside of Portugal. Vespucci played this role to the hilt by relaying detailed information on Brazil to his patron in Florence, Lorenzo di Pierfrancesco de' Medici. In the first letter, he begins by noting that "much time has passed since I last wrote to Your Magnificence," indicating that he had written before, and continues, saying, "the present letter is to give you the news." Vespucci confidently predicts that "Your Magnificence will be pleased to hear of all that took place on the voyage, and the most marvelous things I encountered upon it." The next year, en route to Brazil in 1501, he wrote from the Cape Verde Islands to pass on that he had met part of Cabral's fleet returning from India. This letter describes in considerable detail what he had learned from an informant from one of the ships and concludes with a list of all the goods stowed onboard. When he returned from Brazil, he wrote again, carefully describing the peoples of Brazil.[55]

Vespucci is only the most well known of these representational go-betweens; there were many others. It was sensational news when the first ships from Cabral's fleet returned from India in 1502, and the news quickly left Portugal. Immediately after the first of the ships in Cabral's armada arrived in Lisbon from India, the Italian merchant Giovanni Affaitadi interviewed a sailor from the ship; two days later he had written a full account of Cabral's voyage to India for the Venetian ambassador to Spain. After reading the letter, the ambassador, Domenico Pisani de Giovanni, promptly forwarded the letter to the Doge of Venice. Pisani's own secretary, who was in Lisbon when the ship arrived, wrote to the Doge one day later, including in his letter a key piece of information that Affaitadi had missed: Cabral's discovery of Brazil. "Above the Cape of Good Hope, towards the west," he wrote, "they discovered a new land, that which they call 'of the parrots' . . . they judged this land to be mainland because they saw more than 2,000 miles of coast and did not find an end." The Venetian government quickly sent an agent to Portugal to gather more information.[56]

Information spread rapidly, in part because there were so many sailors with stories of adventure to tell. Soon after Portuguese ships began to visit India, European merchants doing business in Lisbon learned quickly about the new trading routes. Some Venetians feared that the Portuguese maritime route to India would wrest the lucrative spice trade away from them. One Florentine merchant, long resident in Lisbon, estimated in 1501 that the Portuguese could easily supply the west, meaning Europe, with spices, and even Italy, for the sea route was less expensive than the overland route through the Middle East. Venetian merchants had built fortunes by acquiring these spices from Muslim merchants in Cairo and Damascus and introducing them into Europe through Venice. Girolamo Priuli, a Venetian, remarked pessimistically in his diary in August and September of 1501 that the talk on the Rialto was the news of the new route that the Portuguese had navigated to the Orient and whether or not it would be the ruin of Venice. Even though some Venetians thought that Cabral's expedition had not been such a success, since so many ships had been lost and because the actual quantity of spices that made its way back to Lisbon was small, Priuli disagreed. He noted that it was not the amount of spices that Cabral's ships initially brought back; rather, "the importance was the route that had been found and the traffic, which every year will bring back greater quantities of spices." [57]

Merchants not based in Venice were quick to see opportunity in the new route. One was the Frenchman Binot Paulmier de Gonneville, who, in Lisbon in 1501 or 1502, was amazed at the spices and other exotic goods that Portuguese merchants were unloading from their ships. With two partners, he decided to outfit a ship, and they hired two Portuguese pilots at great expense to help the French crew find its way to India. Gonneville's ship, L'Espoir, never reached India, but it was the French ship that did land in Brazil in 1504.[58]

Recognizing the value of information possessed even by sailors on ships, the kings of Portugal may have tried to limit the flow of information about the Portuguese Empire. The Portuguese pioneered new navigational techniques and mapped thousands of miles of previously unknown coastlines, yet virtually all of the maps drawn for Prince Henry, King Afonso, King João II, and King Manuel have disappeared, and there are relatively few known Portuguese maps from the sixteenth century. The absence of such maps has led historians to claim that there was a royal policy of concealment. They argue that King João II cloaked the discoveries by Portuguese mariners, and especially the maps they used to navigate, in secrecy, as did his successor, King Manuel.[59]

According to Portuguese cartographic historian Armando Cortesão, there is little doubt that the maps existed, for the information they carried is reflected in other European maps drawn in the fifteenth century. For example, on the world map drawn by Fra Mauro in 1457–1459 appears a legend that reads: "His Highness the King of Portugal sent his ships [and sea captains] to discover and to see with their own eyes . . . and they [the sea captains] made new maps of these voyages and they gave new names to the rivers and coasts, capes and ports, of all of which I had a copy." [60]

Vespucci often alludes to "a small work" that he was writing, but that he was unable to send to his Florentine patron because King Manuel of Portugal had taken it from him. "When he returns it to me," Vespucci wrote optimistically to his patron, "I shall send it." Vespucci again referred to this work in a later letter, this time reiterating to his patron that "I ask your forgiveness for not sending you this last navigation, or rather this last 'journey,' as I had promised to do in my last letter: you know the reason, since I could not yet have the original back from His Most Serene Highness [King Manuel of Portugal]." But more recent scholarship questions the existence of a policy of secrecy, or at least its effectiveness, since so much information on the new discoveries rapidly left Portugal.[61]

In Portugal, as later in Spain, there was a *padrão real*, or a "master map" kept by the king; on this map, cartographers recorded all new discoveries and all new information as soon as it reached the king. Through the shrewd agency, and perhaps bribery, of diplomatic agents and spies, the Venetian Alberto Cantino somehow managed to have an artist in Lisbon copy a Portuguese nautical chart that showed the new Atlantic discoveries of Cabral, as well as recent discoveries in India (Map 2.2). According to Cortesão, it is highly likely that Cantino's map was copied directly from the padrão real, kept in Lisbon. How Cantino got access to this map is unknown, but Cortesão states that Cantino paid twelve gold ducats for the map and sent it to his patron in November of 1502.[62]

The Cantino World Map provides fascinating insights into the Portuguese mapmakers, who were representational go-betweens, translating new information into a dramatic new vision of the world. The map is itself extraordinary. The careful detail that it reveals about the world reflects the combined knowledge of one hundred years of Portuguese navigation and discovery. The entire coast of West Africa is clearly drawn and fully named. This is not surprising, for Portuguese ships had sailed to such ports for decades. But the east coast of Africa, only recently navigated by Portuguese sea captains, as well as India, are also drawn in considerable and confident detail. Even more striking is the location of places that the Portuguese had not yet seen—China, Malaysia, and Indonesia.

The Cantino World Map, according to Luís de Albuquerque and J. Lopes Tavares, was the first to deviate from the traditional representation of Asia based on the work of the classical geographer Ptolemy.[63] Instead, the Cantino World Map combined information from European sailors, pilots, and navigators with information obtained in India from Muslims to represent Asia in a radically new way. The map reflects the acquisition of information from Muslim pilots and traders, whom the Portuguese met in East Africa and India, about ports farther east—in China, Malaysia, and Japan. The Muslim merchants had their own

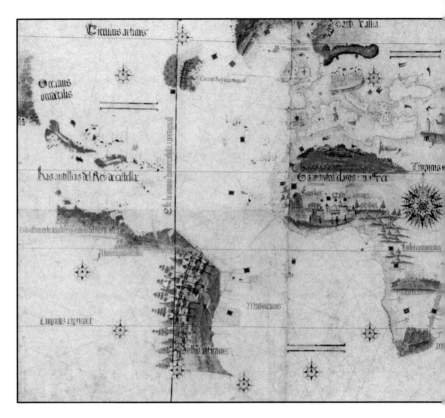

navigational strategies, which the Portuguese learned and translated into their own system. This information, deemed more important than the classical model of Asia drawn from Ptolemy, created the highly original, and far more accurate, projection of Asia.

Reflecting the Portuguese cartographic tradition, which stressed that maps should record only what was known (and not imagined), only the coastline of Brazil appears on the Cantino World Map. The mapmakers paint Brazil as a landscape of parrots and trees, but they make no effort to project it as a continent. The coastline seems to float unconnected to the islands of the Caribbean, which, by 1502, were well known in Spain and Portugal. Brazil is located quite precisely between the equator and the Tropic of Capricorn. The placement of the Portuguese flag and the clearly drawn line of demarcation between the Spanish and Portuguese discoveries claim Brazil for Portugal. According to Cortesão, the coast of Brazil was redrawn in the Cantino World Map, and a second, updated version was pasted over the original. The first version, no longer visible to the naked eye, names only two places along the coast of Brazil: Porto

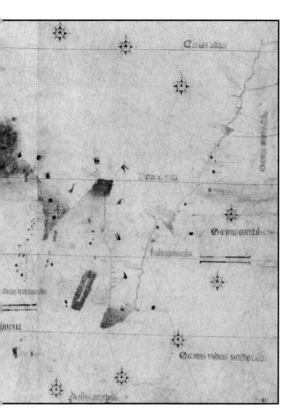

Map 2.2. The Cantino World
Map, 1502. Biblioteca Estense
Universitaria, Modena.

Seguro and the Cabo de São Jorge. The second version, the one visible today, contains these two place-names in addition to the names of two rivers (the São Francisco River and the Rio do Brasil), a second cape—Cabo de Santa Maria—and two place-names: the Bay of All Saints and San Miguel. Cortesão suggests that this correction reflects the new information that had arrived in Lisbon from the 1501–1502 voyage (Map 2.3). [64]

In addition to the named places on the Cantino World Map, there appear legends, written in script, that describe the wealth of the lands, information about when they were discovered, and accounts of the people who lived in them. Opposite the *feitoria* (trading post) of São Jorge da Mina in West Africa, a legend reads:

Whence they bring to the most excellent prince Dom Manuel King of Portugal in each year twelve caravels with gold; each caravel brings twenty-five thousand weights of gold, each weight being worth five hundred *reis*, and they further bring many slaves and pepper and other things of much profit. [65]

Map 2.3. Brazil as represented in the Cantino World Map, 1502. Biblioteca Estense Universitaria, Modena.

This was not particularly new information, but the recording of the exact number of ships, the amount of gold, and the value of each weight suggests the value accorded to concrete information coveted by merchants. Many legends appear in the map opposite India; for example, next to Calicut the legend states, "Here is Calicut, a most noble city discovered by the most illustrious prince King Dom Manuel of Portugal. There is much *benzoim* [balsam] . . . and pepper and many other kinds of merchandise coming from many parts, to wit, cinnamon, ginger, clove, incense, sandalwood, and all kinds of spices and stones of great value . . . and seed pearls." Legends also appear beside places that the Portuguese had not yet visited but had heard of—Sumatra, Malacca, Cambodia, China, and the Malay Peninsula. These legends record valuable information obtained from merchants in India and sure to be of interest for Portuguese merchants interested in trade.[66]

The legend off the coast of Brazil reflects no information about possible trading relations; rather, it is a succinct characterization of the discovery of Brazil, then known as the Land of the True Cross, and a brief description of the peoples living there:

> Found by Pedro Álvares Cabral, a nobleman of the house of the king of Portugal, who discovered it when he went as captain-major of fourteen ships which the said king was sending to Calicut. . . . there are many people who go about naked as their mothers delivered them; they are more white than brown and have very long hair.[67]

Kings, noblemen, and merchants valued the information coming from these new lands, but so, too, did a much wider readership. The letters of Amerigo Vespucci became a widely read source of information about Brazil. Two of Vespucci's letters were published during his lifetime; these letters became extremely influential in shaping how Europeans perceived these recent discoveries. One, addressed to Lorenzo di Pierfrancesco de' Medici, was printed in 1502 or 1503 and "enjoyed an immediate and lasting renown," becoming known as the *Mundus novus* letter, for in it the term "New World" was popularized for the first time. The second, printed in Florence in 1504 or 1505, known as the *Lettera,* is addressed to a "Magnificent Lord," whom scholars believe to be Piero di Tommaso Soderini, successor on the death of Lorenzo di Pierfrancesco de' Medici to the office of Gonfalonier of Justice (the head of the Florentine Republic).[68]

Vespucci's letters reflect the challenges that the discovery of the Americas posed for the European view of the world. Vespucci's *Mundus novus* letter directly contradicts the ancient authorities in their geographic depiction of the world. Vespucci argues that the classical geographers erred in their view that there was

no continent in the Atlantic south of the equator. After the salutation, the letter begins, "But this last voyage of mine has demonstrated that this opinion of theirs [the ancients] is false and contradicts all truth, since I have discovered a continent in those southern regions that is inhabited by more numerous peoples and animals than in our Europe, or Asia or Africa."[69]

The German popularity of the letter brought it to the attention of the mapmaker Martin Waldseemüller, who used Vespucci's accounts to name America in his magnificent map of the world published in 1507. Waldseemüller makes Vespucci the modern (i.e., sixteenth-century) heir to the great classical cartographer Ptolemy. Vespucci appears at the upper right, next to the modern discoveries of the "new" world, whereas the ancient authority, Ptolemy, appears to the left, next to the "old" world he had mapped. Though Waldseemüller acknowledges the new information supplied by the Portuguese discoveries in his depiction of Africa and the coast of Brazil, he remains wedded to Ptolemy's representation of Asia. As compared to the Cantino World Map, Waldseemüller's representation of Asia is less accurate because it is based on classical cartography rather than on the information supplied by seamen and merchants (Map 2.4).

Waldseemüller is quick to imagine and to name America; he gives Vespucci's name to the new world, not Columbus', not Cabral's, not Pinzón's. Because

Map 2.4. Waldseemüller's
World Map, 1507. Martin
Waldseemüller, *Universalis
Cosmographia Secundum
Ptholemaei Traditionem Et
Americi Vespucii Aliorumque
Lustrationes* (St. Die, 1507).
Map Division, The New York
Public Library, Astor, Lenox
and Tilden Foundations.

Vespucci popularized the information of the new world in the old, Waldseemüller gives him credit for the discovery, whether or not he rightfully deserved the
honor. On Waldseemüller's wall map, as on his globe gores, America is assigned
prominently to the lands that Vespucci had written about (Map 2.5).[70]

Letters and chronicles, translated into several languages, disseminated information, perceptions, and interpretations about America to a large European
public. So, too, did some of the first visual images of the Americas. A few maps
circulated to a general public, and on these maps appeared miniature scenes of
the landscape and customs of the Americas and its peoples. Woodcuts—black
and white or crudely colored—accompanied the publication of letters and
chronicles. Invariably, these visual images portrayed cannibalism as the defining
feature of life in Brazil.

References to cannibalism appeared in Vespucci's first letter about Brazil (1502)
when he writes that "they dismember and eat their dead enemies" and when he
elaborates that "we bought ten creatures from them, both males and females,
who were destined for sacrifice." Vespucci saw cannibalism as primarily a form
of nourishment. He declares, "the meat they most commonly eat is human flesh,"
and "they take captives and keep them, not to spare them, but to kill them for
food," or "human flesh is common fare among them." He superimposes on the

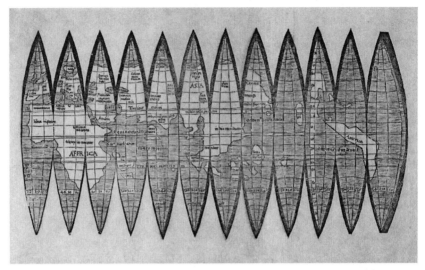

Map 2.5. Waldseemüller's globe gores showing America, 1507. From the collection of the James Ford Bell Library, University of Minnesota, Minneapolis, Minnesota.

peoples of Brazil the ways that meats are prepared in Europe. He writes, "in their houses we found human flesh hung up for smoking," and "I saw salted human flesh hanging from house-beams, much as we hang up bacon and pork."[71]

One of the German editions of Vespucci's *Mundus novus* letter carried a broadsheet depicting cannibalism in Brazil. The colored woodcut portrays Brazilian men, women, and children adorned with beautiful feathers around their waists and ankles, but this exotic scene also features a man gnawing on a human arm; a human head, leg, and arm hanging from the beams of a hut over an open fire; and a human leg resting on a table (Fig. 2.1). The text matter-of-factly states that "[t]hey eat each other, those that they kill. They place that flesh in fire."[72]

The visual depiction of a human skewered as a pig might be for roasting made its way onto one of the earliest depictions of Brazil, the anonymous world map drawn between 1502 and 1506, known as the "Kunstmann II" (Map 2.6). Believed by scholars to be an Italian copy of a Portuguese original, this map records information known as a result of Vespucci's expedition of 1501–1502. Whereas kings are drawn in Africa, as is the case opposite the feitoria of São Jorge da Mina, Brazil is portrayed pictographically with a lurid picture of a body being roasted whole over an open fire. The body is thought to be that of a white European, the crew member who went ashore and was killed and eaten in front of his companions, as related by Vespucci or by Pietro Martire d'Anghiera. The vividness of the drawing, coupled with errors in the presentation of cannibalism, suggests, according to Suzi Colin, that the illustrator "probably based his portrayal on accounts that had been embellished by various intermediaries." Such intermediaries might have heard stories from eyewitnesses—sailors or merchants—who had seen cannibalism.[73]

The rapid dissemination of cannibalistic images and descriptions of Brazil through printed books, maps, and engravings created a shared image of Brazil that was held by Europeans of very different backgrounds and nations. Waldseemüller's giant world map of 1516 depicted cannibalism as a defining feature of Brazil. This map sold so well that a second edition appeared in 1525, and according to one scholar, it became "one of the most influential representations of Indians in Renaissance map illustration."[74] Lurid depictions of cannibals feasting on human flesh sold well in Europe and reflected the power of the representational go-betweens to shape the image of Brazil in the imaginations of Europeans. By reducing Brazilians to simplified caricatures, it proved to be easy to rationalize their exploitation.

Figure 2.1. Illustration depicting cannibalism, 1505. Spencer Collection, The New York Public Library, Astor, Lenox and Tilden Foundations.

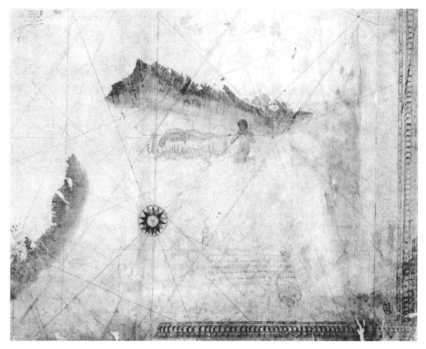

Map 2.6. Anonymous—Brazil as represented on the "Kunstmann II" World Map, 1505–1506. Bayerische Staatsbibliothek, München.

European men, serving as sailors, dominated the roles of physical go-betweens during the time of exploration and first encounters. But not all physical go-betweens during this time were Europeans. Native Brazilians sailed across the Atlantic, as did Africans. Taking captives back to Portugal was a custom followed by the Portuguese in Africa, and indeed, it is not surprising to see it adopted in Brazil, even though Cabral's captains did not elect to do so. When Columbus returned to Spain after his first voyage, he had with him at least seven Indians whom he intended to train as interpreters. Vicente Yáñez Pinzón carried thirty or thirty-six Indians from Brazil back to Spain in 1500. Anghiera describes these Indians as "captives"; most of them certainly became slaves in Spain, including one who might have been used as an interpreter. After describing a successful encounter with the Indians of Brazil, Vespucci writes that "we decided to take a couple of men from this place to teach us their language, and three volunteered to come with us to Portugal." Similarly, the report of the French ship captained by Binot Paulmier de Gonneville that landed in Brazil in 1504 notes that taking natives to Europe was a common procedure. "And because it is a custom," the report states, "among those who visit the new lands in the Indies, to take a few Indians back to Christendom, so it was done." [75]

Native Americans were objects of great wonder in Lisbon and other European ports. An expedition to North America led by Gaspar Corte-Real returned with more than fifty men, women, and children. Alberto Cantino wrote to his Italian patron, the Duke of Ferrara. "These people," he commented, "I saw and touched and contemplated." Gonneville took the son of Guarani chief Arosca back to France with him. Arosca agreed to allow his son, a youth named Essomericq, to leave on Gonneville's ship, along with a companion, a man of thirty-five to forty years named Namoa. Apparently Gonneville promised that Essomericq and Namoa would return in "twenty moons" with knowledge of artillery, which Arosca greatly desired in order to defeat his enemies, as well as how to make "mirrors, knives, axes, and all the things that they saw and admired of the Christians." At a subsequent stop in northern Brazil, the French captain attempted to take two more Indians from Brazil, but the two men jumped overboard at night and, to the amazement of the crew, swam three French leagues (*lieües;* approximately 13 kilometers) back to shore.[76]

Albrecht Dürer, who was fascinated by the new peoples and things appearing in European ports, most probably saw some of these native Brazilians taken to Europe. In the illustrated prayer book *Das Gebetbuch Kaiser Maximilians,* opposite the twenty-fourth psalm, Dürer draws a man wearing a feather skirt and a feather collar, and holding a feathered club; above is a large bird, perhaps a toucan (Fig. 2.2). Although positive identification is not possible, scholars do believe that the similarities between this drawing and other examples of Tupi featherwork and depictions of Brazilian Indians make it possible that Dürer intended this man to represent the Tupi peoples of Brazil.[77]

Although Africans, Asians, and Americans crossed the Atlantic, and in increasing numbers with the advent of the slave trade, they sailed in ships built in Europe with European technology, under the command of European sea captains, and in the service of European kings or powerful European merchants. The roles of the early physical go-betweens therefore were dominated by Europeans. This gave the Portuguese a tremendous initial advantage in their relations with the new peoples they met and with whom they intended to trade. Thus, even when Africans and Americans became physical and transactional go-betweens, they most often did so under the control of the Portuguese.

Figure 2.2. A Tupi Indian? *Das Gebetbuch Kaiser Maximilians*, Bayerische Staatsbibliothek, München.

Ordinary sailors, banished criminals, translators, chroniclers, and mapmakers all became go-betweens in the European process of "discovering" and "encountering" Brazil. As we have seen, the Portuguese experience in Africa directly shaped how Portuguese sea captains, merchants, and the Crown perceived Brazil. For nearly a century, the Portuguese had relied on go-betweens to explore, to encounter new peoples, and to develop trade. And go-betweens continued to be at the center of Portugal's first attempts to possess Brazil.

3. Possession

Kill him and eat him, the good-for-nothing, for he is indeed a Portuguese,
your enemy and mine.

Karwattuware, a French interpreter

The magnificent Reinel Map of Brazil (1519) proudly declares the Portuguese claim to Brazil (Map 3.1). Offshore ride two beautifully drawn
Portuguese naus, the large oceangoing ships that by 1519 sailed regularly to India,
each marked with the bold red crosses that symbolized the Portuguese Order of
Christ, which since the days of Prince Henry the Navigator had financed and
benefited from overseas trade and exploration. Between two Portuguese flags
marking the northern and southern limits of Brazil, a detailed and accurately
drawn coastline names more than one hundred bays, inlets, and rivers, reflecting
the work of Portuguese mariners and cartographers. Over the unknown interior
of Brazil, the miniaturist presents a vignette that represents the peoples and landscape of Brazil. The legend that appears at the top of the map proclaims in Latin,
the lingua franca of the educated European elite, that "[t]his is the chart of the
region of Great Brazil and on the western side it reaches the Antilles of the King
of Castile," and toward the bottom of the map, the land is formally named on a
red scroll: "Terra Brasilis" (Land of Brazil).[1]

One easily reads Reinel's map as a "representation" of the Portuguese possession of Brazil. The flags, the ships, the naming of places all convey to the viewer
the Portuguese claim to Brazil. Like other Portuguese maps in the sixteenth
century, the Reinel Map simultaneously reflects two kinds of information: that
delivered by the physical go-betweens—the homens do mar—who explored
by sea, and that supplied by the representational go-betweens who, as cartographers, translated the collected data into a new vision of the world. Although

Map 3.1. The Reinel Map, 1519. *L'Atlas Miller*, Bibliothèque nacionale de France.

it would seem that the Reinel Map documents the Portuguese possession of Brazil, the reality was quite different. By 1519, when the map was drawn, France and Spain competed with Portugal to claim parts of Brazil, a fact that the map minimizes. More important is the obvious fact that sea captains and cartographers had reconnoitered only the coast of Brazil; the interior was still unknown. There were hundreds of indigenous chiefs whom Europeans—whether Portuguese, French, or Spanish—had never met, and the dense coastal forests were filled with flora and fauna unfamiliar to Europeans. Brazil could be discovered, observed, and mapped, but such a representation did not translate into possession. Possession required the presence of transactional go-betweens—who appear nowhere on this exquisite map.

The beauty of the Reinel Map lies with the work of the miniaturist, who depicts a vision of life in Brazil that portrays the Portuguese dream of possession. Choosing a palette of greens to paint the verdant forests of Brazil, and using rules of perspective to suggest the depth and height of the wooded landscape, the miniaturist re-creates Brazil as if it were a stage. On this stage appear a meandering river, cliffs, clearings, and men, parrots, monkeys, jaguars, and even a dragon. Eight men, but no women or children, are deemed important enough to be drawn; some of the men hold poses as actors might, while others are busily engaged in activity. Four of the men might be chiefs, as evidenced by their wearing of feather headdresses, similar to crowns, and long skirts and capes fashioned from brilliant red and blue parrot feathers. Huge parrots—blue, red, and olive green—swoop down from the tree canopy. But though the trees are tall, the forests are not thick, and all the stands of trees show evidence of cutting. Four naked men are chopping, stacking, loading, and hauling enormous logs. The legend summarizes in words what the miniaturist has painted: "Its people are somewhat dark in colour. . . . These same people are most skillful in the use of bow and arrows." The legend concludes with a reference to the logging, which by 1519 was the primary export of Brazil: "and there grows in great quantity the tree called brazil, which is considered proper for dyeing clothes in purple."[2]

Brazilwood (*Caesalpinia echinata*) grew in the Atlantic forests, and when soaked, produced a reddish purple dye much in demand in Europe.[3] The Portuguese intent to possess this valuable commodity is one of the dominant messages of the map. But the miniaturist and the map's legend suggest that its possession will not be easy. The legend characterizes the peoples of Brazil as "savage and very cruel," and states as a matter of fact that "they feed on human flesh." The miniaturist does not emphasize cannibalism in his depiction of the inhabitants of Brazil, but a smudged, triangular shape in the northeast hints at it. Similar to a pictograph that often appears on later maps—wood stacked in the shape of a teepee, with fingers of fire consuming human body parts—it is possibly a direct reference to the place in northern Brazil where one of Vespucci's comrades was killed and eaten in front of his companions.

If mapmakers did not immediately perceive the importance of transactional go-betweens, practical merchants interested in the brazilwood trade quickly did. Even a trade in a simple export, such as tree logs, required negotiation, for merchants well knew that dreams of riches required agents on the ground. The Portuguese Crown drew on its long experience in Africa to develop rules for the brazilwood trade, as did ordinary sea captains and merchants. To facilitate first contacts, sea captains continued to use strategies that had worked well in Africa, such as seizing indigenous boys and men to train as interpreters, and leaving behind expendable European men, such as degredados. Later, the Crown and merchants came to rely on resident middlemen in Brazil, who devised roles for themselves that resembled patterns that had emerged in Africa.

In the fifteenth- and sixteenth-century African trade, European and mixed-race men known as *lançados* and *tangomaos* became important negotiators. According to Walter Rodney, the term "*lançado*" derives from the verb *lançar* (to throw), meaning that these Portuguese men had thrown themselves into the African world, and "*tangomaos*" referred to traders who had tattooed their bodies in the African style. Lançados and tangomaos were initially Portuguese and later Portuguese and/or mulatto men who lived in African communities and served as the middlemen between African chiefs and Portuguese traders. Another historian sees them as the "spearhead of Portuguese penetration" in Africa, India, and Brazil and argues that in many regions, it was only through them that the Portuguese were able to retain their commercial interests.[4]

The lançados come into focus after the initial phase of exploration and contact in Africa, a time when the first interpreters and colonists had been forced into their roles—serving as slave interpreters or penal exiles. As time passed, degredados and translators carved out roles for themselves that compensated for their marginal social status in the Portuguese world, and they found ways to create for themselves considerable independence and autonomy in the African world. Lançados lived in inland villages, as guests of African chiefs, and typically were married to one of the chief's women. The lançado was expected to follow the laws and customs of the region and to submit himself to the sovereignty of the chief. As a result, the Portuguese Crown and its agents had little control over the lançados. In the early sixteenth century, the Portuguese Crown began to legislate against these traders by issuing laws and decrees that forbade unlicensed traders from the Guinea coast and banned direct trade between the Cape Verde Islands and Guinea. However, these measures did little to stop the lançados, who were essential to trade.[5]

Over time, descendants of the lançados continued in their roles as middlemen on the Guinea coast, even after the Portuguese had long since been replaced by other European traders. Mulatto go-betweens continued to trade on a large scale, in slaves for Europeans and in goods destined for Africans—salt, cloth, dyes, kola nuts, palm oil, and rice. Of them, Walter Rodney writes that "the Afro-Portuguese acted as interpreters, and carried out all the tasks of middle-men in coastal trade, from acting as pilots on the rivers to serving as commercial advisers to the local ruling class."[6]

Although the Portuguese Crown regretted the independent roles that such transactional go-betweens had established for themselves in Africa, a similar situation emerged in Brazil.[7] European men who "went native" became the primary transactional go-betweens in the early brazilwood trade. Such men found themselves in Brazil for a variety of reasons: some came as agents of merchants; others, as degredados. A few deliberately jumped ship or had survived shipwrecks. All these men had to ally themselves with indigenous groups in order to survive; if they did, they had the potential to broker the economic and political relationships between coastal Indians and Europeans. Later, men of mixed race—the Brazilian mestizos (of mixed Indian and Portuguese parentage) known as *mamelucos*—dominated this role, as mulatto men had done in Africa.

Transactional go-betweens would fill a void in the Portuguese colonization of Brazil, as they had in Africa, where, lacking administrators for its far-flung empire, the Crown had relied on lançados and tangomaos. The dependence on such intermediaries, however, was not always in the Crown's long-term interests. The *prazeiros* of Mozambique are examples of transactional go-betweens who, though seeing themselves as *conquistadores* (conquistadors) for the king of Portugal, nevertheless adopted many of the cultural characteristics of the African groups with whom they intermarried. The descendants of the prazeiros shifted their loyalties from the Portuguese world to the African and, in the nineteenth century, resisted Portuguese influence by attacking Portuguese administrative centers and Portuguese trade.[8] Similarly, transactional go-betweens in Brazil might initially serve the Portuguese Crown, but over time they might develop their own interests, which did not always square with those of the Crown.

The roles of transactional go-betweens in the brazilwood trade are only dimly visible in the few documents known to historians that describe the trade in the early sixteenth century. Those documents reveal that what became known as the "brazilwood coast" extended from Cabo Frio, just east of present-day Rio de Janeiro, to Paraíba, north of Pernambuco. The Portuguese Crown immediately perceived the value of the brazilwood trade and quickly decreed it to be a royal monopoly. Merchants who wished to trade for the wood had to have a contract from the king. King Manuel granted the initial rights to brazilwood in contracts reminiscent of those granted in Africa. An Italian living in Seville in 1502 thought this news important enough that he provided details about it in a letter that described the arrival of seven ships from India that year. A consortium of Portuguese merchants received a contract for brazilwood and slaves, Pedro Rondinelli wrote, which required them to send six ships a year to Brazil to further explore the coast and to build a fort. News of the trade appears in Vespucci's letters as well. He writes that on his second trip to Brazil, which took place between 1503 and 1504, he spent five months 260 leagues (approximately 1,600 kilometers) from the Bay of All Saints, loading brazilwood and building a fort. In this spot, he claims to have left twenty-four men behind in the fort with munitions and provisions for six months. A Venetian report on the Portuguese regulations on the spice trade, penned in 1505, described the volume of the brazilwood trade as 20,000 *quintais* (hundredweights) per year, most of it destined for Flanders, Spain, and Italy, valued at 2.5 to 3 ducats per *quintal* (hundredweight). The monopoly of the brazilwood trade cost the Portuguese merchant Fernando de Noronha the sizable sum of 4,000 ducats per year; one observer estimated that Noronha made, on average, one ducat per quintal.[9]

The French quickly became involved in the brazilwood trade, too. The French sea captain Binot Paulmier de Gonneville, who arrived in southern Brazil in 1504, traded for brazilwood on his return. But it is unlikely that he was the first French trader in Brazil. The report of Gonneville's voyage explicitly states that on the return voyage, when the crew realized that they were near the place where French sea captains from Normandy traded for brazilwood, they decided to land and to barter for dyewood. At the first place they anchored, however, the Indians refused to trade, but at a second anchorage, they found Indians who would exchange brazilwood and food for European merchandise.[10]

The brazilwood trade developed two distinct patterns, one generally characteristic of the Portuguese, the other of the French. Both depended on transactional go-betweens experienced in Brazil. The Portuguese trade in brazilwood replicated a pattern that the Portuguese had established in Africa: merchants who held contracts from the king traded at a few established *feitorias* (fortified trading posts) built along the coast. In the French style, ships landed and traded, but no permanent forts were built. In both patterns of trade, brazilwood was not the only commodity of interest to the Europeans; peppers, feathers, exotic animal skins, monkeys, parrots, medicinal oils, and Indian slaves were also purchased in Brazil with European trading goods.

The Portuguese brazilwood trade took place in feitorias, where a resident factor supervised the trade. Cristovão Jacques established one such trading post for the king in Pernambuco, and another was located farther south at Cabo Frio. Merchants sent ships, such as the *Bretoa* that hailed the feitoria at Cabo Frio in 1511, to load cargoes of brazilwood. The captain of the *Bretoa* had been directed to submit to the factor once he arrived. "Above all things," his instructions read, "[you shall obey] the factor on the pain of losing your salary." Furthermore, the captain was warned to be vigilant with his crew and to permit them to go ashore only on the island where the trading post lay. By prohibiting the crew from visiting the mainland, the merchants clearly intended to prevent crew members, most of whom were unmarried and some of whom were slaves, from slipping away and remaining in Brazil, which apparently had happened on past trips. This, the captain's orders noted, was considered "odious to the trade and to the service of the King." [11]

In the Portuguese brazilwood trade, only the factor was permitted to play the role of transactional go-between: only he negotiated over brazilwood with the Indians. Yet, it proved almost impossible to prevent the creation of other, rival transactional go-betweens. The trading post was a community of sorts, and the factor did not live alone. From the sources that describe a French attack on the Portuguese trading fort in Pernambuco in 1531, we learn that the feitoria had been founded thirty years earlier. In addition to its fort and trading warehouse, it included a church and houses where the agents and scribes of the king and of Portuguese merchants lived. While this small Portuguese community existed to facilitate the trade in brazilwood, slaves, cotton, cat skins, parrots, and medicinal oils from the trading post, clearly many in the Portuguese community had contact with the surrounding indigenous groups. Although details are slim, the Portuguese living there had established some sort of modus vivendi with neighboring Indians, for when the French attacked, the nearby Indians joined in the battle on the side of the Portuguese. The French succeeded in taking the trading post, but the French possession was short lived, as the Portuguese destroyed the fort in December 1531. [12]

Those who lived in the trading post, or who participated in the brazilwood trade as sailors or merchants, became candidates who, if they remained in Brazil, might become transactional go-betweens. One such man was João Lopes Carvalho, the pilot of the *Bretoa* when it visited Cabo Frio in 1511. At some point in his life, most likely after 1511 but before 1520, Carvalho lived in Brazil for four years. In 1520, when Magellan sailed along the coast of Brazil during the first leg of his circumnavigation, Carvalho was the pilot of the *Concepción*. His son, by a Brazilian Indian woman, accompanied him. Carvalho served as intermediary during Magellan's brief but successful interactions along the coast of Brazil, where, according to Antonio Pigafetta, the crews had little difficulty provisioning their ships and trading for brazilwood. Pigafetta attributes to Carvalho an explanation of cannibalism that was possibly the first that explained to Europeans the meaning of the practice. "They eat the flesh of their enemies," Pigafetta recounts, "not as being good for food, but from custom." Moreover, he explains that the body is not eaten whole, but "piece by piece." These pieces were dried and eaten "with their ordinary food to call to mind their enemies." [13]

The French specialized in a more informal trade in brazilwood that was highly successful along the coast of Brazil. The French left men in Brazil known as *truchements* (interpreters), who lived with Indian groups and facilitated trade when merchant ships arrived, or French merchant ships carried their own interpreters, who negotiated with Indians for brazilwood. How this trade might have been initiated is visible in the log kept by the Portuguese mariner Pero Lopes de Sousa. In 1531, just south of Cabo Santo Agostinho, Indians swam out to the Portuguese ships and asked the crews if they were interested in brazilwood. As it was by now standard operating procedure for ships to have interpreters on board, Pero Lopes de Sousa had no difficulty understanding the Indians and communicating with them. However, Lopes de Sousa was not interested in brazilwood, as the ship he commanded was part of an armada that had a different mission from the Portuguese king, but to a French sea captain, such an overture might well have resulted in trade. [14]

The importance of go-betweens in this informal trade emerges in documents that reveal yet another competitor in the trade: the English. In the depositions given by the first known Englishmen engaged in piracy in the Americas appear references to interpreters and negotiators. The crew of the *Barbara* was tried for piracy on their return from a sea voyage that left Portsmouth in March 1540 and sailed along the coasts of Spain and Portugal, the Canary and Cape Verde Islands, Brazil, and Haiti before returning to England. Because the *Barbara* had attacked several Spanish ships on the voyage, the Spanish ambassador complained, and England's Lord High Admiral arrested the surviving crew members in 1541. The depositions from the trial reveal many details about the *Barbara*'s stay in Brazil. [15]

Three Englishmen owned the *Barbara*, but among her crew of one hundred served twelve Frenchmen, including her pilot, who hailed from Dieppe, a French port in Normandy traditionally involved in the brazilwood trade. When the *Barbara* reached Brazil in 1540, it anchored off Cabo de São Roque, along the northeastern coast of Brazil. The captain of the *Barbara* had engaged, along with the French pilot, a French interpreter, called by the Englishmen on the *Barbara* a "speechman." The speechman and the pilot "went on land to hear news." According to the depositions, the *Barbara* was very well received, but the crew discovered that they had landed too far from the place where brazilwood grew, and "the people said that they would not bring it so far unto us." The crew attempted to sail, against the wind, toward the location where they might trade for brazilwood, but failed. The pilot then convinced the captain and crew to change direction and make for another landing he knew. Captain Phillips then sailed northwest. The *Barbara* landed at an unknown place where the Indians, through the speechman and pilot, "said they were glad of our coming and promised us to have of their commodities for our wares gladly." Instead of brazilwood, however, the English crew traded for cotton, parrots, and monkeys. But the "speechman," who was so crucial to their successful interaction with the Indians of Brazil, along with the other French crewmen, deserted. The crew of the *Barbara* soon found themselves under fire from the Indians, led by those who had deserted.[16]

The English had been trading intermittently along the coast of Brazil at least since the 1530s, and as the *Barbara*'s voyage demonstrates, English captains already appreciated the value of go-betweens. On one of the earlier voyages made by William Hawkins, an Indian chief accompanied Hawkins back to London and met King Henry VIII. Hawkins made three trips from Plymouth to Brazil in the 1530s, stopping first along the coast of Guinea for elephant tusks and other unspecified commodities. On the second voyage, he left behind one member of his crew, a Martin Cockeram, as surety for the safe return of the "Brazilian king" who sailed to England with Hawkins. This chief, with his lip plug and "strange" ways, made a great impression on Henry VIII and the English nobility. After a year, Hawkins shipped out for Brazil, but en route the chief died. Nevertheless, Hawkins found Cockeram, whom the Indians agreed to give up, even through the English could not deliver their chief in return.[17]

Virtually all the transactional go-betweens of the first generation are silent to us, for most were at best semiliterate, hence they did not write about their own lives, their complicated identities, or their perceptions of the worlds changing around them. By midcentury, however, one group of transactional go-betweens appears frequently in the writings of several Europeans who visited Brazil. These go-betweens were the Norman interpreters, or truchements, who lived around Guanabara Bay and served as intermediaries in the French brazilwood trade with the Tupinambá.

In 1554, two Tupinambá brothers kidnapped Hans Staden, a German gunner who was then working at the Portuguese fortress of Bertioga at the Portuguese colony of São Vicente, and took him to their village along the coast, near the present-day town of Ubatuba. Staden later published an account of his captivity, which made him one of the most influential of the sixteenth-century representational go-betweens. Staden represented his whole experience of captivity in Brazil as a witness of his Christian faith for his European readers. More than any other text, Staden's account reinforced the view in Europe that Brazil was a land of savage and cruel cannibals. The tone of Staden's writings has led some scholars to argue that his detailed descriptions of cannibalism were exaggerated and others to contend that Staden's account may not be an authentic, original eyewitness account. Yet, one of the most striking descriptions in his tale is the portrait he draws of a transactional go-between: a Norman interpreter who had gone native in Brazil. The complexities woven into Staden's description of this Norman interpreter make it difficult to imagine that Staden could have invented his tale.[18]

Staden's account takes place in an Indian world bitterly divided between the Tupinikin, who lived on the Piratininga Plateau of São Vicente and who were allied with the Portuguese, and the Tupinambá, with whom the French had established alliances through their Norman interpreters. The Tupinambá lived to the north of São Vicente, along the coast around and just to the south of Guanabara Bay. Both groups shared a common language and culture.[19] Two Tupinambá brothers, Jeppipo Wasu and Alkindar Miri, thinking Staden to be Portuguese, captured him one day when he was out hunting with his Guarani Indian slave in the forest. Staden tells his readers why the two brothers had taken him captive: "The Portuguese had wounded the father of the two brothers, my captors, and had shot off one of his arms so that he died of his wounds, and . . . they intended to take vengeance on me for their father's death." The two brothers then presented their captive, Staden, to their uncle, Ipperu Wasu, brother of their deceased father. Ipperu Wasu, the brothers informed Staden, "would keep me until I was ready to be eaten, when he would kill me and thus acquire a new name." Fearing his fate daily, Staden desperately sought an escape, but simply running away was out of the question, since the brothers, or their uncle, kept Staden under close watch and had bound his neck with a rope. Staden's plan was to insist that he was not Portuguese, and because the Indians who held him were friendly with the French, he intended to pass himself off as a Frenchman. He hoped that a Norman interpreter or a French sailor would come to his aid, out of a common European bond and shared Christian values. He writes that when he "understood that there were Frenchmen among them who came there in their ships, I persisted in my story that I was a kinsman and friend to the French, and that they should leave me alive until the Frenchmen arrived and recognized me." [20]

As it happened, there were Norman interpreters living very near Ubatuba, one of whom Staden's captors knew as Karwattuware, for a chief, Konyan Bebe, who lived in a nearby village, had adopted him as his "son." One day Staden reports that "the savages came running to me and said: 'Here is a Frenchman. Now we shall see whether you are in truth a Frenchman or not.'" Staden tells his readers that he rejoiced, certain that he was about to be saved by the intervention of Karwattuware, for "he was at least a Christian and would do his best for me." But Karwattuware, who might have chosen to use his power in this situation to help Staden, did not. Instead, he spoke to him in French and "when I was unable to reply to him," Staden writes, "he spoke to the savages in their own tongue and said: 'Kill him and eat him, the good-for-nothing, for he is indeed a Portuguese, your enemy and mine.'" Staden did not understand French, but he clearly did understand what Karwattuware had just said in Tupi, and he recalls begging the Frenchman in Tupi, "for the love of God," to order the Indians not to eat him. Karwattuware only replied, according to Staden, "They will certainly eat you." [21]

Staden's account of this meeting reveals the power of the transactional go-between, positioned in between two conflicting parties. In Staden's eyes, Karwattuware could have saved him, but he did not. But from Karwattuware's perspective, he had nothing to gain by saving Staden, and therefore did not wish to risk challenging the customs of the Tupinambá to free Staden. After he recovered from his shock that the Norman interpreter would not help him, Staden realized that he had no other option but to try again. He met Karwattuware some time later and again tried to use him as an intermediary with his captors. This time he had more success. Addressing the Frenchman in their common language, Tupi, Staden purportedly asked him "whether he had a Christian heart in his bosom when he enjoined the savages to kill me, or had considered the [after]life that was to come," which, according to Staden, caused Karwattuware to reconsider. Staden then reported that Karwattuware "began to be ashamed and excused himself, saying that he had thought that I was indeed a Portuguese, who were such scoundrels that if the French could catch them anywhere in the province of Brazil they would hang them forthwith, which was indeed the truth." Moreover, Karwattuware explained to Staden that the French "had to submit to the savages and be content with their treatment of their enemies." 22

After this second meeting, Staden recounts that Karwattuware did have a change of heart and promised to help him. But even Karwattuware could not do anything for Staden. Staden describes him telling his Indian friends, Staden's captors, that Staden was a friend of France and that he would take him to a ship, but Staden's captors would have nothing of it. Staden writes that "the savages refused to deliver me up, stating that if my own father or brother came with a shipload of axes, mirrors, knives, combs, and scissors and gave them these goods, they would not let me go." Several months later, Karwattuware's French ship arrived at Ubatuba. Staden first pleaded with Jacob, one of the crew members who came ashore to trade and who spoke Tupi, to take him to the ship, but that failed. Later that day he ran away and swam out to the ship. But the French sailors refused to take him on board (Fig. 3.1) because, as Staden relates it, "they thought that if they took me thus the savages would rise against them and become their enemies." 23

Staden swam ashore "very sadly" and returned to his captivity. He continued to live with Konyan Bebe at Ubatuba and even accompanied him on an eleven-day war party against his former friends—the Tupinikin and their Portuguese allies—at Bertioga in August of 1554. A short time later, Konyan Bebe decided to give Staden away to another chief, Abbati Bossange, who lived in the environs of Guanabara Bay. Abbati Bossange adopted Staden as his son, but Staden continued to look for opportunities to escape. One came very soon, two weeks later, when another French ship arrived to trade. The men on this ship proved to be more sympathetic to Staden.

Staden designed a little drama that, with the help of the French crew, allowed him to leave Brazil. First he told his "master," Abbati Bossange, that on the ship were his brothers, who had come to buy his freedom, but that he would remain in Brazil collecting until the ship returned the next year. When the ship was fully loaded with goods from Guanabara Bay, the captain of the crew spoke to Abbati Bossange through an interpreter and gave him several chests of trading goods.

Figure 3.1. Hans Staden begging French sailors to take him to France. Hans Staden, *Warhaftige Historia und Beschreibung einer Landtschaft der wilden nacketen grimmigen Menschenfresser Leuthen in der Newenwelt America gelegen* (Marburg, 1557). Courtesy of the John Carter Brown Library at Brown University.

Meanwhile, several of the crew who looked like Staden posed as his brothers and pretended to prevent Staden from remaining in Brazil. Staden promised Abbati Bossange that he would return the next year, although he had no intention of doing so. "All this was ordained so that we might part from the savages on friendly terms," Staden writes. The *Catherine* sailed with Staden aboard on 31 October 1554, and arrived in Honfleur, Normandy, on or about 20 February 1555. But the *Maria Bellete*, which carried Karwattuware as well as the other Frenchmen who had refused to take Staden aboard, had not yet made it back to France, even though she was overdue by three months. In Staden's eyes, the likely loss of the ship was God's punishment for the "godless" behavior of the Frenchmen toward him in Brazil. Staden's account of his travels, illustrated with woodcuts, appeared in Marburg, Germany, in 1557.[24]

Staden's depiction of Karwattuware reveals how transactional go-betweens adapted themselves to the Indian way of life and accepted the power of chiefs in order to make a commercial relationship possible between the Indian and the

European worlds. Although a European, such as Staden, initially saw such a go-between as possessing extensive power, in fact the power of the Norman interpreter was based on the successful negotiation of his place within Indian society. In such a role, Karwattuware could not go against the wishes of his Indian "father," nor was it in his interest to do so. When Staden was traded to Abbati Bossange, he, too, stepped into the role played by Karwattuware and other Norman interpreters. Just as Karwattuware did not want to alienate the chief who had adopted him as his son, Staden likewise wanted to engineer an escape for himself that would allow Abbati Bossange to save face and to remain on good terms with the French captain who carried Staden to safety.

Two French writers, whose texts, like that of Hans Staden, were avidly consumed by European audiences, also provide descriptions of Norman interpreters. A young Franciscan monk, André Thevet, remained in Brazil for three months (November 1555 through January 1556) and wrote *Les singularitez de la France Antarctique (1557)* based on his personal observations of Brazil and on his conversations with Norman interpreters. A year later, Jean de Léry, a Calvinist missionary, left France; Léry remained in Brazil for approximately one year, and after he returned to France, he, too, wrote a richly detailed account of his experience that was deeply influenced by the Norman interpreters.[25]

Thevet provides few details on the Norman interpreters; nevertheless, it is possible to glimpse them through his writings and to understand how much he owed his portrayal of Tupinambá life to them. Some Norman interpreters served as his translators, for Thevet did not speak Tupi well enough during his ten weeks in Brazil to converse directly with Indians; other Norman interpreters provided him with information. Thevet explains in his discussion of religion that "this and many other things were affirmed for me by some Christians [i.e., Norman interpreters] who had lived there a long time." Thevet illustrates how the language ability of the Norman interpreters, as well as their lengthy residence among the Tupinambá, were essential for his own understanding of Tupinambá religion when he writes, "Here is the religion of our barbarians, which I learned by observing and understood through a truchement *français* [Norman interpreter] who had lived there six years and who understood their language perfectly."[26]

Norman interpreters served as transactional go-betweens for Léry as he traveled around Guanabara Bay, and in their ability to translate information for Léry, they reflected their own position as go-betweens between the Tupinambá and the French. Léry frequently notes the presence of interpreters in his narrative, giving us to understand that he was able to acquire much of his information through them. Léry provides a more complete picture of the Norman interpreters. He describes those he knew as men who had survived a shipwreck eight or nine years earlier and "had remained among the savages, where, having no fear of God, they lived in wantonness with the women and girls." Léry visited twenty-two villages during his time in Brazil, always in the company of Norman interpreters, who moved easily from village to village. Léry notes that the interpreters were essential, for "although the Tupinambá receive very humanely the friendly strangers who go to visit them, nevertheless the Frenchmen and others from over here who do not understand their language find themselves at first marvelously disconcerted in their midst." [27]

Through Léry, we learn how the Norman interpreters brokered the trading relationship between the Tupinambá and the French merchants. He makes it clear that the entire French trade depended on the willingness of the coastal Tupinambá to cooperate. It was the job of the Norman interpreter to convince the coastal chiefs that it was in their interest to participate in the trade. Brazilwood was so difficult to cut, haul, and load in the absence of domestic animals such as horses or donkeys, Léry writes, that "if the foreigners who voyage over there were not helped by the savages, they could not load even a medium-sized ship in a year." Why did the local chiefs agree to cooperate? Léry suggests that the chiefs had become accustomed to the trading goods provided by the French. Maintaining the flow of knives, hatchets, axes, scissors, and scythes required good relations with the French. This very basic desire for European goods was, for Léry, the reason why chiefs cooperated: "I will add," he writes, "that the elders especially, who in the past lacked axes, pruning hooks, and knives—which they now find useful for cutting their wood and making their bows and arrows—not only treat visiting Frenchmen very well, but also exhort their young people to do the same in the future." [28]

What the French expected was extensive. Léry describes the exchange as far more favorable for the French: "In return for some frieze [woolen] garments, linen shirts, hats, knives, and other merchandise that they are given," the Indians "cut, saw, split, quarter, and round off the brazilwood, with the hatchets, wedges, and other iron tools given to them by the French" (Fig. 3.2), then "carry it on their bare shoulders, often from a league or two [approximately 4 to 8 kilometers] away, over mountains and difficult places, clear down to the seashore

Figure 3.2. Cutting brazilwood. André F. Thevet, *Les singularitez de la France Antarctique, autrement nommée Amerique* (Paris, 1558). Courtesy of the John Carter Brown Library at Brown University.

by the vessels that lie at anchor, where the mariners receive it." In Léry's eyes, the Tupinambá did so both to receive the trading goods and to maintain their alliance with the French. The alliance with the French affected the position of the Tupinambá vis-à-vis their traditional enemies, the Tupinikin, and their new enemies, the Portuguese, and therefore it was, it seemed to Léry, in the immediate interests of the Tupinambá to protect their alliance with the French. When an elderly Indian man threatened Léry with death after Léry had killed his pet duck, Léry reflected that despite his fear, he had not been in real danger, for "the Tupinambá knew perfectly well that, already having the Portuguese for enemies, if they had killed a Frenchman, an irreconcilable war would have been declared between them and that they would be forever deprived of our merchandise." [29]

To make possible this trading relationship, which carried such high stakes on both the Indian and the French sides, Norman interpreters had to establish a place for themselves within Tupinambá society. To accomplish this, they had to learn to be persuasive through discourse, they had to obtain social status, and they had to be recognized by local chiefs, for local chiefs would not cooperate unless they perceived the Norman interpreters as trustworthy and dependable, and even as their sons. Thus, to be effective as go-betweens, Norman interpreters had to become enough a part of the indigenous society to be seen as trustworthy. And to be seen as trustworthy, Norman interpreters could not challenge the fundamental structures of Tupinambá culture.

Norman interpreters could not, for example, refuse a woman, or women, given to them by chiefs, because accepting the women made them sons-in-law to the chief. This was their most important connection to Tupinambá society, for by accepting a woman, they became a son-in-law of a powerful man. Léry, a Calvinist, describes this practice as "lewd and base behavior" on the part of the Norman interpreters, but seen from the perspective of the Tupinambá, it was a recognized way of integrating adult males into their communities, and from the perspective of the Norman interpreter, it was crucial to his survival.[30]

Similarly, because warfare was such a vital part of the indigenous world of the 1550s, Norman interpreters could not avoid the wars, and many certainly participated in them. Some of the first Europeans in Brazil described exceptionally violent wars between Indian groups,[31] and the insertion of competing European powers (France and Portugal) only intensified intertribal warfare. Given the long tradition of war among Tupi groups, as well as the introduction of powerful new allies and enemies, European go-betweens must certainly have been valued by Indian groups because of their understanding of European arms and fighting. With a companion, Léry observed 4,000 Tupinambá and Margaia in a three-hour combat, after which the Tupinambá took thirty Margaia prisoner. Léry tells his readers that he and his French companion did not participate in the battle and that they did little more than to "hold our drawn swords in our hands, and sometimes fire a few pistol shots into the air to give courage to our side," but nevertheless their presence was interpreted as a sign of great respect by the Tupinambá Indians. Léry then writes, "there was nothing we could have done to give them greater pleasure than to go with them to war," and "they continued to hold us in such high esteem that, since that time, the elders of the villages we visited always showed us the greatest affection." [32] So, too, would Norman interpreters have observed, and have given support to, the battles fought by the Tupinambá among whom they lived.

When the Tupinambá warriors returned home with their captives, the ritual cannibalism ceremony took place. An essential part of developing the trust between Norman interpreters and the Tupinambá was the formers' acceptance of the cannibalism ceremony that followed these intertribal battles. Coastal Tupi groups practiced exocannibalism, or the eating of those from outside their group, such as enemies captured in warfare.[33] Staden's account of cannibalism provides many details of the preparation leading to the ritual cannibalism ceremony. He writes that when the Tupinambá from Ubatuba returned from battle with their captives, another chief, Tatamiri, whom he described as a "king over certain huts," took charge of the ceremonies to come. Staden relates that Tatamiri "caused drink to be prepared, according to their custom, and all the savages gathered together, drinking, singing, and making very merry." Drinking preceded the cannibalism ceremony and was an important part of the social life of the village. Léry describes how as men danced women served them warmed drink, which they had prepared from chewing cooked manioc, boiling the masticated mass, and fermenting it in large vats. Sometimes the drinking lasted for three days, according to Léry, "until the vessels—even if there were a hundred—are all empty." While this drink made from fermented manioc (*cauim* or *caouin* in Léry's account) lasted, the Tupinambá were "singing, whistling, egging each other on, and exhorting each other to act valiantly, and to take many prisoners when they go to war." [34]

Establishing and maintaining their position within indigenous society demanded that Norman interpreters not just observe but participate in this key ritual of Tupi society. Staden perceived the importance of the cannibalism rite, saying that "their greatest honor is to capture their enemies and to slay them; for such is their custom." Léry explains that Tupinambá cannibalism is not for nourishment: "It is more out of vengeance than for the taste . . . their chief intention is that by pursuing the dead and gnawing them right down to the bone, they will strike fear and terror into the hearts of the living." Another German, Ulrich Schmidel, who arrived in São Vicente in 1553 after having traveled overland from the small Spanish settlement of Asunción, described the Tupinikin custom of cannibalism as "a great party." "When they defeat their enemies,"

Schmidel wrote, describing Tupi warfare, "they bring them to their village, with an accompaniment similar to our weddings." [35]

Norman interpreters joined in the cannibalism ceremony. On one occasion early in his stay, Léry arrived at a village with a Norman interpreter, where they "found the savages dancing and finishing up the *caouin* [drink] of a prisoner whom they had killed only six hours earlier." After being greeted in the usual way, Léry recounts that his Norman interpreter, "who was not new to the customs of the savages, and who, moreover, liked to drink and *caouiner* as much as they did," left him in the house with their Tupinambá hosts and "went over to the big crowd of dancers." There the Norman interpreter remained until morning, "carousing" with the Tupinambá. Moreover, Léry, in his disapproving Calvinist voice, tells his readers: "to my great regret I am compelled to recount here that some Norman interpreters, who had lived eight or nine years in that country, accommodating themselves to the natives and leading the lives of atheists … surpassing the savages in inhumanity, even boasted in my hearing of having killed and eaten prisoners." [36]

Tattooing the body of the warriors who had taken war captives was done after the slaying of the prisoner. Staden writes of the warrior who had returned with a captive that "the king of the huts scratches him in the upper part of the arm with the tooth of a wild beast." Later, after the wound had healed, "the scar remains visible, which is a great honor." Léry writes that tattooing occurred the day prisoners were killed, when their captors cut their chests, thighs, and legs and "rub these slits with certain mixtures and with a black powder that cannot ever be effaced," to signify the honor of having taken an enemy prisoner. "The more slashes they carry," Léry noted, "the more renowned they will be for having killed many prisoners, and they are consequently esteemed the more valiant by the others." The tattooing accompanied the taking of new names. According to Staden, "for every foe a man kills he takes a new name. The most famous among them is he that has the most names." [37]

Norman interpreters could only be effective if they were enough a part of Tupinambá society to garner the trust and loyalty of Tupinambá chiefs. Léry writes that when he refused to accept the "human flesh of their prisoners," he recognized that he was not accepted by the Tupinambá, for it seemed to them that he was "not showing proper loyalty." [38]

The accounts of Staden and Léry underscore the power of coastal Indian groups in Brazil at midcentury. Although the brazilwood trade depended on the long and hard labor of Indian men who did the work of locating, cutting, cleaning, carrying, and stacking the brazilwood logs, and although Léry certainly thought the terms of the trade beneficial to the French, both Staden and Léry portray the coastal Tupinambá chiefs as independent, powerful, and shrewd men. Indian chiefs were in a position to demand what they wanted for the brazilwood. But although the sources reflect the authority of Tupinambá chiefs in the brazilwood trade, they nevertheless make clear that the transactional go-betweens worked generally to the benefit of Europeans. Transactional go-betweens became part of Tupi societies and deferred to their fathers-in-law and elders. Yet, while the relationships they facilitated may have served short-term interests of the tribal elders, in the long run, the brazilwood trade benefited European merchants. As the trade increased in value, the indigenous peoples of Brazil would find themselves faced with an increasing demand for logs.

The historian Alexander Marchant argues that as the brazilwood trade brought not only more frequent contact between Indians and Europeans but also increased demands for the logs, the terms of the trade clearly shifted in favor of the Indians. Brazilwood agents had to deliver more expensive and better trading goods to the Indians to maintain the brazilwood trade. Eventually, Indians became "satiated" with trading goods, at which point, he argues, "the Portuguese themselves were no longer a wondrous novelty to the Indians."[39] Yet Léry and Staden both describe the intense competition between Tupinambá and Tupinikin groups, fueled by competing European rivalries. Léry perceives a dependence on the European merchandise that he suggests limits the independence of tribal elders. Similarly, Neal Salisbury argues that in the second half of the sixteenth century in North America, the expansion of the fur trade had a negative effect on Indian societies. As French merchants moved aggressively into North America, seeking to monopolize the fur trade with Algonquian Indians, they drew Indians "into a dangerous dependency on an unpredictable industry and pitted them in unequal, often destructive competition with one another."[40]

European transactional go-betweens understood in ways that their Indian fathers-in-law could not that the local brazilwood trade was intertwined with wider European rivalries. Portugal, France, England, and Spain all sought to possess some part, or all, of Brazil, either through trade or through exploration and settlement. Inevitably, the Portuguese, Spanish, and even French desire to possess more than brazilwood led to colonization.

Thirty years after Cabral's voyage, the fear of French and Spanish claims in Brazil drove the king of Portugal to grant to Martim Afonso de Sousa the right to plant the first official Portuguese colony in Brazil. Just as men who had gone native facilitated the brazilwood trade, so, too, did such men negotiate the needs of the first Portuguese colonists, which were far greater than those of the traders. Colonization initiated a new dimension of possession, one that brought sweeping changes to the worlds of the Tupi and Guarani peoples.

In 1530, King João III (1521–1557) sent Martim Afonso de Sousa in command of an armada that was to explore the Río de la Plata, which the Portuguese Crown contested with Spain, to attack any French merchant ships trading for brazilwood, and to create the first authorized royal settlement in Brazil. Martim Afonso de Sousa chose São Vicente, in southern Brazil, for the first colony. There was a reason for this. São Vicente was already a Portuguese settlement of sorts when Sousa arrived; in 1530, it consisted of a village of ten or twelve houses, and European stock animals (chickens and pigs) had already begun to transform the landscape. The settlement had grown for the very same reason that Sousa had chosen it: it was near the contested southern boundary of Brazil.[41]

The Treaty of Tordesillas (1494) prompted Spain to claim southern Brazil, the Río de la Plata, and Paraguay. The treaty defined a line that separated the Spanish from the Portuguese spheres of influence. Initially, King Ferdinand of Aragon and Queen Isabella of Castile received from Pope Alexander VI a papal bull granting them the rights to all lands west of a line drawn through the Atlantic, 100 leagues (approximately 620 kilometers) west of the Azores and Cape Verde Islands. However, concern in Lisbon about Portuguese rights to African and Indian trade, and perhaps the certainty that a "new land" lay across the Atlantic from Africa, led King João II to insist on a separate agreement with Spain. In 1494, Ferdinand and Isabella signed a treaty with King João II in the Spanish town of Tordesillas that recognized Spain's rights to the lands discovered by Columbus, but pushed the imaginary line "drawn north and south, from pole to pole, on the said ocean sea, from the Arctic to the Antarctic pole . . . three hundred and seventy leagues [approximately 2,300 kilometers] west of the Cabo [Cape] Verde Islands."[42] The Treaty of Tordesillas thereby redrew the line of demarcation, allowing Portugal eventually to claim Brazil, because it lay within the Portuguese sphere. After 1500, Spain and Portugal continually disagreed over where the line fell in Brazil: Spanish geographers invariably claimed that it bisected Brazil farther east, thus making Brazil smaller on Spanish maps.[43] The Portuguese cartographers, in return, claimed that Brazil extended much farther to the north and south. This can be seen in the Reinel Map of 1519 (Map 3.1), in which the Portuguese flags that mark the northern and southern boundaries of Brazil allow Brazil to extend well south of the Río de la Plata and well beyond the mouth of the Amazon River in the north.

Spain defended its claim by sending the armadas of Juan Díaz Solis (1514–1516), Diego García (1526–1530), and Pedro de Mendoza (1535–1537). Moreover, the Spanish Crown outfitted the expeditions of the Portuguese mariners Fernão Magalhães (Magellan, 1519–1521) and García Jofre de Loaisa (1525) and of the Englishman Sebastian Cabot (1525–1530) to find a sea route to the Orient so it could gain access to the profitable spice trade that it believed lay within the Spanish sphere there. European men who had gone native in southern Brazil, in places such as São Vicente or at the nearby harbor of Cananéia, supplied these Spanish armadas with food, water, and information. South of São Vicente at Cananéia lived a degredado known as "the bachelor" (*o bachiller*) with his sons-in-law. According to the first references to him, in 1527 and 1530, he had been living in Brazil for thirty years.[44] Farther south, at the Island of Santa Catarina (today Florianópolis) and the Río de la Plata, also lived a few isolated men, often survivors of past disasters, who likewise served as go-betweens for the Spanish. When Sebastian Cabot arrived at the Río de la Plata in 1527, for example, his interpreters learned from their local contacts that "a Christian captive" lived among them. Francisco del Puerto was a Spaniard who had survived the massacre of Solis' men in 1516 and lived among the Indians at Río de la Plata. Puerto then informed Cabot "about the nature of the country," including how to navigate upstream.[45]

When Sousa selected São Vicente to be the site of the first chartered town in Brazil, he, with the authority invested in him by the king, created a *vila* (town), granted *sesmarias* (land grants), and established the institutions of municipal government characteristic of Portuguese society.[46] But the colony at São Vicente flourished primarily due to the presence of a Portuguese man who had lived for many years among the Indians and who served as a transactional go-between. João Ramalho had lived in Brazil since 1512. Possibly a degredado or a survivor of a shipwreck, Ramalho had married into the Tupinikin Indians of the Piratininga Plateau, becoming the son-in-law to the chief, Tibiriça. In São Vicente, João Ramalho brokered the relations between the Tupinikin Indians of the Piratininga Plateau and the coastal settlement founded by Martim Afonso de Sousa.

Soon after chartering the first colony at São Vicente, but before learning if and how the first colony had fared, the Portuguese Crown announced plans for the colonization of all of Brazil.[47] This scheme granted huge strips of land, from the coast inland to the line of the Treaty of Tordesillas, to private individuals, who would colonize them at their own expense. The Crown's grandiose scheme for dividing Brazil up into hereditary grants to stimulate colonization was never a success, even though a few individual recipients of these grants, known as *donatários*, did succeed in establishing small colonial outposts along the coast of Brazil. The Crown's plan is still visible in the famous map attributed to Luís Teixeira that was drawn later in the century. Like the Reinel Map of 1519, the map shows how the Portuguese imagined its possession. Not only does all the coastline from the Amazon River to the Río de la Plata estuary fall within the line of demarcation established by the Treaty of Tordesillas, but the vast lands of Brazil, already inhabited by hundreds of Indian groups, were summarily granted to individuals through the drawing of lines. These lines, drawn parallel to the equator, bisected the coast at 50-league (approximately 300-kilometer) intervals and extended from the coast to the line of demarcation, which marked the western frontier of Brazil. Although no one knew where the line of demarcation lay in the vast interior of Brazil, the Crown nevertheless granted these broad slices of territory to "men who had well served the kings in the discovery and conquest of the Orient" (Map 3.2).[48]

The Teixeira map conveys the power claimed by the Portuguese kings, a power honed as the Portuguese ships had explored the coasts of Africa, India, China, Japan, the Spice Islands, and Brazil, using their advances in navigation, mapmaking, and shipbuilding. But the mere fact of having things that conferred power in Europe—such as the accumulated knowledge recorded on the map, the rights assigned in the king's donation, the titles granted to administer justice and to distribute land, or the resources of a personal fortune—did not ensure that those favored with such grants could actually possess them. It was only through the intervention of transactional go-betweens, some named but most not, that the successful donatários were able, over many years, to possess a small part of Brazil.

Of the fifteen hereditary grants given by the king, ten were settled in the sixteenth century, and of these, only two, São Vicente and Pernambuco, were successful. The recipients of the grants generally intended to develop a new economic focus in Brazil, and because the Crown monopolized the brazilwood trade, that new focus was sugar. Following the successful production and export of sugar on the Portuguese Atlantic island of Madeira in the fifteenth century, Spanish colonists on the Canary Islands and Portuguese colonists in São Tomé hoped to develop sugar economies in the early sixteenth century. By the 1530s,

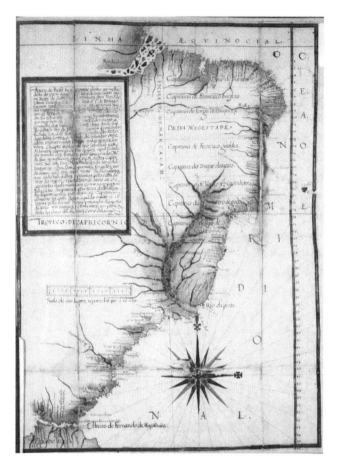

Map 3.2. A map of Brazil, c. 1580. [Luís Teixeira], *Roteiro de todos os sinais, conhecimentos, fundos, baixos, alturas, e derrotas que há na costa do Brasil desde o cabo de Santo Agostinho até ao estreito de Fernão de Magalhães.* Biblioteca da Ajuda, Lisbon.

signs pointed to success in the Canaries, and especially in São Tomé, thus making sugar a logical crop to try in Brazil. But, whereas transactional go-betweens in the brazilwood trade could establish terms of trade that, at least in the short term, were generally seen as favorable to both Indians and Europeans, sugar cultivation was another matter. The cultivation, cutting, and milling of cane and the boiling and dripping of cane syrup to produce sugar required extensive labor that, unlike the labor of the brazilwood trade, could not easily be fit into the extant lifestyle of coastal Tupi indigenous groups, where women were the primary agriculturalists. On the Atlantic islands off the coast of Africa, sugar cultivation had rested on the backs of slaves, imported from other Atlantic islands or from Africa. Those who intended to introduce sugar into Brazil certainly would have planned to use slaves to meet their labor needs there, too. Moreover, sugar cultivation would encroach on lands and forests already claimed by Indian groups. Sugar, therefore, represented a far greater series of demands from Europeans, and Indians were in a position to refuse.[49]

But before sugar plantations could be contemplated, the first colonies had to establish a rudimentary infrastructure. Historian John Monteiro observes that the most successful colonies "were precisely those where significant alliances had been struck between European adventurers and native headmen." Such alliances had been "cemented by marriage strategies, as headmen 'adopted' outsiders as sons-in-law."[50] These outsider sons-in-law served as transactional go-betweens when colonization began.

The agency of Ramalho at the Portuguese colony in São Vicente is clearly visible. By 1548, the captaincy of São Vicente had six hundred colonists, three thousand slaves, and six sugar mills. These slaves were Indians from traditional enemies of the Tupinikin, supplied by Ramalho, who lived on the Piratininga Plateau, above the coastal settlement. Monteiro argues that having such a powerful broker undoubtedly favored the vulnerable coastal settlement, for "Ramalho clearly had appropriated the attributes of a Tupinikin headman."[51]

Other go-betweens, including mamelucos, also helped the colony. When Hans Staden found himself in São Vicente a few years later, some of his closest companions in the settlement were five mameluco brothers. Staden had signed on for a Spanish expedition to the Río de la Plata led by Diego de Sanabria, who had been appointed by the king of Spain as governor of Paraguay. Leaving Spain in 1549, two of the three ships arrived at the Island of Santa Catarina, the agreed-upon meeting place, but the third never arrived and was presumed lost. Because one of the ships was no longer seaworthy, most of the men set out overland for Asunción, while part of the remaining men, including Staden, sailed for São Vicente. The Portuguese colonists there depended on their alliance with the Tupinikin, but at the frontier between Tupinikin and Tupinambá territory, they relied on the five mameluco brothers, who became Staden's friends. These men, the sons of Diego de Praga and an Indian woman, Staden writes, "were experienced both in Christian and savage speech and customs." They protected the passage between the Island of Santo Amaro and the mainland, and they had begun to build a fort, known as Bertioga, where Staden found work as a gunner.[52]

Later, after Staden had been captured, his Tupinambá captors led a war party against the Portuguese in São Vicente. Staden describes how they overtook five canoes in which were two of the Praga brothers, who held off the war party of thirty canoes for two hours with a gun and bows and arrows, but were then overtaken when their arrows ran out. Staden describes the cannibalization of several of their companions, including a cousin. The two brothers were captives but still alive when Staden was traded to another group. Staden believed that they had escaped, although he did not know if they were later recaptured.[53]

At the Bay of All Saints, the Portuguese colony got off to a rocky start, even with the presence of an influential transactional go-between named Diogo Álvares, known as "Caramuru" (Eel) by the Indians living around the Bay of All Saints. Pero Lopes de Sousa, who chronicled his brother Martim Afonso de Sousa's expedition to Brazil, met Álvares in 1531 and wrote in his log that "at this bay [of All Saints] we found a Portuguese who had been here twenty-two years," and he "gave a long notice of what was in this land." Álvares had married the daughter of a local chief in the region around the Bay of All Saints, thereby becoming linked through kinship to many Indians. Before the hereditary grant to colonize the region at the northernmost part of the Bay of All Saints was given to Francisco Pereira Coutinho, Álvares was already active as a transactional go-between, supplying ships with information and most likely food and possibly brazilwood.[54]

When Francisco Pereira Coutinho, the donatário of Bahia, arrived at the Bay of All Saints in 1536 with colonists, Álvares became his ally. In return for facilitating relations with local Indians, Coutinho gave Álvares and his son-in-law land grants in 1536. For nine years, Álvares' brokerage with the Indians was successful, for Coutinho was able to develop cotton and sugar cultivation as well as a small settlement known as Vila Velha (Old Town). But this was to end in 1545. According to the donatários of neighboring Porto Seguro and Pernambuco, Coutinho was a poor leader and in ill health. Dissatisfaction among his colonists led to a rebellion against his authority. Moreover, the Indians attacked Vila Velha, causing the survivors to flee and the donatário to take refuge in Porto Seguro. The donatário of Porto Seguro learned from Álvares, who had traveled to Porto Seguro from the Bay of All Saints to deliver the news, that a French ship had anchored there, and its crew had taken possession of all remaining artillery in the abandoned settlement and had made friends with the Indians. The information supplied by Álvares suggested that the French had promised to return with four or five armed ships and with French colonists who would claim the remains of the settlement and rebuild the abandoned cotton and sugar plantations. Coutinho resolved to return to defend his grant, but on the way back, the ship sank off the coast of the island of Itaparica, and Francisco Pereira Coutinho, the donatário of Bahia, became a prisoner of the Tupinambá, who killed and cannibalized him. Álvares escaped, according to a sixteenth-century chronicler, because of his "good language." The Indian attack, the threat of the French takeover, and the death of the donatário at the hands of the Tupinambá all seemed to doom the colony at Vila Velha.[55]

Duarte Coelho received the captaincy of Pernambuco, the site of one of the king's brazilwood feitorias. The success of his colony may have depended in part on his brother-in-law, Jerônimo de Albuquerque. Coelho embarked for Pernambuco accompanied by his Portuguese wife, Beatriz de Albuquerque, and other family members, including Jerônimo. Jerônimo established a long-standing liaison with an Indian woman who was the daughter of the local chief, Arcoverde. Presumably, Coelho was able to build on existing relationships with the Indians living in the region, as well as new ones, such as that of his brother-in-law with the Indians.[56]

Coelho's grant lay in a prime region for trading brazilwood, but as brazilwood was a royal monopoly and could only be harvested with permission from the king, Coelho and his colonists intended to build a sugar economy. Before leaving Portugal, Coelho had negotiated with investors for the sugar mills, and soon after he arrived, he ordered the construction of these mills. By 1542 he reported that a substantial amount of cane had been planted and that "a very large and perfect" sugar mill was almost completed, with others to be started. In 1550, five sugar mills were grinding cane, and others then under construction would mill in the future, if the king were to respect the rights and privileges initially granted by Coelho to the sugar mill owners.[57]

Coelho's letters to the king indicate that he dealt carefully with the neighboring Indians and that he resented the competing demands for Indian labor posed by the brazilwood trade. The brazilwood trade had become so onerous that the Indians did not do the "hard" and "dangerous" work willingly unless they were paid well. As a result, Coelho wrote to the king, "since they are glutted with tools . . . they stir themselves up and make themselves proud, and rebel." The Indians who had formerly brought Coelho and his colonists food to exchange for tools, and who had done the hard work of clearing and building the mills, now no longer wished to work, for they had enough tools and no longer wished to trade their labor for them. Relations with Indians deteriorated as degredados continued to arrive in Coelho's captaincy as colonists. Coelho had little use for the degredados; he complained to the king that they committed "much evil and damage" and because of them, Coelho wrote, "we have lost the trust which we have had until now with the Indians."[58]

The roles of transactional go-betweens in the other captaincies where settlements began—Porto Seguro, Espírito Santo, Ilhéus, and Paraíba do Sul—are shrouded in uncertainty. A reference to the role of interpreters, who were certainly present in all the initial settlements, appears in a letter from Pero de Góis, the donatário of Paraíba do Sul, to the king. Góis worked hard to build sugar mills, attract settlers, import slaves, and recruit skilled workmen in order to be able to export sugar. He saw that good relations with the local Indians were essential. He hired an interpreter to work with his overseer and two other men with the Indians. Their job was to persuade Indians to clear land and to plant cane and foodstuffs. The interpreter received a higher salary than the overseer. After leaving the settlement, known as Rainha, for a while, Góis returned from Portugal only to find that in his absence the people he had left behind had fled, leaving his captaincy "wasted" and "in rebellion." He established a second settlement farther inland, where the colonists planted sugarcane and Góis worked to build a mill. The work was for naught, however, as relations with the neighboring Indians broke down after a Portuguese man from another captaincy enslaved a powerful chief. The chief's people attacked one of Góis' villages, killing men, burning the canefields, and taking the artillery. A few years later, Góis abandoned Paraíba do Sul and returned to Portugal.[59]

Pero do Campo Tourinho received the grant that encompassed the shore where Cabral landed in 1500, known as Porto Seguro. A native of Viana do Castelo, Tourinho spent eleven years building his captaincy. In 1545, the donatário of Bahia took refuge with him after the colonists of Bahia had rebelled against him and the Indians had attacked his settlement. Tourinho wrote the king in 1546 describing the dangers in Brazil, especially those posed by the attack of the Indians and the designs of the French. Three months later, in November 1546, Tourinho found himself at odds with his own colonists, a group of whom took him prisoner and sent him to Lisbon in chains to be tried by the Inquisition. Those who imprisoned him accused him of blasphemy against the church. The ensuing trial by the Inquisition reveals a conflict between Tourinho's desire to work his slaves and servants hard, even on Sundays and holy days, to build the colony, and the proper deference that sixteenth-century Portuguese, even in the colonies, were required to show toward clergy and traditional Catholic beliefs. Tourinho never returned to Brazil.[60]

When the Portuguese Crown recognized the failures in its private colonization initiative, it decided to send its own royal governor and to build its own capital in Brazil. King João III first reclaimed the captaincy of Bahia from the heirs of the first donatário, the deceased and cannibalized Francisco Pereira Coutinho, and then prepared to build a capital city to house a central government for Brazil. The new royal governor, Tomé de Sousa, possessed a *regimento*, or a series of instructions from King João III, that ordered him to proceed directly to the Bay of All Saints in command of an armada of six ships and 1,000 men, 320 of whom were soldiers. The armada arrived in the Bay of All Saints in March 1549, after eight weeks at sea. On arrival, the king instructed Sousa to peacefully disembark the men of his armada. The king had reason to believe that Sousa would find some Portuguese colonists living in the remains of the small walled settlement of Vila Velha, begun by the former donatário of Bahia, Francisco Pereira Coutinho. By virtue of his regimento, Sousa had the authority "to make war against any who resisted him." [61]

But the king and Sousa hoped that war would be unnecessary. To ensure Sousa's initial success, the king had written ahead to Diogo Álvares, making him aware of the armada that would arrive in Bahia and the plans for building a new capital. Recognizing Álvares' "great knowledge and experience" of the land, the peoples, and their customs, the king ordered him to approach Tomé de Sousa as soon as his armada arrived and to help him in every way. King João III explained that he wrote "because I am informed that through the great experience and knowledge that you have of these lands, and of their peoples and customs . . . as soon as the said Tomé de Souza arrives there, I order you to go to him, and help him . . . because in doing this you will do great service." [62]

When Sousa landed, the forty to fifty Portuguese colonists living in Vila Velha "happily" welcomed him. With no need to prepare for war, Tomé de Sousa turned to the second part of the king's directives. With the help of Álvares and his son-in-law, Sousa reconnoitered the Bay of All Saints, seeking a "healthful place with good airs," well watered, and near an anchorage that would become the capital of Brazil. Of the six hundred colonists who accompanied him, the majority were degredados sent as forced colonists to Brazil. Care had been taken to enlist carpenters, blacksmiths, sawyers, and stonemasons who would oversee the construction of the capital, and work on it soon began. The tiny city was given the full name of Nossa Senhora do Salvador da Bahia de Todos os Santos (Our Lady of the Savior of the Bay of All Saints), which was subsequently known as the City of Salvador, and the surrounding region as Bahia.[63]

Tomé de Sousa also carried instructions to visit the other Portuguese colonies in Brazil. When he visited São Vicente, he recognized the importance of João Ramalho. Tomé de Sousa wrote the king in 1553 that he ordered a town founded above the coastal settlement, on the plain of Piratininga, so that those who were living scattered on the plain would be united in one walled settlement, and over this settlement he placed João Ramalho as captain. A German soldier who passed through Ramalho's town in 1553 commented on the great power of Ramalho, who could call up five thousand Indian warriors on a day's notice.[64]

At midcentury, the French also tried their hand at colonization. In 1555, under the leadership of Nicolas Durand de Villegagnon, the French proposed to establish a colony in the Bay of Guanabara (present-day Rio de Janeiro) that would, in addition to protecting French interests in the brazilwood trade, harbor French Protestants. Accompanying Villegagnon was the Franciscan André Thevet; a year later, three ships left France for the French colony, carrying three hundred soldiers, sailors, and missionaries, among whom was Jean de Léry, the Calvinist missionary.[65]

Villegagnon depended on the Norman interpreters for the survival of his colony. But early on he made the mistake of alienating them. The Norman interpreters revolted against Villegagnon a few months after his arrival in Brazil, in February 1556. Rashly, Villegagnon had decreed that no Frenchman might live with an Indian woman, including the Norman interpreters, unless they were properly married. One Norman interpreter who had lived with his Indian woman for seven years decided to turn on Villegagnon. In the words of Villegagnon's pilot, Nicholas Barré, the truchement lived "without God, Faith, or Law" and did not wish to leave his "whore" or his "superior life" to live in the company of Christians. The Norman interpreter recruited thirty artisans and laborers in Villegagnon's company who had come to Brazil hoping to become rich, but instead found themselves worked very hard building a fort and given very little food. The Norman interpreter promised them "great liberty" and "riches" and the freedom to "live as they wished" if they would rise up against Villegagnon.[66]

A plot to blow up the powder in the fort's cellar failed, as did the attempt to slit Villegagnon's throat, and the ringleaders were clapped into irons. The Norman interpreter who started the rebellion was not there to be captured, probably because, as might be expected, he was safe among his Tupinambá family. He then turned the Norman interpreters living in Tupinambá villages on the mainland against Villegagnon. Barré writes that he "has corrupted all the other interpreters of the said land, who are in number twenty or twenty-five; these do and say all the bad that they can to surprise us and make us return to France." [67] Villegagnon had challenged one of the sources of power wielded by the Norman interpreters, and in return, the Norman interpreters refused to continue as his transactional go-betweens with the surrounding Tupinambá villages. Villegagnon returned to France in 1559; the next year, the Portuguese would attack the colony and expel the surviving French.

The men who played the roles of transactional go-betweens during the first generation relied on Indian women who are almost totally silent in the historical sources. Yet their presence, and their roles as go-betweens in their own right, can be read between the lines. A few of these Indian women are named. One was Paraguaçu, the Indian wife of Diogo Álvares. Álvares had liaisons with various Indian women, but he was married to Paraguaçu, whom he took to France and who was baptized in Brittany in 1528. A baptismal record for "Catherine du Brazil," recorded in St. Malo in 1528, is considered to be that of Álvares' wife, known as Catarina Paraguaçu. Catarina Paraguaçu returned to Brazil with Álvares, where she was part of the transaction of the relationship between her husband and her father and between her husband and her larger kin group. When Tomé de Sousa arrived, along with the first Jesuits to set foot in Brazil, Álvares sent his wife and daughters to the Jesuit school, where they were instructed in the Christian faith. [68]

In São Vicente, Ramalho also had liaisons with several women, but he had a long-lasting alliance with one woman, Bartira, later baptized as Isabel. Bartira, like Paraguaçu, was the daughter of a chief: Tibiriçá of Piratininga. Ramalho never married Bartira, even after the arrival of Catholic clergy, as he had been married in Portugal and his wife was still alive there. In Pernambuco, Jerônimo de Albuquerque's liaison with the Indian woman who was the daughter of the local chief is another example of the same pattern. According to legend, on one occasion she intervened and saved the life of Jerônimo. Baptized with the name Maria do Espírito Santo, she never became Albuquerque's wife.

Figure 3.3. Transactional go-betweens. Vallard Atlas, 1547. This item is reproduced by permission of The Huntington Library, San Marino, California.

Through these Indian women, all three men attained the status and power of an Indian chief, expressed especially in their large clan of descendants. Tomé de Sousa dared not even estimate the size of João Ramalho's family. His descendants, both by Bartira and by other women, formed the basis of his powerful clan in São Vicente.[69] The daughters of these men became highly desirable marriage partners for Portuguese men who arrived in Brazil. Of Diogo Álvares' sixteen known children, twelve were women, and all twelve women married Europeans, some of whom became prominent men in the colony. Three of Álvares' sons were later knighted by the king.[70] Jerônimo de Albuquerque's liaison with Maria do Espírito Santo, as well as with other Indian women, similarly resulted in the births of many mameluco children; he had at least twenty. Before marrying a Portuguese woman at the request of the queen of Portugal, Albuquerque legitimated his mameluco children. These mameluco children married Portuguese colonists and founded many prominent families in Pernambuco.[71]

The strategies of the first generation of transactional go-betweens proved crucial as Europeans sought to possess Brazil. Although the Reinel Map does not include them in the depiction of Brazil, two maps drawn several decades later, in the style of the Dieppe School in France, do. The maps appear in an atlas dated 1547 that was owned or drawn by a Nicholas Vallard, of Dieppe. The maps are clearly derived from Portuguese knowledge, for place-names along the coast, not only of Brazil but of other regions, appear in Portuguese, but the nautical tables and other cartographic terms, such as the equator, are written in French. Who might have drawn the fascinating interior landscapes is not known, but they were clearly influenced by firsthand information. In the map of southern South America, European men positioned to the north of the Río de la Plata negotiate with Indian men and women (Fig. 3.3).

A second map in the atlas depicts the coast of northern South America from the Caribbean to the Tropic of Capricorn, and places the Tropic of Capricorn

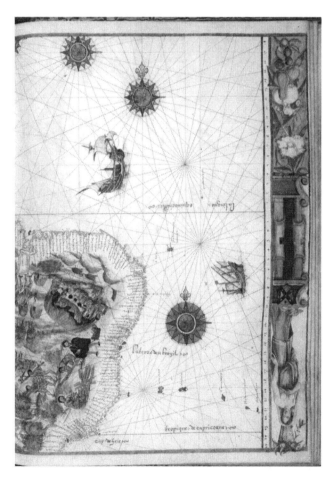

Map 3.3. Northern South America (inverted), 1547. Vallard Atlas, 1547. This item is reproduced by permission of The Huntington Library, San Marino, California.

at the top of the map and the Caribbean at the bottom. Inland from the Brazilian coast, just above the Bay of All Saints, appears the single man dressed in black who was illustrated in the first chapter as an example of a go-between in sixteenth-century Brazil (see Fig. 1.3). Seen in the context of the whole map, it is clear that the miniaturist recognized his importance. Not only does he interact with the men collecting brazilwood, but he is positioned next to a domestic scene — a shelter with a hammock and fires and several Indians relaxing — which suggests his contact with Indian villages, where he most certainly met chiefs and women (Map 3.3).

The vignettes painted over Brazil in the Vallard Atlas visually illustrate that the possession of Brazil required go-betweens, such as men who crossed the ocean, negotiators and traders, and men who allied themselves with native women in the villages. The first colonies demanded much more, however, from the coastal Indian villages than had the brazilwood trade, and thus the transactional go-betweens who arbitrated for the European side became even more important. The justification for the colonization of Brazil, as articulated by the king of Portugal, was not simple possession but evangelization. It quickly became apparent that it was not enough for the Tupi-Guarani-speaking peoples to supply brazilwood, food, and labor for the Portuguese. They were now expected to accept and to practice Christianity. Converting the indigenous peoples of Brazil to Christianity would require a new sort of transactional go-between: the missionary. Missionary priests of a newly founded religious order, the Society of Jesus, would soon fill this role.

4. Conversion

We are beginning to visit their villages . . . and to converse intimately with them . . .

Manoel da Nóbrega, Bahia, 1549

In 1549, a new and very different kind of go-between appeared on the scene in Brazil: the missionary priests and brothers of the Society of Jesus.[1] At first glance, the Jesuits hardly seem to resemble the go-betweens of the Portuguese maritime world, most of whom rarely chose their role; rather, as survivors of shipwrecks or as degredados, they found themselves with the stark choice of adapting or dying. The bachelor of Cananéia, João Ramalho, or Diogo Álvares "Caramuru" had begun as simple physical go-betweens but had parlayed their social position and linguistic ability into effective new roles for themselves as transactional go-betweens. Such men seem very different from the intense men of the first generation of the Society of Jesus. Jesuits came to Brazil not to adapt to Indian society as a means to survive, but rather to create the means for the spiritual salvation of the Indians. But the Jesuits clearly perceived the power of the role of translation and mediation. They sought to convert through persuasion, which made language and example essential to their mission. In Europe, a prominent historian of the Jesuits writes, "Their ministries were characterized by discourse"; so, too, would their ministries in Brazil be defined.[2] Jesuits deliberately sought to become the mediators between Indians and God, because they saw in that role the means to effect the salvation of the Indians of Brazil. Later, Jesuits would become self-conscious representational go-betweens, using their correspondence with powerful men in Europe to influence European perceptions of Brazil. Through their religious dramas, sermons, and schools, they sought to shape the behavior of Indians and colonists in Brazil. In all three roles—physical, transactional, and representational—Jesuits were some of the most powerful go-betweens of the sixteenth century.

The first Jesuits arrived in Brazil in 1549 with the newly appointed royal governor, Tomé de Sousa. The six Jesuits who disembarked with Tomé de Sousa were among the earliest members of a new religious order unlike any other. Jesuits did not live in monasteries, nor did they participate in the communal chanting of the liturgical hours (matins, lauds, vespers) characteristic of the medieval monastic orders. Rather, they dedicated themselves to ministry in the world, and to those peoples who had no one to minister to them. In Europe, these included prostitutes, the sick, the poor, heretics, and outcasts in general. The first Jesuits were indefatigable preachers, holding forth in villages, in streets, in public squares, on ships, in hospitals, and "wherever men and women gather," in the words of the Society's secretary.[3]

The Jesuits sailed with Tomé de Sousa because King João III of Portugal ardently supported the new order. King João took as his confessor the Jesuit Simão Rodrigues, who lived at court, tutored the king's son, and served as the head of the Portuguese assistancy of the Society, founded in 1546. King João offered the new order the possibility for overseas missions in the vast new areas that Portuguese exploration had opened up in the fifteenth and sixteenth centuries. Historian John O'Malley observes that "the initiative for the Jesuits' most spectacular 'missions' during these early years—to India, Brazil, Ethiopia— came not from the reigning pope but from King John [João III] of Portugal." The sixteenth-century Jesuits who left Portugal to bring Christianity to the king's overseas colonies, men such as Francis Xavier or Manoel da Nóbrega, in O'Malley's words, "fulfilled the evangelizing aspirations of the first companions, and they set a powerful example for the generations to come."[4]

On arrival in Brazil, the Jesuit fathers and brothers with Tomé de Sousa undoubtedly were an integral part of the Portuguese Catholic culture that the king intended to foment in Brazil. Two days after their arrival, on Sunday, the Jesuits performed this role by celebrating their first mass in Brazil. Nóbrega preached to the governor and his party, while the Basque Jesuit, Juan de Azpilcueta Navarro, who became known in Brazil as João de Azpilcueta, preached to the colonists living in the settlement, Vila Velha. Yet the Society was so new, and overseas missions such uncharted territory, that the institutions for which the Jesuits would later become known, such as schools, did not yet exist. The Jesuits, therefore, experimented freely in these first years, seeking to define their mission to Brazil.

The great lack of morality encountered in the Portuguese settlement surprised the first Jesuits: "The people here all live in mortal sin," Nóbrega wrote in his first letter from Brazil, "and there is not one man who desists from having many Indian women, all of whom have many children. None of them have come to confess yet." Although Nóbrega saw that there was much spiritual work to be done among the Portuguese colonists, the Jesuits had not come to Brazil to minister to them. In his official instructions (regimento) given to Tomé de Sousa, King João states that the "principal reason that moved me to order the settlement of Brazil was so that the people [i.e., Indians] of that land would be converted to our holy Catholic faith." Immediately, Nóbrega outlined the role that the Jesuits would play in Brazil, and it required that they leave the Portuguese settlement and seek the Indians. In his first letter he writes, "We have resolved to go and live in the villages when we are more settled, to learn with them the language and to teach them little by little." Moreover, the Jesuits would move beyond the new capital to be built, Salvador, and would disperse themselves along the coast of Brazil. Soon after arriving in Brazil, the Jesuits began to leave Bahia. Nóbrega sent Jesuits Leonardo Nunes and Diogo Jacome to Ilhéus in August 1549; Nóbrega himself left Salvador in November and visited first Ilhéus, then Porto Seguro. Leonardo Nunes continued from Ilhéus to São Vicente with ten or twelve children to begin a mission there. In 1551, Nóbrega was in Pernambuco with António Pires. By August of 1551, Afonso Brás had established the Jesuit mission in Espírito Santo.[5] These resolutions to go and live among the Indians and to establish missions near all the Portuguese settlements in Brazil laid the foundation for the roles that the Jesuits would play as go-betweens.

Initially, however, Jesuits lacked even the most fundamental requirements of go-betweens: familiarity with language and culture. In India as in Brazil, the first Jesuits had to rely on interpreters, which brought a whole set of new problems. In India, the Jesuits mistrusted the accuracy of the prayers translated by interpreters, and they disliked the fact that good interpreters were not only hard to find but difficult to keep.[6] In Brazil, Nóbrega expressed his frustration at the language barrier when he could not easily translate prayers and devotions into the indigenous language. "They are so primitive (*brutos*)," he complained, "that they don't have the words." Later, in a formal report, he tempered his criticism, saying, "They have very few words through which we can declare our faith." This required compromise and adaptation; as Nóbrega explained, "Some things we must explain by roundabout means."[7] Recognizing the problem and their own deficiencies, the Jesuits first tried to work through go-betweens who were already established in Brazil, such as Diogo Álvares "Caramuru." Nóbrega hoped to enlist the aid of Álvares to translate prayers, but he was already quite busy as the transactional go-between for the governor.

The Jesuits set about, therefore, to learn Tupi themselves. In this they followed strategies similar to those used by the early Jesuit missionaries to India, who reported great success when they could evangelize in the languages of the peoples they hoped to convert. In Brazil, João de Azpilcueta seemed to have the greatest facility. According to Nóbrega, although the rest of the Jesuits were coarse and poorly trained in the language, Azpilcueta soon was able to walk from Indian village to Indian village making himself understood, and even to preach in Tupi. A year after their arrival, Azpilcueta described a church that had been finished near the Indian villages; there he said mass and taught in the Indian language. He had succeeded in articulating the creation of the world, the commandments, the articles of faith, and prayers in the Indian language. Still, Azpilcueta was not completely self-sufficient; one year later, in 1551, he describes traveling with an interpreter.[8]

While the first Jesuits were learning languages, they, in the interim, took advantage of those outside the order who spoke Tupi and Portuguese. In Porto Seguro, Azpilcueta worked with a man who could write Tupi. Azpilcueta preached sermons from the Old and New Testaments and recited various doctrines of the church so that the man could write them down in Tupi. By 1553, these were finished, and a copy was ready to be sent to Portugal. Azpilcueta entrusted to two Jesuit companions the texts that he had in the "language of Brazil," which included "all the prayers . . . the commandments and mortal sins . . . a general confession, the beginning of the world, the incarnation, the judgment, and the end of the world.[9]

The Society greatly benefited when men, moved by the example of the first Jesuits, decided that they themselves had vocations. A few very skilled interpreters joined the Society. One of the best interpreters in São Vicente was a Jesuit novice, Pero Correia. Correia had been in Brazil since 1534 and had formerly made his living as a broker between the Indians and the Portuguese, not unlike the positions of Ramalho or Caramuru. He claimed to have negotiated a peace with the Indians of Bahia, who had rebelled against the first donatário, Francisco Pereira Coutinho, and maintained that the Indians there "made me lord of their land." He had been a slave trader along the coast of Brazil, raiding Indian villages and selling Indian men and women into slavery, but in 1549, he repented and entered the Society of Jesus, quickly becoming their best interpreter. In São Vicente in 1553 he preached every Sunday afternoon in the "language of the land," where many free and enslaved Indians came to hear him. On Fridays, the Jesuits held a conversation, which the fathers gave in Portuguese to the Portuguese-speaking community, while Brother Correia gave another in the Indian language. Nóbrega instantly recognized the value of Correia to the order. He "does more than any of us, because of the language," Nóbrega wrote. Another brother who served as an interpreter in São Vicente described his work: "There, I preached in the language of the Indians that which the father told me, and all the slaves and whites who heard it were moved and edified." [10]

Ideally, Jesuits hoped to convert chiefs to use their example to facilitate the conversion of their families, villages, and regions. In his first letter from Brazil, Nóbrega described meeting an Indian chief who was already baptized a Christian and who, because of his baptism, was looked down upon by his family and kin. Describing him as "very fervent" and "a great friend of ours," Nóbrega took the time to cultivate him, giving him a cap left over from the sea voyage and a pair of trousers. In return, the chief brought the Jesuits fish and other comestibles. The Jesuits taught him early in the morning, because although he had been baptized, "he does not yet have knowledge of our faith." According to Nóbrega, the chief promised that he would make his brothers, his wife, and as many as he could Christians. Encouraged by his example, Nóbrega hoped to make him into "a great means and example to all the others." [11]

Similarly, on missions into the Indian villages outside the Portuguese settlements, the Jesuits paid special attention to chiefs. On arriving at a village, they found the chief, usually lying in a hammock, and received and gave the traditional greetings in Tupi:

Chief: "Ereiube" ("Vengáis en hora buena") [You arrive at a good time; it is well].

Visitor: "Paa" ("Sí") [Yes].[12]

Although the Jesuits recognized that chiefs were their means of entry into the Indian society, more often than not they found it easier to work through their children. The Jesuits received any children sent to them, but they especially wanted to educate the children of chiefs. On a mission into the Recôncavo, the region surrounding the Bay of All Saints, one of the Jesuit missionaries wrote that the chief Grillo gave them a beautiful boy to educate. Through their teaching of children, Jesuits fully intended to break the bonds between children and parents. They consciously saw themselves performing the same role as Jesus, as stated in the gospel of Matthew 10:35: "For I have come to turn a man against his father, a daughter against her mother, a daughter-in-law against her mother-in-law." Jesuits reported with satisfaction times when children prevented their parents from drinking, or when they preferred not to see their kin, or when they did not want to show "filial love" to their visiting parents.[13]

The first Jesuits began to teach children immediately. Sometime during the first weeks they were in Brazil, four Jesuits traveled to the Indian villages that surrounded Vila Velha and the new capital city that was being built and invited the Indian boys to study reading and writing, which the Indians greatly admired and wanted to learn. Soon, Indian boys wearing lip plugs came daily to Brother Vicente Rodrigues and Father João de Azpilcueta to learn to read and write Portuguese; those lessons also included memorizing prayers. The boys quickly began to conform to the Jesuit ways. Nóbrega writes that their lip plugs caused problems with their pronunciation, and Azpilcueta "made them understand the impediment." Then one of the boys' mothers came and removed his plug and threw it away, and the others followed suit. As a by-product of teaching reading and writing in Portuguese, the Jesuits imparted essential Christian doctrine. This seemed to work so well that Nóbrega, excited by the possibilities, proclaimed in a letter that through knowledge, which the devil had used to defeat humankind, the devil himself would be defeated.[14]

The receptivity of Indian boys to their teaching caused the Jesuits to consider using Portuguese children as a way to draw in even more children. The Jesuit house in Lisbon raised orphans; seven of these children came to Brazil in 1550. A Portuguese Jesuit praised this strategy in a letter sent to the founder of the Society, Ignatius de Loyola, in Rome: "I have letters [from Brazil] of the great good that they [the seven orphans] are doing there. When one of these children goes forth, more than two hundred Indian children come to him, embrace him, and laugh with him, and have great fun." The children from Portugal taught Christian doctrines to Indian children, who in turn taught others in the village. By teaching the Indian children in the villages, the Portuguese child missionaries learned the Indian language as well. Three years after arriving in Brazil, Nóbrega summed up the Jesuit strategy of working through Indian children: "We intend to raise Indian children because they are many and we are few and we know how to speak poorly in their language." By the time that Nóbrega penned these words, the Indian children assisted with sermons and singing, in both Portuguese and Tupi. They served as translators in confession for Indians, slaves, the newly converted, and even the wife and children of Diogo Álvares "Caramuru," who did not speak Portuguese. By 1552, the Society of Jesus had raised and educated approximately two hundred orphans, who, they claimed, received an education equal to what was given in Portugal. Thus did children become transactional go-betweens for the Jesuits.[15]

Jesuits recognized that mamelucos, children as well as adults, would also make excellent interpreters. In early sixteenth-century Brazil, Portuguese settlers and traders used the word "mameluco" to describe the children of Portuguese men and Indian women. The term, which came from the Arabic *mamluk*, "to be possessed," suggested slavery, military service, and "white" slave.[16] It is difficult to know how much of this history the Portuguese saw in the newly emerging social and ethnic group in Brazil or why they chose this name for the children of mixed race. Many mamelucos certainly were the sons of Indian women who were servants and slaves. Despite their proximity to slavery, the Portuguese in Brazil commonly considered mamelucos to be "white," which may reflect the early meaning of "*mameluk*" as a Caucasian slave. Many adult mameluco men did make their livings from service as warriors, although they were never slaves.

The first generation of mamelucos lived in the Portuguese settlements as well as in the Indian villages. When the first Jesuits arrived in Brazil, they commented on the mamelucos living as Indians. Leonardo Nunes wrote from São Vicente that he wanted to send a very tall and very cheerful mameluco back to Portugal so that his Jesuit companions could see for themselves "what there is here." The youth had lived naked for ten years among the Indians; he spoke no Portuguese; he knew nothing of Christianity. In Pernambuco, Nóbrega found "many children of Christians lost in the wilderness among the Indians," both boys and girls, whom he wanted to return to Christian virtues.[17]

Jesuits sought to educate mamelucos as interpreters, and even as potential novices for their order, to press their language ability into the service of evangelism. Nóbrega worked with one youth in Pernambuco whom he described as "lost" because he "ate human flesh as the Indians"; Nóbrega planned to send this youth out into the wilderness to persuade the other mameluco children to return to Christianity.[18]

Mameluco children attended Jesuit schools along with Indians; in many ways the groups were indistinguishable. Both Indian and mameluco children sang in Latin at mass and sang in Tupi on missions to the Indian villages. As time passed, the Jesuits saw the mameluco children, though born into "the most dissolute people of this land," as holding the future of Brazil in their hands. The influence of the mameluco children, the Jesuit José de Anchieta suggested, would play a great part in the "edification or the destruction of the land." Therefore, he recommended that Jesuits take as many pains to educate mameluco children as they took with Indian children. He recognized, too, that their language skills would make them invaluable interpreters who could help the Jesuits in the conversion of the Indians. Some, he thought, might even find vocations in the Society of Jesus.[19]

Nóbrega seriously considered recruiting mamelucos into the Society. He wrote to the head of the Jesuit order in Rome that "it has always seemed to me that they, Indians as well as mestizos, would be very useful workers, because of the language and because they are themselves natives of this land." But, for this to work, he believed that the candidates must be sent to Europe to be educated in "letters and virtues." In 1555, he had two mamelucos prepared for Coimbra, the site of Portugal's university. In 1561, Nóbrega proposed two more mamelucos, who, pending final approval from Rome, would travel to Evora, another city noted for its learning in Portugal. Not all of Nóbrega's colleagues agreed with him. Nóbrega's successor, Luís da Grã, doubted that mamelucos were what the Jesuits needed. The mamelucos "do not have talent," he remarked, and those whom the Jesuits had received into the Society "had not lived up to expectations."[20]

Jesuits doubted the trustworthiness of mamelucos within their society for the same reason that they were drawn to mamelucos. Because of the mamelucos' ease within the Indian world, they could help the Jesuit missionaries change that world. But, on the other hand, that same ease with which mamelucos fit into the Indian world might be used against the mission of the Jesuits. Anchieta confirmed these fears in a letter from São Vicente in 1555. Deep in the interior, mamelucos had destroyed a mission begun by two fathers and had "corrupted, with the venom of words and the example of bad life, those whom we had already subjected to the yoke of Christ."[21]

Despite these reservations, some mamelucos did enter the Society of Jesus and became "tongues" in service to God. By 1574, 110 men served in the Society of Jesus in Brazil; the majority (65%) hailed from Portugal, and the second-largest group (14%) was Brazilian born—usually, but not always, of Portuguese parents. Among this 14 percent numbered the mamelucos who had joined the Society in Brazil, and most of these were known within the Society as *línguas*, or "interpreters." But the gradual entry of mamelucos into the Society during the first two decades was later reversed during Everard Mercurian's term as father general of the Society of Jesus. In 1574 Mercurian wrote to the Jesuit provincial (head of the Society) of Brazil stating that the sons of Portuguese men and women in Brazil might be admitted into the Society if they had shown extensive proof of their virtue, constancy, and desire to leave the world and to live a religious vocation. Although the ability to speak the Indian language was valuable, Mercurian cautioned that it should not be given too much weight. The sons of Indians were not to be considered at all for admission. A few years later, the tide had turned even against the Brazilian-born sons of Portuguese colonists. At the same time that Mercurian barred Asians and Eurasians from joining the order in Asia, he also barred those born in Brazil. "The experience of many years has shown," he wrote to the provincial of Brazil, "that they are not fit for our Institute." [22]

The first Jesuits consciously worked with Indian and mameluca women, who became some of their most ardent early converts. When the Jesuits arrived in Brazil, they found that the vast majority of the women living in the Portuguese settlements all along the coast were Indian and mameluca women. Many of these women were baptized Christians, living as the concubines of Portuguese men. Because the Jesuits disapproved of the way Portuguese men in Brazil lived with many women, in "the custom of this land," they focused their initial preaching to the Portuguese colony on the sinfulness of such a state. The Jesuits urged the men to marry one woman. By introducing changes in the accepted social mores, the Jesuits inadvertently created a new group of potential go-betweens: Christian mamelucas and Christian Indian women who were no longer part of the households of Portuguese men.

The attention paid by the Jesuits to the sins of Portuguese men had an impact on Indian and mameluca women, who formerly had little choice but to accept their state as free or enslaved concubines. With the arrival of the Jesuits, however, new opportunities opened up for these women, and many became vocal Christians and strong supporters of the Jesuits. In Bahia, the Jesuits taught women as well as children; ten months after arriving in Brazil, Nóbrega wrote that the "children and women already know how to pray well." Christian Indian and mameluca women came to the Jesuits to be taught about Christianity, some even risking beatings from their husbands. In Pernambuco at least forty women had been brought from the Indian villages to be baptized by Portuguese priests and kept as concubines. Many of these came on their knees to the Jesuit house, asking "for the love of God" to be further taught. These women brought their children to be educated as well. Nóbrega encouraged the women to formalize their unions in marriage, and he hoped to use some of these women to preach in their home villages in the interior. A recently converted Indian woman preached with such fervor one night in the streets of São Vicente that she unsettled many men and women of the town. Such women were like "mirrors," a Jesuit wrote, "not only for their kinfolk, but for the women of Portugal, too." [23]

Indian and mameluca women soon became interpreters for the Jesuits. In Pernambuco, the interpreter for the sermons and doctrines taught by António Pires to the Indian and African slaves was an honorable married woman, who also served as interpreter when Father Pires confessed Christian Indian women. "I believe that she is the best confessor that I have because she is so virtuous," Pires wrote. [24]

The essential message brought by the Jesuits was that Indians must be persuaded to convert to Christianity in order to enjoy eternal life. In the early letters from Brazil, Jesuits constantly describe how they talked, presented arguments, preached, taught through dialogues, and recited prayers to the Indians. A Jesuit in Lisbon, who met with Tomé de Sousa on his return to Portugal in 1554, wrote to Rome that Sousa described Nóbrega's method in Brazil as follows: Nóbrega surveyed an area, ascertained those "who lived in evil ways," and divided them among Jesuits who then visited them daily. In these visits, Jesuits exhorted the men and women to give up sin and to confess, "and if they had not persuaded them, they returned to the beginning to speak to them again, and so they importuned them until they converted to our Lord." In Brazil, António Pires summed up the approach in a sketch of an exchange with an Indian, wherein he [Pires] convinced the Indian through his arguments: "What is lacking here," Pires wrote, "is a continual conversation" that would put the Indians on the road to heaven. [25]

José de Anchieta, who arrived in Brazil as a young brother in 1553, provided many of the tools that would make this conversation possible. First a teacher in the Jesuit school in Piratininga, Anchieta quickly learned Tupi-Guarani, the *língua da terra* (the language of the land), and wrote a grammar and dictionary that were used by Jesuits throughout the regions where what the Jesuits called the *língua geral* (universal language) was understood. Anchieta's grammar, which was used to teach Jesuits the língua geral, was followed by other manuals, such as a catechism, a dialogue of faith, and a manual to aid in the confessional. [26]

To Jesuits such as Anchieta fell the task of translating Christian concepts of heaven and hell, God, the devil, the resurrection, and other ideas into words that Tupi-Guarani-speaking peoples could understand. Such translations appropriated elements of Indian culture and gave them new meanings. "Tupã" was the word Anchieta used to translate "God"; in Tupi cosmology, Tupã created thunder and lightning from the sky. Anchieta used "Añánga," which among Tupi-Guarani-speaking peoples referred to dangerous spirits of the forests, to represent "the devil." He retained Jesus and Santa Maria, but defined Jesus as "Jandé Jára" (Our Lord) and Mary as "Tupãsy" (Mother of God).[27]

Jesuits developed persuasive arguments to kindle a desire among Indians to convert to Christianity. Leonardo Nunes wrote that the Indians "greatly fear death and the day of judgment and hell," and that this led many to convert so as to be saved. Nunes ordered his interpreter, the skilled Brother Pero Correia, "always to touch on this in the conversations, because the fear puts them in great confusion." Another theme stressed by Vicente Rodrigues through his child interpreters was that "the time of dreams had passed" and that it was time for Indians to "wake up and hear the word of God, our Lord." Pero Correia promised Indians that "if they believed in God, not only would our Lord give them great things in heaven . . . but that in this world on their lands he would give them many things that were hidden." [28]

Similarly, on the other side of the world, a Jesuit in Hormuz described the debates that he held weekly with learned Muslims, Jews, and mystics. Mondays, he debated with mystics (*iogues*) and others he calls gentiles (*gentios*). Fridays, he debated a Muslim philosopher, and Saturdays, he went to the synagogue. One of the debates with a Jew drew a large audience, which the Jesuit preacher saw as particularly beneficial for the Christians.[29]

But language sometimes was not enough, and Jesuits had to work on their form. As Jesuits changed the traditional means of delivering Christianity—that is, the rituals familiar to the faithful in Portugal, Spain, France, or Italy—they instinctively built on the tried and true ways of go-betweens. Translating Christianity required more than the simple exchange of one set of words for another; Jesuit missionaries had to present Christianity in ways that appealed to the Indians of Brazil. One Jesuit believed of the Indians that "because they love musical things, we, by playing and singing among them, will win them." Azpilcueta adapted the Pater Noster (Lord's Prayer) to "their way of singing" so that the Indian boys would learn it faster and enjoy it more. The Portuguese orphans went from village to village "singing and playing in the way of the

Indians and with their very same sounds and songs, moving the words in praise of God." They shook rattles (*maracás*) and beat thick canes on the ground and sang at night, in the Indian style. Nóbrega even disclosed that the "songs of Our Lord" the Jesuits sang in Indian tones and to the accompaniment of Indian instruments came from "their celebrations when they kill enemies and when they walk around drunk." But to Nóbrega it was perfectly justifiable because it attracted Indians. In the Jesuit mind, if Indians gave up certain customs, such as cannibalistic ceremonies, they might retain other customs, such as their music, if turned toward different, spiritual ends.[30]

Similarly, when the Jesuits recognized that the Indians had developed effective ways of persuading through preaching, they imitated the Indian style. They used the Indian intonations, preached while walking around, and even beat their chests for emphasis.[31]

Using their newly developed techniques and their go-betweens, Jesuit missions set out from Portuguese settlements to Indian villages. In São Vicente, where Leonardo Nunes had begun the Jesuit mission, his interpreter, Brother Pero Correia, described a mission into the interior in 1553. Six brothers and Father Nunes traveled the Tietê River by canoe for eight or nine days, then walked overland. At every village, Nunes ordered Correia to preach for two hours at dawn "because that was the time that the chiefs and shamans customarily preached."[32]

A letter from Bahia vividly describes the early missions to Indian villages outside the new capital of Salvador. These missions were led by one of the Jesuit fathers, accompanied by the children whom the Jesuits had been educating. The procession left the settlement with a cross, decorated with brilliant feathers, held high. A baby Jesus in an angelic pose held a small sword in his hand at the top of the cross, while below, the children walked two by two or three by three, preaching in loud voices in the Indian language something resembling the following:

> Christ is the true God who made the heavens and the earth and all of the things for us, so that we would know and serve him. We, whom He made of earth, and to whom He gave everything, do not wish to believe in him or to know him. We obey instead witchdoctors and evil ways. But from here forward there is no excuse, because God has sent the true holiness, which is the cross and these words and songs. God has life for those who believe, there, where He is, in heaven.[33]

Such missions went from Indian village to Indian village, singing in the Indian style and playing Indian instruments, using, a Jesuit reflected, "their own sounds and songs, with the words changed to praise God." When the group arrived at the villages, the Jesuit priest addressed the Indian chiefs, admonishing them to become Christians and to prepare for the arrival of the *pajé guaçu,* or "Great Chief." This was the bishop, newly appointed to the city of Salvador. But the Jesuit counseled them not to become Christians as their forebears had done: in exchange for a shirt, for which they had been punished with death. Rather, the Jesuit priest exhorted them to become Christians for the love of God and promised them that if they believed in the true holiness and did the things of God that they were taught, they would receive life everlasting in the heavens while the evil ones who died would go to hell to burn with the devil.[34]

Using their facility with language and their willingness to incorporate indigenous ways of persuasion, the Jesuits quickly moved to seize the ground they desired: to be the intermediaries between Indians and God. Their agency would make it possible for Indians to meet the true intermediary: the Messiah, as in the words of Timothy, "For there is one God, and one mediator between God and men, the man Christ Jesus" (I Timothy 2:5).

The Jesuits could not simply step into this role of spiritual intermediary, however, because that role was already taken by Indian shamans. Five months after arriving in Brazil, Nóbrega described how he sought to break the power of a shaman through reason and persuasion. Nóbrega described the shaman as "the greatest witchdoctor [*hechiӡero*] of the land"; their encounter took place in an Indian village. Quoting from scripture, Nóbrega reportedly asked the shaman "by what authority are you doing these things," and whether he had communication with God and the devil. To Nóbrega's horror, the shaman replied that he was God, and that he was born God, and that the God of the heavens was his friend and appeared to him in clouds, thunder, and lightning. Nóbrega immediately called together the whole village, and for a long time, through his interpreter, contradicted all that the shaman had said. Nóbrega describes his interpreter as saying all that he said in a loud voice with the same signs of great sentiment that Nóbrega himself had expressed. The effect of all this, according to Nóbrega, was that it confused the shaman, who retracted all that he had said, beseeched Nóbrega to ask God for his pardon, and requested baptism.[35]

Through preaching, debating, teaching, admonishing, and praying, the first Jesuits immediately began to have an effect on the cultural and religious landscape of coastal Brazil and the inland Piratininga Plateau of São Vicente. Through their multiple intermediaries, they made an impression on Indians, mamelucos, and Portuguese alike. The Jesuits initially reported positive, even glowing, results among Indians. António Pires wrote that "the Indians at first did not believe us, and it seemed to them that we lied to them and deceived them . . . as had the lay ministers of Satan, who in the beginning came to this land and preached to them in the interest of their abominable slave trade." But, he continued, now that the Indians were learning the truth, and recognizing the love that the fathers had for them and the trouble they went to in seeking the salvation of their souls, "they understand and want to be Christians with much greater desire and with much greater purpose than at first." Similarly, Jesuits wrote of great gains made among the Portuguese men, who had been accustomed to live publicly with many women. Leonardo Nunes counted up the number of men who had married their concubines (fifteen or sixteen, with seven or eight ready to marry) and noted that other men with wives in Portugal had ceased living with their concubines in Brazil and that several single men left Indian and slave concubines to marry the daughters of Portuguese men who had arrived on the fleet with Tomé de Sousa.[36]

The first Jesuits saw concrete results from their mission among the Indians. Nóbrega believed that through their preaching, the fame of the Jesuits had spread through the Indian villages, such that Indians came from very great distances to hear the Jesuits. "We tell them," Nóbrega wrote, "that on their account principally we came to this land and not for the whites." This clearly had resonated with the Indians, Nóbrega reflected, because the Indians showed great willingness for the Jesuits to talk to them and to teach them. With enough missionaries, Nóbrega thought that it would be easy to convert them all. Other Jesuits similarly depicted early successes in the evangelization of Indians. "The Christians who remain with us," António Pires wrote, "are so much ours that they fight with their brothers to defend us."[37]

Although the first Jesuits seemed pleased with their early successes among the Indians, criticism from an unexpected source upset them. This criticism came from the first bishop named to Brazil, Pedro Fernandes Sardinha. The bishop found fault precisely with the Jesuit strategy of becoming and using go-betweens. In his very first sermon, the bishop spoke out against the adoption of Indian customs by "white men." He particularly objected to the indigenous customs that the Jesuits had adapted in their evangelization mission. In a confidential letter he wrote to Simão Rodrigues, principal of the Jesuit Portuguese province, he questioned the way that the orphans, whom the Jesuits raised in Bahia, sang "in the Indian tone" and played the instruments "that these barbarous [Indians] play" in their drunken and cannibalistic ceremonies. Such music was so dissonant and against reason that the bishop did not know "what ears could tolerate such sounds and such coarse playing." It was even worse, the bishop continued, that the Jesuit priest Salvador Rodrigues "played, danced, and leaped about with them." In the bishop's opinion, this went too far in favor of the Indian customs and had little benefit for their conversion. He also found it odd that the children cut their hair in the Indian way, and he raised concerns about the way Jesuits were burying baptized Indians. These criticisms sparked an angry exchange between the bishop and Nóbrega, in which the bishop indignantly informed Nóbrega, "I did not come here to make Christians Indians, but to accustom Indians to being Christians!" [38]

The bishop objected especially to interpreters in confession. Nóbrega's use of mameluca women as interpreters caused rumors to spread, the bishop wrote, because "it is something so new and never used in the church." If an interpreter must be used, the bishop opined, the interpreter must be an "approved honest man," not "a ten-year-old child"; moreover, the interpreter must be selected by the penitent, not by the confessor. Henceforth, he forbade Nóbrega from using women and mameluco children as intermediaries in confession.[39]

Nóbrega struggled with his anger. In his letter to Simão Rodrigues, he defended the position of the Jesuits in Brazil. He thought the cutting of hair "not very different from our custom" and justified the use of Indian music and instruments as something that "attracted the hearts of Indians." He supported the children who translated confessions, arguing that they had been carefully raised by the Jesuits, and that they aided in the confessions of slaves, newly converted Indians, and mamelucos who spoke no Portuguese, all of whom who would not otherwise have any spiritual care. "It is a very beneficial thing and of great importance in this land," Nóbrega wrote, "because there are not many priests who know the [Indian] language." Besides, to ban the use of interpreters would mean that the grace of the sacrament would be taken from those who did not speak Portuguese. He rejected the bishop's view that interpreters were never used in the church and asked his superior to send theological opinions on the subject to Brazil.[40]

With the arrival of the bishop, the Jesuit mission began to falter in Bahia. Within a year, Nóbrega decided to leave Bahia and to concentrate on the Jesuit mission in São Vicente. Nóbrega cited the lack of good interpreters and the unleashing of "such cruel" intertribal wars, in addition to conflicts with the bishop, as reasons why the Jesuits could no longer make headway with the Indians of Bahia. He wrote the king that the bishop "wishes to follow a different style than our way of doing things," adding diplomatically and with self-deprecation that "his must be the better way, because he is very virtuous, zealous, educated, and experienced." Leaving Bahia to the bishop, Nóbrega sailed south to São Vicente, a place he believed better suited to the Jesuit mission. There, he had excellent interpreters. The Indians of Piratininga lived under one chief, Tibiriçá, who was a baptized Christian. Perhaps most important to Nóbrega's thinking, São Vicente lay at the entrance to the *sertão*, or "wilderness," where Nóbrega hoped to launch many missionaries among the Guarani peoples.[41]

Leonardo Nunes had led the mission to São Vicente, which almost never arrived, due to the absence of an interpreter. About 10 or 12 leagues (approximately 60 to 74 kilometers) from São Vicente, the ship carrying Nunes spotted seven canoes, each with thirty or forty paddlers, the Indians painted with black or with other colors and covered with feathers. Fearing them, the ship's crew changed course and headed out to sea. As Nunes told the story, the Indians gave pursuit, paddling so hard that they overtook the sailing ship and demanded to know who they were. "And because we did not have an interpreter who knew how to respond," Nunes wrote, "they took us for Frenchmen" and immediately attacked. As the arrows fell on them like rain, Nunes retreated to a corner of the ship, fell to his knees, and prayed for help from God. Eventually, the Indians realized that they were Portuguese and let them continue on to São Vicente. There, Nunes found three "Portuguese" towns in the region of São Vicente, in each of which the inhabitants lived "in very grave sin," not only because they were living outside of marriage, but because they had not confessed for thirty or forty years. Above, on the plateau, Nunes visited the Indian village, known as Piratininga, where he found some white men. These were João Ramalho and his mameluco sons. The Jesuit residence in São Vicente quickly became the largest in Brazil, with fourteen brothers, many of whom were excellent interpreters. Nunes hoped to use the interpreters for missions into the wilderness once more Jesuit priests arrived from Portugal. He planned to dispatch two brothers with each priest, and in this way begin the evangelization of the Indians of São Vicente and the wilderness beyond.[42]

Nóbrega's arrival in 1553 was as dramatic, if not more so, as Leonardo Nunes' had been three years before. Nóbrega traveled from Bahia to São Vicente in an armada led by the governor, Tomé de Sousa, who was visiting all the Portuguese settlements in Brazil. The armada included *desterrados* (banished persons, i.e., degredados), who were to be distributed in settlements beyond Bahia. Among the degredados on Nóbrega's ship were women, whom Nóbrega ordered to sleep covered and in locked chambers at night. The voyage took place in the late summer. It was very hot, and Nóbrega had come down with a fever and had to be bled along the way. When the ships arrived in São Vicente, Leonardo Nunes came out in a small boat to meet Nóbrega, still weak from his fever, to take him ashore. But a storm blew up, the boat capsized, and Nóbrega did not know how to swim. Somehow, the Indians with Nunes managed to get Nóbrega ashore to a nearby island.[43]

When he had recovered, Nóbrega found the mission thriving in São Vicente. The church, built by Leonardo Nunes, Nóbrega characterized as better than any other in Brazil, and the Jesuit house had fifty children in the school and frequently supported up to one hundred persons. Nóbrega now saw the early work of the Society in Bahia as having been a training ground for their true mission, which would be in the wilderness, in the lands of the Guarani, where few Christians had been before. The Jesuits whom the Society sends to Brazil, he argued to his superior in Lisbon, should come to São Vicente, "because in the other captaincies I believe now that they will do little more than teach children." Nóbrega was impressed with the interpreters in São Vicente, especially with Pero Correia, whom he named "the best interpreter in Brazil." Nóbrega was eager not to lose time and to use the "authority" and "respect" that Correia enjoyed among the Indians to begin the real mission of Jesuits in Brazil. Nóbrega wrote to Luís Gonçalves da Camara in Lisbon that they had determined it to be God's will that they go 100 leagues (approximately 600 kilometers) into the wilderness and build a house where they would gather the children of the Indians, teaching and joining together many Indians in "a great city" where they would live "in conformity with reason."[44]

But the governor, Tomé de Sousa, was uncomfortable with the Jesuits living deep in the wilderness, practically in Spanish territory. He wrote the king in June of 1553, shortly after the armada brought him and Nóbrega to São Vicente, that "the Jesuits have great desire to go into the wilderness and to establish houses among the Indian, and I forbade it." The governor would allow two or three Jesuits to go into the wilderness with their interpreters to preach to the Indians, but he thought erecting residences so distant from the Portuguese settlement would be too dangerous. The governor also feared that the entrance of the Jesuits into the wilderness would draw with them many evildoers and debtors from São

Vicente, attracted by the reports of gold and silver in the mountains. He therefore closed the overland road, or trail, that ran from São Vicente to Asunción in the Spanish zone of influence in Paraguay. One year later, the king himself decreed that the Jesuits might not enter the wilderness without the permission of the governor of Brazil. In spite of this setback, the Jesuits continued to organize short missionary expeditions into the wilderness and did in fact establish a residence 50 leagues (approximately 300 kilometers) from São Vicente, where the two priests and brothers taught Indian children. Nóbrega continued to dream about a mission to Paraguay.[45]

The Jesuit mission in São Vicente soon conflicted with João Ramalho, who already served as an established go-between, mediating Indian and Portuguese interaction. After Jesuit Leonardo Nunes arrived in São Vicente, Nunes decided to found the shrine of Santo André on the Piratininga Plateau when Ramalho and his mameluco descendants refused to move to the Christian settlements of the coast. Ramalho and his sons, in Nunes' view, "lived a life of savages." Later, Tomé de Sousa would reinforce Nunes' actions by choosing the chapel as the site of the town to be called Santo André. This was the seat of Ramalho's influence, and the chapel would have been built with his consent and support. Father Nunes visited the chapel from time to time, but on the third visit, he had an altercation with Ramalho. The problem for Father Nunes was that Ramalho, who had left a wife behind in Portugal many years before, had been excommunicated by a local priest for the mortal sin of fornication. While Father Nunes was celebrating mass inside the chapel, Ramalho entered, and Nunes ordered him to leave, saying that he could not celebrate mass in his presence. Ramalho stepped outside and two of his sons followed him out, with the intention, according to the Jesuit writing about the event, of striking Nunes when mass had ended.[46]

When Nóbrega arrived in São Vicente, he immediately heard much about Ramalho, whom he described as the "oldest European resident here." Whereas he saw Álvares as the means through which he would be able to communicate with the Indians in Bahia, he saw Ramalho as a "rock against which we stumble" because "[h]is lifestyle, and that of his children, is Indian." Because Ramalho had such an extensive network of kin, he held great influence. Before he had met Ramalho, Nóbrega wrote of him in 1553:

He and his sons have many women, and they sleep with sisters [of these women] and they have many children with them, both the father and the sons. His sons go to war with the Indians and go to their festivals, and they live naked, as do the Indians.[47]

When Nóbrega met Ramalho two months later, he moderated his account, apparently deciding to try to win Ramalho over to use him to reach the Indians. Nóbrega took the oldest of Ramalho's sons on a mission into the wilderness so as to "give our ministry more authority" among the Indians because he is "well known and venerated." Moreover, at the same time that the governor of Brazil judged Ramalho's descendants too numerous even to estimate, Nóbrega stated in a letter that all of Ramalho's sons and daughters came from one Indian woman, the daughter of a chief. "We hope that in him and in her and in their children to have a great means for the conversion of the Indians," he wrote.[48]

Ramalho's primary Indian wife is identified by genealogists as Bartira, daughter of the chief of Piratininga, Tibiriçá, and baptized as Isabel Dias. The year that Nóbrega arrived, Ramalho's "woman" had an encounter with the bailiffs of the secular clergy. This unnamed woman may well be the woman whom genealogists name as Isabel Dias. According to Pero Correia, when the Jesuits preached against the sin of living with women outside of marriage, they promised those who did not mend their ways that punishment would come from the hand of the secular clergy. The bishop sent his agent through Brazil to mete out punishments, but Correia was deeply disappointed by what happened in São Vicente. He cites the case of Ramalho's woman as an example. The bishop's agent assessed Ramalho a fine of one slave for living with an Indian woman outside of marriage. Correia writes that Ramalho's woman objected, because the slave taken was a woman "whom she cared for" and who had helped her to raise several of her children. Ramalho's woman planned to complain to Governor Tomé de Sousa. But, Correia noted, someone told her that she should be quiet, for by letting the slave be taken, she could be assured of never being separated from Ramalho. For Correia, the lesson learned by the errant colonists from this and similar actions of the bishop's agent was that sins could be paid for: "The law of the Church did not come to this land to separate them from sin and to heal their souls, but to take their properties from them," he wrote in one of his letters.[49]

Nóbrega very much wanted Ramalho's marital status to be resolved. He asked that it be verified immediately in Vouzela, in the diocese of Viseu (in northern Portugal), whether Ramalho's wife of forty years ago was still alive. "If this man were in a state of grace," he wrote, "Our Lord would do much through him." Assuming that Ramalho's wife had died, Nóbrega also wanted a dispensation so that Ramalho could marry his Indian woman, even though he had had carnal knowledge of her sister and other kin. Presumably, Nóbrega had worked out a deal with Ramalho, for he added that money was not a problem: Ramalho was prepared to send payment in sugar for the expenses of obtaining the documents.[50]

The Jesuits established their own base, 2 leagues (approximately 12 kilometers) from Ramalho's town of Santo André, on the site that would become the future city of São Paulo. Nóbrega wrote to the king, two months after he had met Ramalho, and expressed satisfaction with the small and attractive settlement that was forming around the church. But one year later, José de Anchieta revealed that the relationship between the Jesuit settlement and Ramalho's town had deteriorated. The mamelucos, Anchieta wrote, "never cease from striving, along with their father [Ramalho], to cast out from the land the work which, with the help of God, we are trying to build." Ramalho's sons openly defied the Jesuits' evangelism and even exhorted those Indians to whom the Jesuits were directing their mission "to leave us and to believe in them, who use bows and arrows like the Indians, and not to trust in us who were sent here for our own evil purposes."[51]

Ramalho's sons did not seem ready to exchange the power they derived from Indian society for the salvation preached by the Jesuits. Anchieta, horrified, wrote about the open acceptance of cannibalism by Ramalho's sons. He described how one of Ramalho's sons killed a war captive "with greatest cruelty," colored his legs red, and took the name of the one he had killed as a sign of honor. Anchieta would not go so far as to accuse Ramalho's son of cannibalism, but in his mind, the point was moot: "and if he did not eat of the war captive, he at least gave him to the Indians to eat, exhorting them not to let be lost he whom he had killed, but to cook him and take him to eat."[52]

Very early on, Anchieta perceived the threat posed by the mameluco sons of Ramalho to the Jesuits. In essence, they were competitors who might use their language ability and knowledge of the Portuguese world to work for the Indian world rather than for the European one. Anchieta claimed that he feared less their threats, "even to death," than he did their cultural influence. Far worse than death threats, in his view, was the way they undercut the Jesuit teaching of Indians. "If this pernicious plague is not extinguished," he predicted, "not only will the conversion of the infidels not progress, but it will debilitate itself and it will diminish more and more."[53]

The Jesuits understood that the character of their mission brought many dangers. The first martyr of the Society, Antonio Criminali, was killed in India in 1549. In 1554, Pero Correia became the first Jesuit martyr in Brazil. On a mission south of São Vicente, he died, with his companion, from wounds received from Guarani bowmen. Nóbrega, intent on expanding the Jesuit mission among the Guarani, whom he saw as the Jesuits' best hope for evangelism in Brazil, had sent Correia with two brothers to preach to villages of Indians along the coast and to open a door for a future mission to the Ibiraiara Indians. While on their mission among the Guarani, Correia and João de Sousa learned that the Guarani had two Europeans living with them who acted as their interpreters. One was a Spaniard who had lived for many years among them, "adapting their customs but exceeding them in corruption," Anchieta writes in a letter describing Correia's death, and the other was a Portuguese. The Spaniard "had great authority among them," Anchieta reports, and urged the Indians to attack Correia and Sousa because they were opening up a road that would be used by their enemies to make war against them. As Correia and Sousa were making their way back to São Vicente, the Guarani Indians, incited by the Spaniard, shot them both to death with arrows. A seventeenth-century Jesuit martyrology portrays the men dying, one with his body pierced with arrows, the other dying from a blow delivered by a war club (Fig. 4.1).[54]

The Jesuits had complex reactions to these deaths. On the one hand, they were greatly saddened by the loss of their best interpreter and by the treachery exhibited by the Guarani. But, on the other hand, in ways that are difficult for modern readers to understand, they saw the deaths not as tragic, but rather as "glorious" and worthy of emulation. "These blessed brothers suffered death in holy obedience, in the preaching of the gospel, in peace, and for the love and charity of their neighbors," José de Anchieta wrote to Loyola, and "all of us wish mightily and ask God through constant prayer that we might die in this way." The chief of Piratininga, Tibiriçá, Anchieta reported, expressed his feelings in the Indian way. From midnight to dawn, he walked the house repeating many times: "The prince of the true speech, the only one who tells us the truth, the one who loved us with sincere love from the heart, has died."[55]

Tibiriçá characterized Correia as a "prince of speech," and Anchieta, Nóbrega, and Loyola recognized him as the "best interpreter" in Brazil.[56] Through his great facility with language, Correia connected very different and often hostile worlds. He was fluent in indigenous languages and cultures, which allowed him to translate Christianity into concepts and rituals that could be understood.

Figure 4.1. The martyrdom of Pero Correia and João de Sousa, 1554. Mathias Tanner, *Societatis Jesu. Americana.* Prague: Typis Universitatis Carolo-Ferdinandeae, 1675. Courtesy of the John Carter Brown Library at Brown University.

Through his powerful preaching, which he modeled on the great chiefs of indigenous society as well as on Jesuit traditions of preaching in Europe, Correia achieved the first objective of the Jesuits in Brazil: to bring Christianity to the Indians through persuasion, not force.

After Correia's death, however, a tone of discouragement sets into many of the Jesuit letters as the fathers and brothers of the Society of Jesus recognized that the conversion of the Indians of Brazil would not be as easy as they had first thought. Several more prominent Jesuits died, among them Leonardo

Nunes, the founder of the mission in São Vicente, who drowned at sea when his ship wrecked en route from Brazil in 1554; and João de Azpilcueta, gifted in languages and preaching, died from a fever he contracted in 1557. Moreover, the first bishop of Salvador, with whom Nóbrega had tangled earlier, was called back to Lisbon and died when his ship sank off the northeastern coast of Brazil. Bishop Sardinha's death was particularly traumatic, as he, along with most of those on the ship, was cannibalized by Caeté Indians. Nóbrega's own health began to deteriorate, and many thought that his end was near.

Nóbrega returned to Salvador following the death of Sardinha and found the new governor of Brazil, Mem de Sá (1557–1572), prepared to force the Indians living around Salvador into submission. A combination of his deteriorating health and setbacks in the Jesuit mission in Bahia led Nóbrega and other Jesuits in Bahia to see the governor's planned use of force as a step forward in the conversion of Indians. Nóbrega had already articulated the need to congregate Indians into villages, where they would live under Portuguese law as well as under the control of the church. This would be beneficial, he believed, for the evangelism of the Indians, and it would protect them from the unscrupulous colonists, who continually sought Indian labor. But in May of 1558, a disillusioned Nóbrega recommended defeating the Indians militarily to achieve this goal. He expressed anger that the Portuguese, who came from a nation feared and obeyed around the world, were nevertheless suffering in Brazil and were accommodating themselves to the ways of Indians—"the most vile and sad people of the world." Were the Indians to be subjugated, Nóbrega believed that many of the problems faced by the Jesuits would cease. The conflict between the Jesuits and Portuguese colonists over Indian slavery would be resolved, because subjugating the Indians would require the declaration of "just wars," the defeated parties of which could legally be enslaved. Many more sugar mills and cattle ranches could be established, causing the income of the Crown, and of the Portuguese population of Brazil, to rise. Nóbrega believed that the subjugation of the Indians would not be that costly, for the Portuguese colonists would help the governor with their slaves, as would Indians allied with the Portuguese.[57]

Mem de Sá's military campaign brought war the likes of which had not been seen before in Bahia. He ordered the men of an entire Indian village killed and the women and children brought back to Salvador as war captives. "Never has another such war been waged in this land," wrote a Jesuit, and "not only these Indians, but the whole coast will be shocked and afraid."[58] The Portuguese exploited the power of their horses, ships, and guns in battle and gained an edge over the coastal groups in Bahia and Ilhéus. Mem de Sá's campaign eliminated many formerly independent and powerful Indian chiefs around Salvador who used to negotiate directly with the governor.

The campaign also led to the consolidation of the formerly independent Indian villages, as well as a few villages where the Jesuits had already begun evangelization by building small churches and schools, into large mission villages (*aldeias*) under the control of the governor and the Jesuits, who not only taught them Christianity but transformed their ways of life. The aldeias of São Paulo, Santiago, São João, and Espírito Santo were established along the coast in 1557, Santo Antonio was founded in 1560, and Santa Cruz on the island of Itaparica was set up in 1561.[59] The aldeias were to become a hallmark of the Jesuit mission in Brazil.

The first Jesuits accepted Mem de Sá's violent campaigns with little if any criticism. José de Anchieta later wrote a long poem in Latin praising the exploits and sacrifices of Sá and lauding the creation of the first aldeias in Bahia. Sá appears in the poem as a hero, a pious and magnanimous governor, a bringer of laws, and the one who put an end to cannibalism. Other Jesuits agreed. Sá had "punished some" and "yoked all," wrote a Jesuit to Lisbon in April 1558, which opened up a "new way of proceeding" that had not been seen before in Brazil. Through fear and subjection, wrote another Jesuit in September of the same year, the Jesuits were beginning to harvest the "fruit" promised by the land of Brazil.[60]

That force had been used to create the foundation for the first Jesuit aldeias did not mean that the Jesuits had entirely abandoned their belief in the power of persuasion. From the Jesuit letters, it appears that most Jesuits saw Mem de Sá's campaign as inevitable, and they welcomed the new beginning that the creation of the mission villages afforded. Within the more controlled environment of the villages, Jesuit evangelists could return to their preferred approach: persuasion through teaching, preaching, and conversation. The new beginning allowed the Jesuits to regain their optimism, which had wavered as their first decade in Brazil came to an end.[61]

Some of this optimism, as well as the return to the Jesuit strategy of converting through persuasion, can be seen in what was one of the first Jesuit plays performed in Brazil. On Christmas night in 1561, in Piratininga, José de Anchieta's *Pregação universal* (Universal Sermon) was performed outside the Jesuit church. The three-hour, five-act play was directed at Indians and Portuguese alike, and it used three languages: Portuguese, Tupi, and Spanish. The play made use of a character familiar in Portuguese drama of the time—a miller—who jealously guards his beautiful coat. In Anchieta's drama, the miller, named Adam, appears humbled and ragged in act one because his Sunday clothes (symbolic of Divine Grace) have been stolen by his sins. In act two, the devil, named Guaixará, the name of an Indian chief, appears along with his ally, Aimbiré, who also bears the name of a powerful chief; both speak Tupi.[62]

This second act, spoken only in Tupi, takes the form of a long dialogue that repeats many of the themes that Jesuits stressed in their mission. First the chiefs / devils celebrate the Indian ways, proclaiming that it is good to drink cauim, to dance, to tattoo the body in red and black, to cover the body in feathers, to be a curer, to inhale smoke, to live for killing and eating prisoners, and to live with many women. When the guardian angel of the Christian Indian village appears, also speaking in Tupi, a dialogue ensues between the chiefs/devils and the angel. The angel questions the right of the chiefs/devils to treat the Indians of the village as their property. But the chiefs/devils then proceed to list all the failings of the Indians to the angel, underscoring how far Indians are from the Christian ideal. At first the angel responds only that confession exists as a cure for all ills. But then, unwilling to listen to any more of the chiefs'/devils' speaking, the angel throws them out of the village, sending them to hell, and declares to the audience:

> Be happy my children and rise up!
> To protect you, I am here; I come from heaven!
> Gather round me; I will give you all of my aid!
> (2.393–398)
> Believe in the Creator, and accept his law
> with submission and with love.
> Obey the doctrine, from the Priest,
> your instructor.
> (2.426–430)

Act three returns to the sins of the Portuguese in Brazil. Although this part of the play is largely lost, it is thought that twelve sinners process, speaking of their sins in Anchieta's poetic verse. In act four, twelve Indian children, students from the Jesuit school, dance and sing. In act five, the miller regains his Sunday dress, much more beautiful than the original, for it has been woven by his daughter, Maria, with the help of her son, Jesus.[63]

Performed at night, with music and costumes, such a theatrical piece undoubt-edly was a powerful teaching tool for the Jesuits. Their representation of Indian chiefs as devils, and the Indian ways of life as evil, underscored the role that Jesuits saw for themselves as interpreters of God's will for the Indians. The guardian angel declares in the play that the Jesuits are instructors—the inter-mediaries who make it possible for Indians to learn the Christian doctrines.

The Jesuits also saw themselves as the preferred, and indeed crucial, inter-mediaries between colonists and Indians. This can clearly be seen in 1563, when Nóbrega and Anchieta led a mission to establish peace with the Tupinambá Indians living on the coast to the north of São Vicente and around Guanabara Bay. This episode well demonstrates how go-betweens played pivotal roles in the negotiation of power between the Indian and European worlds.

Nóbrega, ordered to turn over the leadership of the Brazilian province to Luís da Grã and to retire to São Vicente to improve his health, arrived in São Vicente sometime before 1 June 1560. Nóbrega quickly perceived danger in São Vicente. He had sailed from Bahia with Mem de Sá, who led an armada to expel the French from their colony founded by Villegagnon in Rio de Janeiro. Sá attacked and took possession of the French fort in March of 1560 but retreated to São Vicente to repair his ships and regroup. Nóbrega wrote from São Vicente to Dom Henrique (known in English as Cardinal Prince Henry), then regent of Portugal, explaining that it was very necessary to settle Rio de Janeiro and to create another city like Salvador there to protect São Vicente to the south and Espírito Santo to the north.[64]

The Tupinambá, the traditional allies of the French in Rio de Janeiro, were the major source of concern, for they were the mortal enemies of the Tupinikin, who had allied themselves with the Portuguese in São Vicente. The attack on the French fortress by Mem de Sá did not stop the Tupinambá from continuing to raid the Portuguese farms and settlements in São Vicente. In the words of one Jesuit, the Tupinambá attacked incessantly the "slaves, women, and children of the Christian" settlers of São Vicente. A more dangerous situation arose the next year when a faction of the Tupinikin Indians of the Piratininga Plateau turned against the Portuguese. In July of 1561, the town of São Paulo found itself under attack from this rival group of Tupinikin, who had acquired allies among their former Tupinambá enemies. Only the leadership of Tibiriçá saved the settle-ment. When Tibiriçá died the next year, the need for a peaceful overture to the Tupinambá seemed clear.[65]

In a detailed letter to the head of the Society of Jesus in Rome, José de Anchieta recounts how he and Manoel da Nóbrega served as hostages so that a peace deal with the Tupinambá could be struck. Nóbrega and Anchieta left the fort of Bertioga in São Vicente in April of 1563 as passengers on two ships that headed 20 leagues (approximately 124 kilometers) north along the coast, past São Sebastião Island, and anchored off Iperoig, the very place where Hans Staden had been held captive nine years before. Canoes of Tupinambá met the Portuguese ships, and after various verbal exchanges, as well as the taking of hostages on each side to ensure peaceful intentions, and after an Indian woman vouched for the Jesuits, the Tupinambá invited the Jesuits ashore. With eight or nine Portuguese, Nóbrega and Anchieta visited two villages in the vicinity. Anchieta describes himself as "speaking in a loud voice from house to house in their custom," telling the Tupinambá that "they should be happy with our arrival and friendship" and that "we wished to stay among them and teach them the things of God so that God would give them abundant food, health, and victory over their enemies." Twelve youths of the villages boarded one of the ships and returned to São Vicente to serve as hostages for the lives of Nóbrega and Anchieta while peace was being discussed. Iperoig was the southern frontier of the Tupinambá, and the second ship, which also carried hostages, continued north for Guanabara Bay, where another peace overture was also planned.[66]

Nóbrega and Anchieta went to live in one of the houses of the Tupinambá and began the now familiar Jesuit strategies for evangelization. They gathered the children, boys and girls, as well as some adults, and taught basic doctrines. They set up an altar, and Nóbrega began to say daily mass at dawn. They advised continually that cannibalism must be ended. In return, the Tupinambá treated the Jesuits well, even offering them women to be their wives. Anchieta writes that he understood this custom to be an honor, and noted that European men who accepted Indian women in this way became sons-in-law and brothers-in-law; nevertheless, he describes himself as insisting over and over again that this was, in their case, an offense to God.[67]

The two Jesuits had arrived during a time when a large war party was away, and Nóbrega and Anchieta knew that when the warriors returned, they might well be put to death. Two canoes arrived in the vanguard of the war party, one carrying the "great chief" named Pindobuçu, and the second, the brother of the man who had allowed the Jesuits to stay in the house in the village. When this man heard that there were Jesuits in the house, he gave an order for them to leave. His son-in-law appeared while Anchieta was packing, and the following dialogue repeated by Anchieta purportedly took place at the doorway of the longhouse while the son-in-law held his sword in hand:

Son-in-law: "Who is this?"

Father-in-law: "The Portuguese."

Son-in-law: "A Portuguese?"

Anchieta: "I am your friend and will be with you in the future."

Son-in-law, haughtily and indignantly: "I don't want your company." [68]

Chief Pindobuçu, however, according to Anchieta, did desire peace and made no move to expel the Jesuits from the village. Anchieta describes this chief as very interested in talk, and he quickly fell into conversation with the Jesuits about heaven, hell, and how the Jesuits controlled their desire for women. A few days later, ten more canoes arrived, led by a chief known to be a great enemy of the Portuguese and a loyal ally to the French. This chief had a French son-in-law and a French-Tupinambá *métisse* (mixed-race) granddaughter; his French son-in-law was following with four more canoes of warriors. The chief, as Anchieta tells it, had learned of the presence of the Jesuits in the villages and had resolved to kill them. But his French son-in-law met the ship that had left Anchieta and Nóbrega at Iperoig and that was heading for Rio de Janeiro to make peace overtures there. The captain of the ship was not a Portuguese, but a Genoese by the name of José Adorno who owned a sugar mill in São Vicente.[69] Because he was Italian and spoke French, when the Frenchman boarded the ship, he persuaded him to agree to a peace. The Frenchman sent a message to his father-in-law with one of his Indian brothers-in-law, counseling him to accept the peace, while he turned back to Rio de Janeiro with letters from the Genoese captain requesting peace with the French. The Frenchman further recommended that the ship from São Vicente not proceed any deeper into Tupinambá territory until the peace could be concluded. Adorno's ship then headed back for Iperoig.

Back in the villages, however, the Frenchman's father-in-law mistrusted the Portuguese offer of peace. Anchieta describes him as sitting in a hammock, dressed in a shirt, with a bow and arrows in his hand, stubbornly reminding Anchieta and Nóbrega of the many evils he had suffered at the hands of the Portuguese. One such episode included a time when he had been taken as a slave, but he had escaped by diving off a Portuguese ship and swimming ashore, despite the fact that his feet were shackled with iron. That night, some of the men in the villages hatched a plot to take over the Portuguese ship and to kill Captain Adorno as well as the Jesuits. The next day, the chief arrived dressed in a very fine black coat (*sayo negro bien fino*), which Anchieta's words make clear was a European garment, armed with a sword, and surrounded by many of his armed men. Anchieta implies that his men only waited for the first word uttered in Portuguese, which would unleash an instant, violent death. But the chief first talked things over with another Frenchman who accompanied him, and asked him to point out the captain of the ship. The Frenchman intervened on the side of the captain, explaining that he was a man who spoke French well, and that he had come to make peace with the Tupinambá, as well as with all the French in Rio de Janeiro. Anchieta then clued Captain Adorno, who did not speak Tupi, to explain, in French, that he was not a Portuguese but a Genoese, and a great friend of the French. Only then would the chief begin to discuss peace.

According to Anchieta, the price of peace demanded by this chief was to be paid in captives—the Tupinikin allies of the Portuguese and the enemies of the Tupinambá. In particular, Anchieta writes, the chief wanted the chiefs so that they could be killed and eaten. Captain Adorno made his exit by saying that he had no authority to promise such things, but that he would return to São Vicente and present the demand. Anchieta and Nóbrega remained behind, making clear that no Indians should be given in exchange for the peace, and that if lives were to be given, it would be those of the Jesuits.

Their position in the villages remained tenuous, but time after time Anchieta describes how he and Nóbrega were able to continually avoid what seemed to be certain death. Although Anchieta attributes their safety to Divine Providence, it is clear that the Jesuits' ability to speak Tupi and the protection offered by powerful men in the villages saved them. In addition to Pindobuçu, Anchieta introduces another chief by name, Cuñambeba, who had a small church built for Nóbrega to say mass in and ordered that no one harm or speak ill of the Jesuits. But his protection, Anchieta believed, was not the reason that they were not killed and cannibalized by "such an evil, bestial, and bloodthirsty people." Rather, much like Hans Staden, Anchieta saw their survival, among many who would have liked to kill them, as evidence of the hand of God. Nóbrega decided to return to São Vicente in June of 1563, leaving Anchieta in Iperoig with another Portuguese man as principal hostages. Anchieta remained a hostage until September 1563, when Cuñambeba and twenty others brought Anchieta by canoe to the fortress of Bertioga in São Vicente.[70]

Anchieta's sojourn among the Tupinambá was intended to be a symbol of the goodwill of the Portuguese as they lobbied for peace, but Anchieta later realized that it was more a case of "an end of peace and a beginning of a new war." While the Tupinambá of Iperoig with whom Anchieta lived kept the peace, other Tupinambá did not. Anchieta spent little time lamenting the failure of the peace to take hold. He remarks in a letter that this is what one expects from "a people so bestial and bloodthirsty."[71]

The negotiated peace broke down as the Portuguese made their move into Guanabara Bay. Anchieta describes how he and Nóbrega sailed back up the coast, stopping briefly in Iperoig to collect Anchieta's books, reaching Guanabara Bay in March of 1564. There, an armada led by Mem de Sá's nephew, Estácio de Sá, had attempted to take possession of the island where Villegagnon had once built the French colony. Anchieta and Nóbrega found clear signs that the Tupinambá resisted the disembarkation of the Portuguese fleet: they found houses burned and corpses exhumed. Despite this unsettling beginning, Anchieta nevertheless viewed a settlement in Rio de Janeiro as highly desirable. Not only would it extinguish the influence of the French Calvinists, but he believed that it would serve as a "great door" for the conversion of the Tupinambá.[72]

The men of the Society of Jesus who disembarked in Brazil in the 1550s set themselves the impossible goal of converting all the native peoples of Brazil to Christianity. To begin their mission, they saw the need to turn themselves into go-betweens. Correia, Brazil's first Jesuit martyr, symbolized this role, as did Anchieta and Nóbrega in Iperoig. Most Jesuits were transactional go-betweens in far less visible, but no less important, ways. Teaching, translating, praying, absolving, the Jesuits created roles for themselves as mediators between Indians and God. But Jesuits filled yet another role as go-betweens: just as any European who crossed the Atlantic became a physical go-between, so, too, did they. Physical go-betweens were biological go-betweens, and as biological go-betweens, they unwittingly and unknowingly forever altered the biology and ecology of Brazil.

5. Biology

. . . dysentery, cough, headache, fevers, and other sicknesses from which we die!

Chief Pindobuçu, 1563

When José de Anchieta wrote the long letter about his residence as a hostage among the Tupinambá, he quoted Chief Pindobuçu, preaching through the village:

> If we are afraid of our shaman, how much more should we fear these [Jesuit] priests . . . because they have the power to bring to us the dysentery, cough, headache, fevers, and other sicknesses from which we die! [1]

As remembered and recorded by Anchieta, Chief Pindobuçu spoke these words to impress upon his villagers the power of the Jesuits, but in so doing, Pindobuçu identified one of the most powerful and devastating roles of the go-between: that of disease carrier.

Geographer Alfred Crosby pointed out in 1972 that Europeans brought more than their weapons, their religious worldview, and their desire for wealth to the encounter between the "old" world and the "new"; they brought their diseases, foods, and domestic animals. Disease, argues Crosby, was a major factor in the rapid Spanish defeat of the indigenous cultures of the Americas. [2] Whereas outbreaks of epidemic disease accompanied colonization in the Spanish Caribbean, Mexico, and Peru, in Brazil the pattern was different. The first outbreaks of disease in Brazil did not lead to the immediate demise of indigenous groups. It was not until significant colonization began fifty years after the discovery of Brazil that disease, in conjunction with the introduction of European and African domestic animals, sugar cultivation, and slavery, wreaked havoc on the independent and autonomous Tupi-Guarani-speaking peoples of Brazil. Sustained European settlement, with its concomitant ecological change, violent warfare, and slavery, all intensified the effect of disease after 1550.[3]

The history of disease in sixteenth-century Brazil, as well as the transformation in the landscape, remains largely unstudied. Compared to Spanish America, Brazil has far fewer sources from which to reconstruct the biological and ecological changes of the sixteenth century, and it has generated less interest among historians.[4] "Snatches" of conversations and observations of reactions remain from the indigenous side, but these are generally filtered through European eyes, such as Anchieta's record of Pindobuçu's speech. Undoubtedly, dreams, myths, and oral histories became vehicles through which representational go-betweens on the Indian side recorded and interpreted the changes to their worlds; fragments of such representations might still survive that could be analyzed today.[5] Far more comprehensive and accessible is the European record—the letters of the Jesuits after 1549 in particular—that enables modern historians to reconstruct the changes taking place in Brazil.

Physical go-betweens—European and African—introduced new diseases to Brazil; they imported the first cattle, horses, sheep, goats, and chickens; they planted new, non-native plants, such as sugar and wheat; and many men fathered children of mixed race. Transactional go-betweens also spread disease. Because they facilitated contact between the European and the Indian worlds, and typically through language in face-to-face situations, transactional go-betweens created situations in which diseases could be exchanged. Representational go-betweens sought to explain the meaning of enormous changes, especially the shocking epidemics that decimated the indigenous populations.

Unlike Spanish America, where epidemics accompanied colonization, the first epidemics that likely occurred in Brazil before 1550 did not destroy the political or social structure of independent indigenous groups. Nor did the introduction of European and African domestic animals immediately degrade the coastal forests. But the increasing intensity of colonization after 1550 made outbreaks of disease more frequent and more severe. Simultaneously, imported Iberian pastoral traditions greatly increased the negative impact of domestic animals on the landscape. Between 1550 and 1580, Brazil began to follow a pattern similar to that seen in the Spanish Caribbean in the thirty years after 1492: significant outbreaks of disease coincided with the ratcheting up of the tempo of colonization.

The broad contours of the history of epidemic disease in the Americas are well known. Scholars agree that at least five diseases arrived in the Americas from Europe and Africa in the sixteenth and seventeenth centuries: smallpox, measles, influenza, scarlet fever, and yellow fever. Many medical historians add to this list mumps, rubella, pneumonia, pertussis, anthrax, bubonic plague, malaria, and typhus. Humans themselves hosted more than half of these disease agents, and the others were carried to the Americas in nonhuman hosts—in insects and animals brought to the Americas as a result of human action.[6] Many of these diseases were "habitually prevalent," or endemic, in Europe, Africa, and Asia, where they erupted periodically and largely sickened children, allowing those who survived to harbor immunities against subsequent outbreaks.[7] But when human and nonhuman hosts carried the viral, bacterial, and protozoal agents that spread these diseases to the Americas, they became epidemic, affecting all age groups with very high mortality.[8]

That these diseases were endemic among European, African, and Asian peoples but not among the peoples of the Americas is partially due to what Crosby terms the biological ally of the European conquistador: his domestic animals—pigs, cattle, horses, goats, sheep, and chickens.[9] Many human diseases originate in animals, especially domesticated animals. Horses, cattle, and sheep were, according to William McNeil, "chronic bearers of viral and bacterial infections capable of invading and reinvading people." The long coexistence of Europeans, Africans, and Asians with their domestic animals led to cycles of transfers of infectious agents from animals to humans, resulting in epidemics with "heavy die-offs of hosts and of disease organisms." As cities grew in Europe, Africa, and Asia, diseases spread through person-to-person contact, contaminated water, and insects. Three major diseases that thrived among crowded human populations were smallpox, measles, and bubonic plague. According to McNeil, each major civilized region developed "its own peculiar mix" of diseases, each becoming a "diseased and disease-resistant" human population that in time became "biologically dangerous to neighbors unaccustomed to so formidable an array of infections." Contact between previously isolated regions—through war, trade, migration, or colonization—created a breeding ground for the spread of disease. New trading routes fostered contact and spread epidemics, as did war. But over a long period of time, the devastation once caused by epidemic diseases greatly lessened as these diseases became endemic in the populations of Europe, Asia, Africa, and the Middle East.[10]

The Americas, isolated from the rest of the world, did not participate in this exchange of diseases. Moreover, medical historians long assumed that the disease environment in the Americas was more benign. Fewer domestic animals meant that human populations in the Americas were less at risk. Wild herds of llamas and dogs in the Americas, it seemed, did not transfer infectious parasites to humans in the ways that had occurred in Europe, Asia, and Africa. McNeil writes that "with the possible exception of the guinea pig, the Amerindians' domesticated species . . . were incapable of supporting infectious chains" such as had characterized Europe. Similarly, medical historians have argued that dense urban settlements in the Americas "suffered little from disease." [11]

Recent scholarship modifies this picture of the benign American health environment and suggests, on the contrary, that American indigenous populations before 1492 also suffered from epidemics, nutritional deficiencies, and famines. These historians and archaeologists maintain that infant and child mortality was high, and life expectancies were low. The major diseases in the Americas were bacterial and parasitic infections. Bacterial pneumonia, tuberculosis, typhus, and influenza all likely caused epidemics in the Americas before 1492. But major killers, such as smallpox, measles, bubonic plague, and cholera, did not develop. Although indigenous Americans shared many disease patterns with the rest of the world, as Suzanne Austin Alchon writes, they "were not immunologically prepared for the devastation that lay ahead." [12]

William Denevan argues forcefully that the American landscape was not "pristine" in 1492, but that it had been affected by the humans—the Native Americans—who lived in it. Similarly, Warren Dean makes clear that the coastal Atlantic forest of Brazil had already experienced degradation at the hands of the Tupi groups living there.[13] The first French and Portuguese ships that saw Brazil, therefore, saw a landscape that had been shaped by hunters, gatherers, and agriculturalists. A major difference between the American landscape and that of Iberia and West Africa was the absence of domestic animals, in particular, hoofed animals, or ungulates.

Little is known about disease and the impact of domestic animals in Brazil during the first decades of the sixteenth century, but the same period in the Caribbean is well studied, providing a useful counterpoint. Medical historian Kenneth Kiple asserts that no other region has experienced "such a sudden and devastating ecological assault as the islands of the Caribbean with the arrival of the Europeans." Although estimates of the population of the island of Hispaniola in 1492 vary wildly, its decline is clear. According to data compiled by historical demographer Noble David Cook, estimates of the Indian population in 1508 placed it at 60,000; in 1510 it had fallen to 33,523; in 1514, to 26,334; in 1518–1519, to 18,000; and by 1542, to less than 2,000. The first outbreak of disease arrived with the 1,500 men on the seventeen ships that formed Columbus' second voyage of 1493. This expedition had the goal of establishing Spain's first American colony; hence the colonists brought with them plants and animals, among them pigs and horses. Cook sees many possibilities for this first epidemic: it might have been influenza or swine flu, smallpox, meningitis, typhus, dysentery, or malaria, or a combination of several of these in conjunction with malnutrition. Mortality among Europeans was high— even Columbus was very sick. Soon the indigenous population of the Caribbean was in alarming decline from subsequent sicknesses that were described as fevers in 1500 and 1502, influenza in 1514–1517, and smallpox in 1518–1525. An epidemic thought to be measles struck in 1529. Simultaneously, Spanish cattle, horses, and hogs from the Canary Islands overran the traditional *conucos,* or "mounds," planted by the Native Americans. Native grasses were degraded by the new ungulates, while non-native grasses, accidentally introduced, took root. According to Caribbean historian Carl Sauer, "The pattern of livestock ranching for the New World was formed here." [14]

It is highly likely that the ships in the brazilwood trade—the Portuguese naus and *caravelas* and the French *barques*—introduced diseases into Brazil in the first half of the sixteenth century. [15] The lack of data makes it impossible to know the effect of these diseases on coastal indigenous groups, but it seems clear that for the first half of the century Brazil did not follow the Caribbean pattern. The primary reason for the difference was that many more physical go-betweens sailed to the Caribbean, as compared to Brazil. Warren Dean estimates that more than 330 ships landed along the Tupi coast of Brazil in the fifty years after 1500. This number is far smaller than the ships headed for India during the same period: 319 departures from Portugal between 1500 and 1529, and 192 from 1530 to 1559. The number making the voyage from Spain to the Caribbean was even higher. Pierre and Huguette Chanu count 185 ships that sailed from Spain to the Caribbean between 1509 and 1515 alone. The smaller number of sailings to Brazil suggests that the impact of disease on Brazil was more limited than had been the case in the Caribbean. [16]

Moreover, the first outbreak of disease in the Caribbean coincided with the arrival of a large expedition of men and domestic animals to a circumscribed and highly localized area: an island. Subsequently, the independent indigenous chiefs of the island were rapidly deposed and the population divided into gangs of laborers serving the Spaniards. Then, the many sailings between Spain and the Caribbean reproduced these initial patterns on other islands.[17] In contrast, the initial contact between Brazil and European and African ports took place on a much smaller scale over a long coastline. No immediate conquest of indigenous groups was attempted, and fewer domestic animals were immediately introduced into Brazil. The thinly scattered Europeans who lived in Brazil, with the possible exception of those living at trading posts, assimilated themselves into indigenous groups by marrying Indian women.

Although sailing the Atlantic was hardly healthy, predictable, or safe, the very first voyages to Brazil appear to have been disease free. Caminha's letter makes no mention of sickness breaking out during the first visit to Brazil. The anonymous account of a Portuguese man on the expedition mentions disease only when the armada reached East Africa, three months after they had left Brazil. This disease seems to have been scurvy, for the men improved rapidly after the king of Malindi sent lemons and oranges. Cabral commanded a large armada, which increased the possibility of introducing disease. Most of the subsequent sailings to Brazil were, in contrast, smaller in size. Vespucci made two trips to Brazil. The first, in 1501, had three ships. Two years later, six ships, one of which was under the command of Vespucci, set out from Portugal. But en route, the flagship sank and three others were lost before reaching Brazil. Only two of the six original ships actually reached the Bay of All Saints. On each voyage out, Vespucci describes the mood of the men. Commenting on the first voyage in his *Mundus novus* letter, Vespucci writes that "anxieties beset our spirits" on the sixty-odd-day voyage across the Atlantic and that "fear so overwhelmed us that we had almost abandoned all hope of survival." Regarding the psychological state of the men on the second expedition, Vespucci describes them as "unhappy" and "so afraid that I could not console them" when they feared the loss of the flagship. But Vespucci makes no mention of illness among the crew on either of the expeditions.[18]

Early accounts of Brazil extol the health of the land and its people. Caminha thought the fresh air of Brazil was the reason the bodies of the Indians "were so clean, so fat, and so beautiful that they could not be more so." One of the men on Cabral's voyage described the Indians as hale and hearty. Amerigo Vespucci describes a "very pleasant and temperate and healthy" land whose inhabitants "do not sicken either from pestilence or corruption of the air, dying only natural deaths." Vespucci comments on the longevity of the Indians, many of whom "had up to four generations of descendants." One of the oldest men he met explained that "he had lived seventeen hundred lunar months, which by my reckoning must be 132 years, counting thirteen moons for every year." Even accounting for Vespucci's exaggeration, the clear impression he conveys is that Brazil was a land "filled with countless inhabitants," one in which there was "no pestilence or illness" and the Indians, "unless they die a violent death, . . . live a long life." [19]

Vespucci relates intimate contact between the indigenous peoples of Brazil and his European companions on his two voyages to Brazil. On the 1501–1502 expedition, sailing 1,800 leagues along the coast of Brazil (approximately 11,000 kilometers), the men landed on "several occasions," and at one point the men lived among an Indian group for twenty-seven days. Vespucci writes, "I ate and slept among them." He alludes also to sexual contact between Indian women and European men. On the 1503–1504 expedition, Vespucci remained at the Bay of All Saints for two months and four days waiting for the other ships in the original fleet; when they did not arrive, he sailed south 260 leagues (approximately 1,600 kilometers), where he built a fort and left behind twenty-four men. [20] This proximity between the European crew and Indians laid the groundwork, as did subsequent European expeditions, for miscegenation and the sharing of disease.

The first Brazilian Indian known to have sickened and died from an illness shared with Europeans was the Guarani Namoa, who died when Binot Paulmier de Gonneville, the French sea captain who made landfall along the coast of Brazil in 1504, attempted to take him to France. An experienced captain, Gonneville knew well that not all lands were healthy for European crews. In 1503, heading to India, he decided, after provisioning his single ship in the Cape Verde Islands, not to call along the shore of Africa because of the "dangers and diseases" there, but to sail well out into the ocean. Nevertheless, two-thirds of the crew came down with the "illness of the sea," and six men died. Later the chief pilot died of "apoplexy," possibly a stroke. The ship began to float, at the mercy of the sea, and lost its course, "which grieved all, given the necessity they had for water and to reprovision themselves on land." Only the accidental discovery that they were near land saved the men on this ship, which anchored south of the Tropic of Capricorn, in what is today Santa Catarina in southern Brazil, in 1504. [21]

The expedition resided for six months among the Guarani, but the French account makes no mention of disease while there. After making the vessel

seaworthy, the French prepared to set sail, and the Guarani chief, Arosca, agreed
to allow his son, a youth named Essomericq, to leave on the ship, along with
a companion, a man of thirty-five to forty years named Namoa. Two months
after they left the Guarani, a malignant fever spread through the ship and many
Frenchmen and the two Indians became ill. Essomericq and Namoa were so
stricken that the French crew debated whether to baptize them to save their
souls, even though they had not been instructed in Christianity as was required.
At first, the crew decided not to baptize the Indians, but after Namoa died, they
changed their minds when Essomericq in turn lingered near death. Essomericq
recovered, but the fever killed three Frenchmen, as well as Namoa, before it
ran its course. The crew believed the "wasted and fetid" water of the ship was
the cause of the fever and desired to land to obtain the meats and fresh water
"that cure all the sick." This ship made two subsequent stops in Brazil, possibly
spreading the fever that had already struck many on the ship.[22] Why a fever
suddenly erupted on this ship, when the French crew and the Guarani had been
living together for six months, apparently disease free, is an unsolved puzzle.
Possibly the ship itself was the culprit, still carrying bacterial, viral, or protozoal
agents festering in the bilgewater. Alternatively, one of the men was an asymp-
tomatic carrier, and in the close quarters of the ship, the disease spread.[23]

The known written historical record falls silent after Namoa's death, and we
learn of no more diseases in Brazil for twenty years. Yet, during this time, individual ships were calling regularly along the long brazilwood coast, making it
likely that outbreaks of disease occurred. Still, Antonio Pigafetta does not mention disease while Magellan's expedition of five ships and 237 men briefly called
along the coast of Brazil in 1519. Pigafetta did pay attention to disease, for he
relates the fact that later men did sicken and some died while in the Pacific. These
men were ill from lack of food and scurvy. Twenty-nine men died, including an
Indian whom they had taken from the coast of Brazil and a "giant" they had
taken from Patagonia, south of the Río de la Plata.[24]

Evidence of the introduction of disease in the very south of Brazil emerges
when larger Spanish expeditions were sent to navigate the Strait of Magellan or
to secure the Río de la Plata. García Jofre de Loaisa commanded an armada of
seven ships and 450 men that had as its goal retracing Magellan's route to reach
the Moluccas, the spice islands of Indonesia. Leaving Spain in 1525, the seven
ships first hailed the Canary Islands, then an island called San Mateo, located—
men on the expedition later testified—off the coast of Africa near the equator.

There many men became sick from diarrhea and recovered after "many days." Then the seven ships sailed across the Atlantic for Brazil, and continued south to the Strait of Magellan, making it possible for the men to carry disease. The next year (1526), when Sebastian Cabot's fleet of four sailed for the Moluccas via the Strait of Magellan, disease was recorded among the crew after they arrived in southern Brazil. Luis Ramírez, a man on the expedition, wrote to his father that after arriving at Santa Catarina, he was "sick with fever." Ramírez was "still unwell and exhausted" one month later. The trading log kept by a Spanish official in 1527, when the Spanish armada was anchored at Santa Catarina, confirms the presence of disease. The captain sent one of his men 35 leagues (approximately 194 kilometers) into the interior to find chickens for the ill; the factor traded for honey to make special syrups and acquired yams for a diet deemed better for the infirm. Numerous references indicate that Indians in Santa Catarina came into direct and indirect contact with these sick Europeans, even though we have no accounts of sickness among them.[25]

The Spanish expedition of Pedro de Mendoza to the Río de la Plata, which left Spain in 1534, was sufficiently large to spread disease. It consisted of an armada of fourteen ships, 2,500 Spaniards, 150 Germans, and seventy-two horses. Unable to survive where Mendoza founded Buenos Aires in 1536, the men traveled nearly 1,000 miles up the Paraguay River and founded Asunción in 1537. Ulrich Schmidel, a German on this expedition, described three "very ill" Spaniards who were left among the Payzuno Guarani in approximately 1538. By the 1540s, Schmidel describes many occasions when the Spaniards in Paraguay, including the captain general, Cabeza de Vaca, were "very ill" or "with fever" or "ill to the point of death." [26]

The ships that called along the coast of Brazil carried domestic animals as part of their food supply. Pero Vaz de Caminha notes that Pedro Álvares Cabral showed the Indians of Brazil a sheep (*carneiro*) and a hen (*galinha*). Magellan's armada of five ships carried six cows and three pigs when it left Spain in 1519, but these animals were intended for the consumption of the crew and would not have been left ashore by choice. From Luis Ramírez we learn that his ship headed for the Río de la Plata carried dogs, one of which had to be killed and eaten because the men were starving. Rats and mice were common fellow travelers; when they had run out of food in the mid-Pacific, Magellan's men caught and sold the rats living on the ships. The rats had eaten much of the biscuit stores; what was left had turned to powder and stank of rats' urine. Whether carried intentionally, and even if reserved only for the crew, some of these domestic animals could and did swim ashore following shipwrecks.[27]

Chickens appear to have been some of the first European domestic animals introduced into Brazil. Considered to be food especially beneficial to the sick, chickens were commonly carried aboard ship. In Santa Catarina in 1527, a Spanish official traded fishhooks, knives, mirrors, and combs for food, much of which was native to Brazil (venison, oysters, corn, fish meal), but among the items obtained were chickens, ducks, and pigs. In 1530, when the Portuguese settlement of São Vicente consisted of no more than twelve houses, "chickens and pigs from Spain" were abundant, and an entire small island had been turned over to the pigs.[28]

When the first Portuguese settlements began, the numbers of domestic animals increased, but the nature and toll of disease, even on the few Portuguese in Brazil, remains unknown. Only a few scattered references appear in the written sources. When Martim Afonso de Sousa made his expedition along the coast of Brazil before founding the colony at São Vicente, his brother, Pero Lopes de Sousa, wrote in his diary that Martim Afonso put ashore the ill on his expedition; he left them at the brazilwood feitoria of Pernambuco. Later, Sousa described how he and his men were sick with fever near Guanabara Bay. The sixteenth-century historian Oviedo writes that as soon as Martim Afonso arrived at the Río de la Plata, some of his men began to get sick and die.[29]

A few sketchy references allude to the existence of disease among European colonists in the 1540s, suggesting that the healthy picture of Brazil painted by Vespucci and Caminha was changing. Newly arrived Portuguese now generally required a year of "seasoning" before they could function normally. In 1545, the donatário Pero de Góis wrote his business partner about the need to recruit millers for the sugar factories; the men should be sent a year early, Góis recommended, because "the first year is always wasted by sickness and getting acclimatized."[30]

The introduction of hoofed herbivores into Brazil most probably began with these first settlements and sugar plantations. Warren Dean believes that Martim Afonso de Sousa introduced cattle as part of the first royal colony at São Vicente, in 1532. By the time the Jesuits arrived in Brazil in 1549, stock populations were well established. In Nóbrega's "Information of the Lands of Brazil," penned in 1549, he states that oxen, cows, sheep, goats, and chickens were already present in Brazil, and increasing. In 1551, the Jesuit Afonso Brás, in extolling the fertility of Espírito Santo, stated that there were many wild pigs there. In 1554, the

Jesuit Luís da Grã commented that "all kinds of domestic animals are raised in great numbers . . . because the Christians [i.e., Portuguese colonists] have a great many pigs, oxen, goats, hens, ducks, etc." [31]

The impact of ungulates on indigenous groups is unknown; however, by the 1550s, European domestic chickens had become common among coastal Tupinambá. André Thevet describes chickens that had been brought to the Tupinambá by the Portuguese, but noted that women would not eat their eggs. "Women absolutely will not eat them," he states, "rather they become angry when they see a Christian eating four or five eggs at a meal . . . because they feel that for each egg, they are eating a chicken, which would be sufficient to feed two men." Léry attributes the Tupinambá's interest in chickens as related to their love for feathers; he recounts how they plucked the white down, dyed it red with brazilwood, cut the feathers into little pieces, and attached them to their bodies with a gum. In Bahia, an Indian youth from one of the surrounding villages presented Nóbrega with a hen in 1552; six years later, following the defeat of Indians in Paraguaçu (Bahia), the Indians were required to pay part of their tribute in hens.[32]

The small Portuguese colonies began to transform the surrounding landscape with their agricultural practices. With slave labor, sugar became the essential cash crop of Brazil in the sixteenth century. Beyond sugar, Portuguese settlements were slow to develop other European and African food crops. By 1554, "beautiful" wheat grew in São Vicente, but bread baked from wheat flour remained a luxury, available only in Bahia and Pernambuco. Instead, colonists adapted to the Indian staples of manioc flour and corn. Orchards that grew Mediterranean fruits— oranges, lemons, limes, citrons, figs, and quinces—were soon planted, as were grapes and vegetables commonly grown in Portugal. By the early seventeenth century, several plants had been introduced from Africa: the Angolan pea (pigeon pea), and *nachenim* (a grass), which slaves called *masa* (possibly millet).[33]

Miscegenation was very much a part of the biological story of Brazil in the first half of the sixteenth century. Mixed-race and bicultural children became an integral part of the Portuguese settlements and were possibly part of the changing nature of Indian village life, too. Very few Portuguese women sailed to Brazil before 1550, and as a result, Portuguese men first began living with Indian women in Indian villages, beginning with João Ramalho and Diogo Álvares. With the founding of the first Portuguese settlements, Portuguese men continued to live with Indian women; Jerônimo de Albuquerque and his alliances with Indian women in Pernambuco is one such example. The mameluca daughters of these unions between Portuguese men and Indian women proved to be attractive marriage partners for the next wave of European men who sought status in the growing settlements.[34] Other Portuguese men in the first settlements simply lived with their Indian slave women. A shocked Nóbrega noted during his first year in Brazil that Portuguese men believed that by baptizing their female slaves, they lessened their sin of living with several women outside of marriage.[35] The mameluca daughters of Indian slave women remained in Portuguese settlements, where they stepped into the role left vacant by the absence of Portuguese women. Mameluca women still spoke Tupi, but they were among the most ardent supporters of the first Jesuits. To them fell the task of shaping the identities of the first generations of children born in the Portuguese settlements in Brazil.

Less known, but potentially no less important, was the sexual contact between Indians and Africans, or Africans and Europeans. Miscegenation may have been one reason why the biological and ecological changes of the first half of the sixteenth century were absorbed by indigenous groups. Mixed-race children may have inherited some genetic resistance to disease, and the alliances between European men and Indian women facilitated the transfer of knowledge about the new domestic animals, seeds, and foods that were unloaded off the ships.

After Tomé de Sousa arrived in the Bay of All Saints in 1549 with soldiers, colonists, and the Jesuits, the pace of biological and ecological change accelerated rapidly. The arrival of significantly more physical go-betweens—Europeans and Africans—introduced wave after wave of epidemic disease that brought high mortality, especially to Indians. The Jesuits inadvertently intensified the severity of epidemic disease by creating large aldeias that congregated what had been separate and smaller independent Indian villages. Similarly, as sugar plantations spread, the number of Indian slaves on the plantations increased, creating ideal conditions for epidemic disease. After 1550, the numbers of domestic animals increased, and the pastoral tradition quickly grew. Land grants distributed to colonists for sugar plantations and ranches occupied lands formerly used for indigenous hunting grounds or as buffer zones between hostile groups.

Although there is no record of an immediate outbreak of disease in the Bay of All Saints after the arrival of Tomé de Sousa, the greater contact between Europeans, Africans, and Indians considerably increased that possibility. Tomé de Sousa first describes a "fever" in 1551, two years after his appearance in

Brazil; this fever affected an Indian group not allied with the Portuguese. It erupted after several degredados who deserted from Salvador approached an enemy village by boat. There, because they were seen as enemies, the Indians killed and cannibalized them. To punish the Indian village for their cannibalism, Governor Tomé de Sousa sent Pero de Góis, his captain who patrolled the coast by ship, to burn the village and imprison the chiefs. Subsequently, the governor reported that those whom Góis had spared had died from fever.[36]

Beginning in 1552, three years into the Jesuits' mission in Brazil, their letters regularly comment on diseases among the Indians. A Jesuit letter written in May of 1552 begins with the statement that many Indians in Bahia had recently died in such great numbers that it seemed to be an "odd thing." This "great mortality" affected four Indian villages where the Jesuits had been preaching, where "the young as well as the adults died," but especially infants. A powerful chief of Bahia, called Puerta Grande by the Jesuits, died in "a terrible death" in four days; another chief and his wife fell into an illness that "left them dry"; and a son of a chief became sick with a long illness until he became skin and bones. In a summary letter, also written in May of 1552, brother Vicente Rodrigues called the epidemic a "general cough from which many died." The result was that the Indians began to associate the Jesuits, Christian baptism, and Latin prayers with disease and death. Jesuit letter writers recounted that when the Indians saw the Jesuits arriving at their villages, they fled and hid their children or burned peppers, which, with their stinging smoke, kept the Jesuits from entering the villages. This high mortality suggests the outbreak of an epidemic, possibly influenza. It is likely the first recorded epidemic in Brazil.[37]

Governor Tomé de Sousa undertook a visitation of all the settlements along the coast of Brazil in 1552–1553 immediately after this epidemic swept the Indian villages of the Bay of All Saints. His armada left the diseased environment of Bahia sometime after September 1552, encountered disease near Rio de Janeiro, and arrived in São Vicente before February of 1553. Sousa's retinue included many degredados destined to be colonists in the southern settlements. This armada hailed the ports of Porto Seguro and Espírito Santo and entered Guanabara Bay on its way to São Vicente. Also accompanying Souza were Manoel da Nóbrega, Francisco Pires (another Jesuit priest), and several young Indian boys who were being raised by the Jesuits to serve as interpreters. In Guanabara Bay, an illness broke out, and many became sick. The Jesuit fathers on board, fearing that death would come to many, confessed all of the sick. None died; but shortly thereafter the Jesuits visited some inland Indian villages that were allied with the Portuguese. After the ships sailed from Rio de Janeiro, Nóbrega became sick, as did Pires. Nóbrega had a fever and had to be bled twice; Pires had *câmaras* (diarrhea).[38] Thus, the men and women in the armada, as well as the Jesuits, quite likely carried disease along the coast of Brazil in 1552 and 1553, and introduced it into São Vicente, where by 1554 a major epidemic raged among the recently converted Indians of Piratininga.

These first illnesses described in the Jesuit letters were undoubtedly similar to, but most likely more severe than, previous outbreaks of disease in the first half of the sixteenth century. The greater numbers of physical go-betweens in Brazil, the larger size of settlements, and the growing contact between coastal regions of Brazil increased the possibilities for diseases to spread. Even so, independent indigenous groups were still able to absorb the epidemics in the 1550s. Unlike the first outbreaks in the Caribbean, which accompanied an almost total breakdown in indigenous social structure, coastal Tupi groups withstood the first epidemics. Hans Staden witnessed firsthand the outbreak of illness among the Tupinambá, making his account important for assessing the impact of disease on an independent Indian village. The many details Staden provides make it possible to see how disease might have spread along the coast, through trade, warfare, and cannibalism. His account also makes clear that the Tupinambá weathered the disease without complete social disintegration.

The Tupinambá held Staden captive in 1554 at the same time that an epidemic was consuming Indians in Piratininga. The Jesuit interpreter Pero Correia wrote that in July 1554, almost every day, death struck among "those whom we had made Christians." Three chiefs died, as did many Indian men and women. Two months later, after Nóbrega decided to send several Christian Guarani Indians along with some Jesuits on a mission to the Guarani, "an illness attacked them suddenly from which nearly all died." The next year, at a mission that the Jesuits had established even deeper inland than their residence at Piratininga, nearly all the Indians became sick, and the greater part died.[39]

The village of seven longhouses, Uwattibi (Ubatuba), where the Tupinambá held Staden, had plenty of contact with outside groups, any one of which might have introduced disease. Not only had they recently captured Staden on a raid outside the fort of Bertioga, near São Vicente, but the Norman interpreter Karwattuware visited them regularly. A Guarani Indian slave who had lived among the Tupinambá group holding Staden became sick six months after Staden had been taken prisoner. When the slave had been ill for nine or ten days, Staden writes that the Indians wanted him to bleed this "man who had lost an eye from his disease" and whose "appearance was horrible." Unable to draw blood, the Indians decided, according to Staden, to "kill him before he is dead." Staden, observing that his Tupinambá hosts planned to eat the body, writes, "I warned them that he was a sick man, and they might also fall sick if they ate him." Despite his warning, Staden reports that "they devoured everything except the head and intestines, which they did not fancy, on account of the man's sickness." [40]

In Staden's eyes, the cannibalism of this sick Guarani was further proof of the savagery of the Tupinambá, but cannibalism may have been another means for the spread of disease. Prisoners captured in war by enemies were a kind of physical go-between, because they lived in intimate contact with an indigenous group before they were put to death. Moreover, cannibalism has been associated with the spread of a disease known as kuru among the Fore peoples who are based in modern-day Papua New Guinea. [41]

Immediately before illness broke out among them, the villagers of Uwattibi (Ubatuba) had had recent contact with two groups, an Indian war party and a ship, both from São Vicente. The illness began a little more than two weeks after a war party of Tupinikin attacked the village, and on failing to defeat Uwattibi, the Tupinikin war party moved on to the village of Mambukabe, some four miles away, and burned it. Staden's captor, Jeppipo Wasu, went to Mambukabe to help rebuild it. In his absence, a Portuguese ship from São Vicente stopped "within speaking distance" of Uwattibi, and a verbal exchange took place between the Portuguese on the ship and the Tupinambá on land. [42] Staden relates that soon after this, Jeppipo Wasu's brother returned from the village of Mambukabe with the news that "the others were all sick": Jeppipo Wasu himself, his mother, and his children. Soon the ill returned to Uwattibi and began to die: "a child died first, then the king's mother, an old woman . . . some days later a brother died, and then again a child, and then another brother, that one who had first brought me news of their illness." Jeppipo Wasu eventually recovered, as did one of his wives, but Staden writes that "there died of his family some eight persons." [43] A woodcut in the Marburg edition of Staden's account depicts the mourning of the dead in Uwattibi (Fig. 5.1).

The illness that threatened the family of Jeppipo Wasu in Uwattibi may have been the same devastating sickness occurring on the Piratininga Plateau in that same year. Yet, when Anchieta became a hostage among the Tupinambá in 1563,

Figure 5.1. Mourning the dead in Jeppipo Wasu's family. Hans Staden, *Warhaftige Historia und Beschreibung einer Landstschaft* (Marburg, 1557). Courtesy of the John Carter Brown Library at Brown University.

the tribal social structure was still functioning, and some of the same chiefs appear to have been alive still.[44] Similarly, when Nóbrega returned to Bahia in 1557, the epidemic of 1552, and possibly others, had not weakened the Indian villages so as to destroy their threat to the Portuguese settlement. Nóbrega despaired at the proud and stubborn independence of the Indian chiefs who led the villages in the Bay of All Saints, and as a result gave his support to Mem de Sá's military campaign to subjugate them.[45]

Colonization brought an increased pace of transatlantic crossings. Although it is difficult to estimate the number of ships crossing the Atlantic after 1550, it is very clear that their number increased dramatically and that the incidence of disease on the transatlantic voyages became the norm rather than the exception. The colonization enterprise launched by the French immediately introduced, or coincided with, an outbreak of disease. In 1555, when the French established a colony in Rio de Janeiro under the leadership of Nicolas Durand de Villegagnon, one of Villegagnon's two ships arrived in Brazil carrying disease. The ships had provisioned themselves in the Cape Verde Islands. André Thevet described the air at Cape Verde as "pestilential and unhealthy" and commented that "hot fevers" and the "*flux de sang*" (bloody flux, or dysentery) were very common there, especially among the slaves. After leaving Cape Verde, the ships were unable to find the winds to take them across the Atlantic, and they continued south along the coast of Guinea, where they "lingered little because of the infection of the air," to São Tomé, inhabited by peoples whom Thevet describes as "much more subject to illnesses than those north [of the equator]." Men on one of the ships came down with a fever, believed by the men to be caused by the extreme heat of Africa, but the pilot also noted that the water on board was "stinking and foul" and that "the men on board could not refrain from drinking" it. The men on the second ship, however, remained "healthy and fresh." This "pestilential fever," wrote Nicholas Barré, a pilot on the second ship, "was so contagious and deadly that of one hundred persons, it did not spare but ten who did not become sick; of the ninety who became sick, five died." They ran out of fresh water in the mid-Atlantic, when all that remained was the stagnant water collected in the gutters. When Villegagnon's two ships reached the coast of Brazil in November of 1555, some men were still ill. The Franciscan André Thevet was so sick that he could not participate in the celebration of the Christmas mass one month later.[46]

After Villegagnon arrived in Brazil, "pestilential fever" broke out among the Tupinambá allies of the French living around Guanabara Bay. Thevet describes meeting one of the chiefs, named Pindahousou, whom he found "sick in his bed with a continual fever."[47] Because Thevet was only in Brazil for ten weeks, this illness had to have been sometime between 10 November 1555 and 31 January 1556. Nicholas Barré, Villegagnon's pilot, credited this fever as the reason why the Tupinambá did not rise up against Villegagnon and force him from Guanabara following the souring of relations between Villegagnon and the Norman interpreters. He wrote to his friends in France: "The Savages have been persecuted by a pestilential fever since we arrived here, from which more than eight hundred have died."[48]

Using the descriptions of Staden, Léry, and Thevet, Warren Dean calculates the size of the Tupinambá population living on the coast of Rio de Janeiro in 1555 at between 57,000 and 63,000 persons, with a population density of 4.8 / km². Since the Tupinambá resided in villages where individuals lived in close proximity to one another in large multifamily longhouses, known as *malocas*, the disease could spread easily. According to Staden, each village had up to seven malocas, which formed a sort of square, around the whole of which was a wooden palisade. Each maloca was 14 feet wide and up to 150 feet long; inside, the chief of the hut had his space in the center, while couples strung their hammocks along the sides.[49]

Two years later a terrible illness erupted on the ship that carried the third governor to Brazil, Mem de Sá. In April 1557, Mem de Sá set out from Lisbon with 336 persons, and according to brief accounts of a few on board, nearly everyone became sick, including the governor himself, and 44 died. The ship apparently sailed from Lisbon to the Cape Verde Islands and from there attempted to cross the Atlantic, but because the weather was unfavorable, or because they had become lost, the ship stopped at the island of Príncipe, where the crew again provisioned the ship. Leaving Príncipe, they again failed to find favorable winds and put in at São Tomé, where they remained for a time. The entire voyage lasted an unprecedented eight months. Exactly when and where the illness broke out is unclear, but it seems to have come from one of the Atlantic islands.[50]

More ships brought more Europeans—colonists, degredados, and crew—and African slaves, all of whom increased the probability of the introduction of disease. Port cities hold important clues to understanding the transfer of disease. For example, Caribbean historians can link outbreaks of plague in port cities with Atlantic sailings.[51] Ships sailing to Brazil from Portugal typically began their journey in Lisbon and stopped at the Atlantic islands off the coast of Africa, such as the Cape Verde Islands, São Tomé, or Príncipe, before crossing the Atlantic. French ships also followed this route. Outbreaks of illness in the ports that typically sent ships to Brazil, such as Lisbon, Dieppe, Honfleur, São Tomé, Príncipe, or the Cape Verde Islands, would be an important piece of information in the puzzle, but it still remains unknown.

Ships themselves bore much of the blame. Not only did the transatlantic ships sail from port cities, often the most disease-ridden places in Europe, but they became physical floating links between worlds. As early as the fourteenth century, Europeans recognized the role of ships in transmitting disease, notably plague. Historians have long thought that the bubonic plague that raged through Asia, the Middle East, North Africa, and Europe in the mid-fourteenth century appeared first in the ports, carried by ships that harbored infected rats. Ships carried humans, animals, plants, and insects, as well as trash, water, and food—all hosts for viral, bacterial, protozoal, and botanical agents that would impact the biology and ecology of the places where they landed.[52]

Fevers, dysentery, and diarrhea seem to have been some of the most common diseases in sixteenth-century Brazil, and all of these were aided in their spread by the cramped quarters found on ships. When dysentery (*câmaras de sangue*) and diarrhea broke out at sea, the conditions quickly became deplorable. The lack of clean drinking water and the close contact with human feces are obvious factors in their spread. On one ship headed for India in 1551 traveled several Jesuits, who wrote accounts of the voyage after they arrived in India. Off the coast of Africa, they report that eighty on board became sick, and the Jesuits began to nurse the ill. Antonio de Heredia describes the sick lying in the filth from their intestines; Manuel Teixeira describes having to beg for food for the ill, who had little to eat. Some disease-ridden ships headed for India visited Brazil en route. One such ship left Lisbon in April of 1560 and, unable to catch the right winds, became lost off the coast of Guinea during the month of June. More than four hundred people became sick with fever, and some died. Because the ship could not make it around the Cape of Good Hope, it sailed to Brazil, where the ship arrived in August of 1560. There, the Jesuit Manuel Álvarez was still so sick with fever that he could hardly walk to the Jesuit residence.[53] After the ill disembarked, the lack of adequate sanitary disposal meant that drinking water and food could easily become contaminated.

An epidemic that might have been dysentery struck Espírito Santo in 1559, claiming the lives of free and enslaved Indians, affecting babies and adults alike. Jesuit António de Sá described it as "*prioris,*" possibly pleurisy, and "dysentery so severe that it seemed like a plague." The illness lasted for six days. On some days they buried thirteen bodies, and because there was not enough room, they placed two to a grave. In all, he estimated that the epidemic took the lives of six hundred Indian slaves. The epidemic had begun south of the settlement, between Rio de Janeiro and Espírito Santo. There a French ship had been loading brazilwood, raising the possibility that the ship had introduced the disease. A few months later, the disease had nearly run its course, for in the month of March, only eight had died. An epidemic of dysentery spread in Piratininga Plateau in 1561, especially among the Indian slaves, and so many died that José de Anchieta thought it was "like a pestilence." Dysentery caused the death of the powerful Indian chief of Piratininga, Martim Afonso Tibiriçá, according to Anchieta. Tibiriçá died in December of 1562.[54]

Jesuits suffered from dysentery, too. A Jesuit interpreter sent to confess the soldiers and to teach the Indians who accompanied Mem de Sá on his attack against the French colony at Rio de Janeiro returned to São Vicente very ill in 1560. In Rio de Janeiro he had become sick with fever and dysentery, but he recovered in São Vicente. In the outbreak of dysentery in Piratininga in 1561, two of the Jesuit brothers also became sick with dysentery.[55]

Jesuits constantly refer to "fevers" in their letters, fevers that sickened both Indians and Jesuits alike. Some of these fevers are described as acute and resulting in death; others endured for several weeks at a time. The detail in Jesuit letters makes it possible to see that all these new illnesses quickly spread within and between Indian villages. In Piratininga, for example, José de Anchieta described a girl who was sick with fever and who was brought by her parents to the Jesuits to be cured. The Jesuits tried the remedies they had, but the girl did not improve. She went to live in a nearby village with a sister, where the Jesuits visited her "many" times. When she was "out of her mind for half of a day," the Jesuits judged her near death and moved her to Piratininga, baptized her, and watched her die two hours later. A few days later, two of her sisters became sick with the same fever, and both subsequently died.[56] Fevers also affected Jesuits, and it is certain that they affected Portuguese colonists, too. João de Azpilcueta preached his last sermon in Vila Velha (Bahia) on Maundy Thursday 1557; he immediately became sick with acute fevers that led to his death fifteen days later. Similarly, a severe fourteen-day fever led to the death of father João Gonçalves in Bahia in 1559. Other fevers were less severe but still debilitating. Brother Gregorio had "some good fevers" for three months; when he recovered, he was very thin.[57]

Although Jesuits used "fever" generically, sometimes they did provide more detail in their letters, making it likely that these fevers were malaria. Explicit references to tertian and quartan (in Portuguese, *terçãs* and *quartãs*, respectively) fevers appear in Jesuit letters, which are clear indicators of malaria. Luís da Grã and Brás Lourenço became ill with fever at the beginning of Lent in 1555. Both were bled and recovered, but when Grã's fever returned, he thought it would remain "*tercãas*" (terçãs), or tertian (recurring every three days). Luís de Grã later became the provincial of the Society of Jesus and lived in Bahia, where he undertook periodic visits to the aldeias. He arrived from one such visitation "very sick" with fevers from mid-December until Easter week in 1561. These fevers were described in a letter as *"quartenaryo"* (quartãs), or quartan (recurring every four days). A Jesuit who became sick with fevers that quickly became *"cartãs"* (quartãs, or quartan) was Diogo Jácome in Espírito Santo, who died from them in April of 1565. José de Anchieta is described as sick with *"tercianas"* (terçãs, or tertian) fever in November of 1566.[58]

Malaria begins with a chill, followed by headache, nausea, and vomiting. A spiking fever then develops, accompanied by profuse sweating. The attacks then recur every seventy-two hours in a quartan periodicity or every forty-eight hours in a tertian periodicity. There are four species of protozoal parasites that cause malaria, and three of them are associated with tertian or quartan malaria. Tertian malaria can be benign or malignant.[59] In the early seventeenth century, Ambrósio Fernandes Brandão refers to those who live in Brazil as suffering from tertian and quartan fevers that he calls *"maleitas,"* which modern dictionaries translate as "malaria," from *maldita febre* (accursed fever).[60]

Malaria is spread by mosquitoes; the vector is an infected female mosquito of the genus *Anopheles*, species of which were native to the Americas. Since malaria is thought not to have been present in the Americas before 1492, it had to have been introduced by infected humans. It required only that individuals suffering from malaria arrive in Brazil and that female native anopheline mosquitoes bite them and subsequently bite other individuals for the disease to emerge in Brazil. Because historians now believe that the first outbreak of malaria in the Americas occurred on the fourth voyage of Columbus, it is certainly plausible that malaria reached Brazil very early in the sixteenth century.[61] Outbreaks of malaria would have followed periods of rain, when standing pools of water provided mosquitoes with breeding grounds. José de Anchieta references in passing that "fevers and other pains" are produced by the heavy and frequent rains.[62]

Another "fever" might have been yellow fever, which is characterized by fever, headache, jaundice, and hemorrhaging into the stomach and intestines. Later, in the Caribbean, yellow fever came to be known as Black Vomit (*vomito negro*) because of the hemorrhaging of black blood. In Brazil, there is no definitive evidence of yellow fever in the sixteenth century, yet it seems probable that it must have made the transatlantic crossing. In the seventeenth century, it was also associated with worms (*doença de bicho* or *mal do bicho*), and was identified as a disease of Africa and Brazil by Aleixo de Abreu, a physician, in 1623.[63] Manoel da Nóbrega's illness in 1557 is usually interpreted to have been tuberculosis, but symptoms are also suggestive of yellow fever. Nóbrega thought that he was near death in Bahia in August of 1557 from continual fevers and vomiting blood ("deitando muito sangue pela boca"). A doctor who attended him in Salvador thought that he had a broken vein, but what Nóbrega most felt was "the fever wasting me little by little." In the 1580s, a Jesuit report states that the fathers and brothers of the Society ordinarily "do not throw blood from the mouth" ("ni echan, de ordinario, sangre por la boca"), possibly indicating that such symptoms were seen in Brazil. The illnesses most common among the fathers and brothers, the author notes, are fevers, especially in Bahia.[64]

Yellow fever is a viral hemorrhagic fever also transmitted by mosquitoes, the female *Aedes aegypti*. This species of mosquito, however, was not native to the Americas, and the mosquitoes themselves had to make the transatlantic voyage. The environment offered by ships' water casks certainly favored mosquitoes. Outbreaks of yellow fever on board ship might last for weeks, even months at a time, which would have enabled both the mosquito and the fever to establish themselves in Brazil. Kenneth Kiple and Brian Higgins locate and date the first recorded yellow fever epidemic in the Caribbean to Barbados in 1647. At that time, the sugar boom stimulated both a denser concentration of population on Barbados and a sharp increase in the slave trade. Kiple and Higgins cite a yellow fever outbreak in Pernambuco in 1685 and attribute its origin to a slave ship from Africa. Subsequently, they claim that Brazil was free from yellow fever until the nineteenth century, when again a ship introduced the fever, this time from North America—from New Orleans or Havana. But, given the repeated contact between Brazil and Africa, it seems more likely that yellow fever reached Brazil in the sixteenth century.[65]

Yellow fever and malaria are thought to have been endemic in tropical Africa in the sixteenth century, and as a result, many Africans from that region possessed acquired immunity to yellow fever and innate resistance to malaria. Many Africans who contracted yellow fever as children possessed resistance as adults. Repeated exposure to malaria can also confer immunity, and the sickle-cell trait found in people of African, Mediterranean, or southwest Asian ancestry is known to offer protection against malaria. Portuguese residents in Africa, on the other hand, who were usually adults who had not lived there as children, typically suffered from fevers that erupted after torrential rains broke the droughts. These tropical fevers did not affect Africans, nor even Afro-Portuguese, in the same ways. The fact that ships loaded with slaves sailed quickly and directly from Africa to Brazil suggests that slave ships, slaves, and the European crews of slave ships transmitted African diseases, such as malaria and possibly yellow fever, to Brazil in the sixteenth century.[66]

The Jesuit letters reveal that African slaves suffered from illnesses, some of which most certainly came from either Africa or the transatlantic passage. One of the three slaves that the Jesuits in Bahia received from São Tomé in 1552 died immediately after the Jesuits took possession of him. Nóbrega reported that the same fate befell other slaves from the same ship. "Many others died who arrived already sick from the sea voyage," he wrote to Simão Rodrigues. In another letter, Nóbrega mentioned that an André Gavião had eight African slaves in Ilhéus who were sick and depressed; these were later killed by Indians who had risen up against the Portuguese in 1559. By the 1580s, Anchieta noted that it had become the custom for the Jesuit fathers and brothers to attend to the arriving slave ships from Africa to see if there were any sick slaves who needed baptism. Two thousand slaves entered Salvador in 1581 alone, he estimated, and of these, "many" were sick and brought to shore to die.[67]

According to African historian Joseph Miller, the first generation of African slaves in Brazil was a diverse population that came, primarily but not exclusively, from Central Africa. Most of the Africans had been taken from the coast south of the Kwanza River in present-day Angola. A smaller group of Africans came from the lower Congo River, in present-day Republic of the Congo and Democratic Republic of the Congo, and still others came from West Africa. These were agricultural peoples who lived on savannahs or in tropical forests in "small to moderate-sized village communities of kin, in-laws, clients, and others of familiar backgrounds." The areas of greater population density were located in mixed savannah and forest regions, especially along the rivers. In West-Central Africa, outbreaks of disease followed droughts, for those weakened by famine physically migrated to river valleys or to the coast. Miller hypothesizes that the slave trade "flowed in part from the tides of drought and disease that swept repeatedly through West-Central Africa" as hunger drove "starving people into the hands of slavers." Moreover, epidemics increased the supply of slaves, because slave traders in Africa sought to quickly dispose of sick slaves; but since the transporters of slaves did not bear the cost of slave mortality, the slave ships carried healthy as well as ill slaves.[68]

The devastating killer smallpox is recorded very late in Brazil. Whereas smallpox decimated Arawak, Aztec, and Inca populations after its arrival in the Caribbean in 1519, there is no known record of it in Brazil until Jesuits described it in the 1560s. Letters written in 1563 describe the illness striking in the previous year, 1562. In a long letter, Jesuit Leonardo do Vale describes a plague "so odd" and so unlike any other in Brazil. He thought it had arrived on the ship that first landed south of Salvador, in Ilhéus, but a young man from Pernambuco told Vale that the plague had come from Pernambuco, because he had been trading for slaves along the coast between Pernambuco and Bahia and had seen great mortality among the Indians. So many had died, he reported, that the living could not bury the dead. Where there had once been five hundred warriors, there were now only twenty. After this conversation, Vale thought that the plague simultaneously moved south from Pernambuco and north from Ilhéus. He describes the plague spreading into the wilderness of Ilhéus and to the Jesuit aldeias of São Miguel, Santa Cruz de Itaparica, and Nossa Senhora da Assunção. In each of these aldeias, one-third of the Indians died. He estimated that in only one of the aldeias, eighteen hundred Indians died in a two-month period. The plague then spread to Salvador, where it decimated Indian as well as African slaves. Moving still farther north toward Pernambuco, the plague first infected and killed many Indians in the mission villages of São Paulo and Santiago.[69]

Another Jesuit account from Bahia notes that a pestilential fever preceded the outbreak of smallpox in Bahia and attacked the heart such that there was nothing that could be done. Smallpox, which the Jesuit named *viruelas* or *bexigas*, followed, bringing with it great horror and death. All dancing ceased, he wrote, for "everything was weeping and sadness." The Jesuit school became a hospital where the fathers and brothers tried to nurse the sick.[70]

After Anchieta returned from residing as hostage among the Tupinambá in September of 1563, he describes a fearsome plague of smallpox in São Vicente. His letter is particularly detailed and horrifying. The disease (Anchieta identifies it as smallpox, "viruelas") sometimes caused benign (*dulces*) and known (*acostumbradas*) sores; from these he notes that recovery was easy. But there were other new sores that were "a horrible thing." These sores covered the body from head to toe, he writes, similar to fatal leprosy, and resemble *cuero de cazón* (dogfish skin).[71] The sores entered the mouth, covering the throat and tongue. Many died in three to four days; those who lived longer, he explains, suffered as their skin and flesh began to rot and the terrible stench attracted flies and worms. Pregnant women usually died; for those who gave birth, their babies were born with terrible deformities.[72]

Pedro da Costa describes the arrival of smallpox, which he called "bexigas," in Espírito Santo in early 1564. The plague began in the Aldeia Nossa Senhora da Conceição, where two Jesuits resided, and soon became widespread. All the longhouses seemed to become hospitals, he wrote, so full were they of the sick. As in Bahia and São Vicente, the epidemic was characterized by a terrible stench as the skin and muscle of the diseased began to rot and the bones began to show. Three or four died per day, and the Jesuits spent much of their time confessing, baptizing, and burying the dead. After the illness passed, the Indians chose to move the aldeia. In another aldeia, São João, of the more than four hundred that the Jesuits baptized, "a good part" died during the smallpox plague.[73]

All routine ceased as the Jesuits ministered to the sick during the smallpox plague. Leonardo do Vale wrote that the Jesuits were exhausted from squatting for hours preparing the sick for baptism and confession. Although Vale describes the Jesuits as working day and night to bury the dead, they could not keep up, "for if twelve died, twenty fell sick." Soon, there was no one to dig the graves, and the bodies began to be dumped in the trash heaps.[74]

Twenty years later, when the Jesuits began writing their own histories of their mission in Brazil, they recognized this first smallpox plague as especially horrifying. One report cites a mortality of 30,000 Indians in two or three months.[75] A second epidemic that might have been smallpox erupted in Pernambuco in 1578–1579 and particularly affected Indian and African slaves. Beatriz Mendes described the illness, which she also called "bexigas," as poisonous and revolting, and pointed out that it had carried away many of her own slaves.[76] Smallpox returned to Ilhéus in 1585, and a third epidemic of the disease was thought to have been brought by a French ship that had provisioned itself in Arguim before landing to collect brazilwood off the coast of Rio Grande do Norte in Brazil in 1597.[77]

By the early seventeenth century, smallpox in Brazil was associated with Africa and the slave trade. Ambrósio Fernandes Brandão comments that smallpox and measles particularly attacked the Indians of Brazil. "[T]hese diseases, especially smallpox," he writes, "are foreign diseases which generally are communicated to them [the Indians] from the Kingdom of the Congo and from Arda [West Africa] by the blacks brought from there." The mortality of smallpox, he notes, is very high among Indians and Africans, but not among the Portuguese. He references an outbreak of smallpox the year before, 1616–1617, in which "many rich men in this State of Brazil became poor," because so many of their slaves died. What struck Brandão as particularly odd was the way that smallpox did not seem to have the same effect on those born in Portugal as it did on Indians, Africans, and those of Portuguese or mixed Portuguese and Indian descent born in Brazil. He observes that it is a "curious thing" that smallpox is contracted by "the heathen natives of this land and those from Guinea, and among persons who are children of white men and natives, who are called *mamelucos*, and, further, among all those born in this country, even though of white parents." But, he continues, "those who come out from Portugal and were born there of either Portuguese or some other European parentage never catch the disease—although I have seen perhaps two or three of them die from it."[78] Brandão observed what modern historians can explain: smallpox, endemic in Portugal, was a disease of children, who, if they recovered, harbored immunity as adults. In Brazil, the disease was epidemic, and therefore all, except adults born and raised in Portugal, were at great risk.

In January of 1582, Anchieta described a terrible epidemic in Bahia that might have been measles. In September of the previous year, a terrible epidemic broke out that Anchieta called *sarampão* (measles), which turned into câmaras (diarrhea). The illness was so severe that he thought it had to be a kind of plague. He estimated that this epidemic took the lives of six hundred Indians in one mission village in two days. Indian slaves on the Portuguese sugar plantations also died in such great numbers that the mills had to stop grinding cane for lack of laborers. The Jesuits suspended studies in the college of Salvador so that all priests, brothers, and students could minister to the dying. Just in the environs of the city of Salvador, Anchieta thought that more than nine thousand Indians died. An epidemic "like the measles, but as bad as the plague" hit Guanabara Bay in 1599. It erupted immediately after a ship from Spain, carrying a bishop and officials for Spanish colonies in Southeast Asia, called at Rio de Janeiro. In three months, three thousand Indians and colonists died, according to the English pirate Anthony Knivet.[79]

Another possible source for disease transmission in Brazil lay with Asia. As the Jesuits made their way to India and beyond in the middle of the sixteenth century, their letters reflect contagion there, especially what they called *mordexim*, which medical scholars see as a precursor to epidemic cholera. One Jesuit in India wrote that in the winter of 1552, "an illness, which is known by its old name in this land, mordexi," had spread in Bassein [today Vasai] "as if it were a branch of plague." Another Jesuit described the disease, noting also that it killed men in twenty-four hours and that "many people of the land died." There is no evidence of mordexim in Brazil in the sixteenth century, but Ambrósio Fernandes Brandão describes dysentery similar to mordexim in the early seventeenth century. As with the disease in India, it was characterized by a twenty-four-hour diarrhea. Brandão notes that although "in India this illness, which they call *mordexim*, is fatal, here it is not, for, when the period of the accident is over, the patient gets well without any kind of medicine." [80]

After 1550, the more systematic and intense colonization of Brazil made outbreaks of disease more frequent and more severe among the Indians. Coastal Indians were no longer isolated regionally, as ships began to call more regularly along the coast. The greater movement of Portuguese colonists, the Jesuits, and Indians themselves spread disease within Brazil. Two features of Portuguese colonialism worked in tandem with disease to undermine the autonomy of traditional Indian life: slavery and the aldeia system. Both disrupted the traditional way of life of indigenous groups and concentrated the effects of disease.

Indian slaves lived in close proximity to Europeans and to mamelucos on sugar plantations, where they slept in large slave houses similar to their traditional malocas. On plantations, Indians from many different regions might live together, which undermined traditional family ties and contributed to the spread of disease. Additionally, slaves did not have the freedom to manage their food supply through hunting, fishing, and planting, which certainly caused a decline in overall health and nutrition. The Indian slave trade, which initially took the form of raiding or barter along the coast, also increased contact between indigenous groups and Portuguese and mameluco colonists.

Early Jesuit letters are full of descriptions of the "great number of ill" and the "great death" in the population of Indian slaves all along the coast of Brazil. On the Piratininga Plateau, in the village first founded by João Ramalho, the Jesuit José de Anchieta wrote that "although we help them in their illnesses, even at night in very thick forests," nevertheless many Indian slaves from Santo André died before the Jesuits could baptize them.[81] On the coast of São Vicente, Anchieta described a mission directed at slaves who lived on farms where their masters, the Jesuits continually noted, rarely attended to their spiritual needs. There are always some slaves there "sick near death," Anchieta wrote, who needed the attention of the Jesuits. Among the Indian slaves who came from the coast of São Vicente to aid the uprising of Indians on the Piratininga Plateau, many became sick in 1561 with serious fevers. During the smallpox epidemic in Bahia, the Jesuit provincial sent three Jesuits, with an interpreter, to minister to the slaves on several sugar plantations. The Jesuits were shocked to see the number of slaves who were sick from smallpox. In one day on one estate, they baptized seventy slaves whom they deemed near death. On their way back to Salvador, they were called to another sugar plantation, where smallpox had also spread among the slaves. The Jesuits went, but they were so exhausted that they could hardly sit on their chairs.[82]

Many Indian slaves lived on sugar plantations, where epidemic disease spread even more rapidly than in traditional villages. On the Sergipe do Conde estate in 1572 lived just over three hundred slaves, nearly 90 percent of whom were Indian. The slaves lived in three straw houses, two of which resembled the traditional maloca. In a new straw house lived twenty African slaves, but in the two large, older straw houses (casas de palha grandes) lived all of the Indian slaves. As a slave barracks, the traditional maloca became a potential magnet for disease because Indian slaves on the plantation lived in closer contact not only to Portuguese and to Africans but also to Indians from multiple regions. That a sugar planter could be ruined by an outbreak of disease among the plantation slaves was not an idle fear. In 1581, when Anchieta described the measles epidemic, he painted a vivid picture of the colonists of Bahia crying bitterly because their mills could not grind and their fields could not be planted. On one plantation alone, the provincial judged that fifty Indians died.[83]

Mortality was high also in the Jesuit mission villages. Following the wars against independent Indian groups in Bahia waged by Governor Mem de Sá, the Jesuits and the governor created the aldeia system, staffed by resident Jesuits, to replace the independent and autonomous Indian villages. In each aldeia resided two Jesuits. In these aldeias the Indians continued to live in large malocas.[84] Jesuit letters report numerous diseases in the aldeias, some of which may well have been introduced by the Jesuits. The Jesuits were highly mobile individuals in Brazil, and as they visited aldeias, or moved back and forth between the aldeias and the nearby Portuguese settlements and plantations, they could easily transfer disease. Much of the Jesuit mission involved close human contact, such as speaking and baptizing. Moreover, Jesuits organized large baptisms, processions, and even special religious celebrations known as jubilees in the aldeias, which were attended by Indians from other aldeias as well as by colonists. Such congregations encouraged the spread of disease.

The connection between the Jesuits' illnesses and those of mission Indians can be seen in the Jesuit letters. In 1558, father João Gonçalves went to the aldeia of

Espírito Santo in Bahia to teach Christianity and to baptize babies, who, the Jesuits recognized, ran a high risk of death. On 8 December 1558, the day of Our Lady of Conception, Gonçalves had planned a baptism of the boys he had educated in the school, as well as the baptism of babies and a special mass. In the middle of the day, he came down with a serious fever, but he continued and finished the mass with difficulty. Thirteen or fourteen days later, having been taken back to the college of Salvador, he died. Following his death, nearly all of the Jesuits in the college became sick. Back in the Espírito Santo aldeia, others who worked there became sick, and many, including the governor, thought that the place ought to be quarantined. Nóbrega disagreed. He wrote that "I trusted in Our Lord," and he resolved to send two Jesuits, each of whom had been sick with fever, to the aldeia of Espírito Santo. He justified his action, writing, "from whence the others fled in order not to become sick, I sent the sick there to be cured." [85]

Soon after, the Jesuit João de Melo went to Espírito Santo and wrote that the entire time he was in the aldeia, from January to April 1560, "there were a great number of sick and many of them died." João de Melo himself became sick and could not participate in the Maundy Thursday procession on 11 April of that year; his fever was worsening so much that the vice provincial of the Jesuits ordered him back to Salvador, where he arrived in time for Easter Sunday. The plagues stunned the Indians, who had never before experienced such illness. António Blázquez wrote to Rome the next year that the Indians of Espírito Santo had become so depressed from seeing so much death that they had given up singing and dancing. All that could be heard, he wrote, were cries and lamentations.[86]

Jesuits who were sick, but not near death, continued to work in the mission villages. At the Bom Jesus aldeia in Bahia in 1561, Jesuit António Rodrigues described how he maintained the mission despite the fact that he was sick. He wrote that there was a continual flow of ill persons brought to the church for him to baptize, as well as calls for him to personally visit the ill from house to house. The latter ministry of visiting house to house to baptize the sick had become onerous: "As you know," he wrote his fellow Jesuits in Salvador, "I am very sick and I do not have the strength that I had in times past. I sit down in a chair in the church and I have them bring the sick who can come, and I baptize them there." [87]

While Jesuits on the brink of death returned from the aldeias to die, others who were less ill were often sent from the city of Salvador to the aldeias to get well. When Brother António Gonçalves arrived ill from Portugal, he was sent to one of the larger aldeias of Indians in Bahia to convalesce. In 1562, two Jesuits arrived in Brazil from Portugal. On their outbound sea voyage, many had become sick off the coast of Africa, including BrotherCiprião. Ciprião arrived in Bahia still sick, and as soon as he had recovered sufficiently, he asked for permission to visit the Indian aldeias.[88]

In 1564, the Jesuits organized jubilees at the Bahian aldeias of Espírito Santo, São Paulo, and Santiago that drew many colonists from Salvador. Over very rough, muddy, and flooded roads, residents of the city arrived by foot, on horseback, in carts, or in hammocks. At the aldeias there was singing and dancing through the night, followed by confessions that began at three in the morning and continued until the mass began at dawn. The procession before the mass included delegations of children from the aldeias, Jesuit priests and brothers, other clergymen from Salvador, Indian chiefs, and at one, even the bishop of Salvador. The Jesuits recognized that these events, with their singing, chanting, processing, and dancing, made a great impression on Indians, mamelucos, and Portuguese alike. Such gatherings, however, created settings where diseases could easily spread. The bishop, who had had his hand kissed by many, found himself to be ill (*mal dispuesto*) at one, but this did not prevent him from preaching. At another, a Jesuit describes the sick who despite their illness had come to the aldeia in order to participate.[89]

In many letters, the Jesuits make it clear that though they were often sick, the illnesses of the Indians did not have the same effect on them. For example, when an illness of shivers and chills killed sixty Indians in the São Paulo aldeia in Bahia during the month of June 1560, the Jesuits did not become sick, even though they spent nearly all of their time among the Indians, bleeding the sick, providing remedies such as oranges and sugar, baptizing those on the brink of death, and burying the dead, sometimes four per day. And only one Jesuit became ill during the smallpox outbreak. Gregorio Serrão, a Portuguese Jesuit who served as the translator (língua) in the aldeia of Itaparica, Bahia, lingered near death but recovered. In Espírito Santo, a Jesuit became sick during or soon after the smallpox plague, but from fevers that were likely malaria.[90]

Jesuits saw their own illnesses as yet another burden that those dedicated to the Brazilian mission must bear. Writing about them conveyed to their readers (usually Jesuits in Portugal) the great obstacles that must be faced in Brazil. Jesuits were especially affected by fevers, diarrhea, and an illness that affected the eyes. One of Anchieta's letters is directed to sick brothers in Portugal, and its theme is that illness perfects the virtues. In a letter to the father general of the Society in Rome, Anchieta comments that illness is just another suffering in the Jesuit mission for God. That Jesuits should not interrupt their work of teaching, baptizing, taking confession, and preaching because of their illnesses is a common theme in many Jesuit letters. The example was set by the first leaders of the Society in Brazil, Manoel da Nóbrega and Luís da Grã, both of whom were often ill, but they did not stop preaching, visiting aldeias, saying mass, and baptizing new converts.[91]

Many Christian Europeans in the sixteenth century believed that illnesses, particularly epidemic illnesses, were punishments from God. This view was held also in the Muslim world, where illnesses were attributed to God's will.[92] As a result, when Europeans arrived in Brazil, divine will became a frequent explanation for the pernicious effects of disease on Indians. Villegagnon, for example, recognized the debilitating effect of disease on the Tupinambá Indians living around Guanabara Bay, and accepted it as a personal favor from God. In a prayer, which Léry purportedly heard in 1557, Villegagnon gave thanks:

And to restrain their brutal violence, Thou hast afflicted them with cruel maladies, preserving us from the same all the while; Thou hast removed from the earth those who were the most dangerous to us, and hast reduced the others to such weakness that they dare undertake nothing against us.[93]

Jesuits, who had extensive contact with disease, perpetuated this view. They interpreted the epidemics with their high mortality as punishments from God, who was angry at the Indians for their failure to give up their old ways. When the first signs of illness struck, Jesuits used the outbreaks to reinforce their evangelical message: unless Indians fully left their ways, all-powerful God would strike them dead. As representational go-betweens, Jesuits proclaimed in sermons, speeches, and letters that terrible illnesses were sent by God.

The Jesuits described the first epidemic in Bahia in 1552 as a punishment from God directed at Indians who refused Christianity or who had left Christianity. One proud chief, who had rejected the Jesuit attempts to convert him, died four days after the Jesuits had visited his village preaching of God and death. Vicente Rodrigues noted with satisfaction that the effect on his people was "to fear us greatly, especially our Father Nóbrega." When what Jesuits called dysentery and pleurisy reached the Portuguese settlement of Espírito Santo, Brother António de Sá likened it to the "sword of God's anger" and believed that when the Jesuits baptized those who were near death, the "children of anger" were transformed into "children of grace" before they died.[94]

Through the representation of sickness as a punishment from God, Jesuits characterized the shocking mortality in Brazil as a moral flaw of the Indians. Their deaths were unfortunate but to be expected, Jesuits reasoned, given their failure to fully embrace Christianity. Because the first smallpox plague observed by the Jesuits came at a time when the Jesuit mission was meeting roadblocks on all fronts, Jesuits even attributed it as a punishment from God. Leonardo do Vale described it as a "whipping from the Lord"—a punishment meted out against certain Indians from the aldeias who were drawn to a false prophet in the wilderness of Ilhéus who led a "*santidade*," a millenarian messianic movement. When he learned from a trader that the smallpox plague may have in fact begun in Pernambuco, he modified his view such that God had allowed the plague to break out in two places simultaneously to better punish both the Indians in the aldeias of Ilhéus and the Caeté Indians (who lived between Bahia and Pernambuco) for their cannibalization of the first bishop of Brazil. José de Anchieta also saw the smallpox epidemic as sent from God. "Our Lord has visited and punished this land with many illnesses," he wrote, "from which a large part of the slaves of the Christians [i.e., colonists] have died."[95]

Yet some Jesuits in the early days wondered why God punished so many young children, "who, it seems, are not at fault." Francisco Pires explained the great mortality as God's way of separating the good from the bad and of teaching those who wished to become Christians that they had to do more than receive baptism and wear clothes. "Our Lord wished that the children of these, who were baptized in innocence, would die in that same innocence," he wrote, "and in this way He punished the parents and saved the souls of the children."[96]

The Jesuit mission was to convert as many Indians to Christianity as possible; it would seem, then, that epidemics posed a major threat to this mission, since Indians would die before Jesuits had time to evangelize them. But, paradoxically, imminent death presented an opportunity for Jesuit missionaries. Jesuit letters make clear that their frequent discussion of death, disease, and epidemics was partially due to the fact that those events were intimately connected with their rates of baptism. Faced with those near death, Jesuits quickly baptized them to save their souls. Infants and young children would need little instruction and therefore could die "baptized in a state of innocence."[97] For adults, a simple consent to be baptized on the brink of death often sufficed, even if they had had only rudimentary instruction in Christianity. By counting the number of souls saved rather than the number of living converts in their missions, Jesuits believed they were fulfilling their charge, even though their villages had fewer and fewer Christian Indians in them. In this way, Jesuits accepted—and rarely questioned—the shocking mortality of Indians. At a time when Italian towns and cities were beginning to take steps to control the spread of infectious disease, notably the plague—by forced quarantine, isolation, regulated burials, destruction of personal possessions, and provision of food to the needy—the Jesuits saw no reason to implement such measures in their aldeias. When the governor thought that the aldeia of Espírito Santo in Bahia should be quarantined, Nóbrega counseled the opposite.[98]

Major changes in the Brazilian landscape visibly accelerated in the environs of Portuguese settlement from the 1550s on. The introduction of new foods, cash crops, fruits, and even weeds into the Brazilian ecosystem had profound consequences for biodiversity. The planting of sugarcane required the felling of large stands of trees that were part of the Atlantic forest. The voracious fires that boiled the cane juice in order to make sugar required cords of wood. Though it would seem that new plants would increase biodiversity, in fact the opposite was true. The introduction of non-native plant species was a major factor in the loss of biodiversity, for sugar plantations, fruit orchards, and wheat fields, even if small, competed with native plants. The introduction of ungulates—cattle, horses, sheep, and goats—degraded the original landscape.

Colonists accumulated cattle and other domestic animals on lands granted to them by Crown officials. Land grants (*sesmarias*) given to António de Taíde and to Álvaro da Costa in 1552 and 1557, respectively, refer specifically to the fact that the recipients would place herds of cattle on the grasslands, which suggests that the custom of keeping cattle was now recognized and rewarded in Bahia. When the third governor of Brazil, Mem de Sá, wrote his will in 1569, he declared that he owned 500 head of cattle in Bahia, not counting the animals born that year, and 150 head on his ranch on the Joanne River, north of the city of Salvador. The inventory of his Sergipe do Conde estate in 1572 included seventeen head of sheep, thirteen oxen, and two doves, while on his Santana estate in Ilhéus, there were eight oxen and three sows. In the 1570s, Pero de Magalhães Gandavo reported that stock raising was "general throughout all the Captaincies," with "cows and oxen being especially abundant; and they are increasing rapidly." [99]

By 1587 cattle and horses were part of the urban landscape of Salvador. Gabriel Soares de Sousa, a Portuguese sugar planter, describes the capital city, remarking that bullfights take place in the central square and mounted equestrian festivals (*festas a cavalo*) take place in the larger square in front of the Jesuit church and school. He describes cattle corralled around the mouth of an excellent spring that gave rise to the small river that bordered the city. Their trampling, and the fact that pigs drank there too, made the water undrinkable. The richest families of Salvador own "many horses," he writes, and estimates that five hundred mounted men can be called up if necessary.[100]

By the time that Fernão Cardim, a Jesuit who arrived in Brazil in 1583, wrote his history of the land and climate of Brazil sometime before 1601, he could declare enthusiastically that "This Brazil is already another Portugal," because of all the things, such as fine cloth, that come from the kingdom. These words ring true with the domestic animals that had quickly adjusted to Brazil. No longer was it just the governor, or the Jesuits, who could own large herds of cattle. There are men with "500 or 1,000 head of cattle," Cardim explains. Although Cardim thought the pasture of Brazil poor, he notes that "there is a great quantity of cattle." "Brazil is full of great ranches," especially the Piratininga Plateau, which "looks like Portugal." Pigs do very well in Brazil, and in Cardim's opinion, give the best meat. Sheep are abundant in the south and in Rio de Janeiro. Although goats are still few, Cardim thinks that they will soon flourish. Cardim describes horses as abundant in Bahia, remarking that "handsome jennets are bred that are worth two or three hundred cruzados." Cardim writes that chickens "are infinite and larger than in the kingdom" and dogs of many breeds have multiplied. But of all these domestic animals from Europe, Cardim observes that only chickens and dogs were adopted by Indians. He goes on to say that Indians raise chickens "three to four hundred leagues [approximately 1,850–2,500 kilometers] into the wilderness," and that Indians value dogs because of their use in hunting. "Women carry them on their backs, and raise them as children," he claims, even "nursing them at the breast." [101]

The negative environmental effect of the rapid spread of European domestic animals, especially ungulates, results from a natural phenomenon known as an ungulate irruption, which occurs when hoofed animals have more food than is needed to replace themselves. Elinor Melville documents how ungulate irruptions

radically altered one region of Mexico in the sixteenth century. In such an irruption, Melville explains that the animals "increase exponentially until they over-
shoot the capacity of the plant communities to sustain them." When the animals
have overtaxed the carrying capacity of the land, "their populations crash" and
eventually reach an accommodation with the "now-reduced subsistence base at a
lower density." The ungulate irruption is intensified by pastoralists, who deliberately concentrate more animals per unit of land. The effect on the land is severe.
Melville's detailed study of the introduction of sheep into the Valle del Mezquital
in Mexico reveals that what had been an intensively irrigated and densely populated region when the Spaniards arrived became a "sparsely populated mesquite
desert" one hundred years later.[102]

Although the concomitant process has not been studied in Brazil, and it
most certainly differed from that of Mexico, it is likely that ungulate irruptions
occurred in horse, sheep, and cattle populations. Evidence of rapid increases in
the size of animal herds emerges from a variety of sources. The Jesuits became
interested in cattle early on, as they rarely had enough income to support themselves and their ministries. In Bahia, the Society obtained twelve cows from the
king in 1552, which they intended to milk for the children they were raising in
their residence. Similarly, a gift from Pero Correia, the interpreter who joined
the order in 1549, included ten cows to supply milk for the children living in the
Jesuit residence. Nóbrega quickly saw cattle as beneficial for the Jesuits, "because
they multiply rapidly and require little work," he wrote in 1561. The original ten
cows given by Pero Correia in 1553 had grown to more than one hundred by
1563. The cattle "give meat and leather and milk and cheese, which if there are
many, can support many people," Nóbrega argued in support of the Society's
acquiring even more cattle. By 1587, Gabriel Soares de Sousa estimates that the
Jesuits in Bahia had more than two thousand cows "who calve every year."[103]

Cardim notes that "there is a great abundance" of horses in Bahia; that the
sheep in Rio de Janeiro became so fat that they "exploded with fat"; and that
goats "are multiplying greatly and soon there will be a great multitude" of them.
Pero de Magalhães Gandavo makes a revealing statement when he notes that
goats and sheep "are beginning to multiply again," which suggests that there
may have been a crash in their populations. Similarly, in 1618 Brandão notes that
horses "formerly abounded in countless numbers," likewise suggesting that the
population of horses in Brazil had once been large and then had crashed, as in an
ungulate irruption.[104]

The possible effects of such ungulate irruptions are visible in Soares de Sousa's descriptions of the lands surrounding Salvador. He describes the sugar plantations that dotted the Recôncavo, the hinterland along the Bay of All Saints, and evaluates the lands in terms of their suitability for sugarcane cultivation. What he called "poor" land was good "only for cattle." Similarly, in Melville's study of Mexico, land that had been degraded by the ungulate irruption was no longer suitable for agriculture and became "fit only for sheep." [105]

In the 1580s, sparked by the visit of the Jesuit official Cristovão de Gouveia, who came with his secretary Fernão Cardim to assess the mission in Brazil, Jesuits began to write extensively about the history of their mission. One theme that emerges throughout these histories is the Jesuit awareness of tremendous decline in the Indian population. In a report authored by Fernão Cardim, he writes that there were once more than 40,000 baptized Christian Indians in Bahia, but that at the time when he was writing, there are not more than 10,000 "because they have died from many diseases." The author of a history of the Jesuit aldeias in Bahia notes that twenty years before (1563), there were fourteen aldeias with 40,000 Indians, yet in 1583, there were but three aldeias with no more than 3,500 Indians. The Indians of Bahia "are now depleted," the history states, and "no one could ever imagine that so many people would be depleted, even more so in such a short time." While the Jesuits recognized that the Indian population around Salvador and the coast had declined, they perceived that Indian population in the wilderness was still very large and that it had not suffered the same decline. Cardim states that the number of Indians was "uncountable in the interior, of many nations, customs, and languages." [106]

This view was shared by the Portuguese colonists as well. By the 1580s, because the coastal populations of Indians had declined, Portuguese colonists financed slaving expeditions to bring Indians from the vast interior to the coastal sugar plantations. Rather than having the diseases come to them, as had happened to the first generations of coastal Indians, by the 1580s, the Indians of the interior were forced to march to the coast, where they entered a disease-ridden colony and quickly fell victim to the epidemics that continually broke out. The Indian slave trade, coupled with the onslaught of epidemics, led to what Stuart Schwartz has called a "wasted generation." [107]

As Suzanne Austin Alchon argues, the magnitude of the demographic decline of the Native American populations resulted because of the intersection of disease with colonization. "Violence, slavery, and migration," which came with

European colonization, she writes, led to the failed recovery of indigenous American populations.[108] Before systematic colonization began at midcentury in Brazil, its indigenous populations undoubtedly suffered from disease, but they were able to maintain their culture and keep their social and political organization intact. Similarly, diseases undoubtedly followed trails into the wilderness and sickened peoples very distant from the Portuguese settlements, but independent and autonomous indigenous nations, described as "uncountable," still populated the nearby wilderness in the last decades of the sixteenth century.

After midcentury, the sheer magnitude of the European and African migration to Brazil, in contrast to the tiny migration from Brazil to Europe and Africa, meant that the influence of the physical go-between redounded to the European and African side. Every European and every African who stepped ashore in Brazil, whether a penniless degredado or a starving slave, potentially brought unknown diseases or soon worked cultivating foreign seeds or tending European and African hoofed animals or felling parts of the Atlantic forest. Often unaware of the roles they played, physical go-betweens contributed to the increasing power that the Portuguese settlements wielded in Brazil. Moreover, go-betweens carried coastal patterns of disease and ecological change deeper into Brazil. Jesuit missionary priests saw their mission as opening up "doors" into new Indian populations so that Christianity might be preached; in so doing, they not only introduced disease but paved the way for more contact between Indian and European and African peoples.

The foremost representational go-betweens of the second half of the sixteenth century, the men of the Society of Jesus, recognized and accepted the Indian population decline from disease. But the Jesuits also understood that the enslavement of Indians was part of their rapid decline. Jesuits did not question disease, for they saw it as an act of God, but they did question Indian slavery, which they saw as a sin of the colonist. Most of the Indian slaves working for Portuguese colonists had, in the eyes of the Jesuits, been obtained illegally. Jesuits, therefore, accepted the mortality of Indians from disease, but not their mortality from enslavement. The quest for Indian slaves was a crucial, driving characteristic of the Portuguese colony. How slavery became entrenched in Brazil and why the influential Society of Jesus was unable to prevent the illegal enslavement of Indians in Brazil are the subjects of the next chapter.

6. Slavery

All Indians purchased today are legally acquired . . .

Pero de Magalhães Gandavo, 1574

When Pero de Magalhães Gandavo returned to Portugal from Brazil in the 1570s, he wrote two accounts about life there, becoming a new kind of representational go-between, one who reflected the perspective of Portuguese colonists. In a treatise presented to King Sebastião and Sebastião's uncle, Dom Henrique (known in English as Cardinal Prince Henry), he proclaims that as soon as a colonist arrives in Brazil, no matter how poor he may be, if he obtains slaves, "he then has the means for sustenance; because some [slaves] fish and hunt, and the others produce for him maintenance and crops; and so little by little the men become rich and live honourably in the land with more ease than in the Kingdom." In his history of Brazil, published in 1576, Gandavo adds that many colonists in Brazil own two hundred, three hundred, or even more slaves. Colonists generally "treat each other very well" and "are happy to help others with their slaves," he claims, and they "greatly favor the poor who come to settle." In Gandavo's eyes, the acquisition of slaves in Brazil brought wealth, and with it came status and honor, even for the most impecunious of Portuguese colonists.[1]

Gandavo's representation of Brazil as a place where the ownership of slaves was the means for the Portuguese colonists to live honorably reveals a fundamental truth about sixteenth-century Brazil: the unquestioned acceptance of and reliance on slavery. Soon after Cabral's landing in Brazil in 1500, slavery became firmly rooted in Brazil, where it would be the foundation of Brazil's economic development for nearly four hundred years. The first slaves in Brazil, and indeed the slaves about whom Gandavo writes in the 1570s, were not African; rather, they were Tupi, Guarani, Gê, and Arawak peoples indigenous to Brazil. Indian slaves cleared the first fields and planted them with sugarcane; Indian slaves built the first mills and produced the first sugar harvests. African slaves joined Indians on the sugar plantations in the first half of the sixteenth century, and their numbers increased rapidly after 1550. By the last three decades of the sixteenth century, African slaves began to outnumber Indian slaves on the sugar plantations of Bahia and Pernambuco. Yet neither the expansion of the slave trade with Africa nor the devastating decline in the coastal Indian population ended Indian slavery—nor did a series of laws promulgated by the king. On the contrary, Indian slavery existed alongside African slavery throughout the sixteenth century, and indeed throughout the entire colonial period of Brazilian history.

The actions of go-betweens at all levels established slavery, Indian and African, as a fundamental part of the Portuguese colonization of Brazil. Slavery is often portrayed as a dyadic relationship between two parties—the master and the slave. But third parties are inevitably part of the complex nature of slavery, and especially so as slavery becomes established and accepted as a social and economic institution. As the Portuguese developed the maritime slave trade with Africa in the fifteenth century, the roles of physical, transactional, and representational go-betweens were indispensable. Sea captains and their crews transported slaves. Translators and bilingual agents negotiated the complex exchanges that underlay a trade in slaves. But perhaps the most powerful go-betweens in the origins of slavery were those like Gandavo, who, through their writings, articulated the arguments that justified the enslavement of one group of people by another. Gandavo could unabashedly declare that owning slaves was an "honorable" occupation because he had been shaped by a tradition that represented slavery as such. Lawyers, theologians, and historians in Portugal provided the legal and moral framework for African slavery in the fifteenth century; their writings led to an almost universal acceptance of African slavery in the Portuguese world and laid the foundation for the immediate and unreflective enslavement of Tupi, Guarani, Gê, and Arawak peoples in Brazil after 1500.

The sea captains and merchants who immediately began to enslave indigenous peoples from Brazil were familiar with slavery and with maritime slave trading. They were also aware that a slave trade from Brazil might potentially be quite profitable. They believed, too, that slavery and a slave trade were

legitimate commercial practices. Such attitudes had been encouraged by an official ideology that surfaced in Portugal a half century before and that legitimized
the seaborne slave trade between sub-Saharan Africa and Portugal. Constructed
by representational go-betweens in the employ of the Portuguese Crown or the
mercantile elite of Lisbon, this ideology drew on the arguments of classical philosophers, early Christian theologians, and traditional Iberian customs to justify
the initiation and expansion of the African slave trade. These arguments used
representations of Africans, of slavery, and of the Portuguese in such a way as to
portray slavery as morally uplifting rather than dehumanizing. Either because
the arguments were so persuasive or because dissent from them was heavily cen-
sored, there was little debate in Portugal over the morality of enslaving Africans
in the fifteenth century. Similarly, no moral debate seems to have characterized
the initial enslavement of Indians in Brazil, in contrast to the early Spanish experience, in which Antonio de Montesinos, Bartolomé de Las Casas, and other
theologians vociferously challenged the enslavement of Indians.[2]

Although the Portuguese developed the powerful arguments that would
underlie the transatlantic slave trade from Africa and that would lead to the
enslavement of indigenous peoples in Brazil, they did not need to legitimize the
existence of slavery, nor even the idea of a slave trade by sea. Both slavery and a
slave trade were already well established in the Mediterranean world. Although
slavery had disappeared from much of Western Europe by the fifteenth century,
that was not the case on the Iberian Peninsula. In Iberian kingdoms, such as
Portugal, Castile, or Aragon, slaves worked as domestics, in artisanal trades, or
as heavy laborers. The Spanish law code of the thirteenth century, known as the
Siete Partidas, clearly spelled out the status of slaves and the power of masters.[3]
For the Portuguese, as well as for other Iberians, there was nothing unusual
about the existence of slavery, nor was there the need to comment on its morality. The arguments of classical philosophers and early Christian theologians carried great weight, and they had already discussed slavery in detail.

Aristotle and early Christian theologians such as St. Augustine and St. Thomas
Aquinas had established that slavery was a "natural" state, acceptable to God.
From Aristotle arose the conviction that natural law sets aside part of mankind
to be slaves. In *The Politics*, book one, chapters 4 and 5, Aristotle argues that "a
slave is a living possession," and "the slave is not only the slave of his master, but
wholly belongs to him." He poses the question: "Is there any one thus intended
by nature to be a slave, and for whom such a condition is expedient and right,

or rather is not all slavery a violation of nature?" And he answers clearly: "That some should rule and others be ruled is a thing not only necessary, but expedient; from the hour of their birth, some are marked out for subjection, others for rule."[4] In the early Christian era, Augustine connected slavery with sin. He writes, "We believe that it is with justice that a condition of servitude is imposed on the sinner," and "[t]he first cause of servitude, therefore, is sin." Slavery, in Augustine's eyes, is "a condition which can come about only by the Judgment of God, in Whom there is no injustice, and Who knows how to distribute different punishments according to the merits of the offenders."[5] Aquinas accepted Aristotle's notion of natural slavery and explored some of the complexities of slavery in the middle ages. He discussed whether slaves might marry, whether slavery was inherited from the mother or father, and whether slaves were entitled to justice.[6]

The Portuguese did not need to justify the slave trade, even by sea, for they were not the first maritime slave traders. The Canary Island archipelago, known during Greco-Roman times as the Fortunate Islands, was rediscovered by seafaring Western Europeans in the fourteenth century. Claimed in the fifteenth century by the Kingdom of Castile, the islands became a destination for Italian and Iberian merchants who mounted slaving expeditions aimed at the indigenous peoples, known as the Guanche. In addition to this Atlantic trade, Genoese merchants participated in a slave trade in the eastern Mediterranean, using their ships to carry peoples from the Black Sea hinterland—often Eastern Orthodox Christians—to Mediterranean ports. The Genoese, as well as other Italian and Iberian merchants, also purchased slaves from port cities of North Africa and resold them in other Mediterranean markets. These slaves came from sub-Saharan Africa via the overland trans-Saharan trade. "Captives," who frequently became slaves, were also a common form of booty trafficked by Mediterranean pirates. Christian as well as Muslim pirate-merchants were guilty of attacking coastal settlements and kidnapping unsuspecting residents, who, if not exchanged for a ransom, were sold as slaves in Mediterranean ports.[7]

But Portuguese merchants were the first Europeans to systematically export slaves by sea from Africa. Arguim (1448), in present-day Mauritania, was the first Portuguese feitoria in Africa, and by the 1450s, a regular commerce in slaves had begun there.[8] Several decades later, the Portuguese king ordered a feitoria to be built farther south, at Mina, the "mine" where for a decade the Portuguese had traded for gold. The building of the trading post was carefully planned.

The captain charged with this undertaking left Lisbon not only with detailed instructions from the king but with much of the hardware, timbers, gates, tiles, bricks, and even pre-cut stones for the fortress. He had with him five hundred soldiers, should it become necessary to resort to force to carry out his mission. The Portuguese captain negotiated with the African chief Caramansa, and through interpreters gained his support, albeit begrudgingly, for the fort.[9] Thus began in 1482 the infamous feitoria of São Jorge da Mina, which would later become one of the most prominent ports in the transatlantic slave trade.

Even though there had been a long-standing tradition of slavery in the Mediterranean, the advent of this Portuguese slave trade from Africa was something quite new. This trade took into captivity peoples who did not threaten the Portuguese militarily and who often willingly accepted Christianity. Moreover, the trade was not undertaken by pirates, but was fully licensed and encouraged by Prince Henry the Navigator, who prided himself on being a devout Christian. Not only was Prince Henry a major investor in the slave trade, but the Portuguese Crown continued to benefit from it after his death. The reputation of the Portuguese Crown thus required that the enslavement of Africans in this new commercial venture be seen within Christendom as legal, moral, and just. Therefore, Portuguese kings and princes took pains to obtain from the ruling popes the rights to engage in the new slave trade and to insist on the legal status of African slaves.

Not surprisingly, the task of constructing coherent arguments on the legality of African slavery fell on the shoulders of lawyers, theologians, and historians, often those who sought and received the favor of the Portuguese Crown.[10] Their arguments reflected the specific historical traditions and customs of Iberia, especially the legacy of *convivencia*, or "co-existence," of Christians, Jews, and Muslims, and the centuries-long Reconquista of Muslim Iberia by Christian kingdoms. Most importantly, the arguments carried the seal of the papacy, expressed in a series of papal bulls that granted the Portuguese Crown permission to enslave Africans.

Gomes Eanes de Zurara, a royal chronicler and an aide to Prince Henry the Navigator, is the most well known of these writers. In his chronicle of Guinea, Zurara describes the early Portuguese slave raids in West Africa and the subsequent auctioning of West African slaves in Portugal. In telling this story, Zurara defines the arguments that justified the enslavement of Africans between 1434 and 1447. According to Peter Russell, a modern biographer of Prince Henry,

Zurara was "no mere palace clerk but a person of consequence at court, a protégé of princes who were very much aware that it lay in the hands of the chroniclers such as he to determine if and how posterity would remember them."[11]

The first references to slaves in Zurara's chronicle are not to sub-Saharan slaves, but to slaves brought from the Canary Islands by Gil Eanes in 1433. Zurara spends little time in his narrative discussing these slaves, for they were part of an established slave trade that supplied the already extant custom of Iberian slavery. The second set of references in Zurara's chronicle is to captives and appears during his discussions of the sailors who successfully sailed past the Cape of Bojador and who were entreated by Prince Henry to capture one or two local inhabitants to serve as future translators. In describing the failure of one captain to successfully capture a youth, Zurara writes that the captain, Afonso Gonçalves, was not content "because he had not captured one of those Moors."[12]

By defining those who were to be captured as Moors—that is, Muslims from North Africa—Zurara has little need to justify their enslavement. Hostility between Christians and Muslims in Iberia was long-standing and often led to enslavement through piracy, raids, or outright war. The practice of freeing those so captured was known as *resgate* (ransoming). Following battles in the Reconquista, Iberian families from the Christian kingdoms offered ransom for their captive kin through a bilingual intermediary, known as an *exea* (from the Arabic *shī'a*, or "guide") or an *alfaqueque* (from the Arabic *al-fakkāk*, or "redeemer"), a classic example of a transactional go-between.[13] Capturing a Moor and holding him as a captive who could be ransomed later was not an act that required justification to Iberian Christians.

Zurara does provide justifications for enslavement when the Portuguese moved beyond capturing individual Moors, who might easily be ransomed by their families. After describing the capture of a group of men and women in an out-and-out raid, Zurara reminds his readers that Prince Henry's most important motivation for undertaking the exploration of the coast of Africa was to bring Christianity to the lost souls of Africa. Zurara describes how Prince Henry sent an ambassador to the Vatican to ask for indulgences for those engaged in crusades under Prince Henry's leadership. Zurara includes a Portuguese transcription of part of this papal bull (*Illius qui se pro divini*, of Eugenius IV, 1442) to underscore the great work of Prince Henry as a leader against the Moors, the enemies of Christ. Although this bull says nothing about Africa, or indeed slave raiding there, its placement in the text clearly conveys to the reader that the pope recognized the right of Prince Henry to extend the crusade against the Moors to Africa. The next year, in 1443, when Prince Henry received the monopoly over the African trade south of the Cape of Bojador from the regent of Portugal, documents submitted by Prince Henry clarified that two voyages had brought back a total of thirty-eight Moors from Africa as captives.[14]

As Zurara builds up to his most famous passage in his chronicle, which concerns the first landing of a significant cargo of sub-Saharan Africans in southern Portugal, he references a biblical story that justifies the slave status of Black Africans. One of the Moors whom the Portuguese had captured was a free man of status among his own people in Africa, and he sought to ransom for his freedom. He proposed to exchange five or six slaves in his homeland for his own freedom. Zurara writes of these slaves whom the Moor proposed to exchange, "These blacks (*negros*), even though they are Moors as the others, are nevertheless slaves (*servos*) of them by the ancient custom which I believe is because of the curse that after the flood Noah threw on his son Cain." [15]

With these words, Zurara references what was to become one of the most powerful justifications for the enslavement of Black Africans: the so-called Curse of Ham. "This biblical story," writes David Goldenberg, "has been the single greatest justification for Black slavery for more than a thousand years." [16] The text in Genesis first explains that "the sons of Noah who went forth from the ark were Shem, Ham, and Japheth. Ham was the father of Canaan. These three were the sons of Noah; and from these the whole earth was peopled." But when Noah, the first farmer, drank too much wine from his vineyard and fell asleep drunk, the text from Genesis relates that Ham "saw the nakedness of his father," and "told his two brothers." When Noah woke up from his sleep and learned what his youngest son had done, the biblical text preserves his response verbatim: "'Cursed be Canaan; a slave of slaves shall he be to his brothers'" (Gen. 9:18–25, RSV).

Jewish, Christian, and Muslim scholars through the ages pondered the meaning of the story. According to Goldenberg, Ham was taken to mean "dark" or "hot"—as in living in the hot country—by generations of textual scholars, but this is a misreading of the original Hebrew. He argues, on the contrary, that "[t]he name Ham is not related to the Hebrew or to any Semitic word meaning 'dark,' 'black,' or 'heat,' or to the Egyptian word meaning 'Egypt.'"

Goldenberg's thesis is that Ham did not represent the father of Black Africa to the early Hebrews and that "there is no indication from the biblical story that God intended to condemn black-skinned people to eternal slavery."[17]

Goldenberg further argues that the "Curse of Ham" is a misnomer. Although many interpret the passage to mean that Noah cursed and condemned Ham, the biblical text actually says that Noah cursed Canaan, Ham's son. Why Canaan should receive the curse for his father's sin sets the stage for the extension of the curse to all of Ham's descendants. Zurara states that he believes the curse falls on "Caym," which is certainly Cain, and not Cão (Ham) or Canaã (Canaan), as the biblical text reads. Cain was also cursed, and according to interpretations of the curse dating back to the sixteenth century, the mark of the curse made him black, too.[18]

Coupled with these two misreadings—equating Ham with black and condemning Ham not Canaan—Goldenberg argues, was the increasing identification of Black Africans with slavery. It was the growing presence of Black African slaves, he suggests, that led to the "introduction of blackness" into the biblical story. Gradually, the curse of Noah came to be understood as a curse of blackness and slavery in seventh-century Islamic texts, which coincided with the increasing numbers of Black African slaves in the Middle East as a result of Muslim conquests in Africa. "From this time onward," Goldenberg writes in his conclusion, "the Curse of Ham, that is, the exegetical tie between blackness and servitude, is commonly found in works composed in the Near East, whether in Arabic by Muslims or in Syriac by Christians. The increasing reliance on the Curse coincides with the increasing numbers of Blacks taken as slaves."[19]

Zurara's use of the Curse of Ham provides his Portuguese readers with a powerful interpretation of a sacred text that implied that slavery and blackness were entwined. Black Africans were already slaves to the Moors, Zurara explains, and were so because of a biblical curse. While Zurara cites as his reference Archbishop Dom Rodrigo de Toledo, other scholars suggest that his use of the story was also influenced by "the attitudes of his native Muslim informants."[20]

Zurara, like other Iberian Christians, came of age in a southern Mediterranean world influenced by Islamic law, culture, and commerce. Muslims, Christians, and Jews lived together in an uneasy coexistence in late-medieval Iberia, and, as a result, Iberian Christians had more contact with Islamic philosophy and cultural traditions than did Christians in Western Europe. Islamic teachings clearly specified that only infidels might be enslaved, with the hope that slaves would gradually convert to Islam. This Muslim attitude toward slavery would greatly influence the attitudes of Christians in Iberia and later in Western Europe, as Christians came to adopt the view that "infidels," not fellow Christians, should be enslaved. Christian and Jewish Iberians living under Muslim rule, as well as Christians and Jews living in the Christian kingdoms that bordered the Muslim kingdoms, were exposed not only to Muslim attitudes toward slavery but to the ambiguous position of Black Africans in the Islamic world. While all races were welcomed into the Islamic faith, and though slavery was never the predominant labor system in Muslim society, nevertheless, a slave trade had existed from sub-Saharan Africa to Egypt and the Middle East since well before the rise of Islam. Africans had, for example, labored as slaves under the Greeks and Romans. But the numbers of African slaves in the Middle East increased with the Islamic conquests of North Africa and the subsequent expansion of the trans-Saharan trade. Over time, sub-Saharan Africa became an important source of slaves for the Middle East. The enslavement of West Africans served to demean the social position of Black Africans, even when Black Africans converted to Islam. By the eleventh century, most slaves in the Muslim world originated from sub-Saharan Africa. Racial stereotyping in the Muslim world denigrated Blacks, and blackness came to be equated with slavery. As in the Muslim world, the Curse of Ham would be used to justify the enslavement of Black Africans at the very time when African slavery began to expand into Portugal.[21]

In a famous chapter, Zurara recounts the arrival of an expedition led by Lançarote de Freitas (or Lançarote da Ilha) in 1444. Zurara represents these events so as to persuade the reader that slavery is bittersweet but nevertheless just. Lançarote, the royal tax collector of the southern Portuguese port of Lagos and a man close to Prince Henry, had returned from West Africa with a significant cargo of slaves. Early on the morning of 8 August, Zurara writes, sailors began to unload more than two hundred slaves from six ships in the port of Lagos. Zurara describes the slaves as ranging from "reasonably white, attractive and of good appearance" to "as black as Ethiopians and so disfigured." He asks his reader a rhetorical question: "What heart could be so hard as not to be pierced with piteous feeling to see that company?" before describing how the slaves were divided up randomly into five lots, "children separated from fathers; and women from their husbands; and brothers and sisters from each other."[22]

Zurara's detailed re-creation of the scene suggests that it was not an ordinary sight. The division of the slaves took place outside the town gate in a field that was filled with townspeople and people from nearby villages who had come to celebrate the safe return of the ships. Even Prince Henry was there, watching the spectacle mounted on a horse, and bestowing favors and gifts; he was to receive one-fifth of the slaves. But according to Zurara, it was not a happy scene. As the Africans were divided up into lots, many cried, groaned, beat their faces with their hands, and threw themselves on the ground. Others sang lamentations, and though none of the Portuguese could understand the words, Zurara believed that no one could miss the deep sadness expressed. Women who refused to give up their children were beaten. The Portuguese common people who saw this apparently were shocked and revolted at the sight. Zurara, describing the townspeople and villagers who had given up their work for that day to see "this new thing," recounts, "And with these things that they saw, some crying and others being separated, they made a great disturbance which interrupted the officials of that division." [23]

Some historians see Zurara's portrayal of this auction as an important statement, arguing that it reflects that the slave trade with Africa was not initially accepted in Portugal. Russell disagrees, believing rather that there was nothing unusual about the auctioning of slaves in Lagos. Russell suggests instead that Zurara describes a special occasion that was "intended to celebrate the fact that Portugal had now joined the Genoese, the Catalans and Valencians as a serious slave-trading nation." Prince Henry's presence there, he maintains, was intended to underscore the importance of this event and to silence his critics. Russell writes that the prince sought to let the crowds at Lagos "see for themselves that, contrary to what his many critics had been suggesting, the exploration of Guinea was not the risky and useless waste of effort and money they complained about." [24]

Russell cites a similar scene described by Zurara the next year when ships returned loaded with slaves, this time to Lisbon, to underscore his argument that Zurara had no intention of raising moral objections to the slave trade. Zurara describes the scene in the Lisbon harbor as the ships anchored and crowds gathered to see what their cargo was. "Who would be he who would not take pleasure to see the multitude of people who ran to see those caravels?" Zurara asks. The next day an equally large crowd lined the streets along which the slaves were marched and noisily praised the wisdom of Prince Henry, silencing all critics. In Zurara's words: "The shouts of the crowd praising the great virtues of the Prince [Henry] were so loud when they saw those bound captives being taken along those streets that if anyone wished to dare say the contrary, he would have to retract it immediately." [25]

Zurara's description of the slave auction in Lagos does suggest that village peasants and ordinary townspeople, who were unlikely to benefit from the slave trade, initially found the slave trade from Africa repulsive. But his description of a similar arrival in Lisbon, a city of merchants, clearly conveys the recognition by its more mercantile populace of the financial profits to be realized from the trade. Zurara expresses the view that the plight of the slaves was to be pitied and lamented, but those lamentations were tempered by his certainty that blackness "equaled ugliness and servility" and that through slavery the Africans would become Christians, bringing their souls salvation.[26]

The spiritual benefit to be gained by slaves is one of Zurara's most important justifications for the slave trade. At the arrival of the slave ships in Lagos, Zurara portrays Prince Henry as disinterested in his material profit (which came to forty-six slaves) but taking pleasure instead in the "salvation of the souls that before were lost." Zurara claims that many years later he saw with his own eyes, in the town of Lagos, children and grandchildren of these very slaves who were "such good and such true Christians." Yet, as his description of the arrival of slaves in Lisbon reveals, material rewards were handsome for merchants and investors. Zurara has no reservations about this fact. He tells his readers that Prince Henry was not present in Lisbon when the slaves arrived, but he nevertheless sent for his fifth of the slaves. The rest of the slaves were sold in the city, "from which all generally received great benefit and gain." [27]

Zurara recognizes the financial success of the slave trade, but he is also careful to emphasize that the slave trade was moral, acceptable, and even honorable. He employs the arguments that would uphold the slave trade for centuries: Black slaves from Africa were "disfigured" and already slaves because they had been cursed to servitude by Noah; moreover, slavery would bring Christianity, and ultimately salvation, to heathen Africans. Thus, following Zurara's logic, slavery was a noble, honorable cause. The pain felt by slaves would be more than compensated by their spiritual gain.

The theory of the just war also served as a powerful religious justification for the Portuguese enslavement of sub-Saharan Africans and later of the indigenous peoples of Brazil. Classical philosophers and early Christian theologians had debated the morality of waging war. Augustine argued that war, although abhorrent, was permitted when undertaken by proper authorities for a just cause, such as to establish peace and order. Thomas Aquinas established three conditions for war to be just and therefore not a sin. First, he argued that "the authority of the sovereign by whose command the war is to be waged" must be obtained. Second, "that those who are attacked should be attacked because they deserve it." And third, "the belligerents should have a rightful intention, so that they intend the advancement of good." From such ideas developed the legality of waging a just war.[28]

The kings of the Christian kingdoms of Iberia never doubted that the Reconquest fit the rules developed by Augustine and Aquinas for a just war. As the crusading monarchs of Iberia began to assert their right to extend the Reconquest to North Africa, the concept of the just war began to coincide with the enslavement of Africans. The raids, attacks, and pitched battles of the Reconquest in Iberia had always created prisoners of war or captives, who were held by both sides. These captives lost their freedom and became slaves unless they were ransomed by their families or religious leaders. After the Portuguese attacks on Muslim cities such as Ceuta in 1415, Tangier in 1437, and Alcácer-Ceguer in 1458, prisoners of war taken by the Portuguese in North Africa became slaves. After the assault on Ceuta, the Portuguese king sought a declaration from the pope declaring that it had been a crusade, thereby laying to rest any question of the justness of the war and entitling the soldiers to special indulgences. Once the declaration of a just war had been made, it legitimized not only the violence but also the enslavement of the prisoners of war. In 1441, after the Portuguese attacked Mauritania, the Crown again sought and received (ex post facto) papal confirmation that the war was just. In 1442, Prince Henry requested and received a papal bull that declared the raids along the coast of West Africa a crusade. Ten years later, the famous papal bull "Dum diversas" granted the Portuguese the right to enslave all "pagans and enemies of Christ."[29]

Warfare and slave raiding were not practical means to obtain slaves over the long run, however, and sea captains sought to trade, rather than to fight, for slaves. Trading for slaves replaced overt slave raiding along the coast of Africa in the 1450s. But a peaceful slave trade required a new justification for enslavement, as sea captains were no longer obtaining their captives through wars claimed to be just. In another famous bull, "Romanus pontifex," Pope Nicholas V ruled in 1455 that the slave trade was permitted because good came from it, and he gave the Portuguese the monopoly over the slave trade in West Africa henceforth. This idea that slavery enabled Christian evangelism appeared in official documents as an unquestioned assumption. For example, when Prince Henry rewarded the Order of Christ with certain rights, the official document states that along the Guinea coast, "as in the beginning through war as later through trade and ransoming, a great number of captives has come to Christianity." The idea that slavery and evangelism could work together became another fundamental justification for the slave trade in the sixteenth century when a law requiring the baptism of African slaves was included in the compilation of laws by King Manuel in 1514.[30]

While the early slave raiding along the coast of Africa depended on physical go-betweens who sailed the ships, charted the waters, and violently captured the first slaves, once trade replaced raiding, transactional go-betweens—some of whom were themselves slaves—became essential. Often seized by force, these interpreters paved the way for a commercial slave trade by making contact with local groups, negotiating with chiefs, and clarifying the terms of trade.[31] Later, resident middlemen became the crucial transactional go-betweens in the slave trade with Africa. In traditional African societies, enslavement occurred as punishment for indebtedness or crimes, or as the result of wars; these slaves could then be traded. The African kings controlled this intertribal slave trade, as they did the early trade with the Portuguese. But the slave trade with Portuguese merchants required an intermediary who acquired slaves from African kings and transferred them to European sea captains. By the sixteenth century, lançados were established in upper Guinea and were accumulating slaves— those deemed "criminals" in traditional African societies, those captured in war, and those overtly stolen in slave raids. Lançados assembled slaves to await ships from Portugal, and they sold goods brought by Portuguese ships to Africans.[32]

Similar patterns soon emerged when Benin, Kongo, and Angola became sources of slaves for the Portuguese trade. *Falantes* (speakers; interpreters) were important in the Benin slave trade, whereas *pombeiro* was the name given to the "middleman," often mulatto, who supplied merchants with slaves from the interior of the Kongo and Angola. The falantes and pombeiros spoke African languages and were acculturated in African ways. The pombeiros in Angola often came from São Tomé, were themselves of Kongoese ancestry, and used their knowledge of Kongo customs and language in the slave trade.[33]

The slave trade brought increasing numbers of West Africans not only to Portugal but also to Western Europe. In the early sixteenth century, the German painter Albrecht Dürer drew two portraits of West Africans. One is

Figure 6.1. Albrecht Dürer's *Portrait of a Black Man*, 1508. Albertina, Wien.

a charcoal sketch of an African man (Fig. 6.1), which bears a date of 1508 but may have been drawn earlier, when Dürer was in Venice (1505–1506). He also drew a silverpoint portrait of an African woman in Antwerp in 1520–1521. Antwerp was then a very cosmopolitan city filled with Portuguese merchants. Katherina (Fig. 6.2) was a slave or servant of his friend, the Portuguese factor João Brandão.[34]

By the early sixteenth century, the Portuguese were not the only Europeans engaged in the slave trade with West Africa. Genoese, Florentine, and Castilian merchants challenged Portuguese merchants there, but the Portuguese dominated the trade.[35] Moreover, the Portuguese Crown became deeply involved. According to the careful recalculation of the rates of the Portuguese slave trade in the late fifteenth and early sixteenth century by economic historian Ivana Elbl, the Crown's share of the slave trade was at minimum an average of one thousand slaves per year, and the private slave trade, whether by Portuguese merchants, Cape Verde Islanders, or the São Tomean and Príncipe traders, was on average nearly two thousand slaves per year.[36] The Portuguese Crown, which claimed one-third of the total trade, considered the trade legal, moral, and lucrative.

Figure 6.2. Albrecht Dürer's *Portrait of Katherina*, 1521. Gabinetto Disegni e Stampe, Uffizi; Fratelli Alinari.

There were voices raised in opposition to the slave trade, but few were heard. One of the most persuasive was that of Fernando Oliveira, a Portuguese clergyman, military theorist, and pilot.[37] Oliveira wrote several major works on Portuguese shipbuilding, but his *Arte da guerra do mar* (1555) explicitly addresses the moral and practical issues that arose when the Portuguese engaged in war at sea. As a former member of the Dominican order, Oliveira was educated, but he deliberately wrote in "short and clear" Portuguese so that "men of war," who rarely read Latin, could benefit. Oliveira immediately tackles the nature of war and the just war. In Chapter 4, titled "What Is a Just War?" Oliveira begins with a statement that Christians may not wage war unless it is just, and a just war punishes those who have offended God—blasphemers, heretics, apostates, and former Christians. "We may not wage just war against the infidels who never were Christians," Oliveira states, "such as Moors and Jews and Gentiles who with us wish to have peace, and who do not take our lands nor by any means threaten Christendom." Then, he proclaims: "To seize lands . . . to capture the peoples of those lands who have not blasphemed Jesus Christ, nor have resisted the preaching of His faith . . . is manifest tyranny." Moreover, Oliveira argues, it is not acceptable for Christians to excuse themselves on the grounds that slavery is a custom among the peoples whom they capture, "because if there were not buyers there would not be evil sellers, nor would thieves steal in order to sell." Oliveira clearly believed that most of the captives acquired by traders had been forced into slavery in response to the demand created by slave traders. He writes, "we give them the opportunity to deceive themselves, to rob each other, and to enslave and to sell." In his most famous words, Oliveira declares: "We were the inventors of such an evil trade, never before used or heard of among humans." Oliveira does not explicitly identify the slave trade he denounces, but scholars have little doubt that he is directly addressing the Portuguese slave trade in West Africa.[38]

Oliveira completely dismisses the argument, advanced by apologists for the slave trade, that slavery facilitated conversion to Christianity. He asserts instead that those who went to Africa for slaves did so for their own material interest, not to save the souls of slaves—"because if their material interest were removed, they would not go there." Moreover, those who owned slaves rarely taught their slaves "how to know or to serve God," nor did they even allow them to hear mass, or permit them to observe Sundays or holy days. Oliveira concludes that "[t]heir captivity is more attributed to the service of their masters than to the service of God."[39]

Oliveira's book received little recognition in Lisbon, and Oliveira found himself imprisoned by the Inquisition soon after the book's publication. Other Portuguese as well as Spanish theologians also questioned the slave trade with Africa, but their works did not have much effect either.[40] Bartolomé de Las Casas, who had considerably more success with the Spanish Crown in his campaign against Indian slavery in the Spanish colonies in the sixteenth century, perceptively notes the power of the historians of the Portuguese court. In his *Historia de las Indias*, Las Casas reviews events along the coast of West Africa, borrowing liberally from Zurara. From time to time, Las Casas reflects on the Portuguese role in the enslavement of Africans and criticizes the representations made by Portuguese historians. After paraphrasing Zurara's account of the first captures of Africans, he writes, "How much the Portuguese historians extol as illustrious these, such evil, deeds, offering them all as great sacrifices to God." And, later, after recounting Zurara's description of the first slave auction in Lagos, Las Casas chides Zurara for not seeing that the good intentions of Prince Henry (to Christianize the slaves) did not excuse the violence, the deaths, the captivity, and the great injustice done to those brought from Africa.[41]

The well-developed justification for slavery and the increasing numbers of slaves trafficked between African ports and Portugal in the fifteenth century explain the immediate, unreflective adoption of slave trading in Brazil. So comfortable were mariners of the early sixteenth century with the slave trade that they immediately saw it as a possible commercial venture in Brazil. When the Society of Jesus arrived in Brazil in 1549, however, questions began to be raised about the legality of enslaving the Indians of Brazil. Although the Jesuits wanted to enlist the support of the Portuguese colonists in their mission to evangelize the Brazilian Indians, a bitter conflict with the colonists over Indian slavery soon ensued.[42]

References to a slave trade from Brazil appear in documents from the first years of contact. When the Portuguese Crown granted to Fernando de Noronha the right to exploit the brazilwood trade in 1502, the contract contained a proviso that allowed him to trade for slaves. The captain's instructions for the *Bretoa* (which partially belonged to Fernando de Noronha) directed that slaves could not be brought back except if ordered by the outfitters (*armadores*) of the ship. Thirty-six Indian slaves were taken to Portugal on the *Bretoa* in 1511. In 1515, a Portuguese ship returned to Portugal loaded not only with brazilwood but with slaves. These slaves, according to a pamphlet publicizing the voyage, cost virtually nothing because parents freely gave their children to the slave traders, thinking "that their children are going to the Promised Land." When Magellan arrived along the coast of Brazil in late 1519 and early 1520, he prohibited his men, on penalty of death, to trade for slaves. His rationale was in no way a moral statement; it was simply to avoid conflict with the Portuguese and to prevent the addition of more mouths to feed aboard ship.[43]

The Indian slave trade in southern Brazil appears to have been established by the 1520s, when a Portuguese degredado known as "the bachelor" of Cananéia was supplying slaves to Spanish and other European sea captains. In northern Brazil, when King João III drew up the charter that granted Pernambuco to Duarte Coelho in 1534, he permitted Coelho to export, free from the usual duties, 24 slaves annually to Lisbon. Beyond these 24 slaves, Coelho was free to send more slaves, provided the duties were paid. Moreover, the king indicated that the sailors and crew were also permitted to bring Indian slaves from Brazil. Virtually nothing is known about these Indian slaves who were sold in Lisbon in the first decades of the sixteenth century, but they were certainly outnumbered by West African slaves. Elbl estimates the annual trade in slaves from West Africa at 2,650 slaves in 1500–1509; that number rose to 3,500 slaves annually in 1510–1515, and to 4,500 slaves annually in 1516–1521. It is likely that the mortality of the far fewer numbers of Brazilian Indian slaves in Portugal was high, given their lack of immunity to European and African diseases. One hundred years later, Ambrósio Fernandes Brandão thought it remarkable enough to comment on the high mortality of Brazilian natives in Portugal. He states, "I have seen some of the native heathen of this land taken to our Portugal, where they do poorly and most of them die very soon."[44]

Demand for slaves soon intensified when the first donatários began to build their colonies in Brazil. In 1548, 3,000 slaves labored in the captaincy of São Vicente, which then had six hundred colonists and six sugar mills. One of the sugar mills in São Vicente, probably the largest and best appointed, had 130 slaves, the vast majority of whom were Indian, for only 7 or 8 were from Africa. The African slaves held the highly skilled jobs, including the crucial role of sugar master. In 1542, the donatário of Pernambuco asked the king for "a few slaves from Guinea"; in 1545, the donatário of Paraíba do Sul wrote his business partner that he had sufficient slaves to work some of his mills, but he wanted to import 60 slaves from Guinea for new mills he was building upstream. When Hans Staden arrived in Pernambuco in 1548, he estimated that 30 "Moors

[African] and Brazilian [Indian] slaves" lived at Iguarassú, a sugar mill outside the main settlement at Olinda.[45]

The first Africans to set foot in Brazil were on the very first expeditions to Brazil: an African interpreter was with Cabral in 1500, and an African slave was present for Magellan's sojourn in 1519–1520. Although it is impossible to date when the first African slaves arrived to stay in Brazil, it is likely that they came in the 1530s. In the earliest settlements, highly skilled African slaves were purchased because of their familiarity with sugar production. African slavery was certainly established in Brazil when the first governor, Tomé de Sousa, landed in 1549 with slaves provided by the king himself.[46]

After the Jesuits arrived in 1549, they immediately perceived that slavery was the preferred labor system used by the colonists in Brazil. "Men who come here," Nóbrega observed, "find no other way of living except to live from the labor of slaves." When the Jesuits first visited Pernambuco, they found a substantial African slave population working and living alongside Indian slaves. In 1552, a Jesuit indicated that Pernambuco had such a large population of Indian and African slaves that every Sunday during Lent of that year one thousand slaves, both men and women, joined in an orderly procession. Even more slaves lived on plantations. So commonplace was Indian slavery in Brazil that the Jesuits immediately dedicated part of their mission to Indian slaves. The slaves were so responsive to the Jesuit preaching, Jesuit Francisco Pires notes, that "they know the catechism better than their masters." Even Hans Staden, who found himself destitute in São Vicente after having been shipwrecked, was able to acquire a Guarani slave who helped him to hunt. By 1556, the town council of Salvador wanted permission from the Crown to institute a slave trade between Brazil and Africa; they proposed to exchange Indian slaves from Brazil for African slaves from São Tomé.[47]

Some of the slaves in Brazil came from the Spanish territories farther south, from the Río de la Plata and Paraguay. There Spanish conquistadors enslaved thousands of Guarani in their expeditions of exploration and conquest. Spanish captains used Indian guides and interpreters to lead them to neighboring villages and settlements, but if the Indians resisted, they were attacked and enslaved. The German Ulrich Schmidel, who arrived in the Río de la Plata with Pedro de Mendoza in 1536 and remained in Paraguay until 1553, frequently comments on the enslavement of Indians. On one occasion, a Spanish captain ordered the Spaniards to kill all the Cario [Guarani] men (who had formerly been their allies) but to enslave the women and children. On another occasion, their captain, Cabeza de Vaca, ordered the men to attack, kill, and enslave their hosts, the Surucusi; according to Schmidel, two thousand men, women, and children were enslaved. After one expedition, Schmidel writes that the Spaniards "won nearly 12,000 persons, between men, women, and children, who must become our slaves"; his own share amounted to fifty slaves. Because of the proximity of Paraguay to São Vicente, Guarani slaves made their way into the Portuguese colony. According to António Rodrigues, a Spaniard who had accompanied the armada of Pedro de Mendoza to Río de la Plata and who later entered the Society of Jesus in São Vicente, Spanish slave traders sold Guarani Indians in São Vicente, as well as in Peru.[48]

Other Indian slaves came from overt slave raiding along the coast of Brazil, a practice not unlike some of the first slave raids along the coast of Africa. Unscrupulous Portuguese slave traders used deception and trickery to capture Indians, whom they sold as slaves to colonists. Slave raiders approached the Indians peacefully, then filled their ships with captives and set sail. Although these raids produced slaves for colonists, they were deeply destabilizing and threatened Indian retaliation against the first settlements. The only voices raised against Indian slavery were those of the donatários, who complained that the actions of these slave traders were ruining the chances for their colonies' success. In 1546, Pero de Góis, the donatário of Paraíba do Sul, described to the king the slave trading of one Henrique Luis. According to Góis, Luis imprisoned "an Indian, the greatest chief in this land," on his ship and demanded a large ransom from the chief's people for his safe return. The chief's people paid the ransom, but Luis broke his word and, "in order to ingratiate himself with other Indians," gave the chief as a prisoner to them. After this deception, the chief's people attacked and destroyed one of the Portuguese villages. Góis wrote the king that "they all said many bad things of us, and that they did not trust us, and that we don't keep our word." Similarly, in the same year, Duarte Coelho, the donatário of Pernambuco, compared those living in the regions south of Pernambuco to pirates, informing the king that they sailed up and down the coast attacking and enslaving Indians. After residing in Brazil only a few months, Nóbrega believed that most of the slaves in Bahia in 1549 had been obtained through such raids.[49]

Unlike the experience in Africa, where Christian evangelism was used as an argument in favor of enslaving Africans, the first Jesuits in Brazil did not advocate enslaving Indians to evangelize them. Nóbrega believed instead that slavery impeded the mission of the Jesuits to the Indians. He wrote his superior soon after arriving in Brazil that the conversion of the Indians depended on the return of enslaved Indians to their homelands. After a decade in Brazil, Nóbrega echoed Oliveira's arguments when he concluded that the enslavement of Indians by colonists "is not to save them nor for them to know Christ nor for them to live in justice and reason, but to rob them of their farms, their sons, their daughters, and their women." The Jesuits urged instead that the king of Portugal limit Indian slavery in Brazil.[50]

Brazil's first governor and judicial authorities took the first steps to place limits on Indian slavery, by directive of the king, who had decided that slave raiding along the coast of Brazil should no longer be tolerated. In the royal instructions (regimento) written for the king's first governor of Brazil in 1548, the king acknowledged that such raiding occurred and outlawed it henceforth. The Crown magistrate subsequently wrote from Brazil to his sovereign that slave raiding was the primary cause of Indian unrest in Brazil and informed the king that he had ordered that Indians seized in this way be liberated. And, in fact, Jesuit Leonardo Nunes escorted a group of Guarani, who had been captured south of São Vicente and sold as slaves in Bahia, back to their homeland in southern Brazil. Nunes wrote that raiding against coastal Indians had largely stopped by 1551, "praised be the name of Our Lord."[51]

Following the arrival of the governor and the Jesuits, several basic rules began to be asserted for the regulation of the Indian slave trade. As had happened in Africa, outright raiding was discouraged, and instead, enslavement was to take place through just wars or resgate. Both practices had well-established precedents and well-developed arguments to legitimate African slavery; these were soon modified to apply to Brazil.

As we have seen, ransoming (resgate) was a familiar custom from the Iberian Reconquest, it was a well-known practice in the Mediterranean, and it had characterized some of the first interactions between Portuguese and North Africans. In Brazil, it took on an added meaning because it was associated with the cannibalistic ceremonies of coastal Tupi groups. Later, cannibalism would be used as an argument in favor of enslaving Indians, but in the beginning, resgate was simply a means of obtaining prisoners slated for sacrifice. Through resgate, captives held for a cannibalism ceremony were purchased from an Indian group. Since Tupi groups obtained these captives from their intertribal wars and raids, such captives were prisoners of war in the eyes of the Portuguese as well

Figure 6.3. A captive in a cannibalism ceremony. André F. Thevet, *Les singularitez de la France Antarctique, autrement nommée Amerique* (Paris, 1558). Courtesy of the John Carter Brown Library at Brown University.

as the French. Because the captives were, in the minds of the colonists, already slaves, ransomed captives could then be legally owned as slaves. Moreover, since the prisoners so obtained were rescued from certain death and cannibalism, the Portuguese and the French saw slavery as an act of charity, infinitely better than death through cannibalism. Jean de Léry described how he obtained slaves after the Tupinambá returned from a ferocious battle with the Margaia. They had thirty prisoners with them, reports Léry, and a few days later "our interpreters entreated them to sell some of them to Villegagnon." Léry himself bought "a woman and a little boy of hers who was less than two years old," and this purchase "cost me about three francs' worth of goods." Léry saw his new slaves as having been "rescued by us out of their [the Tupinambá] hands."[52] Depictions of captives, secured by cords, before they were about to be killed for cannibalism ceremonies, appear as illustrations in both Léry's and Thevet's works (Fig. 6.3).

At first, the Jesuits accepted resgate as a legitimate means for obtaining slaves, and they saw it as a means of reducing and eventually replacing cannibalism. Léry describes how resgate was already undercutting the traditional Tupinambá ritual of cannibalism. He writes that one of the Tupinambá men told him that since Villegagnon had arrived, "we have scarcely eaten half of our enemies." The man further reflected to Léry, "I don't know what will come of all this." Jesuits capitalized on this moment of change in Indian society and preached to Indians that they must sell captives to the Portuguese as slaves; they even took a direct role in delivering captives to the Portuguese as slaves. A Jesuit priest in Rio de Janeiro, for example, took eight war prisoners from an Indian group and gave them to the Portuguese, who paid for them. Over time, however, Nóbrega had reservations about ransoming, for he doubted that all the slaves he saw around him were truly captives liberated from cannibalistic ceremonies. He thought it more likely that Portuguese colonists manipulated Indians to obtain slaves. Nóbrega echoes Oliveira's criticism of the African slave trade when he writes that most Indians became slaves through "cunning." Nóbrega alludes to such devious practices when he expresses his belief that the Portuguese had "taught" the Indians how to attack each other and sell captives as slaves, or that the Portuguese had "asked" Indian men for women as wives, giving the women's fathers some trading goods, but then kept the women as "slaves forever." [53]

As in the early days of African slavery, the concept of the just war, the captives of which could be enslaved, became established in Brazil. When the king wrote the royal instructions to his first governor, Tomé de Sousa, he commanded Sousa to inform himself about the Indians who had risen up against Francisco Pereira Coutinho, the deceased (and cannibalized) donatário of Bahia, and who had destroyed *fazendas* and committed other damages. Once he ascertained which Indian groups had rebelled, the king ordered Sousa to "destroy their villages and settlements, killing and capturing those whom you deem sufficient for their punishment." [54] In essence, this was a just war, and the defeated could legally be enslaved.

So, too, was another just war declared in 1562 by the third governor of Brazil, Mem de Sá, who signed a decree proclaiming that all Caeté Indians would be slaves wherever they were found, with no exceptions. This was in response to the death of Dom Pedro Fernandes Sardinha, first bishop of Brazil, at the hands of the Caeté Indians. Sardinha, who had been so critical of the Jesuit mission in Bahia, had been summoned back to Lisbon by King João III. In 1556, Bishop

Sardinha departed Salvador on a ship carrying one hundred persons. The ship headed north but ran into storms near the Cururipe River in the coastal region inhabited by the Caeté Indians. The passengers and crew managed to save themselves, only to be imprisoned by the Caeté. Nóbrega, outraged, wrote to Tomé de Sousa that the Caeté had cannibalized "clergy and laymen, the married and the single, women and children!"[55]

Though the Jesuits agreed in principle with the concept of a just war, they had direct experience with such declarations turning into a free license to enslave. Certainly the Jesuits believed that the cannibalism of the bishop and many other prominent citizens of Salvador was unacceptable and had to be punished. But the declaration of the just war against the Caeté was devastating for their mission. The immediate consequence of the declaration was that Portuguese colonists indiscriminately seized Indians, even those who lived in the Jesuit aldeias, called them Caeté, and turned them into slaves. As a result, according to a Jesuit history written twenty years later, twelve thousand Indians fled the mission villages.[56]

Slavery posed complicated problems for the Jesuits. Through their letters, it is clear that they were virtually the only Europeans in Brazil in the sixteenth century who questioned Indian slavery. This brought them into conflict with the Portuguese colonists when the Jesuits began to refuse to absolve colonists who knowingly held illegally captured slaves. In one letter, the Jesuit João Gonçalves reflects on a recent situation that had emerged in Bahia when a slaver arrived with three boatloads of Indian slaves to sell in Salvador. António Pires, then the only Jesuit priest in Salvador, spoke out against those who sought to buy the slaves, and he refused to confess the crew. Similarly, Nóbrega describes "closing the door" of confession to the Portuguese colonists because of the illegal slave trade. Yet, from his first months in Brazil, Nóbrega believed that slaves were necessary for the Jesuits' own mission. He proposed that the *colégio* (school and residence) of Bahia be supported by ten slaves: five slaves would farm, and five would fish. Nearly a decade later, in 1558, he wrote that the "best thing that could be given to the colégio would be two dozen slaves from Guinea," who would raise food crops and fish to support the Jesuits and their students.[57]

The Jesuits became slave owners even though many early Jesuits had serious reservations about slavery. The first slaves owned by the Jesuits in Brazil were Africans, whose status as slaves was no longer questioned. The king of Portugal provided the first slaves—three slaves from São Tomé—and over the next few years the Jesuits acquired many more slaves, some of whom were Indian. The

legality and morality of holding Indian slaves in Brazil, given the Jesuit position on the illegal capturing of slaves, was a matter referred to Rome. In 1562,
the head of the Jesuit order, Diego Laínez, wrote to Nóbrega authorizing the
Society to own slaves in Brazil "as long as they are obtained justly." Laínez'
successors, however, held reservations about the Society's ownership of slaves
and ordered that the slaves owned by Jesuits in Portugal be freed. Some Jesuits
in Brazil opposed the acquisition of slaves, and some questioned the legality of
African slavery.[58]

By 1570, when Gandavo characterized Indian slavery as widespread and
essential to the survival of the Portuguese colonies in Brazil, and confidently
predicted that even the poor could acquire slaves in Brazil, the reality was that
Indian slaves were becoming harder to obtain in the coastal regions where colonists lived. Mortality among coastal Indians in Brazil had been extremely high
since 1550, such that even Gandavo recognized that the coastal regions around
the Portuguese colonies, with the exception of a few friendly Indian villages,
had been left "unpopulated by the natives." Then, colonists learned that the
young king Sebastião had signed a law (20 March 1570) decreeing the liberty
of the Indians of Brazil.[59] Thus, it would appear that this law, coupled with epidemic disease, signaled the demise of Indian slavery in Brazil. It would seem,
too, that Africans would soon replace Indian slaves on the sugar plantations of
Bahia and Pernambuco. But, in fact, Indian slavery increased after 1570.

Indian slavery did not end with the decline of the coastal populations because
a new slave trade brought thousands of Indians to the coast from the *sertões*, the
"inland wilderness frontiers." The Indian population in the interior remained
high, despite the decline in coastal indigenous populations. A colonist who lived
in Bahia characterized the sertões of the São Francisco River in the 1580s as well
settled by a variety of Indian groups, who competed with each other for waters
to fish and lands to hunt and farm. Fernão Cardim similarly estimated that the
number of Indians in the interior was "uncountable" and of "many nations, customs, and languages."[60]

A familiar pattern soon emerged as transactional go-betweens appeared
to run this slave trade from the sertão (wilderness frontier). Mixed-race and
bicultural mamelucos with great expertise in the sertão became the lançados
and pombeiros of Brazil. The Jesuits became vocal opponents of this trade
and of the mamelucos, very nearly compromising their mission in Brazil with
their stinging criticism of colonists who benefited from the trade. Using many

of the same arguments that had once underpinned the African slave trade, the Jesuits sought to impose limits on the Indian slave trade from the sertão by insisting that just wars and legitimate resgate were the only legal means to enslave Indians.

To be sure, the wealthiest colonists did begin to bring more African slaves to Brazil. From 1550 to 1575, Luiz Felipe de Alencastro documents that 10,000 Africans came to Brazil; that number climbs fourfold to 40,000 from 1576 to 1600. In 1581, the Jesuit provincial wrote in his formal annual letter to Rome that more than 2,000 slaves had arrived in Salvador from ports in Africa that year. In 1583, a Jesuit report estimated the slave population of Bahia at 10,000 African slaves and 8,000 enslaved and free Indians. Pernambuco, according to the same document, had 15,000 African slaves and 3,000 Indians.[61]

King Sebastião's law of 1570 assumed the liberty of Indians; however, it did allow the enslavement of Indians to continue under certain circumstances. Following a just war, duly licensed by the king or by the king's governor, the defeated could be enslaved. Colonists could continue to take captives from certain Indian groups—those who "customarily" attack the Portuguese, those who wage war on other Indians to obtain captives for cannibalism ceremonies, the Indians labeled Aimoré, or "others like them." Colonists might seize such Indians, provided that within two months the captives taken were registered with Crown officials, who would verify their status, and if unsatisfied with the documentation presented, would free the Indians.[62]

Even with these loopholes that clearly maintained the principle and practice of Indian slavery, colonists immediately petitioned the king, stating that it would be detrimental to comply with the law because they needed workers for their sugar mills and plantations. The king then compromised the law further by asking his two governors in Brazil and the Jesuits to come to an agreement such that the colonists would have access to laborers for their estates and that the manifestly unjust taking of slaves would be avoided. The two governors and the Jesuits worked out a compromise that protected the mission villages and reiterated the principle of the just war. Though colonists would risk public whippings, fines, and banishment if they took an Indian from a mission village, an Indian who ran away from a mission village and remained away among hostile Indians for a year could be taken as a slave. Governors had the right to define just wars, but captains, who had previously undertaken slaving expeditions at will, were now forced to obtain permission before they could enter the wilderness.[63]

Just wars declared by the governors of Brazil partially maintained the flow of Indian slaves to the Portuguese colonies following the proclamation of Sebastião's law. The Jesuits quickly learned that the just wars waged after Sebastião's law were legal but brutal affairs; they saw firsthand what could happen in the wilderness north of Rio de Janeiro in 1575. There a Jesuit father witnessed a massacre and the violent enslavement of several thousand Tamoio Indians in a so-called just war. The Jesuit provincial described in detail this deeply disturbing war in his annual letter. The letter apparently caused such consternation when it was read in Lisbon and Rome that the father general of the Jesuits in Rome asked his provincial in Brazil to henceforth limit his annual letters to more uplifting topics.[64] The war began when the Tamoio, who had been the allies of the French, captured seven Indians, including a chief, from a mission village founded by the Jesuits. This deed, and the belief that the captives would surely be cannibalized, gave the governor of the south a pretext to declare and to wage a just war. He recruited men from Rio de Janeiro and São Vicente, and one of the Jesuit fathers, Baltazar Álvares, accompanied the armed force that headed north by land and by sea. Arriving at a fortified Tamoio village nearly a month later, the governor decided to surround the village, which he estimated at one thousand archers strong, and to cut off water and food. In the Jesuit account of what happened, Álvares served as a negotiator who moved between the ranks of the governor and the Tamoio stronghold. He convinced the Tamoio chief, Ião Guaçú, to surrender to the governor.[65]

The results of Álvares' intervention, however, were disastrous. The chief had to hand over five hundred Indian allies, who were then slaughtered by the governor's soldiers in order to defeat the enemy. The Jesuit annual letter of 1575 states that "it caused great pain to the father [Álvares] to see so many killed with such great cruelty, without being able to aid their souls, because even though he tried to teach them something so that he could baptize them, the fury and the speed with which they were killed was such that they did not give him time to do that which he wished." Once the warriors had been killed, the rest of the Indians, except for the chief and his family, whom the governor had exempted, became slaves. This also pained Álvares, who saw "the women and children of the killed [being] divided amongst the Portuguese, the women separated from children." Some of the slaves were taken to São Vicente, the rest to Rio de Janeiro.[66] Amid the massacre and the shackling, the remaining Indians fled into the wilderness, but the governor pursued them still, killing some and capturing others. The Jesuits could only criticize the violent nature of this war, for it was a duly declared just war and therefore legal.

But the major source of slaves after 1570 was the new slave trade into the interior. Gandavo presents this trade as a modification on the former ways of doing things. Because of the intervention of the Jesuits, he writes, the old methods of slave raiding and ransoming had ceased. Slaves now came from the sertão, and officials certified that Indians brought from the sertão were legally enslaved before they were distributed to colonists. Gandavo describes the process: "They examine them [the slaves] and ask them questions—who sold them or how they were ransomed . . . or who captured them in a just war—and those who are found to be wrongly acquired are given their liberty." In spite of this change, Gandavo believed that colonists easily maintained their slave labor forces. "All Indians purchased today," he writes, "are legally acquired, and the inhabitants of the land are not failing on this account to increase their possessions." [67]

Fernão Cardim wrote a description of the expeditions into the sertão, known as *entradas*, characterizing them as slave-trading companies, backed by investors and headed by a local citizen, who took the title of captain. The captain obtained permission from the governor for the entrada; permission was given on the condition that the traders bring the Indians without force or deceit. Then the captain recruited men for the expedition, especially mameluco interpreters. The companies included fifty or sixty Portuguese and mameluco men, each carrying his own arms, and many Indian archers. The Indians served as porters, hauling the food and the trading goods for the expedition. On the entrada's return, the leaders of the expeditions divided up the Indians who had been brought out, according to the amount initially invested in the expedition. The men on the expedition also received a share of the Indians.[68]

An important source documents this intercontinental slave trade in detail. In 1591, the visiting inquisitor sent by the Holy Office of the Lisbon Inquisition arrived in Salvador. The inquisitor, Heitor Furtado de Mendonça, became interested in the lapses in religious discipline found on the expeditions that left coastal Bahia and Pernambuco in the 1570s and 1580s in search of Indian slaves in the interior. The trials he initiated reveal the complexity of the roles of the mameluco transactional go-betweens, who led, or were key participants in, the slave trade from the wilderness, a trade euphemistically known in Bahia and Pernambuco as "descending" Indians.[69]

The mameluco línguas (tongues; interpreters) on such expeditions became powerful rivals for the Jesuits because they overtly challenged the monopoly that the Jesuits claimed over the Indians as yet uncontacted in the wilderness. One of these men was Domingos Fernandes Nobre "Tomacaúna"; another was Álvaro Rodrigues, a grandson of Diogo Álvares "Caramuru." Both were nearly the same age—Domingos was born in 1546, and Álvaro in 1547—and both had a strong connection to the Indian world. Álvaro's mother was a mameluca daughter of Álvares, and Álvaro lived on an estate in Paraguaçu, on the fringe of the Recôncavo; Domingos Fernandes Nobre was born in Pernambuco—his father a Portuguese stonemason, his mother a free Indian woman.[70]

Both men entered the wilderness on the large entrada into the sertão led by Antônio Dias Adorno, Álvaro Rodrigues' older cousin. At the request of the governor, Adorno, also a grandson of Diogo Álvares, left the captaincy of Porto Seguro in 1572 in search of precious minerals and gold. One hundred fifty colonists and four hundred Indians headed up the Caravelas River searching for signs of emeralds, sapphires, gold, and other green and blue stones that had been seen there earlier. On this entrada, Domingos Fernandes Nobre and Álvares Rodrigues were young men in their twenties. Nobre later described how he painted himself on the legs with the black and red dyes of *urucum* and *jenipapo* and adorned his head with feathers. He joined with the Indians, singing, dancing, shaking, and drumming. Some of the men returned to Ilhéus by canoe, but Rodrigues and Nobre continued on to the São Francisco River, where they traded swords, knives, and other arms with the Indians for slaves.[71]

Subsequently, both Nobre and Rodrigues led a series of expeditions into the wildernesses behind the coastal settlements of Ilhéus, Porto Seguro, Bahia, and Pernambuco in the 1570s and 1580s. In eighteen years, Álvaro Rodrigues went on seven entradas, leading six of them. Domingos Fernandes Nobre entered the sertão seven or eight times, also serving as captain on numerous expeditions. These entradas lasted from four to fourteen months and often followed one another in quick succession. With the exception of the first entrada of Antônio Dias Adorno, these later expeditions served the sole purpose of descending Indians. In 1576, for example, Nobre went to the sertão of Arabo (Serra do Orobo, Bahia) with the permission of the governor to "descend Indians." This expedition took four to five months and brought two hundred Indians to Salvador.[72]

The visiting inquisitor tried several mamelucos for living as Indians in the interior, and these trials reveal how these expeditions were organized and run. The mameluco Francisco Pires stated the point of the entradas bluntly: "Five years ago he left Pernambuco for the Sertão of Laripe [Chapada do Araripe in

NW Pernambuco] in the Company of Manoel Machado, now deceased, to ransom and buy Indian slaves."[73] Each entrada had a clearly designated captain and included colonists, mamelucos, and armed Indians. The mamelucos who served as interpreters made contact with Indian chiefs, established the terms of trade, and tried to persuade entire villages to willingly leave the interior and resettle on the coast.

Many of the mamelucos had previously lived with Indians in the sertão and, like the French truchements of a generation before, were recognized as powerful men in the wilderness. Nobre characterized his early manhood—the years from his eighteenth birthday until he was thirty-two—as a time when he "lived as an Indian man, neither praying nor commending himself to God." Sebastião Madeira confessed that he lived with the Indians for a year and a half in 1587 or 1588 in the sertão of Serra Pequena; at the same time, he knew of another mameluco, Marçal de Aragão, who was living 7 leagues (approximately 40 kilometers) distant. Lázaro da Cunha entered the sertão of Pernambuco with a company of men in 1585, but he remained behind, living with Tupinambá Indians for five years. The next year, when another company of men arrived to trade for slaves, the men saw Lázaro, naked, with his eyelashes plucked, his eyebrows shaved, his legs painted with genipapo, and his hair cut in the Indian style, and he was living with two women.[74]

While living in the sertão, the mamelucos changed their names and adopted the lifestyles of the Indian groups with whom they lived. Nobre became "Tomacaúna" when he entered the sertão, and though neither he nor anyone else gave a translation of his name, my best guess is that the name combined the Tupi suffix *úna* (meaning "black") with "Tomaca" (meaning "Antbird"). Since colonial scribes often used *m* and *b* interchangeably for Tupi words, "Tomaca-úna" may be the same as "Tobaca-úna." "Tobaca" is a variant spelling of "Tovaca," and "Tovaca" and "Tovacuçu" derive from the Tupi *to'bag* or *tuaku'su*, both types of antbirds that live on the forest floor. Tomacaúna "Black Antbird" described himself as "walking naked as they do" and singing, dancing, crying, lamenting with his Indian hosts. He drank their fermented drink and took their smoke, all "as they did, in their Indian way." Other mamelucos did the same. In 1573, Pedro Bastardo went into the wilderness at the age of twenty-four with Pedro Álvares, André Dias, and other mamelucos and remained there for seven years. There he took the name "Aratuam," which he said meant "Arara" (Parrot; Macaw), and joined in ritual ceremonies in which he drank the Indian "wine" and took their smoke. Domingos Dias, Manoel da Maia, Baltasar de Leão, and Gonçalo Álvares also had Indian names when they entered the sertão. Domingos Dias became "Jocorutu" (Owl), Baltasar de Leão became "Jabotim" (Land Turtle), Gonçalo Álvares became "Pinasamoquu" (Long Line), and Manoel da Maia became "Jaibatinga" or "Jabibatinga" (White Turtle). Another mameluco was called "Marigui" (Black Gnat; Mosquito).[75]

Following the example of others before them, mamelucos allied themselves with powerful Indian chiefs in the sertão by accepting their daughters as wives. Nobre lived with two Indian women, who had been given to him by their fathers, in the sertão of Arabo in 1576. On subsequent expeditions he acquired more wives. In 1577 he lived with three women in Arabo; in 1578 he lived with seven women in the sertão of Ilhéus. All of these things, he later recalled to the visiting inquisitor, he did "so that they would accept him as Indian and so that they would call him nephew."[76]

To present themselves as strong and valiant to Indian chiefs, mamelucos tattooed their bodies, for in Indian society, tattoos indicated bravery in war and therefore marked status for men. The tattoos of Nobre were so notorious in Bahia that his Portuguese wife felt compelled to denounce him to the visiting inquisitor. Using the tooth of the rodent known in Tupi as *paca* to cut his skin, Nobre described to the visiting inquisitor how he sprinkled black powders into the wounds to create permanent tattoos on his legs and arms. He did this, he explained, out of "necessity." Once, for example, he and a companion had themselves tattooed when the Indians rebelled against them. But when the Indians saw the tattoos, he stated, "they fled." Many other mamelucos and white men confessed or were denounced for having tattooed themselves in the sertão.[77]

Mameluco línguas became convincing speakers in the sertão, not only because they spoke Indian languages but because they could imitate the discourse of Indian chiefs. In persuasive language, the mamelucos proclaimed that life would be better on the coast. The Jesuit Fernão Cardim claimed that the mamelucos promised the Indians that they came "for them by commandment of the Governor, that they may come to enjoy the good things of the Sea." Mamelucos told Indian chiefs that they would be able to retain their traditional customs and live in their own villages when they relocated to the coast.[78] This idea resonated with Indians, perhaps because of the existence of long migrations in search of a promised land in their mythology. Periodic migrations undertaken by the Tupi-Guarani-speaking peoples in search of a "land without evil" have been documented by a number of sociologists, anthropologists, and historians.[79]

When Indian chiefs did not want to descend their village to the coast, the mameluco línguas established the terms of exchange between the men of the entradas and the Indian chiefs. Essentially, they created slave trading posts deep in the interior. This trade was highly dangerous. Whereas coastal slave trading and slave raiding had been done by ship, which gave the Portuguese slave traders an advantage, deep in the sertão they lacked an easy escape. The slave trade depended on what the Indian chiefs wanted in exchange for captives and on their negotiation of terms. And what the chiefs wanted were arms. In 1572, in the sertão of Pernambuco along the São Francisco River, Nobre gave swords, knives, shields, and other arms to Indians whom he knew to be hostile to the Portuguese and who "fight and kill them, when they have the chance."[80] Giving arms to Indians known to be enemies of the Portuguese not only was in violation of Crown policy, but immediately put the men on the entrada in danger. Fifteen years later, in 1587, the mameluco Francisco Pires traded three good swords for three Indians in the sertão of Laripe; later, the three chiefs to whom he had given the swords "rose up with their people and made war" against the entrada of "white Christians."[81]

Some mamelucos shifted their allegiance and identities toward their adoptive Indian families, just as the Norman interpreters had done before them. Pedro Bastardo described how he "helped the Indians in their wars with other Indians," and Lázaro da Cunha and Marçal de Aragão not only helped in the intertribal wars but sometimes "fought against the whites" and on at least one occasion "fought and defeated" the "Christians."[82]

But most often, mameluco transactional go-betweens served the interests of the entradas, funded by the coastal sugar planters. The entradas descended thousands of Indians, the majority of whom became slaves in Bahia and Pernambuco. According to a variety of Jesuit sources, the numbers of Indians brought from the wilderness to be slaves ran into the tens of thousands. One Jesuit writer claims that 20,000 Indians had been brought just from the sertão of Arabo to Bahia from 1575 to 1577; from 1577 to 1583, the descending of Indians had continued, with some planters bringing 2,000, others 3,000, and others even more for their estates.[83] The total number seems impossibly high, but it corresponds to the figure given in the reports of one of the Jesuits' own entradas into the sertão, where they, too, sought Indians for their mission villages. When the Jesuit João Vicente went to the sertão of Pernambuco (Chapada do Araripe) in 1580 to convince Indians there to relocate to the Jesuit aldeias on the coast, he had joined together 1,000 Indians whom he intended to bring to Bahia.[84] Jesuit Fernão Cardim estimated that, in all, 40,000 Indians had been brought from the sertão.[85]

The inventory of the Sergipe do Conde estate in the Recôncavo of Bahia provides a small glimpse into the lives of slaves living on one of the larger plantations. Evaluators assessed the plantation's property in 1572, following the death of its owner, the third governor of Brazil, Mem de Sá. Just over three hundred slaves lived on the plantation, nearly 90 percent of whom were Indian. The slave population was overwhelmingly adult and evenly divided between men and women. On the plantation lived a small number of African slaves— twenty—all men. There were no African slave women, but Indian women outnumbered Indian men in the slave labor force. Many of the adult male slaves had occupations related to the production of sugar, and of all the slaves, the African men had the highest assessed value. Of these twenty African men, seven were listed as "married," presumably to Indian women. Most of the Indian slaves, as well as all of the African slaves, had been baptized and given Christian names. But also living on the estate were Indians who had recently arrived in a resgate, that is, from a recent entrada into the sertão. All of these slaves were women, and virtually all had only Indian names.[86]

The large number of Indians who had Christian names on the Sergipe do Conde plantation—214, or 70 percent—reflects the Jesuit mission to Indian slaves. While the Jesuits fought against Indian slavery, they recognized the reality around them. Given the large and increasing numbers of Indian and African slaves in Bahia, the Jesuits directed a mission specifically at slaves living on plantations. Fernão Cardim describes this ministry: "We are in continual mission to the mills and farms of the Portuguese. . . . [T]hese missions have given such benefits that a father who was there for fifteen days baptized two hundred slaves, adults and children, both from Guinea and of this land, and [celebrated] up to one hundred marriages . . . and gave them knowledge of the Creator and of salvation."[87] In four months, he claims that Jesuits had baptized close to eight hundred Indian and African slaves, married five hundred, and heard a great number of confessions. A detailed proposal sent to Rome about these missions to plantations indicates the systematic approach the Jesuits intended to use. A priest of confidence assisted by a reliable companion would be given the responsibility to visit each plantation yearly. On arrival at the plantation, they would take a census of all the slaves and indicate who had been baptized, who was married, and who had made confessions; they were not to leave until all slaves had received the help and correction needed. They were to say mass in the morning on saints' days, because those were the days that the slaves and Indians had off; after mass they were to teach before the slaves left to work their own gardens. They were to encourage the establishment of the confraternity of Our Lady of the Rosary. At night, or during the evening meal, they were to teach again using the approved catechism.[88]

Even though the Jesuits ministered to the plantation slaves, they never believed that the Indians brought to Bahia and Pernambuco after 1570—the year of King Sebastião's declaration of the liberty of Indians—were obtained "justly." A Jesuit history of the mission villages, written in 1583, states that the Portuguese who enter the sertão deceive the Indians there by persuading them to descend to the coast, where they are promised that they will live in their own villages. But when they arrive, the Jesuit report continues, the Portuguese divide up the Indians, separating families, and then they sell them.[89] Nor did the Jesuits believe that the colonists followed the rules for a just war. Cardim writes that although the king had "commanded that no war should be held lawful, but that which should be made by order of the Governor general . . . notwithstanding many times it is not done with such examination as the cause requires." According to Cardim, the governor was to have taken "counsel with the Bishop, and Fathers of the company [i.e., the Jesuits], and experienced persons of the Country, and of good consciences." These men were to determine whether or not a war against a specific Indian group was just. But, Cardim writes that either the Jesuits were not consulted, or if they were, it was simply as a formal courtesy, for those who decided that the war would be just had "more regard to the hope of the profit that is offered them, of getting of slaves in the said war, than unto the Justice of it."[90]

While the Jesuits initially had some success persuading the new governor of Brazil, Manoel Teles Barreto, that the slave trade from the sertão was not a legal trade, Barreto later turned against the Jesuits and sided with the colonists. Barreto, who arrived in 1583 on the same ship as the Jesuit visitor Cristovão de Gouveia, with whom he had an excellent relationship on the Atlantic crossing, at first accepted the Jesuit view that colonists used deception to bring Indians from the sertão. Informing himself on this issue, Barreto determined that "all of the Indians who descend from the sertão are brought down with deception by promises that are made to them—that they will live in freedom and in their own villages." But when the entradas arrived on the coast, Barreto found, the story changed: "They divide them among themselves, separating the men from their wives, the parents from their children, the brothers from their sisters."[91]

The relationship between the Jesuits and the governor deteriorated rapidly, however, as the governor learned more about the bitter conflict between the colonists and the Jesuits. Jesuit criticism of colonists who owned illegal Indian slaves had opened up a wide breach between the Society and the colonial elite. Cristovão de Gouveia notes in his letters that he found a "general aversion" to the Jesuits in Bahia. Gouveia cites two reasons for the colonists' dislike of the Jesuits: first, the hard position the Jesuits had adopted on Indian slavery, and second, the perception that Jesuits harbored runaway Indian slaves in the mission villages. When Gouveia undertook his review of the entire mission field, he found Jesuits everywhere unwilling to hear the confessions of colonists who refused to renounce illegal Indian slavery. Gouveia remarks in a letter to the father general in Rome that in the captaincies of Ilhéus and Porto Seguro, the number of Portuguese men who confessed with the Jesuit priests was few, if any. In some regions, the situation had deteriorated to the point where the colonists were openly hostile to the Jesuits, such as in Porto Seguro, where the colonists and the town council rose up against the Jesuits over the issue of Indian slavery.[92]

The Jesuits used their influence to lobby for a new declaration on the liberty of Indians in Brazil, one that they hoped would close the loopholes left open in the 1570 law. The Jesuits not only questioned the morality of Indian slavery, but they feared that the continued existence of the slave entradas would compromise their mission. Cardim believed, for example, that conversions were becoming less common and that Indians were fleeing from Bahia due to their fear of enslavement. In 1583, he estimated that there were few free Indians within 200–300 leagues (approximately 1,200–1,850 kilometers) of Salvador, which augured poorly for their salvation and the increase of Christianity. "There is no remedy," he states, "until the law, which we ask for from the King, arrives, stating that they may not be slaves." Before leaving Brazil for Portugal in 1584, one Jesuit was instructed not to return without first obtaining this declaration on the liberty of the Indians.[93]

The Jesuits succeeded in getting a second law passed in 1587. Signed by the Spanish king Philip II, now King Filipe I of Portugal, the new law explicitly recognized that Sebastião's law of 1570 had been compromised by the "excesses" of colonists in Brazil. In the preamble, the king states that colonists had brought free Indians by force and by deceit from the sertão, that they sold the free Indians as slaves, and that they received services from the free Indians without paying them for their work. The law then commands that "no one, no matter their social status, may enter the sertão with arms to look for Indians without the license of my governor." The governor could still appoint men to lead expeditions into the sertão. Such expeditions would include two or three Jesuits, who, "because of the good faith that they have among the Indians, can persuade them more easily to come and serve my vassals on their mills and plantations without force or deceit." When an expedition returned, the law specified that the Indians "would not be divided among the colonists" unless the governor, the Crown magistrate, and the Jesuits who had gone on such expeditions were present. The division of the Indians, moreover, would be more for the benefit of the Indians than for the colonists, and no Indian would be forced to work against his or her will. The law mandated a record-keeping system, in which the names and ages of all Indians would be written down, and required the Crown magistrate to verify the accuracy of the list twice per year.[94]

King Philip's law still preserved the concept of the just war and of ransoming. "All Indians are free," the law stated, "except those who were captured in a just war that was undertaken by my, or by my governor's, command or those who were bought in order that they would not be eaten by other Indians."[95] Under the new law, the enslavement of Indians could only continue in just wars or through the traditional ransoming.

If the Jesuits thought that this law would end the enslavement of Indians, they were soon disappointed. When the visiting inquisitor arrived in Bahia in 1591, two expeditions of approximately one hundred men each were trading for Indian slaves in the sertão. One captain, the mameluco Gonçalo Álvares, confessed to the visiting inquisitor that he had failed to abstain from eating meat on holy days while he was in the sertão, but he saw no need to apologize for the fact that he was the captain of an entrada of twenty-five colonists and many Indian archers that entered the sertão "to descend and bring with him Indians from the sertão to the coast." Another entrada into the sertão in the 1590s traded horses, guns, gunpowder, bullets, drums, and silk battle standards to Indian chiefs in return for slaves.[96] Clearly, the intercontinental slave trade was still flourishing at the end of the sixteenth century. The expensive goods traded for slaves—horses, guns, drums, and silk battle standards—suggest that powerful chiefs remained in the sertão who demanded such merchandise in exchange for slaves.

Whether they were conscious of doing so or not, go-betweens set into motion patterns, attitudes, and practices in Brazil that repeated earlier actions in Africa and that would repeat themselves with little reflection for at least three hundred years. Early Portuguese merchants unreflectively adopted slave trading, justifying their trade with arguments used in the African slave trade. The men of the Society of Jesus questioned the legality of the enslavement of many Indians in Brazil, but not the legal and theological principle of the just war or the custom of resgate. In the second half of the sixteenth century, mamelucos carved out roles for themselves that harkened back to those of the African lançados and pombeiros, as well as to the strategies used by the Norman truchements and the first Portuguese men to "go native" in Brazil. Neither Indian slavery nor the go-betweens who facilitated it ended with the close of the sixteenth century. Rather, as the frontiers of Brazil expanded in the seventeenth and eighteenth centuries, so, too, did the enslavement of Indians. Entradas into the sertão to descend Indians continued in the seventeenth and eighteenth centuries in São Vicente, Minas Gerais, Goiás, Mato Grosso, and Maranhão. Organized in similar ways to the entradas from Bahia and Pernambuco in the sixteenth century, the later entradas enslaved thousands of Indians and made use of mixed-race backwoodsmen as guides and interpreters.

One of the few cautionary notes in Gandavo's glowing portrait of slavery in Brazil was that Indian slaves had a tendency to rise up in revolt or to run away. Were this not the case, he was of the opinion that "the wealth of Brazil would be incomparable."[97] Indians challenged not only slavery but the entire Portuguese colonial enterprise. It is now time to turn our attention to the roles of Indian go-betweens—physical, transactional, and representational—and to their resistance to Portuguese colonization.

7. Resistance

> . . . a new kind of superstition that was born among the Indians . . .
>
> *Jesuit Annual Letter, 1585*

In 1585, rumors of a new prophet in the sertão spread through the parishes and sugar plantations of the Bay of All Saints. Coming on the heels of an epidemic of measles, described as the "most cruel illness ever seen in Bahia," and in the midst of repeated entradas into the sertão to descend thousands of new Indians to the decimated slave houses on the coastal sugar plantations, the rumors gave hope to scores of slaves, especially to Indians but also to Africans. For this movement's leader, known as "Pope" to his followers, preached that "God was coming now to free them from their captivity and to make them lords of the white people." Believers would "fly to the sky," whereas "those who did not believe . . . would be converted into birds and animals of the forest." The prophet proclaimed further that on earth the crops of the believers would grow of their own accord and that believers would not want for food or drink. He led rituals through which they achieved a state of true holiness known as *santidade*.[1]

This religious movement, known to historians today as the Santidade de Jaguaripe, is a complex example of resistance to Portuguese colonialism.[2] As the Portuguese committed themselves to Brazil in the sixteenth century, disease, death, and slavery seemed to seal the fate of the native peoples. Faced with new and deadly pathogens, with the insatiable European need for laborers to exploit dyewood and sugar, with moral arguments that justified their enslavement, with the intense men of the Society of Jesus, and with the slow but steady establishment of Portuguese settlements, the indigenous peoples of Brazil found their traditional way of life assailed from many directions. It has been all too easy to characterize this process as the inexorable march forward of Europeans and the rapid retreat of Indians. Lost in this approach is an understanding of how native peoples resisted colonization.

The Santidade de Jaguaripe is not typical of the initial resistance of indigenous groups to Europeans. From the earliest documented encounters, it is clear that when representational go-betweens on the Indian side expressed resistance to the European presence in Brazil, they did so through their traditional religious and political leaders: chiefs, village shamans, and wandering prophets. Chiefs could easily prevent Europeans from landing and getting water, they could refuse to trade, and they could reject the European men left among them. When colonization began and intruded sharply on Indian lands, hunting grounds, personal freedoms, and village autonomy, chiefs frequently resisted Portuguese advances through war. Village shamans also resisted the imposition of colonial rule. When the Society of Jesus arrived in 1549, shamans challenged their message by preaching against Jesuit missionaries. The wandering prophets who arose periodically among indigenous groups also incorporated rejection of colonial rule in their messianic preaching. All these forms of resistance emerged from the traditional Indian village structure and were led by traditional leaders, such as chiefs and shamans.

As the Santidade de Jaguaripe makes clear, however, indigenous resistance to European colonialism in Brazil evolved as circumstances themselves changed. As the presence of the Portuguese grew in Brazil, and as the coastal villages found their social and political structures undermined by war, slavery, and disease, new forms of resistance articulated by new go-betweens appeared. No longer traditional village leaders, these new representational go-betweens led the resistance of Indians who lived not in traditional villages but in Jesuit aldeias or as slaves working on sugar plantations. New wandering prophets led religious movements that encouraged slaves to rebel against their masters, to flee slavery, and to reject the authority of the Jesuits. These wandering prophets were not traditional shamans from the villages, but rather Indians who themselves had been slaves; residents in Jesuit missions; or refugees from epidemics, war, or disbanded villages. They were new kinds of representational go-betweens who, by the time of the Santidade de Jaguaripe in the mid-1580s, preached alternatives to both the traditional Indian village life and the Portuguese colony. In the most developed colonial areas, religious movements of resistance, such as the

Santidade de Jaguaripe, blended Christian, Indian, and possibly African beliefs into a meaningful religious experience for slaves and others marginalized in the Portuguese colony. Because so many slaves fled from the plantations to join these movements, they powerfully challenged the order and authority of Portuguese colonial rule.

At times of contact, the traditional leaders of indigenous groups—the chiefs and shamans—had great power, particularly when Europeans had no interpreters, and they often used it to resist encounters with Europeans. In the far north of Brazil, for example, indigenous chiefs and shamans generally did not welcome Europeans and quickly turned their people against them. Anghiera uses the adjectives "big," "grim," "cruel," and "threatening" to describe the thirty-two men who met Pinzón's men in 1500 and prevented them from approaching a village at night. According to Anghiera, Pinzón's men concluded that "they never wanted peace, agreement, or friendship." Vespucci's account of his first landing in northern Brazil in 1501 illustrates that an Indian group cautiously studied the Europeans and refused to approach the bells and mirrors left as presents until the Europeans were "far out at sea." When two Portuguese men willingly followed Indians inland, they never returned, and Vespucci describes how a third sailor was killed, cooked, and eaten in full view of the men on the ships. Indians in northern Brazil whom Gonneville met on his return voyage to France in 1504 also prevented his landing. At an anchorage in northern Brazil, when several men went ashore for water, the Indians who had been watching them attacked, taking two captive, killing a third, and wounding four others.[3]

In contrast, Pedro Álvares Cabral's landing in central Brazil provoked little hostility. As we have seen, Cabral carefully managed the first encounter, but local chiefs also played a role. Pero Vaz de Caminha singles out several men who might have been chiefs or shamans. One he describes as an older man "covered with feathers"; this man had sheltered the degredado that Cabral had sent ashore. Two others he describes as "talking" among the multitudes. One of these speakers he thought was counseling against interaction; the other, he believed, seemed to be saying that the Portuguese, and the mass he had just witnessed, were a "good thing."[4]

Chiefs could easily turn their warriors against the Europeans and destroy their first toeholds along the coast of Brazil, as Vespucci found out. On his last expedition to Brazil, Vespucci writes that he left twenty-four armed men behind in 1504 with provisions for six months. According to the royal treasurer on Sebastian

Cabot's expedition to the Río de la Plata twenty years later (1525–1527), Indians killed all of these men because of the conflicts that arose.[5]

As contact increased, Indian chiefs often advocated war against the European invaders. War was one of the most powerful tools that chiefs and shamans could wield, because Indians held the early advantage. War was a central part of life among the Tupi-Guarani-speaking peoples living along the coast of Brazil, and coastal Tupi and Guarani were fierce and intimidating warriors, as Europeans immediately noticed. In 1502 Vespucci wrote of them that "they are a warlike people and very cruel to one another" and that "when they fight, they kill one another most cruelly." The report of Binot Paulmier de Gonneville's landing noted that Arosca, who was at peace with neighboring chiefs, nevertheless went to war twice during the six months that Gonneville and his men were living among them. Each time he led five to six hundred men into battle. Part of the reason Arosca agreed to send his son, Essomericq, as well as Namoa, with Captain Gonneville when he set sail, was so they might return with knowledge of European weaponry. Pero Lopes de Sousa recorded in his diary a combat he witnessed in Bahia in 1531 between rival indigenous groups. Each side had fifty canoes with approximately sixty men in each. Armed with shields and bows and arrows, the two armies fought from midday to sunset. The victors took many captives.[6]

As the first settlements grew, the Tupi and Guarani who lived alongside in their traditional villages often turned against the colonists, even though the Portuguese thought of them as allies. Usually the cause was the widespread and indiscriminate enslavement of Indians. These wars doomed some of the early colonies in Brazil, such as that of Pero de Góis, who held the grant of Paraíba do Sul, and who found his colony ruined in 1546 after neighboring Indians, with whom the Portuguese had been living in peace, rose up against his colonists and killed twenty-five of them, burned the canefields, stole the artillery, and left everything else in ruins.[7]

Hans Staden observed resistance from the neighboring Indians of Pernambuco on his first trip to Brazil, when he was a gunner on a ship commanded by the Portuguese captain Penteado. On arriving in Pernambuco in January 1548, Staden reports that the Indians had "rebelled against the Portuguese who had enslaved them" and had attacked the Portuguese settlement at Iguarassú, which was a sugar mill built outside the main settlement of Olinda. The people of Olinda "were powerless to help the settlers [of Iguarassú], for they feared an attack from the savages." At the request of Duarte Coelho, forty of Penteado's men sailed to Iguarassú and joined ninety colonists, thirty African slaves, and an unspecified number of Indian slaves against, Staden claims, eight thousand Indians. The siege lasted one month, during which time the Portuguese were unable to obtain food; the siege was only broken when some of Penteado's crew were able to successfully leave and return with "victuals." According to Staden, once the blockade had been broken, the Indians sued for peace.[8]

Attacks against Portuguese settlements increased as outlying fields, sugar mills (*engenhos*), and roaming cattle spread. In 1553, Indians rose up against the Portuguese colonists in Pernambuco, burning two sugar mills: the one at Iguarassú and another at Olinda. In 1555, fifty Indians who were living in supposed peace with the Portuguese in Bahia attacked the sugar mill of António Cardoso outside of Salvador, saying that "the land was theirs." The Indians then shot at a traveler who was on the road between Salvador and the engenho with three slaves, attacked three cowboys, and took cattle belonging to Garcia d'Avila. Later, on the *roças*, or "cultivated fields," outside of Salvador, they killed an African slave, captured several slave women, and seized a youth working on his father's field. They also imprisoned three men living in the outly-ing Indian villages. Three years later, in Espírito Santo, the Indians, who were also nominally at peace with the Portuguese, rose up against the colonists, killed and maimed many, and surrounded the colonists in the town, attacking them by night and day. If the colonists had not been helped, the new governor of Brazil wrote to the new young king Sebastião, "they could not escape from being killed and eaten." In 1559 a Jesuit wrote to the father general in Rome that the Indians surrounding Ilhéus had burned four sugar mills and had stolen all of the property in them. The colonists had barricaded themselves in the town, but the Indians had them surrounded, so they could not look for food, and many were starving.[9]

Not only were these attacks devastating for the early European settlements, but they clearly reveal the depth and the success of Indian resistance. More than fifty years after first contact, Europeans such as Staden, Léry, or Thevet remained highly impressed with the intensity of indigenous warfare. Hans Staden writes that he accompanied a Tupinambá war party on an eleven-day warring expedi-tion (in 1554) that ventured into Tupinikin and Portuguese territory, very near to where he himself had been captured. The war party consisted of thirty-eight canoes, each with eighteen men. When they spotted their enemy, they gave

Figure 7.1. Indigenous warfare. Jean de Léry, *Histoire d'un voyage faict en la terre du Brésil* (Geneva, 1594). Courtesy of the John Carter Brown Library at Brown University.

chase for four hours, and when their arrows and shot ran out, they stormed the canoes and captured the men. Jean de Léry describes a combat (in 1557) that he viewed as "cruel and terrible beyond belief," with Indian warriors "so relentless in their wars that as long as they can move arms and legs, they fight on unceasingly, neither retreating nor turning their backs."[10] Illustrations of Indians at war appeared in many of these chronicles. In an early edition of Léry's history, the ferocity of hand-to-hand combat (lower half of woodcut) is contrasted with a more relaxed portrait of village life (upper half) (Fig. 7.1).

European observers recognized the role that chiefs and shamans played as they defined the enemy and prepared their warriors for intense combat. Staden and Léry describe how chiefs exhorted their men in long speeches to remember their ancestors and their honor and reminded them of their enemies. In the words of Léry, a Tupinambá chief placed a choice before his men: " 'Let ourselves all be killed and eaten, or avenge our own.' " When chief Konyan Bebe led his warriors on the warpath, Staden describes how he would pace back and forth in the camp each night, "haranguing" the men but also entreating each man "to take note of his dreams that night" and "to see to it that their dreams were good."[11]

In response to the changes of the sixteenth century, chiefs began to define new enemies and to label specific groups of Europeans as friends or foes. When the Tupinambá captured Staden, he reports that a chief approached him and said that "having captured me from the Perot, that is to say the Portuguese, they would now take vengeance on me for the death of their friends." The Portuguese had become enemies, and therefore Staden, who lived among them, would be cannibalized. Similarly, when the war party that Staden accompanied returned with Tupinikin and Christian mameluco captives from the Portuguese colony at São Vicente, the mamelucos as well as the Tupinikin were cannibalized because the Christian mamelucos of São Vicente had also become enemies of the Tupinambá. So, too, did the Tupinambá subject captured Portuguese to the cannibalism ceremony. Thevet describes meeting the Tupinambá chief Quoniambec, "the most feared and dreaded," especially by the Portuguese, because "he had killed many." Thevet characterized his "palace" as a longhouse (loge), just like all the others, and "decorated outside with the heads of Portuguese." [12]

Although war is a violent engagement between two opposing groups and signifies the breakdown of negotiation and exchange, third parties are nevertheless often to be found working for each side as spies, message carriers, interpreters, and sources of information. Indigenous chiefs acquired transactional go-betweens, frequently Europeans or mamelucos, who provided them with arms and battle counsel highly useful for fighting Europeans. There was no lack of such potential go-betweens who might serve on the Indian side. In 1551, the Jesuit brother Pero Correia wrote to the head of the Jesuit assistancy in Portugal that he, along with five other brothers and Father Leonardo Nunes, went looking for a Christian man who had been living for eight or nine years among the Indians. The man was living deep in the sertão, for it took fifteen days, traveling mainly downstream by canoe, to reach him. When Nóbrega visited Pernambuco in 1551, he observed that the sertão was "full of the children of Christians, old and young, males and females, who live in and are being raised in the customs of the Indians." The martyrdom of Pero Correia and João de Sousa in 1554 was partially due to such go-betweens on the Indian side. Both Correia and Sousa were experienced interpreters, but on their mission among the Guarani, they met two Europeans who acted as interpreters for the Guarani. These men urged the Guarani to attack the Jesuits by claiming that Correia and Sousa were opening up a road that would be used by their enemies to make war against them. [13]

When Anchieta and Nóbrega gave themselves as hostages in Iperoig, a Tupinambá chief relied on his French son-in-law and other interpreters for information. Anchieta describes a tense meeting with this chief, known to be a great enemy of the Portuguese and a loyal ally to the French. The chief conferred with a French interpreter who accompanied him. Despite the fact that the chief mistrusted the Portuguese, he accepted advice from the French interpreter, as well as from his French son-in-law, which led to peace negotiations.[14]

European transactional go-betweens certainly helped individual chiefs become more powerful in war in the short run, but over the long term they escalated intertribal warfare by introducing more powerful weapons, by offering strategic counsel, and, most significantly, by drawing chiefs into European rivalries. The increased power of traditional enemies masked the growing presence of the Europeans. The war parties mounted by the Tupinambá against the Portuguese in São Vicente were a form of indigenous resistance to colonization, but they also served the interests of the French. Similarly, Tupinikin attacks on the Tupinambá tribes weakened the French, which aided the Portuguese colonial enterprise.

Indian shamans and wandering prophets were a second major source of traditional indigenous resistance to the Portuguese, a role made clear in Jesuit letters. Shamans and wandering prophets customarily held privileged positions as intermediaries between the sacred and the worldly, the very roles coveted by the Jesuits. The Jesuits quickly recognized their influence: "These are our greatest adversaries," Nóbrega wrote of them in 1549. Using their traditional roles and powers, shamans and wandering prophets represented the Jesuits and the Portuguese colonial enterprise as evil.[15]

According to modern anthropologists and ethnohistorians, the shaman (*pajé*) and the wandering prophet (*caraíba*) were two distinct religious specialties in Tupi societies. A pajé lived in a village and was a healer and interpreter of dreams, whereas the caraíba was a messianic wandering prophet whose power extended beyond the village. The first Jesuits typically called the village shaman "*hechicero*" or "*feiticeiro*," the respective Spanish and Portuguese terms for "sorcerer." They saw them primarily as healers who cured through trickery. By the early seventeenth century, a Jesuit dictionary drew a distinction between the resident pajé *catú* (of good) and the pajé *angaiba* (of evil). The first was in favor of the common good, such as gaining victory in war, whereas the latter could cause sickness and death or cause the fish not to be caught. In one of his texts written after 1583, the Jesuit Fernão Cardim defines "caraíba" as "Santo" or "Santidade" and describes him as a "feiticeiro," usually "an Indian of evil ways" who emerges from time to time in the sertão, deceiving all. A Jesuit dictionary of the early seventeenth century translates "holy thing" (*santa coisa*) as "caraíba." Further complicating the roles of caraíbas, the sixteenth-century Jesuits recognized that Europeans could be seen as caraíbas. Anchieta defined "caraíba" as "holy or supernatural thing" but noted that in the beginning the Portuguese were called caraíba because "they came from afar, from another world, from over the water."[16]

Staden, Thevet, and Léry provide descriptions of the power of the shamans and wandering prophets in traditional village settings. Staden and Thevet fold the two roles of shaman and wandering prophet into one. Staden uses the word "*paygi*" (pajés), but describes caraíbas when he defines them as "certain wise ones among them" who "travel every year throughout the whole country, visiting all the huts." These men have the power to cause the *tammarakas* (*maracás*, "rattles") to speak and to grant "whatever is required of them." Thevet describes "*pagés*" (pajés) as the interpreters of dreams and healers. Each village had two. Thevet introduces "*charaïbes*" (caraíbas), defining them also as pajés. He sees both pajés and caraíbas as very powerful persons, almost demigods, but of "evil ways"; imposters who do not remain in one place and seek to mislead their neighbors as "ministers of the Devil." Jean de Léry draws clearer distinctions between the two: the pajé he defines as a "barber or doctor" (*barbier ou médecin*), and the caraíbas were "false prophets coming and going from village to village" and promising great things through their communication with the spirits.[17]

As the Jesuits began their mission and insisted on acceptance of Christian doctrine, many indigenous shamans and wandering prophets began to challenge Jesuit teachings and interpret them in a negative light. Using their authority as healers, shamans proclaimed that the Jesuits, through their teachings, brought death. One Jesuit wrote that the shamans persuaded the Indians that "in baptism we put death into them"; they told Indians, moreover, that calling on Jesus or making the sign of the cross was the "sign" of death. When an Indian chief in Bahia died after having been baptized, the shamans spread the word that "the holy baptism had killed him." Shamans would persuade the sick that the Jesuits were trying to kill them, and would slyly extract knives, scissors, and fishhooks from the bodies of the ill Indians, claiming that the Jesuits had put them there.

Although the Jesuits would see it only as deception and trickery, the symbolic value of the knives, scissors, and fishhooks—all items that Europeans had introduced into Brazil—powerfully underscored the point of the shaman: that the Portuguese, of whom the Jesuits were a part, were killing Indians.[18]

Many Jesuits saw the shamans as acting for the devil in, as they saw it, the devil's campaign against their Christian mission. "Satan, who rules in this land," wrote António Pires, "ordered and taught the sorcerers many lies and deceptions to impede the good of souls." João de Azpilcueta described how shamans portrayed the Jesuits as little better than the slave-hungry Portuguese colonists. The shamans "tell the Indians that I teach them so that when they are our slaves, I will have less work," he wrote, and continued to explain how shamans dismissed the progress being made as the governor ordered new construction in the city of Salvador. According to Azpilcueta, shamans preached that the fort being built was to be a prison for Indians or a place to kill them, and the fountain under construction was to be a site where Indians would be drowned.[19]

One of the few religious practices that the Jesuits and other Europeans understood about Tupi and Guarani groups in sixteenth-century Brazil was the periodic emergence of wandering, messianic prophets. After residing in Brazil for only a few months, Manoel da Nóbrega wrote in 1549 that the Indians "worshiped nothing nor knew God," but that "from time to time a sorcerer [hechicero] appeared in the villages" and "preached that there was no need to work, that the crops would grow on their own, that arrows would hunt the game, that the old would become young, that warriors would kill many of their enemies, and that the people would eat many captives." After hearing these words, which the caraíba distorted by speaking them through a gourd, the Indians, "especially the women, began to shake, throw themselves on the ground, and froth at the mouth." Then, "the hechicero would cure them and holiness [santidad] would enter them," Nóbrega concludes.[20]

The early Portuguese colonists coined the term "*santidade*," "sanctity" or "holiness," to describe such wandering prophets and their messianic movements. One of the first uses of the term emerges in 1544, after Martim Afonso de Sousa had left São Vicente, and his wife, acting for him, decreed from Lisbon that the Portuguese colonists of São Vicente were permitted to go to the Piratininga Plateau to trade for slaves "except when the Indians of the said plateau are in the midst of a *santidade*." No one could go at that time, she ordered, "because I am informed of the great risk."[21]

Those who had lived in Brazil for a number of years recognized that santi-dades were dangerous for outsiders. The Jesuit brother Pero Correia explained why. In 1551, Correia describes a santidade in a letter, explaining that after the arrival of a "saint" who promised health, and victory in battle, and who deco-rated pumpkins to look like heads—complete with hair, noses, eyes, mouths, and adorned with colorful feathers—the Indians, men and women, danced and sang around them night and day. These dances were accompanied by copious amounts of drinking. Two of the best interpreters of São Vicente, recounts Pero Correia, went to a village where a santidade was going on, and the "saints" ordered them killed, and they were.[22]

Other early descriptions of santidades furnished by the Jesuits stress that the messianic prophets promised to return youth to the elderly, that the santidades appeared from year to year, and that the Indians were incapable of renounc-ing their faith in them.[23] The gifted Jesuit linguist João de Azpilcueta, who participated in one of the first expeditions (1553–1555) into the sertão behind Porto Seguro, describes in detail a festival that had all the characteristics of what the Jesuits and Portuguese colonists called a "santidade." In an Indian village, he writes, where many Indians from different villages had gathered, a large house had been constructed in the plaza. Inside the house was a smaller house in which a pumpkin was dressed to look like a human head. The Indians told us, he explains, that this was our saint, that they called it "Amabozaray, which means a person who dances and fights, and who had the ability to make the old people young again."[24] The Indians painted themselves and dressed themselves in feathers, Azpilcueta continues, "dancing and making many gestures, twisting their mouths, howling like dogs." Each carried in his hand a painted pumpkin and proclaimed that these were saints, "who ordered the Indians not to plant because the plants would grow on their own and [not to hunt because] the arrows would fly to the plains and kill the game." This santidade in the sertão of Porto Seguro also posed great danger to the small group of European men. When the men arrived at an Indian village, they found it full of Indians from other villages, because they had come to attend "the festivals of the sorcerers." Only through the intervention of an Indian chief accompanying Azpilcueta was the expedition allowed to stay in the village, but only for one night.[25]

Jean de Léry gives a detailed description of a ceremony (which would have taken place in 1557) led by caraíbas, and his understanding is enlightened by the Norman interpreters who served as his informants. Léry writes that the rituals were inspired by "certain false prophets that they call *caraïbes*" (caraíbas), who traveled from village to village proclaiming that "by their communication with spirits they can give to anyone they please the strength to vanquish enemies in war, and, what is more, can make grow the big roots and the fruits . . . produced by this land of Brazil." The ceremony that Léry observed began after Indians from neighboring regions arrived at one village. Some ten or twelve caraíbas separated the assembled five or six hundred Indians into houses, one for the men, one for the women, and one for the children. The men began to sing a repetitive "he he he he" from their house and the women replied in turn, "he he he he." Léry, who was with the women, observed that "not only did they howl, but also, leaping violently into the air, they made their breasts shake and they foamed at the mouth." Then, Léry, against the advice of his Norman interpreter, secretly entered the men's house and saw "three circles, and in the middle of each circle there were three or four of these *caraïbes*, richly decked in robes, head-dresses, and bracelets made of beautiful natural feathers of various colors, holding in each hand a *maraca*." The shaman shook the rattles continuously so that "the spirit might thereafter speak." Léry noticed that the shaman would repeatedly take "a wooden cane four or five feet long, at the end of which was burning some of the dried herb *petun* [*petum*, "tobacco"]," and blowing the smoke in all directions they would say, "So that you may overcome your enemies, receive all of you the spirit of strength." When Léry asked his interpreter what was being said, the interpreter replied that the songs lamented the passing of the ancestors and praised the day when the living would rejoin them. The songs referred to a previous flood, the interpreter told him, when the waters "had once swelled so high above their bounds that all the earth was covered, and all the people in the world were drowned, except for the ancestors, who took refuge in the highest trees." [26] An illustration of a caraíba, as it appears in an early edition of Léry, shows the caraíba holding a maracá and wearing a feather crown (Fig. 7.2).

Léry's detailed description brings out the role not only of the caraíba, but also of the maracá, tobacco, and the ancestors. In Staden's far less detailed account of "a great feast" with "drinking, singing, and prophesying, and many other strange ceremonies" orchestrated by the "wise men," maracás and tobacco are also present. In his account, the wise men "ordain a day, and fix upon one of the huts, which they cause to be cleared," and invite the men to come, each with his own tammaraka (maracá). The men of the village offer presents to the wise men, one of whom "takes each Tammaraka separately and fumigates it with a herb

Figure 7.2. A Caraíba holding a maraca. Jean de Léry, *Histoire d'un voyage faict en la terre du Brésil* (Paris, 1594). Courtesy of the John Carter Brown Library at Brown University.

called Bittin [*petum,* "tobacco"]." The wise man then speaks to the rattle, but Staden writes that "the people imagine that the rattle is speaking." [27]

Tobacco appears in several descriptions of santidades. Léry and Thevet both describe how the tobacco leaf, dried and rolled into a large palm leaf, made something resembling a candle. After lighting the end, one received the smoke

Figure 7.3. Smoking and making fire. André F. Thevet, *Les singularitez de la France Antarctique* (Paris, 1558). Courtesy of the John Carter Brown Library at Brown University.

"through the nose and mouth." The Indians say "that it is very healthy," and that taken in this fashion, "it takes away hunger and thirst," writes Thevet, whose account includes an illustration of smoking tobacco (Fig. 7.3). Léry describes constant usage among men, but not women, to the point where warriors went off to war with their tobacco and did not need food for three or four days. Léry tried smoking and reported simply that "it seemed to satisfy and ward off hunger." But Thevet noted that "if one takes too much of this smoke, or perfume, it goes to the head and makes one drunk, like the bouquet of a strong wine." For those not used to it, he informs his readers, "the smoke causes sweating and dizziness to the point of fainting, as I have experienced myself."[28]

Anchieta describes *santidades* as the most important belief of the Tupi-Guarani-speaking peoples in his account "Customs of the Indians," written on the eve of the appearance of the Santidade de Jaguaripe in 1584. "What they most believe," he writes, is that from time to time their "feiticeiros, whom they call pajés, invent new dances and songs . . . and spread them throughout the land, and occupy the Indians in drinking and dancing all day and night." A "feiticeiro," who is also called "santidade," will make many promises, Anchieta explains, for example, that the food will grow on its own, that the hunted game will come right to their houses, or that the old women will become young again. Anchieta describes the pajés as claiming to have a spirit within them and to be able to communicate this spirit to others by fumigating and exhaling over the new disciples. At these times, those who receive the smoke tremble and sweat profusely. Anchieta leaves little doubt that he believes all this to be the work of the devil and the cause of the ruin of Indians.[29]

As more Europeans established themselves in Brazil, their presence diluted the powers of traditional chiefs, shamans, and wandering prophets. Chiefs found that war against the Portuguese increasingly led to disaster. Powerful chiefs had adapted to European warfare and used European and mameluco transactional go-betweens to give them battle counsel. Nevertheless, although coastal Indians saw themselves as braver in battle and as superior warriors to the Portuguese, they were increasingly at a disadvantage when horses, ships, and European weaponry were used against them. The destruction of independent villages in coastal regions led to the loss of the traditional role of the chief, as well as that of the village shaman.[30]

The second and third governors of Brazil, Duarte da Costa and Mem de Sá, used large forces of able-bodied soldiers and colonists, as well as greater stores of artillery, to organize scorched-earth campaigns against threatening Indian villages. These campaigns pitted the governors' entire force against individual villages and chiefs. After the attack on António Cardoso's sugar mill, and the seizing of cattle, slaves, and colonists outside of Salvador in 1555, Governor Duarte da Costa sent his son to head a series of punitive expeditions. On the first expedition, 70 foot soldiers and six horsemen marched against the village from which the war party had come. In addition, a Portuguese ship approached by sea. The soldiers found the village emptied of women and children and surrounded by a strong palisade, with earthen traps dug deep into the earth with sharp spikes at the bottom and covered on top with leaves. After hard fighting, the soldiers entered the village, captured the chief, and burned the village and two neighboring ones, while the captain of the ship captured two small boats and two canoes. A few days later, the governor ordered a force of 160 men to retake all the seized cattle and to free the kidnapped cowboys; subsequently, he sent two armed boats to claim the slaves and others captured by Indians. Then he sent nearly 200 men with some horsemen and slaves to free those still trapped in the engenho of António Cardoso. In this last engagement, five villages around the mill were burned, and the horsemen killed many Indians. On his way back to Salvador, the governor's son burned three more villages, and the following week, his father ordered him to burn five more.[31]

Duarte da Costa's attacks against the surrounding Indian chiefs led to the creation of six companies of twenty men each to defend the fields around the city. But neither this, nor the burning of sixteen villages, completely ended the resistance. When Mem de Sá arrived in Salvador in 1557, he described Bahia as "a land at war." The Portuguese did not dare work their fazendas except just around the city, and they had no slaves to work for them "because the Indians do not want peace." Nóbrega later thought that the colonists of Bahia never believed it would be possible to defeat the Indians of Bahia. The situation was not much different along the coast south of Salvador, where the Indians in Ilhéus and Espírito Santo had risen in rebellion and had completely surrounded the Portuguese settlements.[32]

Mem de Sá's campaigns against Indian chiefs utilized ships, European arms, horses, and Indian warriors. His son commanded six ships and a force of two hundred men that set off for Espírito Santo; there the fighting was so fierce that Mem de Sá's son died in battle and his nephew led the soldiers to what the Portuguese claimed was a victory. The governor wrote that the Indians were "pacified" and that "it seems that they will not soon raise their heads again." But resistance through war was hardly over. There were several subsequent uprisings in Espírito Santo during Mem de Sá's term; in 1560 it was virtually abandoned, and by 1562, there were no working sugar mills. Mem de Sá personally went to Ilhéus with food and munitions to save the colonists there. "God gave him a great victory," a Jesuit wrote from Bahia, and noted that after the Indians had been "well punished," Mem de Sá made peace with them. Sá returned to Bahia and initiated a campaign against the independent chiefs of coastal Bahia and the Bay of All Saints. He sent several large armed expeditions that included large forces of Indian warriors against chiefs in Paraguaçu and Jaguaripe.[33]

War became less successful as a form of indigenous resistance in Bahia when colonists and Crown authorities had fortified the sugar mills, erected walls around their settlements, burned Indian villages, captured powerful chiefs, and organized small companies of soldiers available to be called on in times of necessity. In a Jesuit history of Brazil written in 1584, Anchieta exaggerated the role that Mem de Sá had played in "subjugating nearly all of Brazil," but he was right in asserting that the wars waged against powerful chiefs in Bahia had dramatically deflated their strength. In all, Anchieta estimated that Sá had burned 160 Indian villages.[34] Although war continued to be an important form of indigenous resistance elsewhere, it was less so in Bahia or Pernambuco after the 1560s. Following the pattern in Bahia and Pernambuco, indigenous resistance through warfare continued but gradually became less and less viable as the Portuguese colonies entrenched themselves along the coast of Brazil.

Independent and autonomous Indian villages began to disappear along the coast in the near vicinity of Portuguese settlements in the second half of the sixteenth century. In Gandavo's description of Brazil in the 1570s, he observes that the coast was now "unpopulated" by natives, not only because the "governors and captains of the land overthrew them little by little," but also because many Indians "fled to the sertão." Nevertheless, new forms of resistance began to emerge, such as migration. In the sixteenth century, numerous chroniclers refer to large-scale migrations undertaken by Tupi-Guarani-speaking peoples. Some of these were led by persuasive prophets in search of a "land without evil"; others occurred as Tupi groups fled from the Portuguese and reestablished themselves elsewhere. Still other migrations were initiated when Indian slaves, who had been descended from the sertão with promises of living in liberty, rebelled against their enslavement. One such uprising occurred in Bahia during Holy Week in 1568. Indians rose up on several plantations, killed some Portuguese, and robbed and burned the plantations. The Indians fled to Rio Real, their original homeland.[35]

After the destruction of independent Indian villages, Indians in and near Portuguese settlements tended to live in the aldeias administered by the Jesuits or on sugar plantations as slaves. Adapted resistance that did not rely on the traditional village social and political leadership and customs then began to emerge. In particular, the santidades, which, as we have seen, had their roots in traditional religious life, became a new form of resistance to Portuguese colonialism. In the second half of the sixteenth century, santidades began to reflect the disturbing new realities in the lives of Indians. Caraíbas used santidades to represent the evils of Portuguese colonialism. Anchieta describes a caraíba (he uses the term "feiticeiro") "whom all follow and venerate as a great saint," in the sertão of Piratininga in 1557, who intended to destroy the Jesuit church. "Wherever he goes," Anchieta writes, "all follow and they wander from here to there leaving their own houses." He acquires followers by blowing smoke from his mouth over them, Anchieta explains, and in this way he gives them his spirit and makes them his followers. The people then give to the leader all that they have. From two boys in the school, the Jesuits learned much about this wandering prophet, for he had stopped at their village and stayed in their house. The wandering prophet said that he was on his way to war, to fight his enemies, but on his return, he intended to destroy the Jesuit church at Piratininga. "In no way are we afraid of him," Anchieta concludes.[36]

In 1559, Nóbrega described a santidade that erupted on a plantation in Bahia that clearly articulated resistance to slavery. It was initiated by an Indian who arrived from another village, and it was continued by a slave on the plantation. The slave called together other slaves to listen to the prophet, who predicted that he would destroy the plantation and the master of it, that he would convert all who wished into birds, that he would kill all the caterpillars that were then infesting their food plots, and that he would spare the Jesuits but would destroy their churches. The Indian further preached that the marriages celebrated by the Jesuits were "worthless" and that the men should return to their custom of having many women. The governor's bailiff went to arrest the slave, who escaped twice and hid himself in the forest. The slave eventually decided to turn himself in and ask for mercy, but the Indian prophet who introduced the santidade fled and was never found.[37]

A santidade spread in the sertão of Ilhéus in 1561 or 1562 immediately before the outbreak of the first smallpox plague. Jesuit Leonardo do Vale describes it in a letter as a "blindness" that occurred when an unknown caraíba, calling himself a saint and a prophet from the sky, arrived with predictions of things to come. The santidade in the sertão disrupted the order established by the Jesuits in the newly created aldeias of Nossa Senhora da Assunção and São Miguel. Leonardo do Vale suggests that God punished the followers of the santidade with the smallpox epidemic, which began in Ilhéus and moved up the coast and through the islands of Tinharé and Itaparica, and with a famine that followed in 1563–1564. The epidemic and famine especially affected the very places, Vale writes, where the "pilgrims first began to flee to the santidade." He singles out the aldeias of São Miguel and Nossa Senhora da Assunção as devastated. Soon thereafter, the Indians abandoned the aldeias. In a history of the aldeias of Bahia written in the 1580s, a Jesuit author blames an unnamed mameluco who, with a series of "lies," convinced the Indians to secretly abandon the Jesuit aldeias in Ilhéus. But few of those who fled in this way, the Jesuit notes, escaped from being enslaved. In other words, he implies that the mameluco engineered the flight of the aldeia Indians in order to enslave them.[38]

The power of these santidades spread beyond the aldeias and sugar plantations and into the homes of the Portuguese colonists. A Portuguese woman who had lived in Bahia all her life confessed that she had believed in one of these santidades as a girl. Luísa Barbosa revealed that when she was twelve (which would have been in 1566), a santidade arose in Bahia, and both its Christian and pagan Indian members said that "in their santidade was a God . . . who told them not to work because the crops would grow of their own accord." They also believed that "those who did not believe in the santidade would turn into sticks and stones." This santidade also contained clearly articulated animosity toward the Portuguese. Barbosa said that the followers believed that "the white people would be converted into game for them to eat" and that the "law" of the whites was worthless. At the time, Luísa Barbosa stated that all the Christian and pagan Indians living in her father's household as well as in other Portuguese households said and believed in such things, and she herself believed, too, and joined in the rituals. Only later, after all the followers of the santidade had been "extinguished and punished," did she realize that all of it was false and wrong. Many other such santidades had subsequently arisen in Bahia, she noted.[39]

One of the subsequent santidades mentioned by Luísa Barbosa might have been that of 1568. The uprising of Indian slaves during Holy Week in 1568 was caused, according to a Jesuit, by a "saint" who "spoke" among the Indians descended from a region north of Bahia, Rio Real. These Indians had entered Bahia during the famine that followed the smallpox plague that had devastated the sugar plantations as well as the Jesuit mission villages. The Jesuits believed that the Indians had been "illicitly ransomed," meaning that they had been illegally enslaved. Once the Indians "learned what it was to be a slave," a Jesuit explains, and "when they had experienced it well themselves," they saw no escape. Hence they "imagined" the saint who told them to return to their lands.[40]

When the Jesuit provincial wrote his annual letter in Latin in 1585, he provides the first description of the Santidade de Jaguaripe, the latest of the santidades to sweep Bahia. His précis of the movement outlines many of its most important features and clearly reflects how the Jesuits saw it; it was a new kind of resistance. The Jesuit provincial calls the santidade a new kind of superstition that was born among the Indians (*novum inter Indos superstitionis genus est ortum*) and locates it "in the nearby mainland" (*in Continenti proxima*), in other words, the adjacent sertão. It was a "pestilence" (*pestilentius*) because it imitated Christianity, and it was certainly the work of the devil. The provincial writes that its rites express observances of Christians, such that "the Devil could persuade" the less wise that "our ways in no way differ from their ways; and if there are nevertheless differences, our ways stray from the truth." [41]

The description of the Santidade de Jaguaripe in the provincial's letter emphasizes the extensive imitation of Christianity and of the Jesuits' own missionary practices. The provincial cites the ordaining of "a supreme high-priest of their rites, as we ordain the Pope," the consecration of bishops and priests, and the institution of the confession of sins. He thinks it would truly amaze his Jesuit readers in Portugal, Rome, and elsewhere to know that "they have schools free of charge" modeled after the Jesuits' own schools. They celebrate "masses," and from tiny balls strung together, they create "prayer circlets." They substitute gourds for the altar bell and cymbals. They manufacture books from bark and boards and embellish them with esoteric marks and letters. [42]

The rituals associated with tobacco, which were clearly drawn from the indigenous tradition, the provincial finds disgraceful and bordering on insanity. Introducing the tobacco ritual, he writes: "They think themselves, however, to possess the means of perfectly attaining virtue and sanctity at that time when they are reduced to insanity." This "insanity" emerges after drinking the "juice of a certain herb, which the Indians call petima [*petum*, "tobacco"], of very great strength." After taking the tobacco, he describes that "they fall suddenly, half alive, and tremble in all their limbs." Writhing on the ground, as if "mad," the believers "twist their mouths indecently," stick out "their tongues in an unsightly way," and "speak amongst themselves without moving their lips." The provincial thought all of this was the work of the devil, but the believers, he notes, are convinced that when these agitations end, "they are washed with water and made holy; and whoever has produced the more horrible signs is thought to have attained the more sanctity." [43]

Is this superstition or is this madness, the provincial wonders as he explains the beliefs behind the rituals. The believers say "that their ancestors are to be conveyed here in a ship" and will liberate them from "the most wretched servitude into the sweetness of freedom that they desire," and that "at the ancestors' coming the Portuguese will then at last totally perish," but if any of the Portuguese are to survive, "they will be converted into fish or pigs or similar beasts." Whoever believes all this, the provincial relates, "is promised salvation; anyone who does not will be torn up by wild beasts and birds." [44]

The provincial recognizes the power of the message of the santidade, even though he finds the beliefs absurd. When the Indians heard of the santidade and fled from the Portuguese estates, "they burned the Portuguese houses, laid waste their fields, razed the sugar mills to the ground, and cruelly put to death many Portuguese," he writes. Then he charges that the believers even killed their own children to hasten their flight. He asks rhetorically, "for why should they spare the Portuguese when, so that their own children might not be a hindrance to their flight, they either buried them alive in the ground or slaughtered them in barbarous fashion?" [45]

When the visiting inquisitor arrived in Salvador in 1591, the memory of the Santidade de Jaguaripe of 1585 was still very much on the minds of residents of Bahia. As a result of the inquisitor's call for denunciations and confessions of sins and heresies, residents of the city of Salvador and the surrounding rural parishes denounced those who consorted with the santidade. Although most of the denunciations came from the Portuguese residents of Bahia, who generally did not join the new religious movement, several mamelucos and a few Portuguese came to the inquisitor to confess that they had believed its message and had participated in its rituals. Most claimed that they had pretended to believe—that they followed the rituals on the outside only, remaining firmly Christian on the inside. These denunciations and confessions, as well as several trials initiated by the inquisitor, complement the letter written by the Jesuit provincial. Together they provide enough description to reconstruct how the Santidade de Jaguaripe resisted the expanding power of the sugar planters and royal officials of the Portuguese colony, and how new kinds of representational go-betweens created new religious beliefs and practices that challenged the Society of Jesus. [46]

From the Inquisition trials, it seems that the rumors of the new preacher in the sertão first reached the Indian slaves, African slaves, free Indians, and mamelucos living in Jaguaripe, in the southern Recôncavo of Bahia. The Recôncavo was the rich agricultural hinterland that surrounded the Bay of All Saints. The city of Salvador at the northern entrance to the bay was the "city of the king," the "court of Brazil," and the port where ten or more ships were usually at anchor loading sugar and cotton. But following Mem de Sá's defeat of the chiefs around the bay twenty years before, most of the residents of Bahia now lived outside of Salvador on their sugar plantations, ranches, or farms in the Recôncavo. According to a Portuguese colonist, the city of Salvador had at that time eight hundred heads of households, and the Recôncavo had about two thousand. Three to four thousand African slaves labored on the sugar plantations, and about eight

thousand Indians lived in Bahia, some in the Jesuit aldeias, but a greater number lived on the plantations as slaves. Jaguaripe lay at the southern edge of the
Recôncavo and therefore on the fringe of the Portuguese colony. Gabriel Soares
de Sousa describes the land around Jaguaripe as "very weak," serving only for
pasture for cattle and small ranches worked by "poor people who plant nothing more than food for their own subsistence." Up the wide Jaguaripe River,
however, a little below the waterfall, was the sugar plantation of Fernão Cabral
de Taíde. Soares de Sousa describes it as "very beautiful" and well appointed,
with a sugar mill run by water power, a church, a handsome house, and other
living quarters. Below the plantation lived some farmers who grew food crops
and sugarcane, but the land was so sandy and dry that he judged that it "doesn't
serve for much more than for wood for the mills." South of Jaguaripe the mainland bears the name Tinharé. The Recôncavo appears dotted with trees, parish
churches, and sugar mills in the detail of the Bay of All Saints that accompa-
nies the text and map drawn by Luís Teixeira between 1582 and 1585 (Map 7.1).
The *barra de* (sandbar of) Jaguaripe is clearly marked below the large island of
Itaparica.[47]

In Jaguaripe, the news of the santidade in the sertão did not immediately
cause concern. Instead, the rich sugar planter Fernão Cabral de Taíde decided
to take advantage of it, and he organized an entrada to descend the believers so
he could, many later testified, "acquire many slaves." Cabral asked none other
than Domingos Fernandes Nobre, the famous mameluco interpreter known as
"Tomacaúna," to lead the entrada of one hundred men—twenty mamelucos
supported by eighty Indian archers. With the governor's permission, the entrada
left Cabral's estate and set off into the sertão of Jaguaripe. The following year,
the governor certified that he had approved the entrada as a means to extinguish
the santidade in the sertão. Otherwise, the entrada seemed little different from
others that had headed into the sertão to descend Indians.[48]

But this entrada would pose complicated choices for its mameluco participants. The men on this entrada, mamelucos and Indian archers alike, had
already heard about the pope and his believers in the sertão. Some were inclined
to believe in his message and looked forward to meeting him. Cristovão de
Bulhões, a mixed-race mameluco/mulatto who lived on Cabral's estate in
Jaguaripe, and who would have been nineteen or twenty at the time, described
to the inquisitor that he had heard it said among the Indians that Mary was coming. He believed that "St. Mary, Our Lady, Mother of God" would descend from

Map 7.1. The Bay of All Saints, c. 1580. [Luís Teixeira], *Roteiro do Brasil*. Biblioteca da Ajuda, Lisbon.

heaven and would arrive among the Indians. It would, he thought, be a *"santidade de verdade,"* a "true holiness."[49]

The Indians and mamelucos from Jaguaripe were not the only ones who had heard about the santidade. Not very long after the entrada left Jaguaripe, another mameluco youth of approximately the same age as Cristovão de Bulhões learned from the slaves in the parish where he lived, on the other side of the Recôncavo, that "God was coming now to free them from their captivity and to make them lords of the white people" and that "those who did not believe . . . would be converted into birds and animals of the forest." This youth, Gonçalo Fernandes, was free, but his mother was an Indian slave. He wanted to go and see the pope for himself and asked Cabral for permission to join Domingos Fernandes Nobre's entrada into the sertão so that "with his own eyes he might see" the place where "it was said that God was," because "it seemed to him that this was the true God." [50]

The one hundred men who entered the sertão on the entrada led by Nobre all met the pope, as a few of them later testified before the inquisitor. According to the mameluco Bras Dias, the leader of the santidade was a baptized Christian Indian known as Antônio, who had been raised in a Jesuit mission village and who had run away from the Jesuits and "invented" the movement's beliefs and rituals in the sertão. Paulos Dias reported that his followers called Antônio "God" and said that Antônio claimed to have descended from the heavens and to have created all the animals on earth. Cristovão de Bulhões said that Antônio referred to himself as "God and Lord of the world." [51]

Domingos Fernandes Nobre confessed to meeting two congregations of the santidade: one of approximately sixty believers, and another led by Antônio, the pope. His descriptions evoke the intensity of the adherents who believed that the world as they knew it was about to be destroyed and a new one created. They spent their days in a trancelike state, participating in processions and in rituals. Domingos Fernandes Nobre first met a branch of the santidade that was carrying a sacred statue. He told the inquisitor that he removed his hat and pretended to revere it. Then, the believers showed deference to him and to his entrada of armed men when they asked for permission to hold a procession with the statue. Nobre confessed to the inquisitor that he not only gave his permission but instructed the Indians and slaves on his entrada to "help them." Later, when Nobre met Antônio, he recounted that Antônio also headed a procession. Antônio appeared leading "his followers in orderly ranks of three, the women and children following behind." They approached with their hands raised, "shaking, making movements with their feet, hands, and necks, and speaking a new language." [52]

After Nobre met Antônio in the sertão, Nobre and his men, skilled in the ways of the sertão and in the art of persuasion, convinced Antônio and his followers to descend to Jaguaripe. One of Nobre's men, Pantalião Ribeiro, later told the inquisitor that they knelt before Antônio as "if they wanted to embrace Antônio's feet," in an attempt to deceive his followers. Nobre and his men joined in the santidade. Nobre recounted that he "wailed and lamented" in the Indian custom, "jumped and celebrated" with Antônio in the "Indian way," "played" the Indian instruments, and "sang" their songs. Nobre confessed, too, that he "drank the smoke" with Antônio, "the smoke that the followers of the santidade call sacred." Ribeiro confessed that he not only took the smoke but "howled" and spoke the "gibberish" that only those of the movement understood. Most of the men on the expedition "rebaptized" themselves, adopting the name of Jesus or that of a Christian saint. An Indian rebaptized Ribeiro, giving him the name José; Domingos Fernandes Nobre said that the believers called him São Luís, or "Son of God"; and Cristovão de Bulhões said that Antônio rebaptized him, but that he had "forgotten" his name.[53]

Nobre and his men made many promises to the believers in the sertão. Cabral later revealed in a cross-examination that he had written to Nobre in the sertão and told him to tell the followers of the santidade that if they descended to his estate, he would give them lands where they could live in freedom. Cabral also suggested that Nobre promise them that they could join their church "with that of the Christians." Pantalião Ribeiro explained to the inquisitor that while he was in the sertão he continuously praised the followers of the santidade, telling them that their santidade "was very good" and that "they should come to the whites and do the ceremonies before them" because "it would seem good to them" as well.[54]

Domingos Fernandes Nobre and his men first persuaded the group with the sacred statue, some sixty believers, to descend to Cabral's estate. He sent a letter ahead, to Cabral, explaining that the believers and the statue were en route with some of the men from the entrada, but that he would continue on to meet Antônio. He counseled Cabral to keep the believers in the santidade content while he remained in the sertão. He claimed to the inquisitor that fresh reinforcements had arrived from the governor to aid him in his search for Antônio. Whether Domingos Fernandes Nobre ever convinced Antônio and his followers to descend to Cabral's estate is unclear, but at some point, on the way back to Cabral's estate, according to Paulos Dias, Antônio and his wife and children slipped away from Nobre.[55]

When the believers arrived on his estate, Cabral made no effort to censure the santidade or to isolate it. Instead, he treated them with courtesy and respect, honoring the leaders by receiving them in his house and serving them at his table. He allowed his own slaves to be baptized into the congregation. A woman known as Maria or as "Mãe de Deus" (Mother of God) was, according to several witnesses, the leader of the congregation on Cabral's estate, along with her husband, Aricute, also known as the "second pope." Cabral permitted the believers to build their own church half a league from his own house. In this church, the inquisitor learned six years later, there was an "idol of stone" that resembled "neither a man nor a woman nor any known animal." Cabral's wife confessed to the inquisitor that the woman known as Mãe de Deus came to see her in the company of four others and greeted her reverently in the "Indian custom." She, in turn, welcomed them and had fish and manioc flour served to them. Before they left, she gave Mãe de Deus some ribbons, telling her that with them she would be more venerable. Antônio da Fonseca was a boy of sixteen when "he saw with his eyes" the Indian "whom they called God and the black woman whom they called Mother of God" join with Cabral's own slaves and live in a village on his estate. Antônio's sister Maria, who was then a girl of eleven, often played with Cabral's daughters on Sundays and holy days. Once when she was at the house, she later told the inquisitor, a slave woman came to see Dona (Lady) Margarida, Cabral's wife, and asked for permission to baptize another slave into the religious movement. Dona Margarida, Maria remembered, gave her permission. Another of Cabral's slaves, who was formerly known as "Cão Grande" (Big Dog), was, according to Cristovão de Bulhões, known after his baptism as "Pai Jesu Poco," which he said meant "Tall Lord Jesus." "Poco," from the Tupi *"puku"* or *"pu'ku,"* means "long" or "tall," hence his new name "Tall Jesus" incorporated both Christian and Tupi meanings.[56]

For several months—Cabral's wife said two, Cabral said three, a kinsman said four or five, and the mameluco sugar planter and entrada leader Álvaro Rodrigues said six—the santidade church blossomed on Cabral's estate. During this time, in the absence of Nobre and the other mamelucos from Jaguaripe, Cabral protected the santidade and did nothing to challenge it. Rumors spread in the city of Salvador and through the plantations of the Recôncavo that Cabral entered the santidade church on several occasions, removing his hat as a sign of respect. Cabral at first claimed to the inquisitor that he could not remember if he took off his hat before the statue, but he later admitted that he had done so. It also came out in his trial that he gave his slaves permission to miss mass and that he gave the believers some cloth to decorate their sacred statue. The believers reciprocated by treating Cabral as a patron. Cabral was forced to reveal in his first interrogation that once when he went from his house to the village, the believers came out to greet him, waving branches and playing flutes and singing songs in the language "invented by them." According to Álvaro Rodrigues, who disliked Cabral intensely, the believers called him "Tupante," which he defined as meaning "'True God' in their language," but Cabral denied that he had been given that name. He swore to the inquisitor that he was known simply as "Carabi Poco," an Indian phrase that he said "means 'Tall Man'" (*homen grande*). *Carabi* is most probably *caraíba*, and, as we have seen above, *poco/puku/pu'ku* means "tall" or "long." Since *caraíba* has the sense of an outsider and because white men were sometimes called "caraíbas," Cabral could legitimately swear that his name meant "Tall Man." But Caraíba Pu'ku could also convey the sense of a holy leader, as in "Tall Prophet." [57]

News of the congregation quickly spread to other plantations in the Recôncavo, even though Cabral carefully regulated who visited the village of believers on his estate. Cabral stated that he allowed some Indians "who brought permission from their masters" to visit the church in return for a few chickens, but in the estimation of Fernão Cardim, the rector of the Jesuit college of Salvador, "the greater part of the male and female slaves, Indians of this land, Christian and gentiles," fled from their masters to the santidade in Jaguaripe. [58]

As slaves fled to Jaguaripe, the power of the movement as an act of resistance became clear to sugar planters. Belchior da Fonseca, a Portuguese farmer on the island of Itaparica, denounced Cabral, saying that once the santidade arrived in Jaguaripe, baptized Indian slaves began to run away from their masters. He could not remember how many slaves fled from Gaspar Francisco, who also lived on the island of Itaparica, but he estimated that ten or twelve slaves ran away from Catarina Álvares, the widow of Diogo Álvares "Caramuru," who still lived in Vila Velha, the original Portuguese settlement of Bahia. Two or three slaves ran away from Gonçalo Veloso de Barros, who lived in the city of Salvador, and Alexandre, a slave of Antônio Pires, ran away from Rio Vermelho. João Bras went to Jaguaripe to speak with Cabral, asking him to return two free Indians and a slave, all Christians, who had fled from his estate to join the believers on Cabral's. Álvaro Rodrigues complained in his denunciation to the inquisitor that "nearly all of his Indians, both enslaved and free," had fled from his estate in Cachoeira to Jaguaripe. Moreover, he emphasized to the inquisitor, the beliefs of the santidade had spread to the African slaves. [59]

Not only did slaves escape to Jaguaripe to join the santidade, becoming physical go-betweens, but independent congregations that followed the example of the Santidade de Jaguaripe began to sprout up elsewhere. In these congregations, believers initiated others into the movement and explained the meaning of the prophecies of Antônio, Mãe de Deus, Aricute, and others. Gonçalo Fernandes stated in his confession that the fame of the Santidade de Jaguaripe was so great throughout Bahia that all Indians, both slave and free, either fled from their masters to join the believers at Cabral's estate in Jaguaripe or adopted the beliefs and followed the rituals where they were. Paulo Adorno told the inquisitor that Indian slaves, both Christian and pagan, "secretly met and did the rituals." He had seen such a meeting on an afternoon on a Sunday or a holy day, a time when the sugar mills did not grind and when slaves customarily rested. He related to the inquisitor that in a straw hut on the beach at Agua dos Meninos, he observed a young girl pour water on the ground in certain spots and serve the remaining water to each of the Indians. He saw the Indians giving each other the smoke "of a leaf which they call holy leaf" and explained that "the smoke is their way of baptism." In the parish of Paripe, the believers met secretly at night in the Indian houses so that the whites would not see them. In these meetings, they took the smoke and "spoke in their language" and believed that God was coming. In another parish, Matoim, Maria Antunes denounced a mameluca for joining her slaves at night and "dancing" and doing "the ceremonies and idolatries" of the Indians. In Cachoeira, Pero de Moura saw his half brother, a mameluco, join with the Indians of Álvaro Rodrigues, who were believers. On two separate nights, he saw his half brother take the smoke and perform a ritual with his eyes closed that involved a palm leaf shaped into a ring. Pero de Moura told the inquisitor further that he heard his half brother, who was a believer, say the following: "We are drinking the smoke because this is our God who comes from Paradise." The religion even crept into the Jesuit aldeia of Santo Antônio, where, according to the Jesuits, "the ancient serpent" laid an "ambush" for the Indians when their resident Jesuit father was absent, infecting nearly all with his "poison."[60]

Congregations grew quickly because every believer was a potential minister and could quickly become a transactional go-between who drew in new converts. Manoel, an Indian slave of Antônio Pereira's, preached in the Indian language to Gonçalo Fernandes and inducted him in the parish of Paripe by blowing smoke over him. Gonçalo ran away from home, João Ribeiro told the inquisitor, and joined with the Indians and slaves who practiced santidade. Later, Gonçalo Fernandes inducted an eleven-year-old girl by exhaling smoke over her, telling her that "she was a saint," and giving her a new name.[61] Iria Álvares, an Indian believer in Matoim, tried to get her son to join, and when he would not, she barred him from her house for a month and a half. Others who spread the news of the new religion were teachers and missionaries. The Jesuits claimed that the sect had its own schools to teach the young, modeled after the Jesuit schools. The Jesuits also noticed that the pope, meaning Antônio, sent messengers to "stir up" the Indians who lived with the Portuguese. One such messenger traveled out of Bahia, to the captaincy of Porto Seguro. The missionary, an Indian named Silvestre, had been a Christian for eighteen years, according to his Portuguese master and mistress. In Porto Seguro, he attracted a sizable following as he preached the santidade's message that "the Indians would be the lords of the whites and the whites would be their slaves." [62]

Whether on Cabral's estate in Jaguaripe or in parishes in the Recôncavo, the santidade quickly became a dangerous form of resistance to slavery and to Portuguese colonial rule. Álvaro Rodrigues explicitly described to the inquisitor how the movement violently challenged the authority of slave owners: "If masters prohibited their slaves from following the cult, the slaves rose up against them" and killed, maimed, and robbed them before burning down their estates. In his eyes, the santidade was an "uprising against the whites" in which the believers "created a riot" and "laid waste to everyone." The governor shared his view. "Santidade was the cause of great unrest in this land," he wrote in 1586, because "the greater part of the Indians—both free and enslaved—ran away to it, burning plantations . . . and killing whites." He named two estates that had been torched: that of the Count of Linhares, which was the Sergipe do Conde sugar plantation inventoried in 1572 at the death of Mem de Sá, and that of Garcia d'Avila. [63]

According to the written sources, Antônio was the leader of the original santidade that became the Santidade de Jaguaripe. Antônio's origins reflect how his own life had been influenced by the preaching of the Jesuits and by slavery, disease, and the breakdown of independent Indian villages in the second half of the sixteenth century. Antônio was not raised in a traditional Indian village. Many described him as having been raised in a Jesuit mission village in Tinharé, to the south of Jaguaripe. The Jesuits first contemplated a mission in Tinharé in 1561, at the request of an Indian chief of the region whom they had baptized. When the Jesuits first visited, they estimated that the region—the island and the adjacent coast on the mainland—had twenty-four Indian villages. Soon the Jesuits created two aldeias in the immediate region: Nossa Senhora da Assunção and

São Miguel. Each mission village had a Jesuit father and brother, and between the two mission villages, six thousand Indians. As we have seen, a santidade spread in the sertão of Ilhéus in 1561 or 1562, immediately prior to the outbreak of the first smallpox epidemic. The mission villages of São Miguel and Nossa Senhora da Assunção, where Antônio is said to have been raised, were especially devastated by the epidemic and the famine that followed. The Indians soon abandoned the aldeias; some may have become slaves.[64]

Given this turbulent history, if Antônio indeed was, as Nobre reported to the inquisitor, "raised in the house of the fathers of the Society of Jesus during the time when they had mission villages in Tinharé," he most certainly had direct exposure to Christian doctrine. As a boy, he would have attended the mission school and might even have been a translator. He had certainly heard of the santidade in the sertão. He would have had to have survived the smallpox epidemic, but most likely he lost many members of his family and original village. It seems likely that he fled with the others when the Indians abandoned the mission villages with an unnamed mameluco, and possibly he became a slave. Eventually he fled to the sertão, where his own santidade began.[65]

Little is known about the other two leaders, the "second pope," Aricute, and his wife, the woman known as Maria or Mãe de Deus. Ronaldo Vainfas sees her as both a female shaman who emerged from the indigenous tradition, and the result of Jesuit preaching about Mary. The inquisitor quizzed Cabral about her, in particular regarding what his intentions were when he called her St. Mary and Mother of God. Cabral dismissed her importance. "She was a slave [boçal]," he replied, "who knew no Portuguese." His word choice, "boçal," is intriguing, for boçal (boçal in Spanish) usually refers to a newly arrived African slave, one who has not yet learned Portuguese or Spanish. No other source suggests that Mãe de Deus was an African slave, but we may conclude that Cabral used the word to underscore that she was a newly enslaved woman and therefore without any knowledge of Portuguese ways.[66]

The leaders of the santidade became representational go-betweens who redefined the meaning of life for Indians, slaves, and others marginal to the Portuguese colonial society by freely borrowing from the Jesuits' own teachings and by asserting the importance of Indian myths of origin. Both the inquisitor and the Jesuit provincial accepted as evidence of Christian teachings some beliefs that were more likely inspired by indigenous myths. For example, when the inquisitor heard that the believers proclaimed that a flood had destroyed the earth, he understood them to mean Noah's flood. When summing up the beliefs of santidade, the inquisitor explains that Antônio was also known as "Noah," and that he had escaped the flood "in the eye of a palm tree." But in the indigenous tradition, a common belief was that the earth had been destroyed by a flood and that the ancestors had been saved by floating in the eye of a palm tree. Paulos Dias, a mameluco, said that Antônio "was called in their language Tamanduaré." Another leader, sometimes called the "second pope," was known by the Indian name Aricute. In a Tupinambá myth recorded by Thevet, Tamendonare (Tamanduaré), angry at his brother Aricoute (Aricute), strikes the earth, causing a huge fountain of water to erupt, which floods the land. Tamendonare escapes into the mountains with his wife and they find refuge at the top of a palm tree. Aricoute, similarly, survives by climbing a *jenipapeiro* tree. From these two brothers are descended the Tupi peoples. Cardim records a variation on this same myth sometime after 1583. In summarizing the beliefs of the Indians of Brazil, he judges that they seemed to have no knowledge of the beginning of the world, but some knowledge of the biblical flood. He recounts that in their obscure and confused understanding, the waters drowned all except for one who survived with his pregnant sister, and from them "they have their origin." To the historian Ronaldo Vainfas, the use of these names— Tamanduaré and Aricute—surely means that Antônio and another leader were seen as possessing the divine powers of the heroes of Tupi mythology.[67]

The Jesuit provincial dismissed the use of petum (tobacco) in the santidade rituals as indecent and indicative of madness, but it was a recovery of an important indigenous ritual used by traditional caraíbas. "Drinking the smoke," by which the believers meant inhaling the smoke, had a sacred meaning in the Santidade de Jaguaripe, as Gonçalo Fernandes explained to the inquisitor: the believers "drank the smoke until they fell drunk," and through the smoke, "the spirit of holiness entered them." Drinking the smoke was a means of achieving holiness, of inducting new believers, and of passing the spirit from one believer to another. This is similar to the use of tobacco by caraíbas in ceremonies reported by Léry, Staden, and Anchieta, but apparently not to the general, non-sacred use of tobacco by Indians and Portuguese by the 1580s. In one of his texts, written after 1583, Cardim describes tobacco as the "holy herb" and cites its medicinal qualities. But Cardim's explanation of how the dried tobacco leaves were smoked through a palm straw or cane suggests that addiction had become common. "Sucking and drinking that smoke," he writes, induces pleasure and

laziness, as whole parts of days and nights are spent lying in a hammock smoking. "It is very harmful to some," Cardim explains, and "makes them drunk and
dizzy," and others "drool at the mouth." Cardim relates that many Portuguese
took the smoke for its medicinal value, but it was also seen as a wicked habit
(*vício*) or as slothful because the Portuguese who took it wasted days and nights
smoking.[68] The Santidade de Jaguaripe, in contrast, restored the sacred use of
tobacco in ceremonies led by caraíbas.

In the inquisition trials, the words *abusão*, literally "abusion," and *erronia*,
"error," are used to describe the santidade to the inquisitor, suggesting that
those who participated, or who observed the rituals, clearly understood that
the religious movement directly copied Christian practices, though in faulty or
corrupted ways. The men on the expedition repeatedly told the inquisitor that
the movement "imitated" and "counterfeited" the rites of the Christian church.
Bras Dias reported that practitioners placed crosses in piles of rocks, and around
them they drew lines on the ground in all directions. Antônio baptized his wife
and children, Bras Dias continued, by raising a bowl of water and pouring it
over their heads, blessing them. He described baptisms in which men were given
the name Jesus, and women, the name Maria. Domingos Fernandes Nobre noted
that the followers of the santidade built churches with altars adorned with candlesticks, vestries, and baptismal fonts. Diogo Dias reported that the believers had made a chair out of one piece of wood, which they used to confess the
women; he added that the believers used prayer beads and read "in their way"
from books made of leaves of wood. The Jesuits clearly saw the 1585 santidade as
more dangerous than previous santidades because of these Christian influences.
Whereas the belief that there was no need to plant, the use of smoke, the labeling
of the Portuguese as evil, and the belief in the return of ancestors were common
in previous santidades, the Santidade de Jaguaripe copied recognizable Christian sacraments, such as the mass or confession, in such a way that it challenged
the Jesuits' own mission.[69]

The millenarianism of the Santidade de Jaguaripe lay at the core of its spiritual
message and served as its most potent call for resistance. Believers rejected the
authority of slaveholders and predicted the imminent overthrow of slave society.
Christian teachings of the apocalypse, combined with Tupi and Guarani beliefs in
a "land without evil," created the millenarian message of the movement. Periodic
migrations in search of a "land without evil" are, according to anthropologists,
a characteristic of Tupi and Guarani indigenous culture.[70] But the millenarian

message of the Santidade de Jaguaripe also drew from the Christian belief in the second coming of Christ, the dawn of a new age, and the punishment of sinners.

In millenarian movements, believers seek to escape from what Vittorio Lanternari calls a "bitter and painful present" and hope for "a radiant future wherein all evil will be erased." According to scholars, disasters, crises of subsistence, civil wars, colonialism, the rapid spread of capitalism, or relative deprivation can encourage the spread of millenarian ideas because, in the words of Ted Daniels, "old myths about the meaning of humanity do not meet changing circumstances; they are no longer relevant." Believers are prepared to sacrifice to be among those who will be saved in the next world: a world of peace, harmony, equality, and happiness. Sacrifice may take the form of moving to a new holy city, sharing one's possessions, failing to plant the crops needed for survival, or passively withdrawing from the world to await the dawn of a new age. Retribution can be violent or nonviolent, but believers expect a superhuman agent to defeat the evil loose in the world. Because millenarians see the world as fundamentally evil, they desire intensely that those who cause that evil should pay for their sins. Although millenarian movements are religious in tone, they invariably become political, and conflict escalates when movements challenge the right and authenticity of extant political authorities. Not infrequently, this leads to deep and potentially devastating conflicts with established authorities.[71]

The millenarian urgency of Antônio's message can be seen in the confessions of those who believed. Luísa Rodrigues, the mameluca daughter of a Portuguese notary public, confessed that she believed out of ignorance that "Our Lady and Our Lord" would return to walk on earth. The only Indian believer interrogated by the inquisitor was a woman who told him that it was "true" that the followers said that "God Our Lord would descend from heaven, and that God would change this world and that when he came, all would die, and that after they died, they would rise." Gonçalo Fernandes confessed to the inquisitor that the followers believed that "their God was coming soon to free them from slavery" and "to make them lords of the white people." The "whites would become their slaves," he said, while those who did not believe "would be converted into birds and beasts of the forest."[72]

Álvaro Rodrigues, the veteran mameluco slave trader and grandson of Diogo Álvares "Caramuru," saw the millenarianism of the santidade as its most dangerous feature. He described to the inquisitor how the believers no longer planted because they believed that their food and drink would grow for them of their own accord and that their vegetables "would be bigger than those of others," and that they "would not run out." The leaders of the santidade told him, moreover, that "they had no fear of swords nor of chains because the iron would change into wax and would not harm them."[73]

In Christianity, millenarian ideas appear in the prophecies associated with the Day of Judgment, as expressed in the book of Revelation, in which the messiah returns on a white horse leading heavenly armies to make war against a ten-horned beast, the false prophet, and thereafter creates a New Jerusalem where the faithful will live with God, the messiah. Then Jesus inaugurates the "millennium," the one-thousand-year reign of Christ on earth when the devil will be held in bondage.[74] While it is unlikely that the believers in the Santidade de Jaguaripe had read the book of Revelation written in Greek by John of Patmos, they were certainly familiar with the broad outline of the end of the world as Christians understood it, for the missionary priests of the Society of Jesus had preached these Christian beliefs to Indians, Africans, and mamelucos in Brazil for thirty-five years.

Jesuits in Brazil stressed heaven, hell, the Day of Judgment, and the second coming of the messiah in their sermons. In a mission to Indians living beyond the new capital of Salvador in 1552, the children who served as interpreters told the Indians that those Christian Indians who had believed in the "true holiness (santidad)," which was the holiness brought by the Jesuits, were given "life forever in the heavens," whereas the evil Indians died and went to hell, where they "burned with the devil." The Jesuit Pero Correia preached in Tupi in Piratininga in 1554 that "if they believed in God, that not only would Our Lord give them great heavenly things . . . but that in this world, in their lands and places, he would give them many things that were hidden."[75]

A basic part of Jesuit teaching in the *Doutrina Cristã*, the catechism José de Anchieta translated into Tupi, introduces the concept of the Day of Judgment. Taught in the classic question-and-answer dialogue, the *Doutrina Cristã* outlines the scenario in plain language. The Jesuits taught that Christ will return from heaven on a cloud; no one, not even animals, will escape; all will die and then be reborn; the good will be beautiful, and the bad, ugly. Christ will judge all and will take the good to heaven, where they will live forever, and the evil will go to the fire of hell, where they will suffer eternally. The effect of this teaching was profound. Anchieta described the conversion of a very old Indian man who, swayed by the millenarian teachings of the Jesuits, wanted to convert to be part of the millenarian kingdom of Jesus. The man, whom Anchieta judged to be 130 years old, came to the Jesuits with great fervor asking for baptism, because "all night long he was thinking of the wrath that God would have to have to burn the whole world and destroy all things." The Indian then said, according to Anchieta, that "it was enough that the souls of his forebears were in hell, but his, he wanted to go to heaven to be with Jesus."[76]

The Jesuits, moreover, saw signs around them that the apocalypse was not far off. António Blázquez wrote a letter for Nóbrega in which he states that Nóbrega, when he had seen the converts from the mission village of Espírito Santo in Bahia moving through the fields with crosses in their hands, thought that these seemed like signs of the apocalypse. The plays that Anchieta wrote, which were performed in the 1580s in Portuguese, Spanish, and Tupi, dramatize the apocalypse in recognizable terms. In the trilogy *Na vila de Vitória*, Anchieta portrays Bahia as corrupt, ruled by the devil, and in its last days. Redemption comes when the saints Úrsula and Mauricio overthrow evil and begin a new age.[77]

The Santidade de Jaguaripe may also have drawn on religious beliefs brought by slaves from Africa, for African slaves were among its believers. The vast majority of the denunciations of the Santidade de Jaguaripe suggest that its members were Indians, but one of the most important denunciations explicitly described the participation of African slaves. This denunciation, moreover, was that of Álvaro Rodrigues, the mameluco slave trader and sugar planter who lived in Cachoeira on the Paraguaçu River near Jaguaripe. Rodrigues states that the santidade began in the sertão among the Indians, but once it became established on Cabral's estate, Christian Indians and mamelucos "left the faith of Christ our Lord and the *negros cristãos de guine* [baptized slaves from Africa] began to do the same." Another denunciation, that of Maria Carvalha, an eighteen-year-old free servant of Fernão Cabral's, specifically refers to an African slave in the movement. Maria denounced Petronilha, whom she described as a *"negra de Guiné crioula desta terra cristã"* (baptized African slave born in this land). According to Maria, while she was dusting a home altar one day, Petronilha slapped the image of Mary and said that it was worthless and made of wood, whereas hers, the image of the Santidade de Jaguaripe, was better because it moved when they approached. Petronilha, Maria said, was part of the santidade and entered its church and "did the ceremonies with the Indians and the slaves." Cristovão de Bulhões, one of the men on Nobre's entrada, was a mulatto/mameluco. He stated that his father was a mulatto, born in Mina, meaning São Jorge da Mina in West Africa, and his mother was an Indian slave. Diogo da Fonseca, who was also on the entrada from Cabral's estate, was a mulatto. These few written references to Africans or to persons of African descent who participated in the santidade suggest that the presence of other African slaves was certainly possible.[78]

Moreover, the Santidade de Jaguaripe had several characteristics that could have been influenced by Central African beliefs or that, at minimum, welcomed the participation of slaves from Central Africa. The Santidade de Jaguaripe's emphasis on the ancestors' return paralleled the Central African belief in the central role of ancestors in shaping the lives of their descendants. The role of the caraíba resembled the importance of the diviner or curer in Central African societies. Historian James Sweet documents the transmission of beliefs and rituals from Central Africa to Brazil in the seventeenth and eighteenth centuries. Diviners, who were "mediators" between the world of the living and the world of the spirits, "could predict past and future events, uncover the guilt or innocence of suspected criminals, and determine the cause of illness or other misfortunes." In Africa, diviners restored balance and harmony and were particularly important during times of rapid social and political transformation. A diviner/healer received ancestral spirits, who possessed the medium's body, which enabled the ancestral spirits to speak with the living. Sweet cites examples of diviners and spirit possession in the seventeenth century. The *calundú*, or ceremony of divination and spirit possession in Brazil, he argues, took root in Brazil by the middle of the seventeenth century; Sweet documents rituals of possession by African spirit mediums by 1618. However, Laura de Melo e Souza's comprehensive study of sorcery in colonial Brazil describes African practices of divining that were present in the late sixteenth century in Bahia, indicating that African beliefs and rituals were already present in Bahia in the last decades of the sixteenth century. This opens up the possibility that the Santidade de Jaguaripe could have incorporated Central African rituals.[79]

One belief suggestive of African influence is the Jesuit provincial's description of the santidade belief that the ancestors would arrive by ship. In Central African beliefs, the world of the living was separated from the world of the dead by a body of water.[80] That the ancestors would arrive by ship suggests the crossing of a body of water — an ocean, a river, a lake — such as that which separates the land of the living from the land of the dead. Another possible African influence might have been the sacred statue. Sweet describes the importance of "rocks and other objects from the natural world, especially those with cavities for harnessing the power of spirits or special medicines." In the santidades described before the Santidade de Jaguaripe, the "idols" observed by Staden, Léry, and the Jesuits in Brazil were the maracás and decorated gourds. The sacred statue of the Santidade de Jaguaripe was described by Cabral and the men of Domingos Fernandes Nobre's entrada as "of stone" and as not having the shape of a woman, a man, a fish, a bird, or an animal. Two men described it as like a "chimera." It was carried in processions in the sertão and then brought to Jaguaripe. There may have been other sacred statues that looked more like copies of Portuguese statues of saints, for a Portuguese colonist claimed that there was a "wooden idol" that looked like an Indian, and another said that he "saw" the sacred statue when it was in possession of the governor and stated that it was 1 *covado* (approximately 45 centimeters) high, and dressed. One report of the believers in the Santidade de Jaguaripe placing crosses in heaps of stones and drawing lines on the ground in all directions might also be evidence of African traditions. In Central Africa, the cross was known before the arrival of Europeans, and its sign was used to explain the relationship of humans to the world.[81]

The prophecies of the Santidade de Jaguaripe may have made sense to African slaves because they predicted retribution and vengeance for the slave owners, who would pay for the evils of slavery. Sweet argues that Central Africans understood enslavement by Europeans as "the most virulent form of witchcraft, one that required a powerful religious counterattack in order to be freed from the curse." African sorcerers, according to Sweet, used their "most powerful religious antidotes" to counter their enslavement. Laura de Mello e Souza documents early examples of African sorcery in Bahia, some of which may have been a part of the Santidade de Jaguaripe.[82]

The millenarianism of the Santidade de Jaguaripe may also have found fertile soil among African slaves because they, like Indian slaves, had been exposed to the preaching of the Jesuits. African slaves who lived on the sugar plantations of Bahia had received rudimentary exposure to Christianity from the Jesuit missions to the plantations. The Jesuits addressed slaves from Africa through interpreters—there was at least one interpreter for African slaves in Bahia and one in Pernambuco in the 1580s—and the Jesuits recognized the need to translate the catechism they used in Brazil into a language that the African slaves could understand. Jesuits had created a lay confraternity for Africans devoted to Nossa Senhora do Rosario and encouraged African slaves to participate. Although this evangelism was rudimentary, and can hardly be construed as evidence that African slaves had embraced Christianity, it nevertheless reveals that some slaves did have some exposure to Christian ideas. Christianity, moreover, had been introduced by the Portuguese in Africa, in particular in the Kongo kingdom, and slaves were required to be baptized before being transported across the Atlantic. Millenarian movements are known to have later emerged in Central Africa in the late seventeenth century. All of these factors suggest that the millenarian tone of the Santidade de Jaguaripe would not have been totally unfamiliar to African slaves and that it was certainly possible for African slaves to identify with the millenarianism of the Santidade de Jaguaripe and to have influenced it with their own rituals.[83]

Clearly, the Santidade de Jaguaripe was not a return to traditional indigenous beliefs, nor was it simply an imitation of Christianity. While Antônio claimed, or was granted, the powers of a traditional caraíba, he and other leaders became powerful new representational go-betweens who reinterpreted traditional Tupi beliefs and Christianity. They did not come out of traditional Indian villages, but from the sugar plantations and Jesuit aldeias. In the santidade, they created new identities for themselves—who they were and how they would live—and new religious rituals that connected them with the sacred. These beliefs and rituals resonated with the many slaves living in Portuguese colonial society. Slaves lived not only far from their original homelands but in an alien world where they toiled unceasingly on fields and in sugar mills. Around them, many died in alarming numbers from epidemic disease, and new slaves constantly arrived to take the places of those who had died. For the slaves of Bahia, the message preached by Antônio created a new mythology and offered hope. He prophesied that in the coming new world, evil would be eradicated, oppression would be ended, and wrongs would be avenged. When believers fled to Antônio in the sertão or to Mãe de Deus in Jaguaripe, they resisted slavery, the Jesuit mission, and the Portuguese colonial enterprise. When ministers carried the beliefs of the santidade outside Bahia, they made what had been localized resistance even more serious, because it threatened to become general.

The Santidade de Jaguaripe met its fate sometime during 1586. In his annual letter of 1585, likely written early in 1586, the Jesuit provincial states that a leader of the Santidade, who may or may not have been Antônio, had been captured by Indians from the aldeias, who then "dragged" him through the aldeias "for the mockery of everyone." He states approvingly that the governor sentenced to death the one "who a little before had made himself God" and allowed the Indians to hang him. The provincial thought it entirely justified that he should "perish at the hands of those to whose souls he had brought destruction." But the provincial also noted that the fathers and brothers are still "totally occupied" with "suppressing" the sect.[84]

From the Inquisition records, a few more details emerge. The governor ordered the church on Cabral's estate burned and the runaway slaves returned to their owners. He sent the woman known as Mother of God, her husband (the "second pope"), and a third leader to Lisbon. He dispatched an entrada led by Álvaro Rodrigues, the mameluco sugar planter of Cachoeira, to find the remaining congregations in the Recôncavo and the sertão. By his own admission, and with little remorse, Rodrigues murdered the remaining leaders of the movement in front of their followers. The Inquisition trials leave unanswered the fate of Antônio. The governor claimed that he had escaped, as did Nobre. The Jesuit annual letter seems to say, however, that Antônio was hanged by his followers in or near the aldeia of Santo Antonio.[85]

The Santidade de Jaguaripe shook Bahia to its roots in 1585 not only because it was a new form of resistance but because it was a new kind of religion. Antônio, Aricute, and Mãe de Deus became new religious figures who combined the traditional roles of the caraíba with Christianity and possibly with African beliefs and rituals. Believers became saints in a new religion that promised them what the Jesuits had to offer—salvation in the afterlife—and something more: freedom from slavery in the present life. Anchored by the presence of heroes from indigenous myths, the new religion identified Brazil as a promised land. The certainty that the Tupi ancestors had returned to the sertão, and that the savior and the mother of God described by the Jesuits had also come, fueled a powerful rejection of present conditions. All must be abandoned, for all would be irrevocably changed.

Resistance to Portuguese colonialism took many forms, from the traditional responses by chiefs and shamans to the adapted resistance articulated by Antônio and other leaders in the Santidade de Jaguaripe. Representational, transactional, and physical go-betweens all were part of the creation and expression of resistance to Portuguese colonial rule. The obvious danger of the Santidade de Jaguaripe was, from the point of view of the leaders of the Portuguese colony, that it encouraged slaves to flee the plantations (thereby becoming physical go-betweens) and to reject Christianity. But another danger, which the visiting inquisitor perceived after the fact, was that the Santidade de Jaguaripe also spoke to the mamelucos. Because of their fluidity, bicultural ambiguity, and facility with language, mamelucos were the crucial transactional go-betweens for the Portuguese colony. Go-betweens had power at particular moments in time in a divided and changing world. Which side would they choose to serve? How was their power felt in the colony? The power of the go-betweens, therefore, is the focus of our last chapter.

8. Power

> I worship you, goat, because you will become a wineskin.
> *Domingos Fernandes Nobre "Tomacaúna," 1585*

On 28 July 1591, an elaborate procession and mass honored the first inquisitor to set foot in Brazil, Heitor Furtado de Mendonça. The pomp and ceremony of the occasion underscored that Salvador was more than just a harbor on the Bay of All Saints; it was the capital of Portuguese Brazil. Important institutions of Portuguese society and polity had been transplanted successfully to the colony, and the procession and mass symbolized the growing influence of Portuguese culture. As an official of the Holy Office of the Lisbon Inquisition, the very presence of an inquisitor in Brazil established that henceforth obedience to the teachings of the Catholic Church would not only be expected but assessed. With the full support of the governor, the city council, the Jesuits, and other clerics, the inquisitor could interrogate residents of Salvador and prevent them from leaving the city to conduct their business. He could imprison them and send them under heavy guard to Lisbon. He could sentence them to exile as degredados, or he could levy fines on them and confiscate their property. Clearly, the visiting inquisitor wielded a great deal of power when he arrived in Brazil's capital.

On the surface, the inquisitor's power derived from his position as a representative of the Holy Office of the Inquisition. But on closer inspection, the extent of and the limitations to his power were also affected by the role he played as a go-between. Mendonça, whose title was "visiting inquisitor," headed an inquisitorial *visit* to Brazil; he was in no way authorized to establish a *permanent* office of the Inquisition. On the one hand, therefore, he was one of the few high-ranking agents of a powerful European institution who actually traveled to the colonies and returned with firsthand information. On the other, his influence in Brazil would be temporary. On another level, he was a representational go-between. His job was to set into motion the procedures used by the Lisbon Inquisition to detect, to try, and to punish heresy in Brazil. His work, therefore, led to formal trials that generated pages and pages of written transcripts, all of which are a representation of Brazil—its sins, heresies, and crimes. Although the visiting inquisitor did not translate, mediate, or guide opposing parties in Brazil to settlements, he was nevertheless a transactional go-between. The role sought by the visiting inquisitor was to be the principal mediator between sinful individuals and God. Through his agency, he intended that heretics, blasphemers, and sinners of all stripes would confess their sins, repent through the punishments he imposed, and be reconciled with God.[1]

The role played by the visiting inquisitor in Bahia from 1591 to 1593 tells us a great deal about the power of go-betweens. His power, like that of all go-betweens, depended on a particular moment in time and on a particular physical space. Moments of encounter, of conflict, of change present the socially and geographically mobile individuals who often become go-betweens with opportunities. They are often sought as agents and allies by opposing or distanced parties. The arrival of the visiting inquisitor, for example, presented an opportunity for the Jesuits in their conflict with the sugar planters over Indian slavery. There is every reason to assume that the Jesuits hoped the inquisitor would help them in their quest to censure those who engaged in illegal enslavement of Indians. When conditions change, however, altering the nature of a particular moment or of a physical space, a go-between can lose his or her source of power. In the case of the visiting inquisitor, his power as a go-between was tied to his appointment as visiting inquisitor. His power was greatest when he first arrived in Salvador and established the temporary tribunal of the Lisbon Inquisition. Once he left Salvador and headed for Pernambuco, his influence diminished in Bahia; and once he left Pernambuco, it was greatly reduced in all Brazil. Go-betweens acquire knowledge and information that is potentially very valuable. The visiting inquisitor was privy to much secret information revealed in the confessions and interrogations. Whom the go-between favors with that information and how they represent it can influence the future profoundly. In the case of the visiting inquisitor, his representation of Brazil would clearly influence how high officials of the Lisbon Inquisition perceived the sins of colonists in Brazil, then and in the future. Go-betweens, therefore, have power individually because of their roles as physical, transactional, and representational agents. They operate in moments of time and in physical spaces where vested interests compete and conflict, where violence is possible, and where the outcome (often with huge consequence) is uncertain. The uncertainty of this landscape of power gives the go-between the choice of mediating as a neutral third party or of influencing the outcome by arbitrating in favor of one side.

If the role of the visiting inquisitor helps to explain the power of go-betweens generally, the trials he conducted during that time reveal much about the power of specific individual go-betweens at the end of the sixteenth century. The visiting inquisitor initiated more trials during his brief stay in Salvador than his superiors in Lisbon expected. Many of these trials were similar to the kinds of trials that the Lisbon Inquisition conducted in Portugal. But among them were trials unique to Brazil, such as the trials that investigated individuals who adopted customs of the Indians while in the sertão. Most of those so tried were mamelucos, men such as Domingos Fernandes Nobre "Tomacaúna," or Álvaro Rodrigues, the grandson of Diogo Álvares "Caramuru," who descended Indians from the sertão in the intercontinental slave trade. Another set of trials unique to Brazil were those the inquisitor opened into the Santidade de Jaguaripe. The visiting inquisitor had many reservations about the mamelucos who joined in the rituals of the Santidade de Jaguaripe and about Fernão Cabral. The inquisitor found the behavior of Cabral unacceptable, and Cabral's trial is one of the most lengthy from his visit. In the trials of mamelucos and of those linked to the Santidade de Jaguaripe can be seen the roles played by go-betweens in the landscape of power in Bahia at the end of the sixteenth century. There was no longer any question in Salvador about whether the Portuguese or the Indian world would be dominant. Rather, it was not *if* but *how* Indians living in the sertão would become part of the colony.

By the time the visiting inquisitor stepped ashore, Salvador, the Recôncavo surrounding the Bay of All Saints, and the nearby sertão had a clearly defined social and economic hierarchy. Sugar planters constituted the clear elite; their power derived from their control over land and slave labor and their ability to produce a valuable export crop. In Bahia, thirty-six sugar mills were counted in the Recôncavo in 1587; they produced 120,000 arrobas (1,762,800 kilos) of sugar for sale. In Pernambuco, their dominance was even more pronounced; a Jesuit report cited sixty-six sugar mills at around the same time and an annual

Map 8.1. Bahia: Salvador, the Recôncavo, and the sertão

production of 200,000 arrobas (2,938,000 kilos) of sugar. Although the Society of Jesus was no longer the sole religious order in Brazil, it still remained the most influential representative of Catholicism. The number of Jesuits had grown substantially. By 1586, there were 145 Jesuits in Brazil. Seventy-one Jesuits (49% of all Jesuits in Brazil) lived in Bahia, and the majority (64) resided at the college in Salvador. The Society administered three mission villages in Bahia—Santo Antonio, Espírito Santo, and São João—and in these aldeias lived between six hundred and eight hundred free Indians. Unlike the alliances of the Jesuits with local elites in Europe, in Brazil the Jesuits were highly critical of the sugar planters because of their reliance on illegal Indian slavery to plant, cut, and mill their cane.[2]

The mass in honor of the inquisitor set the stage for the inquisitor's power and the tone for his visit. Its theatrical staging emphasized in a way that few could miss the unique status and powers possessed by the inquisitor. It began with a procession, a visual spectacle, led by the bishop, from the church of Our Lady of Ajuda to the cathedral. The governor, the Crown judge, the members of the city council, the Jesuits, the secular priests, and the lesser clerics solemnly accompanied the inquisitor, who was escorted under a canopy of golden cloth. Inside the cathedral, the inquisitor sat on a red velvet chair beneath a crimson damask canopy in the main chapel. Religious and political language then became important. Mass was said in Latin, followed by a sermon preached in Portuguese by the provincial of the Society of Jesus. The archdeacon of the cathedral mounted the pulpit and read the edicts brought by the inquisitor from King Philip II of Spain, now King Filipe I of Portugal. The inquisitor's notary stepped up to read a document of the late Pope Pius V in favor of the Holy Office of the Inquisition and against those who dared to criticize it. When the inquisitor moved to an altar, richly adorned with a silver cross, four silver candlesticks, and two missals resting on damask pillows, a chaplain carried over the heavy velvet chair reserved for him. One by one, the governor, the judges, the councilmen, and other officials came to the altar, knelt, and swore to uphold the faith. The notary came to the foot of the cross and in a loud voice asked all the people in the cathedral to promise to do so as well. At the end of the ceremony, the notary affixed these documents to the door of the cathedral, along with one that stated that under pain of excommunication, all residents of the city and its environs up to 1 league (approximately 6 kilometers) must denounce within thirty days everything of which they knew, or had seen, or had heard, against the holy Catholic faith. He nailed another document to the church door stating that the king had decreed that "those who accuse themselves and confess their sins during the time of grace to the lord visitor [the inquisitor] will not lose their estates."[3]

With these words, the notary opened Pandora's box in Brazil. The power of the inquisitor was clearly perceived by all. The very next day, residents from Salvador came forward to confess their sins and to denounce the sins of others. The very first depositions, duly recorded by the notary, revealed that the residents of Salvador and the Recôncavo were far from model Portuguese Catholics. Just as the Holy Office of the Inquisition had found in Portugal, a wide gap existed between what the church leaders preached as orthodoxy and the beliefs and behaviors of ordinary people. On the very first day, the sixty-five-year-old parish priest of Matoim confessed that he had had indecent "dishonest contact" with some forty people, the majority of whom were young men. Several days later, a sugar master from Madeira confessed that he had wed a woman on the island of Madeira, only to find out that she was already married. Fernão Cabral de Taíde arrived to confess to the inquisitor that he had allowed the Santidade de Jaguaripe to build a church and to practice its rituals on his estate. A sixty-five-year-old woman known as a New Christian—that is, descended from Portuguese Jews who were forced to convert to Christianity in 1496—explained to the inquisitor in detail how she slaughtered chickens (she ordered their necks cut and their bodies hung so that all the blood flowed out). Although she was a New Christian, she told the inquisitor, she had no Jewish intentions when she had her food prepared in this way. A gypsy woman confessed that ten years ago, on a day when she had been "worn out" and arguing over something with people she did not remember, she angrily renounced God.[4]

A database constructed from the trials of the Lisbon Inquisition, currently held in the Arquivo Nacional da Torre do Tombo in Lisbon, indicates that just less than half of the individuals tried by the Lisbon Inquisition in Brazil were accused of crimes that can be labeled as "heresy." This category includes such things as blasphemy, reading prohibited books, practicing rituals or customs labeled as Jewish, making statements that favored Islam or Protestantism, asserting "false" or "wrong" interpretations of the faith, and treating the cross or other religious images in a disrespectful way. The second largest group comprised a variety of sexual crimes: bigamy, sodomy, male homosexuality, and lesbianism. The inquisitor also tried those who asserted that it was not a sin to have intercourse, or that the civil status of a married person was higher than that of the clergy, who took a vow of celibacy. A third category of sixteenth-century trials encompassed crimes committed against the Holy Office of the Inquisition. These included trials against individuals who had fled the Inquisition in Portugal and were now living in Brazil, individuals who had not denounced crimes of which they were aware, individuals who misrepresented themselves in front of the inquisitor, individuals who publicly insulted or denounced the Inquisition, individuals who aided the escape of others, and individuals who broke the oath of secrecy that surrounded all inquisitorial procedures. Another group of trials concerned individuals who had adopted indigenous customs while living in

Table 8.1. Trials initiated by the Lisbon Inquisition in sixteenth-century Brazil

Crime	N	%
Heresy	76	45%
Sexuality	40	24%
Crimes against the Inquisition	22	13%
Indigenous customs	18	11%
Known trials not in index	12	7%
Total	168	100%

Source: Unpublished data from the Gulbenkian Inquisition Database (1987) coordinated by Robert Rowland

Brazil. These are the transactional go-betweens, in their majority mamelucos, who descended Indians from the sertão in the intercontinental slave trade and who participated in the Santidade de Jaguaripe (Table 8.1).[5]

It is quite possible that the Jesuits encouraged the inquisitor to crack down on the mamelucos, whom they saw as their greatest rival in the sertão. Four prominent Jesuits who resided at the college in Salvador sat on the inquisitorial *mesa*, or "bench": Fernão Cardim, Leonardo Armínio, Marçal Beliarte, and Luís da Fonseca. All would sign the sentences of the trials. All could reasonably expect to have the ear of the inquisitor during his sojourn in Bahia. Jesuits even provided interpreters for the inquisitor when necessary. And some Jesuits, including those who sat on the bench, gave their own formal denunciations to the inquisitor. By censuring the mamelucos, the inquisitor in Salvador would provide the Society of Jesus new leverage in their quest to limit illegal Indian slavery. If mamelucos could be prevented from entering the sertão, then the descending of Indian slaves would be made all the more difficult for sugar planters.[6]

Fernão Cabral was one of the first to voluntarily appear before the inquisitorial bench, on 2 August 1591. His was a shocking confession, both because of what he said and because, as a well-known sugar planter, he was expected to model proper behavior. Cabral's confession took place during the period of grace, which meant that he could expect some leniency from the inquisitor. He admitted that he had financed the entrada into the sertão led by Domingos Fernandes Nobre that sought the believers in the santidade and that when the believers arrived in Jaguaripe, he settled them in a village, permitted them to build a church, and allowed them to continue their ceremonies. He admitted that "once he entered their church, which pleased them." He apparently knew that it was generally said in Bahia that he had removed his hat when inside the church, and he addressed this point to the inquisitor. He claimed that he could not remember if he had removed his hat or not, but asked for pardon if he had done so. Cabral maintained that he disbanded the movement on the orders of the governor and that he had handed over to him the woman known as Mother of God, her husband, and all the slaves who had descended to his estate. He presented a document written by the governor that he believed proved that his intention was to descend the movement from the sertão to destroy it.[7]

Cabral also confessed a horrific crime, which revealed the extent of his power on his estate and probably that of sugar planters generally. One night he had found one of his slave women "swollen" and "very near death" from having eaten earth. Eating dirt, or *geophagy*, is a form of pica, a pathological craving for nonfoods that is often related to nutritional, and especially mineral, deficiencies. To strike fear into the woman, he said to two nearby slaves, both men, "Throw her into the oven." After Cabral left, the two slaves did as they were told. The woman burned to death. Cabral claimed to the inquisitor that he only wished to frighten her and other slaves; his intent was to break them of the habit of eating dirt. He insisted that he did not mean for the woman to die. The next day, when he learned what had happened, he maintained, he was burdened with remorse.[8]

Beyond his own confession, thirty-eight individuals denounced Cabral, including two Jesuits. One of the denunciations against him gave an even more horrifying picture of the slave woman's death and the extent of his power, not only over the slaves but also over the free persons who lived on his estate. According to Nuno Pereira, the slave woman whom Cabral ordered placed in the oven was a baptized Christian. Terrified, she called on "God, Our Lady, and on all of the Saints" to help her. She pleaded with all the Christians and slaves on Cabral's estate to save her. Pereira then said that the woman cried that since neither God, nor the saints, nor the Christians would help her, she would turn to the devils of hell. Still no one came forward, and she burned to ash. Such was their fear of Cabral, according to Pereira. Another denouncer told the inquisitor that the woman was with child. Her denunciation, if true, suggests that the death may have occurred in front of the slaves and free residents of Cabral's estate. This denouncer reported a visual picture of the woman's death that had been repeated throughout Bahia. She said that after the woman's body burst in the fire, the head of her child could be seen.[9]

Cabral had power that extended well beyond his slaves and free dependents. Luísa de Almeida told the inquisitor that one Sunday after mass, she was waiting alone in "Fernão Cabral's church in Jaguaripe." The church, or rather chapel there, São Bento, had its own cleric, but Luísa de Almeida thought of it as Cabral's church. Sugar planters often built chapels on their estates and provided livings for clergy. But Luísa de Almeida had little respect for Cabral's piety. While she waited for her slaves to come with a hammock to carry her back to her own house, Cabral propositioned her "with clear and dishonest words" inside the church. When Luísa de Almeida refused these advances and pointed out that Cabral was her son's godfather and that he had carried the infant to the baptismal font, Cabral replied that it hardly mattered, since fornicating with a *comadre* (godmother) was the same as fornicating with anyone else. Subsequently, Cabral threatened her repeatedly. She had great hatred for Cabral after this experience, she told the inquisitor. A twenty-three-year-old Jesuit denounced Cabral for using sacred words obscenely. He said that Cabral repeated the words that priests used to consecrate the host—*hoc est corpus meum*—during illicit sex. The Jesuit reported that he had heard this from someone he did not remember in the aldeia of Santo Antonio.[10]

The Jesuits had little affection for Fernão Cabral. They had lodged a complaint against him twenty years earlier when he had "taken by force" six free Indians who normally resided in the Jesuit mission village of São João. At the time, the Indians were working for wages on the estate of another planter. The prelude to this episode was that an Indian woman, whom Cabral claimed as a slave, had run away from him and had taken refuge in the Jesuit aldeia of Santo Antonio. The Jesuits turned her over to the local judge, who placed her in the town jail and gave Cabral until a certain Thursday to prove that she was legally his slave. When Cabral failed to appear, the judge returned the woman to the aldeia of Santo Antonio. Cabral wrote to the Jesuit father in charge of Santo Antonio and declared that if he did not return the woman, he [Cabral] would satisfy himself with Indians from the mission villages that were closer to his estate in Jaguaripe. Subsequently, he boldly seized six free Indians from São João and put them in his boat and carried them across the Bay of All Saints to his own plantation, saying that "it had nothing to do with the Jesuits, nor with the governor," for "his power was greater than that of the law."[11]

Fernão Cardim, a prominent Jesuit in Salvador and one of the four Jesuits who sat on the inquisitorial bench, denounced Cabral for his role in the spread of the Santidade de Jaguaripe. Cardim stated that Cabral allowed the movement to have a temple and an idol on his estate and that a great number of slaves and Indians had fled to Jaguaripe to worship the idol at the temple. Moreover, he

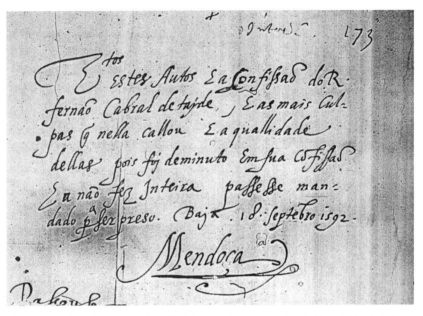

Figure 8.1. Order to imprison Cabral. "Trial of Fernão Cabral de Ataíde," Inquisição de Lisboa 17065. Instituto dos Arquivos Nacionais / Torre do Tombo—Portugal.

said that Cabral went to the temple and worshiped at the idol, just as the Indians did. He offered the name of an eyewitness, a João Bras, who had personally witnessed Cabral take off his hat and venerate the idol.[12]

Cabral soon found himself jailed by the inquisitor, who determined on 18 September 1591 that his confession had not been complete. Mendonça signed an order that authorized the imprisonment of Cabral (Fig. 8.1).

Cabral reappeared before the inquisitorial bench for four sessions of further questioning. Of all his sins, the inquisitor was most interested in the question of whether or not he had removed his hat inside the church of the Santidade de Jaguaripe movement. Cabral contradicted himself, and thereby gave the inquisitor clear proof of perjury. In his trial, Mendonça draws a finger pointing to this slip of Cabral's, with a note saying that "he retracted it in the next [interrogation]" (Fig. 8.2).

While Cabral was in jail, the Jesuits of Bahia first learned of stinging criticisms leveled against them in Madrid. These were brought by Gabriel Soares de Sousa, a sugar planter from Bahia who had written a long treatise on Brazil in 1587, which he presented to King Philip II (now King Filipe I of Portugal) and

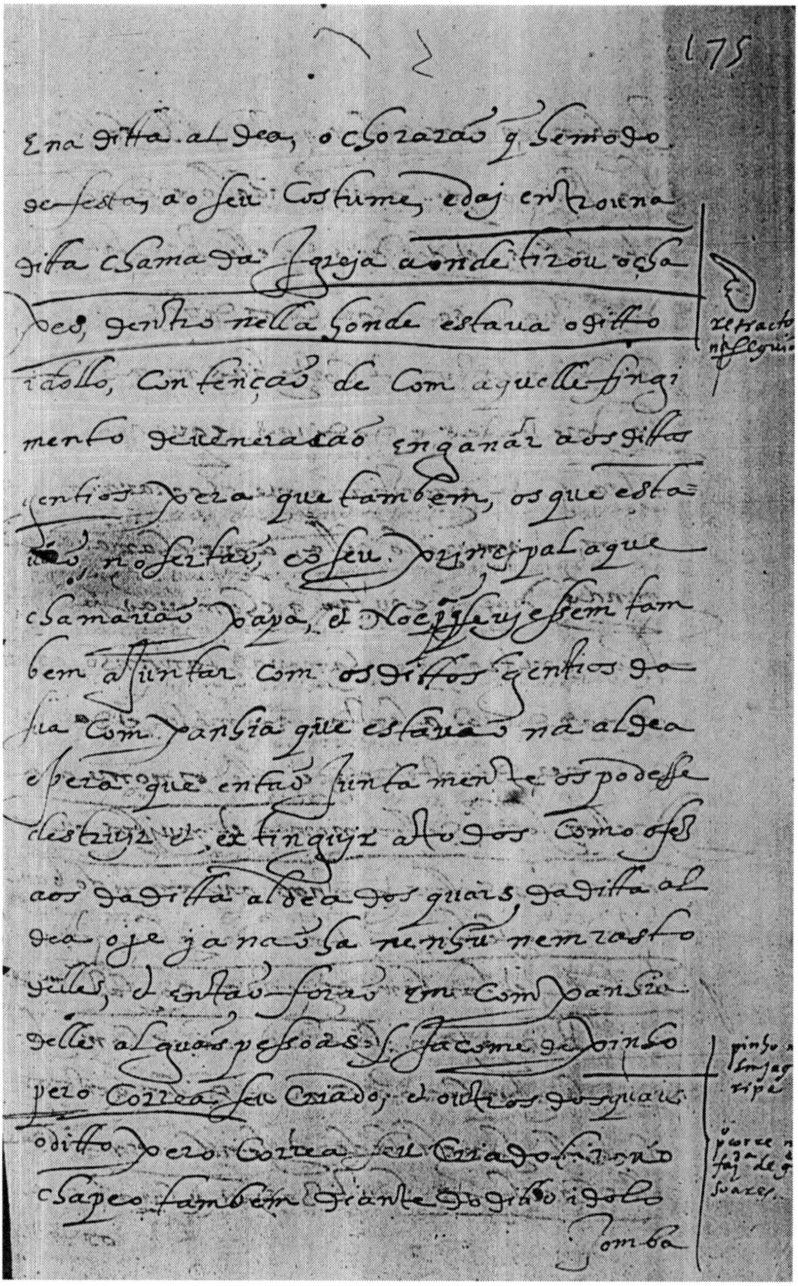
175

e na ditta aldea, o chorarão q̃ he modo de festas ao seu costume, e daj entrou na ditta chamada Igreja aonde tirou o chapeo, gentio nella, onde estava o ditto idolo, com tenção de com aquelle fingimento determinasão enganar aos dittos gentios, pera que tambem os que estavão no sertão, e o seu principal a que chamavão papa, e se quisessem tambem ajuntar com os dittos gentios da sua companhia que estavão na aldea e pera que então juntamente os podesse destruir e extinguir a todos como o fes aos da ditta aldea dos quais da ditta aldea oje ja não ha nenhu nem rasto delles, e então forão em companhia delle algumas pessoas s. Jacome de Pinho, Pero Correa seu criado, e outros dos quais o ditto Pero Correa seu criado tirou o chapeo tambem diante do ditto idolo tomba

Figure 8.2. Cabral's perjury. "Trial of Fernão Cabral de Ataíde," Inquisição de Lisboa 17065. Instituto dos Arquivos Nacionais / Torre do Tombo—Portugal.

which was later published as *Tratado descritivo do Brasil em 1587*. The treatise included history and geography, descriptions of flora and fauna, and sketches of indigenous customs. The second part is wholly devoted to Bahia; here Sousa describes the city of Salvador and the estates of the Recôncavo. The Society of Jesus appears in this work as a prosperous order, well supported by the Crown. Sousa describes a "sumptuous college" with "large dormitories" overlooking the ocean, and a "beautiful and attractive church" with many "rich ornaments" in the center of Salvador. He alludes to the many herds of cattle, farms, and ranches outside the city that supplied the order with food and income. Sousa emphasizes the prosperity of the Society in his treatise, but he does concede that the work of the Jesuits had "gathered much fruit." [13]

In another, apparently secret, document written at the same time and also presented to the king, Soares de Sousa lambastes the Jesuits. It was, according to Serafim Leite, the great historian of the Jesuits in Brazil, "the most anti-Jesuitical document of sixteenth-century Brazil." Soares de Sousa begins by emphasizing that in the beginning the colonists greatly respected the Jesuits, serving them and "adoring them as gods on earth" because of their great virtue and exemplary life. So revered was the Society that governors, bishops, captains, leading citizens, and ordinary colonists gave them everything they needed for their mission. But as the number of Jesuits rose, Soares de Sousa recounts, they became increasingly greedy and disinterested in the lives of ordinary colonists. He cites the colleges, each with its own stipend from the king, and the lands—given to them by the king, governors, and colonists—as extensive. Soares de Sousa argues that despite finding the college in Bahia endowed with a stipend from the king, cattle ranches, farms, and Indians from multiple mission villages, as more Jesuits arrived from Portugal they spent their time on their own material interests, such as demarcating lands, building houses for their recreation, and obtaining rulings against the colonists that restricted their use of Indian laborers from the mission villages. By refusing to allow local judges to hear the claims of colonists or by penalizing poor squatters with excommunication, the Jesuits, Soares de Sousa claims, consolidated much land under their control. He goes on to describe several political battles in which the Jesuits attacked the governors of the king, underscoring his assertion that the Jesuits had abandoned their spiritual mission. [14]

Not surprisingly, Soares de Sousa particularly rejects the position taken by the Jesuits against Indian slavery. He declares that when the Jesuits made their rounds to the sugar plantations to minister to slaves, they asked Indian slaves if they had been captured illegally, and if so, they encouraged the slaves to run away to the mission villages. "They do not want anyone to own an Indian as a slave for any reason," Soares de Sousa complains bitterly, for "they want them all in their mission villages." Soares de Sousa then makes his case that the king should allow the enslavement of Indians. In his view, "their lifestyle and customs certify that they are not fit to be free." He argues that Indians deserve to be enslaved because of their past actions against the Portuguese—"killing and eating many hundreds of them, even thousands of them, among whom were a bishop and many priests." Soares de Sousa closes his document with an argument that colonists would make again and again to the kings of Portugal: without Indian slavery, Brazil cannot be sustained.[15]

Since their arrival in Brazil, Jesuits had written regularly to the Jesuit provincial in Rome, to the leaders of the Society in Portugal, and to the king of Portugal, articulating their views. When Philip II of Spain imposed his claim on the throne of Portugal in 1580, however, the dynasty of the House of Avis, whose last kings had been faithful supporters of the Jesuits, came to an end. According to historian Dauril Alden, "For the first time since the Society's founding they [the Jesuits] were excluded from the highest levels of political authorities." Jesuits in Portugal and Brazil soon found that they lacked access to important information and could not influence the king as easily. Only long after the fact did Jesuits in Brazil learn that Soares de Sousa had the ear of the king and was telling a very different story about Brazil.[16]

Shocked Jesuits began to formulate a defense of their mission in 1592. Six Jesuits, three of whom simultaneously served on the inquisitorial bench, authored the Society's response. The Jesuits open their rebuttal with a reference to the Gospel: "Blessed are you when people abuse you and persecute you and speak all kinds of calumny against you falsely on my account" (Matthew 5:11). Identifying themselves, therefore, as followers of Christ who will be "abused" and "persecuted," the Jesuits nevertheless claim that they are "consoled," for they are "blessed." But to be consoled by the words of the Gospel is not enough, the Jesuits argue; they believe it is important to tell the truth. Immediately, the Jesuits present themselves as the true missionaries of Christ, and they cast Soares de Sousa as a liar who speaks "evil" against them "falsely." The Jesuits then refute his views, one by one. While Soares de Sousa described a sumptuous college, the Jesuits remind the king that the first residences of the Jesuits had been built of mud brick and thatched with straw. And to Soares de Sousa's claim that the Jesuits received labor from the Indians in the aldeias, the Jesuits reply that the aldeias are "the king's" and that the Indians living in them serve everyone, not just the Jesuits. However, the Jesuits note that the aldeias "are being consumed" by the constant demands placed on them by colonists, the governor, and others, including Soares de Sousa. The lands that Soares de Sousa said they coveted are, the Jesuits explain, clearly theirs, and they argue that it is regrettable but necessary for them to assert their clear legal title to them. The Jesuits respond to Soares de Sousa's contention that Brazil cannot be sustained without Indian slavery with this forceful reply:

> The only remedy for this colony is to have many Indians living in peace in aldeias near the sugar mills and estates. This way there will be someone who can resist the attacks of its enemies—whether French, English, or Aimoré—who have already done much damage, and continue to do so. Moreover, the Indians can place a brake on the slaves from Guinea, who are many, and who are only afraid of the Indians.[17]

The visiting inquisitor would not directly enter into this disagreement between Soares de Sousa and the Jesuits of the college of Salvador nor that between the sugar planters generally and the Jesuits over Indian slavery. He would not investigate whether sugar planters were breaking the law by holding Indians descended from the sertão as slaves. He would not consider whether sugar planters allowed slaves, African and Indian, to practice Christianity, or whether they stopped their mills on Sundays and other holy days. But the inquisitor would address this conflict indirectly, because he would focus on certain practices used by mamelucos in the sertão. In the sertão, mamelucos used persuasion rather than overt violence to descend Indians to the coast, but this required cultural hybridity rather than orthodoxy on their part. By placing the mamelucos on trial for their "Indian customs," the inquisitor would attack the very strategies that gave the mamelucos their power in the sertão. The confession and trial of Domingos Fernandes Nobre "Tomacaúna" crystallizes as no other the power of the mameluco go-betweens, who supplied the plantations of Bahia with Indian slaves. Mamelucos did not accept the Jesuit monopoly over the right to descend Indians from the sertão. Nobre directly and openly challenged Jesuit missionary priests in the sertão, and he would successfully defend himself before the visiting inquisitor and his tribunal.

Nobre was deep in the sertão, on yet another entrada to descend slaves, when the inquisitor arrived in Salvador. He missed the mass marking the beginning of the inquisitor's work as well as the period of thirty days of grace conceded to the residents of the city of Salvador. On 12 January 1592, the inquisitor granted an additional period of thirty days of grace, this time to the residents of the parishes of the Recôncavo. Men whom Domingos Fernandes Nobre had known for most of his life, including some who had been with him on the most recent entrada, denounced him for joining in the ceremonies of the Santidade de Jaguaripe. On 21 January, even his own wife, Isabel Beliaga, went to the inquisitor to denounce his tattoos. Isabel stated that she "had heard" that he tattooed himself to show Indians in the sertão that he was brave and to escape certain death at the hands of his Indian enemies. Nobre decided to confess his faults to the inquisitor on the very last day of grace granted to the residents of the Recôncavo, on 11 February 1592. In his confession, Nobre told the story of his entire adult life—a time that he had split between living in the sertão as an Indian and living in Salvador as a married man. His confession reveals the mindset of the mameluco go-between who could fully insinuate himself in both the Indian and the Portuguese worlds.[18]

Nobre confesses many sins. Like Cabral, he did not think it a sin to have sexual intercourse with women to whom he was linked by bonds of godparentage. He cites "a sin of the flesh" with two of his goddaughters, both Indian girls, whom he had sponsored when they were baptized as Christians. He confesses that whenever he entered the sertão, he failed to pray, to abstain from eating meat on holy days of obligation, or to commend himself to God. He recounts in detail his association with the Santidade de Jaguaripe.[19]

Nobre's confession describes how a mameluco go-between adapted to fit into the Indian culture of the sertão and then took advantage of Indians who had limited knowledge of or experience with the Portuguese world. Mamelucos such as he became powerful in the eyes of Indians because they looked and acted like powerful men. Their bodies bore the tattoos that signified their bravery in battle. They possessed multiple women, controlled powerful weapons, sometimes used magic, and could speak persuasively in Indian languages. The mameluco go-between became a chameleon in the wilderness, adapting to, and insinuating himself in, each new situation.

One can imagine the distaste of the Jesuits who sat in judgment on Domingos Fernandes Nobre "Tomacaúna" and the other mamelucos who came to confess their sins in the sertão. Jesuit missionaries had a very different approach for facilitating contact between the Indian world and the Portuguese colony. A Jesuit missionary priest typically entered the sertão with a single Jesuit companion. The two men, dressed in their traditional robes, did not carry arms, nor did they seek to portray themselves as powerful figures. They did not attempt to prove their bravery by tattooing their bodies. They did not remove their robes and walk naked in order to imitate indigenous adult males. Jesuits strove to maintain their vows of chastity and therefore refused to marry Indian women and thereby receive the protection of powerful fathers-in-law. Jesuits eschewed magic and trickery. The cultural characteristics of Jesuit transactional go-betweens constitute a discernable pattern: they avoided adapting to the cultural world of the sertão. In essence, they were "dyed in the wool," that is, faithful to the Jesuit "way of being," when they entered the sertão.

Though striking differences marked the outward manifestation of the dyed-in-the-wool Jesuits and the chameleon-like mamelucos in the sertão, they did share one common strategy: preaching. To be persuasive, both Jesuit missionaries and mameluco slave traders had to know more than just Indian languages; they had to be respected as orators. Jesuits were instantly drawn to the tradition of oratory among the Indians of Brazil and commented on it in their letters and reports. Jesuits described the custom of *senhores de fala* (lords of speech), who, through their speeches, got the Indians to do what they wanted, such as to go to war. Jesuits wrote about "speak offs" in which orators competed to see who was the best speaker. In one of his reports, Fernão Cardim describes how a contender was heard all night and often all day, with no sleep or food or rest. If the speaker did not tire, he was seen as a great man. Though mamelucos had no formal training in language or oratory, nor were they motivated to preach to achieve spiritual growth, they intuitively modeled themselves on these senhores de fala.[20]

Jesuits and mamelucos found themselves preaching against each other in the sertão. This is the principal complaint in a denunciation against mamelucos given by a Jesuit who lived in the aldeia of Santo Antonio in Bahia. The Jesuit was an Englishman by birth and known in Brazil as João Vicente. He stated to the inquisitor that during the fifteen years he had lived in the mission villages of Bahia, "he had heard from the Indians," and it was "public knowledge held as the truth," that the mamelucos who enter the sertão to descend Indians "preach to the Indians not to descend with the priests of the Society [of Jesus]." The mamelucos forcefully argue, he explained, that if the Indians descend with the Jesuits, "they could not have many women, nor drink their smoke, nor dance, nor keep the customs of their forbears."[21]

According to the Jesuit annual letter written for the year 1581, there was a conflict between Jesuit missionary priests and mamelucos in the sertão of Arari (Chapada do Araripe, Pernambuco) in 1580 and 1581. In the letter, the Jesuit provincial describes how a missionary priest undertook a mission to the sertão in November of 1580 after Indians from the highlands of Arari, 180 leagues (approximately 1,100 kilometers) from Salvador, sent emissaries to the Jesuits. The emissaries explained that they wished to descend from the highlands to the mission villages of the coast. But because the Indians were afraid to come alone, citing the danger of the long journey, which involved crossing the lands of many of their enemies, as well as their fear of the Portuguese colonists, they asked for a mission from the Jesuits. Two Jesuits left Bahia and, according to the Jesuit provincial, "passed through lands and nations very strange and barbaric and many of them mortal enemies of the Indians" they were looking for. One of the Jesuits became sick and had to be left behind in an Indian village en route, but when the other arrived at Arari, he preached to the Indians and, as reported in the Jesuit annual letter, motivated several thousand Indians to descend to the aldeias of the coast. But then an entrada of Portuguese and mameluco men arrived and, the Jesuit provincial writes, they "began to use their cunning to preach a thousand deceptions." The effect was that of the thousands that the Jesuit priest had roused with his preaching, only 580 remained with him. But worse was to come: of the 580, the Portuguese and mamelucos "robbed" some 200. After a long and difficult journey back, 250 Indians arrived at the Jesuit aldeias of Bahia.[22]

João Vicente identifies himself as the Jesuit missionary priest who undertook this expedition. He wrote to a Jesuit colleague that he would have descended one thousand Indians to the Jesuit aldeias of Bahia if the men in the sertão had not "hindered him with their lies, thirsting more for the bondage of the people than their salvation." In his denunciation to the inquisitor, João Vicente names five mamelucos who preached against him in the sertão; three were subsequently tried by the inquisitor.[23]

One of the mamelucos was Francisco Pires, who admitted to the inquisitor that he "preached" and "advised" the Indians, telling them not to descend with the priests to the coast, because the Jesuits would "prohibit them from having many wives." He told the Indians that the Jesuits had "stocks in which they would lock them" and whips to punish them. The Jesuits would not allow them "to have their dances and customs of their ancestors," he told the Indians in the sertão, and they would "make them Christians" and not allow them "to live in their Indian ways." Pires estimated that João Vicente returned with "one hundred and some" Indians.[24]

Another mameluco accused by João Vicente was Lázaro da Cunha, whom the inquisitor also tried. Cunha revealed under cross-examination that he counseled Chief Jugasu, the most powerful chief in Arari, that he should not descend with his people with João Vicente. Instead, Cunha persuaded Chief Jugasu that if he wanted to descend to the coast with his people, he should descend to Pernambuco. Lázaro da Cunha claimed that he did this on the orders of his captain, Manoel Machado, and other soldiers in the company. João Vicente denounced two more mamelucos by name, but they were not tried by the inquisitor, and he denounced Domingos Fernandes Nobre as another mameluco who preached against the Jesuits in the sertão.[25]

These conflicts between Jesuit missionary priests and mamelucos in the sertão were nothing new. In his secret report to the king, Soares de Sousa referenced a conflict between Jesuit missionaries and mameluco slave traders that had taken place nearly seventeen years before. Neither the Jesuits nor the sugar planters had forgotten it. It took place in Rio Real, which lay on the coast between Pernambuco and Bahia. It was particularly galling to the Jesuits because the mamelucos not only preached against them, but seemed to have done so with the support of the governor. One of the mamelucos who preached against the Jesuits in Rio Real was Gonçalo Álvares, who confessed his sins to the inquisitor in 1592. At the time of his confession, Álvares had just returned from the sertão, where he had led a company of twenty-five Portuguese and mameluco men and many Indian archers to descend Indians for the Sergipe do Conde plantation, one of the plantations in the Recôncavo that had been burned during the time of the Santidade de Jaguaripe movement. Among the things that Álvares confessed was that many years before, when he went with the governor to make war in Rio Real against an Indian chief known as Surubi, he took the Indian nickname Pinasamonquu, "Long Line." When asked by the inquisitor why he took this name in the Indian custom, Álvares responded that he used the name there because it was how the Indians knew him, and that it meant that he was brave and had killed enemies.[26]

As with the mission to Arari, the Jesuits write that their mission to Rio Real began after the unexpected arrival in Bahia in 1574 of the chiefs of Rio Real, who came to the Jesuits in Salvador and asked for a mission to their homelands. The Indians of Rio Real had been at war with the Portuguese, and many Indian slaves who had fled Bahia in the Holy Week uprising of 1568 had taken refuge there. The Jesuit provincial sent Father Gaspar Lourenço with a companion back with the chiefs to Rio Real. Lourenço had lived in Brazil since childhood, he had been taught in the Jesuit school of São Paulo, and he was a gifted linguist, noted for his great eloquence in Tupi.[27]

According to the Jesuits, at the same time that Lourenço began his mission, the governor of northern Brazil, Luís de Brito, decided to take advantage of the changing political situation. Rio Real lay between Bahia and Pernambuco, and the presence of hostile Indians there had always impeded overland travel and had encouraged French interlopers to trade for brazilwood there. With the seeming "pacification" of the Indians of Rio Real by the Jesuits, Governor Brito sought to capitalize on the situation. He sent a captain with some men to Rio Real to see if a settlement could be made in the region. While Father Lourenço went with the chiefs 6 leagues (approximately 37 kilometers) into the sertão to visit the villages, the Portuguese captain made camp along the coast. Lourenço built four churches in Rio Real, including one in the village of Surubi, a chief greatly feared by the Portuguese and considered to be an enemy. He opened the first school for Indian boys and began evangelism. With this auspicious beginning, Lourenço wrote to the governor that the location on the coast was not suitable for a Portuguese settlement, as the land was sandy. The Portuguese, however, wrote the opposite to the governor, and showed no signs of desiring to return.[28]

In hindsight, the Jesuits believed that the ulterior motive for the presence of the Portuguese settlement was to acquire slaves. In Rio Real lived many runaway Indian slaves as well as many more Indians who might become new slaves. Governor Brito declared a just war against a hostile chief in this region, Aperipê. The governor collected a company of men in Bahia, one of whom was Gonçalo Álvares, who would have been fifteen or sixteen years old at the time, and began to march toward Rio Real. Although Lourenço attempted to persuade the governor that the beginning of the conversion process was a delicate time and that the presence of soldiers would frighten the Indians, his appeal fell on deaf ears.[29]

The battle between the preaching of the Jesuit missionaries and the mamelucos began at this critical moment. A mameluco, whose behavior the Jesuits could only understand as demonic, went through the villages where Lourenço had built the new churches and preached against him. According to the Jesuits, the mameluco said that Lourenço was there to trick them, that Lourenço had joined them together to make it easier to take them as slaves, and that the Portuguese were already on the beach ready to enslave them. Two more mamelucos appeared who also moved among the Indian villages. These mamelucos preached that Lourenço was worthless because he was unarmed and unaccompanied by men who could defend them. These two mamelucos also preached that the governor was on his way from Bahia to take them all as slaves.[30]

The Jesuits believed that the preaching of the mamelucos in Rio Real undermined the work that Lourenço had done, for the Indians soon felt threatened by the presence of the Portuguese and wanted to retreat deeper into the sertão. A Jesuit history records the Indians saying, "Let's go, let's go, before the Portuguese arrive," and Lourenço trying in vain to calm the Indians down. The actions of a third mameluco completely unsettled the Indians. This mameluco arrived at the village of the chief Surubi and kidnapped a woman, saying that she was a slave. The Indians, distraught at the brazen way that the mameluco had seized the woman, abandoned the village and moved to a fortified position deeper in the wilderness. At this point, the governor arrived to attack Aperipê, but seeing that Surubi had withdrawn from the village where Lourenço had built a church, the governor interpreted this as a hostile act and expanded his campaign to include Surubi, too. When the soldiers arrived, Surubi fought back and was killed by a bullet. Some of his people surrendered to a Portuguese captain, who promised to take them to the Jesuits and not to enslave them. But when they arrived at the coastal camp, the governor did enslave them. When the governor left, he ordered the other Indians, whom Lourenço had converted to Christianity, to march to Bahia. On the long march back, some of these Indians were shunted off into the forest and clapped into irons by the Portuguese. Lourenço arrived in Bahia with twelve hundred Indians, who were divided between two aldeias.[31]

As the Jesuits drafted their rebuttal to Soares de Sousa in 1592, they looked back with bitterness to these experiences in Rio Real. They had persuaded thirty Indian villages to accept peace with the Portuguese, and they had founded three new mission villages in Rio Real. But with the aggressive tactics of the governor, not only had the three new mission villages been lost, but the thirty Indian villages had risen up in rebellion. Many of the Indians that Gaspar Lourenço brought to Bahia died later from disease.[32] The Portuguese settlement in Rio Real was abandoned. The overland road to Pernambuco remained very dangerous, and French traders continued to land and trade there for brazilwood.

Not surprisingly, in their rebuttal of Soares de Sousa's charges, the Jesuits identify the "opening of the sertão" by Governor Luís de Brito—in other words, the campaign in Rio Real—as a turning point in their relationship with the colonists. Soares de Sousa had stated that the Jesuits openly preached against Governor Brito from the pulpit and that there had been a formal break between the Society and the governor. The Jesuits did challenge this war, arguing that it could not be considered a just war. In their response to Soares de Sousa's criticisms, the Jesuits remind the king that this war had subsequently been ruled unjust and that the Indians captured in it were ordered to be freed. The Jesuits also accuse Soares de Sousa as one of the captains on the expedition who had killed and enslaved many Indians in Rio Real. They argue that he created his plantation with the Indians he acquired there and that he sold many levies of slaves.[33]

The competition between the Jesuit missionary priests and the mamelucos in Rio Real, in Arari, and in the nearby sertão reveals much about the influence of go-betweens. There was a complicated interplay between persuasion and violence. Deep in the sertão, the power of the go-between rested solely on his ability to persuade, whereas violence was a tool used more commonly in the nearby sertão. In the deep sertão, Jesuit missionaries and mameluco go-betweens approached independent Indian villages and powerful autonomous chiefs carefully and with words rather than with overt violence. Jesuit missionaries entered the sertão alone, entrusting their lives, as well as the success of their mission, to God. Mamelucos such as Nobre recognized that the power of violence lay on the other side—with the powerful chiefs in the sertão. Therefore, they, too, approached Indian groups with words. Later, once initial contact had been established and exchanges such as trade had begun, violence, or its threat, strengthened the Portuguese presence in the sertão. The entradas that descended Indian slaves included a company of Indian archers, and the mamelucos themselves carried arms. But though mamelucos might exploit the threat of force, they did so only with care, because they could easily be overwhelmed if warfare broke out deep in the sertão. In the nearby sertão, however, Indian chiefs no longer had the upper hand. Often they were in open conflict with Portuguese society. Violence was quickly seized as a means to force the defeat of powerful chiefs. For example, in Rio Real, when an unnamed mameluco seized a woman by force, he did so because he was backed up by the governor, who was camped on the coast with a troop of armed men. Unlike the distant sertão, Rio Real was not far from

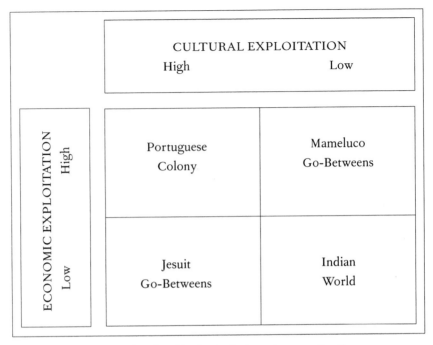

CULTURAL EXPLOITATION
High   Low

Portuguese   Mameluco
Colony   Go-Betweens

Jesuit   Indian
Go-Betweens   World

ECONOMIC EXPLOITATION
High
Low

Figure 8.3. Go-betweens and modes of domination in sixteenth-century Brazil

Salvador; it was on the coast, and the villages where Lourenço was evangelizing were only a short distance inland.

The Jesuit and mameluco go-betweens in the sertão represent two approaches for contacting, interacting, and ultimately dominating the Indian world. One mode, symbolized by the chameleon-like mamelucos, emphasized high economic exploitation and low cultural exploitation. The other, symbolized by the dyed-in-the-wool Jesuits, emphasized low economic exploitation and high cultural exploitation (Fig. 8.3). As Figure 8.3 illustrates, the Jesuit go-betweens represented a high level of cultural conformity by insisting on the primacy of the Portuguese Christian tradition. But because Jesuits did not seek the economic exploitation of Indians and defended the right of Indians to be free, Jesuits favored low economic exploitation. Mameluco go-betweens, on the other hand, had no qualms about the economic exploitation of Indians. Yet, mamelucos did not insist on cultural conformity. In their lives and in their behavior, cultural norms were relative to situations and not absolute, thus they were more tolerant of cultural difference.

Which of these two major transactional go-betweens would succeed in controlling the relationship between the Indian and the Portuguese worlds in the sertão? To answer this question requires returning to the distinction made by Georg Simmel between mediation, which implies neutrality on the part of the third party, and arbitration, which results when the third party chooses a side. The Jesuit missionary priests and most (but not all) of the mamelucos arbitrated; they did not mediate. Both took the side of the Portuguese colony. But the way they arbitrated and the interests of those for whom they arbitrated were quite different and profoundly significant. If Indians chose to trust mameluco go-betweens, their destination was slavery on the sugar plantations; if they chose the Jesuit go-betweens, they would find themselves relocated to aldeias. Both led to the domination of Indians by the Portuguese colony, but with very different results. The mamelucos were slave traders, but they did not seek to convert the Indians to a Portuguese way of life. The Jesuits would not enslave Indians, but they desired to change Indians fundamentally through the regimented life of the mission village.

Sugar planters favored the arbitration of the mamelucos rather than that of the Jesuits. As a result, the successful arbitration of the mamelucos influenced the nature of the colonial society in formation. The actions of planters such as Fernão Cabral, Gabriel Soares de Sousa, or Álvaro Rodrigues illustrate how the domination of Indians followed in the path blazed by the mameluco go-betweens. Once descended from the sertão, their Indian slaves would live in villages on their plantations where they were not expected to become model Christians. Cabral, Soares de Sousa, and Rodrigues all discouraged the missions of the Jesuits to their estates. Instead, they preferred to let their slaves express their religious beliefs as they pleased, as long as they worked on the plantations and accepted the lordship of the sugar planter. Their villages would become places where high economic exploitation would coexist with an acceptance of cultural differences.

The fate of the believers in the Santidade de Jaguaripe movement clearly reflects this strategy, as it was used by Fernão Cabral. The detail in the Inquisition records makes it possible to carefully reconstruct how the santidade came to his estate and flourished there. The competition between Jesuit and mameluco go-betweens is visible, as is Cabral's willingness to tolerate cultural differences for the larger goal of economic exploitation.

Cabral allowed the santidade to come to his estate because he accepted that economic exploitation did not require cultural domination. As we have seen, when rumors of the movement first appeared in the Recôncavo, Cabral decided that it was perfectly appropriate for him to take advantage of the situation. His kinsmen related to the inquisitor that Cabral wanted laborers for his estate. With his own financial backing and with the permission of the governor, he organized the entrada led by Domingos Fernandes Nobre. Nobre used words, not violence, to persuade part of the santidade to descend to Jaguaripe.

Nobre's account of his meeting with Antônio, the wandering prophet "pope" of the Santidade de Jaguaripe, is the closest we can come to understanding how a mameluco transactional go-between perceived his agency. The meeting that Nobre describes to the inquisitor occurred after he had sent ahead a message to Antônio that included a sketch outlining where they should meet and his gift of a suit of clothes. The encounter between the two men is characterized not by violence but by the exchange of gifts and the sharing of language and other forms of communication: smoke, music, and worship. Nobre describes how Antônio approached the agreed-upon place at the head of a long procession of men, women, and children, who followed him in ranks of three and with their hands held high. Of particular interest to Nobre, who was renowned as a translator, is the fact that they spoke in a new language, a language "invented" by the believers in the santidade. Nobre confessed to the inquisitor that on his knees before Antônio he worshiped Antônio and said, "Adoro-te, bode, porque hás de ser odre" (I worship you, goat, because you will become a wineskin). Then Nobre confessed that he joined in all the rituals of Antônio's movement: he "wailed and lamented," he "played and sang," he "jumped and celebrated," he "drank the sacred smoke," and he "allowed them to adore him and to call him son of God."[34]

Domingos Fernandes Nobre's companion, Pantalião Ribeiro, confessed to the inquisitor that he said virtually the same thing when he greeted Antônio: "Beijo-te, bode, porque hás de ser odre." The phrase has the ring of a proverb, which it is. The proverb "Beijo-te, bode, porque hás de ser odre" (I kiss you, goat, for you will become a wineskin) was common in Spain and Portugal. To interpret the proverb we must begin with the symbolic meanings of the goat and the wineskin. In Mediterranean cultures, the goat is suggestive of the ugly and the devilish, whereas the wineskin is seen as something valued because it holds something desirable—wine. One reading of the proverb in a European/Mediterranean cultural context is "I don't like you, but you have your uses"; another is "Even ugly things have their value."[35]

Pantalião Ribeiro, who was not a mameluco, told the inquisitor that he said the words to mislead Antônio the "pope," and that when he said them he would kneel before him, trying to embrace his feet. As a Portuguese immigrant, Ribeiro most likely meant the proverb to mean the obvious: I will kiss you now, you ugly goat, because you will be valuable to me in the future. Ribeiro was born in Portugal, where his father worked for the customs house of the city of Porto. Like the go-betweens who appear in works of fiction in the late fifteenth- and sixteenth-century Iberian world, Ribeiro had a great deal of physical mobility and an ill-defined social status. He had been born in Portugal, which conferred on him a certain prestige in Brazil, yet at the same time he was a farmer (*lavrador*) who lived in the not very prosperous parish of Jaguaripe; he was neither a sugar planter nor a man of means. Similarly, the classic go-between in Spanish literature—La Celestina—also has fluid social status, which enables her to move freely as a matchmaker in a highly stratified world. Another literary go-between with social mobility is Philtra in the sixteenth-century Portuguese play *Comedia Eufrosina*. Philtra uses the very same proverb—"Beijo-te, bode, porque as de ser odre"—in a scene where she makes it clear to the audience that she will play a character for all he is worth.[36]

What Nobre "Tomacaúna" meant when he said the proverb to Antônio is more difficult to understand. Given that Nobre had never been to Portugal; that he probably did not habitually drink wine, as a Portuguese laborer might; and that he had not herded goats, as might a young peasant boy in Portugal, it cannot be assumed that his use of the proverb reflects its original Mediterranean cultural meaning. In Brazil, not only was the goat one of the newly introduced domestic animals that was rapidly changing the landscape and providing new means of wealth for those living in or on the margins of the Portuguese colony, but wine was a foreign element, too. In sixteenth-century Brazil, wine was imported, expensive, and not widely used outside the centers of Portuguese settlement. Soares de Sousa writes that wine from Madeira and the Canary Islands was sold in stores in Salvador, but Jesuits outside Salvador frequently lamented that they did not have wine to celebrate the mass.[37]

Taking the Brazilian setting into consideration, other interpretations of the proverb emerge. The goat is not so much ugly as valuable, and the wine is precious, unattainable, and sacred. This, combined with the fact that the proverb clearly implies transformation (the goat turns into the wineskin), can suggest a very different meaning. The goat is valuable now, but it will be transformed into something even more valuable, perhaps even sacred, in the future. Moreover, we must take into account that Nobre does not recite the proverb exactly: he says "Adoro-te" (I worship you), whereas the common usage of the proverb is "Beijo-te" (I kiss you).

As a mameluco, Nobre possessed more complex and shifting loyalties than his Portuguese companion Pantalião Ribeiro. While Nobre served as an agent of sugar planters, he also had a profound tie to the indigenous world. An opportunist in order to survive, Nobre lived on the margins of respectability in Salvador. Although he was well known in Salvador, the Recôncavo, and Pernambuco, he gave his occupation to the inquisitor as "none." He was married, but his body was tattooed. When Nobre said "Adoro-te, bode, porque hás de ser odre," he used language rather than force to achieve his ends. The actual words state his strategy: he will worship (becoming a chameleon) because he is sure that in the future he will be rewarded. The substitution of the word "*adoro*" for "*beijo*" can alter the meaning of the proverb, because Nobre does not explain what his reward is to be. The reward can be material or it can be sacred. Nobre's ambiguous proverb plays to his advantage, both before Antônio and before the inquisitor. When he meets Antônio, he is among the intense believers in a new religion, and that means that he must worship, so he says "I adore you" to Antônio. It would not be too far-fetched to interpret the proverb in this setting to mean: "I worship you now, for you will become Christ." However, when he repeats the proverb before the inquisitor and the Jesuits sitting on the bench, the proverb retains its Mediterranean meaning: he will exploit an ugly goat for a material reward.

If we consider Simmel's definition of the tertius gaudens (the third who rejoices or enjoys), one more interpretation of this proverb uttered in the sertão comes into focus. That is that, as the go-between, Nobre is making a joke and enjoying it. The encounter between Nobre and Antônio has a theatrical quality about it. The procession, singing, and dancing and the formal greeting all seem to have taken place before an audience of believers. The fact that one phrase from the meeting—the proverb—survives verbatim in Nobre's trial further underscores the importance Nobre ascribed to that moment. At that moment, when Nobre "Tomacaúna" is the third party, the intermediary between the dyad of Cabral and Antônio and between the santidade and the Portuguese colony, he is, in Simmel's words, "the egoistical exploiter of the situation," and his situation "gives him at least the feeling of a slight ironical superiority over the parties."

Much is at stake for Antônio but not for Nobre. The proverb recited to Antônio and then repeated to the inquisitor is Tomacaúna's joke. He knows that he is the master of the situation, and he enjoys the role. In his moment of power, he has his fun.

In their aldeias and on their missions to the sugar plantations, the Jesuits saw the Santidade de Jaguaripe in a completely different light. It was a "superstition," a "plague," a "madness," and an "error." They blamed its outbreak on the devil. It was not appropriate in their eyes to fraternize with its followers nor to deceive them or joke with them, and certainly not to enslave them. Rather, as the Jesuits saw it, what was needed was to lead those blinded by the devil back to the true faith. According to the Jesuit provincial, the fathers and brothers "devoted great effort to suppressing these uprisings," seeking to "snatch souls from the snares of the devil." The Jesuits sought to dissuade the followers of the santidade by preaching against it. The provincial writes that they succeeded in persuading "many both from killing Portuguese and from the flight that they are meditating."[38]

But when the santidade arrived on his estate, Cabral did not follow the strategies of the Jesuits and seek to lead the believers back to Christianity. Instead, he welcomed the leaders—Mãe de Deus and Aricute—and he allowed his own slaves and runaway slaves from plantations in Bahia to baptize themselves into the movement. Cabral allowed the followers of the santidade to establish themselves in their own village on his estate, where he permitted them to build their own sanctuary.

Similar kinds of villages existed on sugar plantations elsewhere in the Recôncavo, particularly on the estate of Cabral's neighbor, Gabriel Soares de Sousa, who also lived in Jaguaripe, and on the estate of Álvaro Rodrigues, who lived in Paraguaçu. According to the Jesuits, Soares de Sousa prohibited the Jesuits from ministering to the village of Indians on his lands in Jaguaripe. On their periodic visits to plantations, Jesuits commonly asked Indians how they had descended from the sertão. In the eyes of the Jesuits, many of the Indians Soares de Sousa claimed as slaves were in fact free. The mameluco sugar planter Álvaro Rodrigues had a similar kind of village of Indians living on his estate in Cachoeira on the Paraguaçu River. A Jesuit denounced him for allowing the Indians in this village to live too much like Indians, including having multiple wives and continuing the custom of killing war captives in public ceremonies. Jesuits saw such Indian villages under the control of sugar planters as obstacles to creating a free Christian Indian population living in aldeias administered by the Jesuits.[39]

During the time when the Santidade de Jaguaripe freely practiced on his estate, Cabral stepped into the role of transactional go-between and arbitrated the relationship between the Santidade de Jaguaripe and the Portuguese in ways favorable to his own interests. He, too, egotistically exploited the moment by having his own joke. He made the santidade a spectacle, an entertainment, for his friends. Cabral allowed some from Salvador and the Recôncavo to visit the village of believers as long as they did not openly make fun of the rituals. Pero de Novais, who called himself a friend of Cabral's, made an additional trip to the inquisitorial board to make this point. He remembered that once, on Cabral's estate during the time of the santidade, he and António Lopes Ilhoa, a sugar mill owner and merchant, were invited by Cabral to visit the church of the santidade. Before he took them, however, Cabral made them promise not to laugh or to poke fun at the rituals. Novais decided not to go, but he told the inquisitor that Ilhoa did. Several others visited the church, including a judge, a notary, and the nephew of the governor.[40]

The accounts of the destruction of the Santidade de Jaguaripe, as recorded by the Jesuits and as revealed in the Inquisition trials, make clear that only when many colonists complained to the governor that their slaves had fled to Jaguaripe did Governor Manoel Teles Barreto command Cabral to dismantle the movement. Cabral did not immediately do the bidding of the governor. Instead, he stalled, saying, according to his kinsman Francisco de Abreu, that if he disbanded the santidade, when the news of this reached António in the sertão, "they would hurt and kill the white men [i.e., the men on Nobre's entrada] who were with him."[41] The governor then ignored Cabral and went around him. He ordered Bernaldino Ribeiro da Grã to go to Cabral's estate, where he was to tell Cabral that "there is no time to wait for Tomacaúna." Grã told the inquisitor that when he arrived, Cabral refused to help him unseat the movement, saying that they would be killed. But Grã went to the temple of the santidade with a companion but without Cabral. In the Indian language, which he told the inquisitor "he knew well," he persuaded them to surrender. He told them that they were completely surrounded by Christians, who would capture them and kill them if they tried to fight. He then burned the temple and took away the sacred stone, the books, and other ritual items. He ordered Cabral to shackle the believers and to take them in chains to the governor.[42]

Meanwhile, after many of his own slaves had run away to Jaguaripe, Álvaro
Rodrigues, the veteran mameluco Indian slaver and sugar plantation owner in
Cachoeira on the Paraguaçu River, presented himself to the governor. He suggested that he be appointed to put down the movement outside of Jaguaripe.
Rodrigues later claimed to the inquisitor that the governor and the city council
gave him their support, as did the Jesuits, who allowed him to take a levy of
Indian archers from the mission villages. Álvaro Rodrigues described how he
led his own Indians, as well as the mission Indians, many of whom still believed
in the santidade, through the Recôncavo and then the sertão of Jaguaripe.

Rodrigues represented competition for Cabral and for Nobre, who, as go-
betweens, still hoped to control how the believers in the santidade would descend
into colonial society. Rodrigues testified to the inquisitor that while in the wilderness he intercepted several letters from Cabral to Nobre. The letters, he
said, warned Nobre that he, Rodrigues, was on his way to capture him by order
of the governor. The letters also recounted, Rodrigues said under oath, how
in the past few days a judge (Bernaldino Ribeiro da Grã) had gone to Cabral's
estate with a request that he disband the santidade, but that Cabral had sent
him "to all the devils." One of the men on Rodrigues' entrada testified that as
they approached Nobre, who was with Antônio and the followers of the santidade, Nobre fled from them and took the followers of the movement, including
Antônio, with him.[43]

Then Rodrigues unleashed a new strategy, one that showed that the moment
in time and the physical space were changing. When Rodrigues encountered
congregations of the santidade, he took prisoner its leaders, whom he calls feiticeiros (sorcerers). But this, he told the inquisitor, did little, for it did not destroy
either their faith in the santidade or the faith of the believers. The sorcerers,
he reported, told him that they would "fly to the sky" and that "they were not
afraid of swords or chains because they would turn into wax." To break the
faith of those he held prisoner, as well as the faith in the santidade by his own
company of Indian archers and slaves, he had to preach to them in their own
language, "which he knows well," and convince them of the falsehoods of the
leaders. Rodrigues then describes his own drama, complete with persuasion and
violence. He ordered all to assemble so they might hear him preach. Then, in
front of them all, Rodrigues ordered the sorcerers' heads smashed. He told the
inquisitor that only "after they [the sorcerers] died, when the believers saw that
what they said was false," did he have control over them. So shocked were they,

he stated, that "many died on their feet out of fear of punishment and amazement, with no sign of any illness."[44]

Bernaldino Ribeiro da Grã and Álvaro Rodrigues used persuasion and violence to destroy the Santidade de Jaguaripe. They saw themselves in competition with the Jesuits, Nobre, and Cabral, all of whom had interacted with the movement's adherents primarily through language. Rodrigues' actions reveal that, in his view, simply preaching was not enough to control the movement. He believed that only violence could achieve that end. His methods were not those advocated by the Jesuits, nor those of the chameleon-like Nobre. Álvaro Rodrigues' strategy, though successful in defeating the movement, bore a high cost. By using violence, Rodrigues destroyed precisely what was desired by the Portuguese colony. By murdering the leaders, and by indirectly (or directly) causing the deaths of other believers in the Santidade de Jaguaripe, he killed potential slaves for the sugar plantations.

Álvaro Rodrigues' and Bernaldino Ribeiro de Grã's accounts of how they destroyed the Santidade de Jaguaripe with persuasion and violence reflect the growing influence of the Portuguese colony in the nearby sertão. Rodrigues defeated unarmed believers in a millenarian religious movement, not a tribe ruled by a powerful chief deep in the sertão. Grã obtained the surrender of an unarmed religious congregation on a sugar plantation. In both situations, the agents of the Portuguese colony recognized that they were powerful enough that they did not need the persuasiveness of the Jesuit missionary priests or of the mameluco línguas. By 1586, in the immediate sertão surrounding the settled areas of the Recôncavo, colonists had little need for the services of transactional go-betweens like Nobre or the Jesuit missionary priests. The situation had changed. Only in the distant sertões, where they were still faced with powerful chiefs, did the colonists depend on the transactional go-betweens and their strategies of persuasion.

The inquisitor's visit began to wind down in the second half of 1592 as he sentenced those whom he had tried. After a lengthy trial, during which Cabral had remained in prison for almost a year, the inquisitor sentenced him in August of 1592 and explained his rationale. Although Cabral's sins on the outside were very serious, his social status and circumstances were such that the inquisitor believed he could be shown a certain measure of mercy. The inquisitor fined Cabral 1,000 cruzados, which was approximately one-twentieth of the value of his estate, compelled him to attend the public ceremony of penitence held in the cathedral of Salvador, and sent him into forced exile as a degredado for two

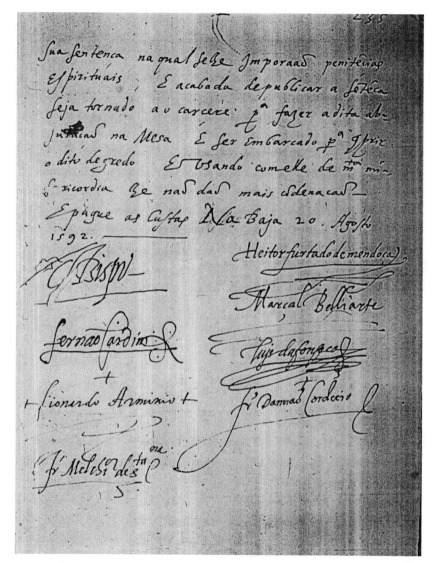

Figure 8.4. Four Jesuits sign Cabral's sentence. "Trial of Fernão Cabral de Ataíde," Inquisição de Lisboa 17065. Instituto dos Arquivos Nacionais / Torre do Tombo—Portugal.

years.[45] The inquisitor, the bishop, four Jesuits—Fernão Cardim, Leonardo Armínio, Marçal Beliarte, and Luís da Fonseca—and two other clerics, all of whom sat on the inquisitorial bench, signed his sentence (Fig. 8.4).

A month later, in one of his last letters, José de Anchieta wrote that a humbled Cabral publicly received his sentence, "giving thanks to the inquisitor" for the mercy he had been shown.[46]

In March of 1593, Domingos Fernandes Nobre received his sentence. His punishment was considerably lighter than Cabral's. Of all Nobre's sins, the inquisitor was most interested in his failure to abstain from eating meat on days of obligation in the sertão. But Nobre had convinced him that since he was such a big man, vegetables were not enough to sustain him. The inquisitor ordered him to perform various penitences, to pay the costs of his trial, and never to return to the sertão. The other men on his entrada who were tried by the inquisitor likewise received minor punishments and were also ordered never to return to the sertão. The mameluco Lázaro da Cunha had confessed his sins during the time of grace, and as a result, he, too, received leniency. Even though he told the inquisitor that he had been present when the Indians of the sertão ate human flesh, the inquisitor did not follow up on this piece of information. Cunha claimed that when in such situations, he ate pork, pretending that it was human meat. The inquisitor accepted this at face value and ordered him only to perform various spiritual penitences, to pay twenty cruzados to the Inquisition, and never again to return to the sertão.[47]

Francisco Pires, the mameluco who had preached against the Jesuit João Vicente, received the harshest sentence. The inquisitor ordered Pires to appear at the cathedral on a Sunday, barefoot, with his head uncovered, and with a lit candle in his hand, to hear his sentence. Not only was he never to return to the sertão, but he was to pay 30 cruzados to the Inquisition and to be whipped in public. His heavier punishment owed to his failure to confess during the period of grace and to a petition he had filed with the inquisitor. The inquisitor interpreted his petition (which asked for a rapid closure to his case in view of his impecunious state) as insolent.[48]

Álvaro Rodrigues, who saw himself as the one who had successfully defeated the congregations of the Santidade de Jaguaripe in the sertão, also found himself at the center of his own Inquisition trial. But the inquisitor did not find the evidence against him—that he allowed Indians to live in their traditional ways on his estate or that he had been excommunicated for robbing slaves from a kinswoman—to be extensive enough to condemn him. He did, however, assign Rodrigues spiritual penitences and ordered him never to return to the sertão without the express permission of the bishop of Salvador.[49]

In the midst of doling out these sentences, the inquisitor found himself the target of reprimands from Lisbon. He had sent two prisoners to Lisbon, but when their cases were reviewed by the tribunal there, the inquisitors deemed that there was not enough evidence against them. Both were set free. The cardinal who served as head of the Lisbon Inquisition wrote him in April of 1593, telling him not to imprison anyone else unless he had sufficient proof, for to do so would tarnish the reputation of the Holy Office. He assumed that Mendonça had already made his way to Pernambuco, where he wanted the inquisitor to undertake the "shortest possible visit" and then to return immediately to Lisbon. Although Mendonça was to have traveled to São Tomé and Cape Verde after he finished his work in Brazil, the cardinal ordered those two visits cancelled. Accompanying the cardinal's letter was another from inquisitors on the Lisbon tribunal that stated that the evidence Mendonça had collected against two more residents he had imprisoned was also judged to be insufficient. A letter from September of 1593 ordered him to proceed directly to Pernambuco, if he had not already done so, because he had been in Bahia for two and a half years and had "caused much expense." A letter from March 1594 acknowledged the receipt of several mailings from Mendonça, but again criticized his handling of a sentence. Mendonça had sentenced Marcos Tavares, the mameluco son of Iria Álvares (the only Indian believer in the Santidade de Jaguaripe tried by the inquisitor), to a public whipping and had sent him as a degredado from Brazil. The tribunal in Lisbon believed, however, that Mendonça should not have publicized Tavares' sin—sodomy—because "of the scandal that arises from knowing that there are delinquents in this crime." His seniors in Lisbon again ordered him to "quickly finish" his work in Pernambuco and to return to Lisbon. In December of 1594, they told him curtly to cut his Pernambuco visit short, because he had "spent much time and caused much expense."[50]

When the inquisitor arrived in Salvador in 1591, his power seemed limitless, but when he left Bahia in September of 1593, it seemed considerably less so. Several of those he had imprisoned had been freed, and three individuals were actively petitioning the Inquisition in Lisbon for a reassessment of their sentences. The letters sent to him by his superiors repeatedly asked him for transcripts of these trials. One of those who had filed a petition was Fernão Cabral. Cabral deeply resented how he had been imprisoned and sentenced, and he had set about challenging his trial in 1593.[51] Although the sentences given to the mamelucos, with the exception of Francisco Pires', were milder than Cabral's, it is unlikely that they were fully carried out. The men did perform their spiritual penitences, but they most probably did return to the sertão. On 2 August 1593, before the visiting inquisitor left for Pernambuco, the inquisitorial bench met to consider whether to enforce the ban on mamelucos returning to the sertão. The bench agreed that if the governor needed them to destroy a santidade or to provide help in war or to discover mines of metal, the men could obtain permission from the bench, or from the bishop, to return. Domingos Fernandes Nobre later received a land grant in Sergipe—as the region north of Rio Real came to be known—the very place where the Jesuit father Lourenço had battled the mamelucos in 1574.[52]

When Inquisitor Mendonça left for Pernambuco, his moment in Bahia was over and much of his power as an individual go-between was lost. Similarly, the strategies of persuasion used by mamelucos or by the Jesuits were no longer needed in the nearby sertão by the end of the sixteenth century. There, too, the moment of the persuasive transactional go-between had passed. Yet, the influence of the Inquisition in Brazil had hardly ended when Mendonça left Brazil, just as, deep in the sertão, strategies of persuasion continued to be used by mamelucos and Jesuits alike. And, even when individuals had lost power as go-betweens, the consequences of their agency could still be felt among those for whom they had arbitrated.

The lingering influence of the transactional go-betweens can be seen in another set of laws on Indian slavery in Brazil. In 1597, a ship anchored off Salvador that was carrying a document eagerly expected by the Jesuits. That document clarified a new law, signed by the king in November 1595, stating that all Indians of Brazil were free and that no one might go into the sertão to enslave them. In the new law of 1595, the king explicitly recognized that the colonists of Brazil had manipulated the "words" and "meaning" of "just war" doctrine to enslave Indians. The king now placed the right to declare a just war in his hands solely. The only Indians who could be enslaved were those captured in a war ordered by the king, and such a war would be announced in an official document, duly signed by the king. All Indians enslaved through other means were to live in freedom, and if colonists wished to take advantage of Indian labor, they must pay the Indians for their work.[53]

Another document signed by the king eight months later, in July of 1596, went even further. This document addressed the practice of descending Indians from the sertão. The 1596 document clearly states that for there to be "good communication" between the Indians of the sertão and the colonists, the king designates the Society of Jesus as the ones who should have the "care" of "descending" the Indians from the sertão. Only the Jesuits would go to the sertão to convince the Indians to come and live and interact with the colonists. The governor and the Jesuits would determine where villages of Indians might be created, and the Jesuits would declare to the Indians in the sertão that they were free, that they would live as free persons in the newly created villages, and that they "would be masters of their property, just as in the sertão." "The Indians will not be able to say," the king's document reads, "that they were descended against their will or through deceit."[54]

"Now," Pero Rodrigues, the Jesuit provincial of Brazil, wrote confidently in 1597, "from here forward the priests of the Society will be able to perform their ministry without the opposition of the people."[55] By 1597, Soares de Sousa's pointed criticisms of the Society had been refuted, and the Jesuits had regained the favor and respect of the Crown. Three years before the end of the sixteenth century it seemed that the Jesuits had finally won their battles: against Indian slavery, against the mamelucos in the sertão, and against the sugar planters of the coast.

But the Jesuit provincial was wrong. Though the new law seemed to say that the Jesuits had won the battle for the Indians by dislodging the mamelucos in the sertão and by discrediting those who held Indian slaves in the colony, the Jesuits had not won. The law did little to help the Jesuits hold on to their desired position as the sole intermediaries between the Indian world and the Portuguese colony. Nor could the Jesuits keep the role they coveted as the chief intermediaries between the Indians and God. Where the social and political structures of traditional Indian society remained intact, village shamans and wandering prophets resisted them; where traditional Indian village structures had been destroyed, new kinds of religious leaders, such as Antônio in the Santidade de Jaguaripe, challenged them. Although the Jesuits continually won the war on paper, by persuading the Crown and the pope to issue laws and bulls in their favor, mameluco go-betweens outmatched them in the sertão time and time again. There were too few Jesuit línguas and missionary priests to maintain the aldeias, to minister to slaves living on plantations, and to mount an active missionary campaign in the sertão. Even as the numbers of Jesuits in Brazil grew, as Soares de Sousa perceptively saw, Jesuits spent increasingly more time in their colleges than in missions to the sertão. For their vision to be effective, Jesuits needed the full support and cooperation of the colonial elite.

Instead, the future would hold even more brutal battles between Jesuit missionaries and mameluco slave traders in the sertão, and between the Jesuits and the colonists in the Portuguese settlements. In the seventeenth century, entradas known as *bandeiras* began a whole new cycle of Indian slavery that affected tens of thousands of Guarani. Mamelucos organized these bandeiras from the towns of the Piratininga Plateau in São Vicente. The competition with the Jesuit missionaries reached the point of open conflict when the bandeiras attacked the

Jesuit missions and enslaved the Indians. In the Amazon, when the great Jesuit visionary of Brazil, António Vieira, arrived in 1653 to reestablish the Jesuit missions, he faced many of the same controversies that had plagued his forerunners in Bahia. Vieira stepped into controversies over whether Indians could be enslaved, who controlled Indian labor, and how entradas into the sertão to descend slaves ought to be organized.[56]

When the visiting inquisitor, sick from the Atlantic crossing, stepped ashore in Salvador in July of 1591, his encounter with Brazil was markedly different from those of the first Europeans nearly one hundred years before. He was welcomed into a Brazil that was now a well-established Portuguese colony. The earlier conflicts between the Portuguese and the Indian worlds had retreated far from Salvador and were visible only in the distant sertões. The go-betweens on the Portuguese side had fundamentally changed the direction of coastal Brazil, and though the Portuguese colonies were still small enclaves, clustered like islands along the coast, certain patterns had been set in motion that, like living organisms, would continue to reproduce themselves. The way the Portuguese colony would interact with the Indian world in the seventeenth and eighteenth centuries followed the pattern set by the mameluco transactional go-betweens of the sixteenth century. New go-betweens emerged who used very similar strategies for arbitration in the new encounters between the Indian and the colonial worlds in subsequent centuries.

I began this book with the story of an unnamed Indian woman who negotiated such an encounter in the first years of the seventeenth century: a peace between the Aimoré and the governor of Brazil. The Jesuit historians Pierre du Jarric and Fernão Guerreiro never name this woman, but they do provide more details about her life that are worth pondering. Both Jesuits give the credit for the peace not to her, but to "a man of honor and of means," a man now well known to readers of this book: Álvaro Rodrigues. Guerreiro describes how in 1602, Álvaro Rodrigues, still living in Cachoeira on the Paraguaçu River, made peace with the Aimoré by sending a woman to them with presents. Guerreiro notes that Rodrigues had obtained this woman (and another who died) "in an attack against the Aimoré." A third Jesuit, Pero Rodrigues, who had been the Jesuit provincial of Brazil at the end of the sixteenth century, leaves no doubt about her status: she was Rodrigues' slave. Pero Rodrigues calls the woman a "Christian slave of the same nation [Aimoré]."[57]

Vicente do Salvador, a Franciscan who lived in Salvador in the early seventeenth century and who wrote a history of Brazil, tells us even more, including the name of the Aimoré woman. Her baptismal Christian name, he writes, was Margarida. As a girl, Salvador continues, she had been captured by Rodrigues in a raid against the Aimoré and had been brought back to his estate. There she learned not Portuguese, but Tupi, and she wore the cotton shirt (or cotton sack) that Indian slave women wore once they had become Christians.[58]

Like most in Bahia, Álvaro Rodrigues did not speak the Aimoré language because the Aimoré were of the Gê linguistic family, not of the Tupi-Guarani. Rodrigues thus sent Margarida as the go-between. Bearing a hammock, mirrors, combs, and knives, she returned to the Aimoré and initiated the encounter. Later, when the first Aimoré approached Rodrigues' estate, he gave them more gifts and dressed them in red cloth. When Rodrigues ferried them across the Bay of All Saints to the city of Salvador, Vicente do Salvador tells us that "there was not a single shop or tavern that did not invite them in and toast them." After the agreement was worked out between the chief and the governor, the Aimoré came to the island of Itaparica, where the Jesuits began to teach them Christianity.[59]

Despite the joy of the Jesuits, and even of the people of Bahia, who celebrated the peace made with the Aimoré, Guerreiro and Jarric report a tragic but familiar ending to this story. The Aimoré who arrived to settle on the island of Itaparica soon became very sick. The disease is left unnamed, but it could have been one of any number. The Jesuits worked day and night for two and a half months taking care of them during the epidemic and trying to save their souls before they died. When the epidemic subsided, many Aimoré fled back to their homelands. But, having made contact, the Jesuits subsequently sent a missionary priest to the Aimoré to live among them and to learn their language.[60]

Through her actions, an Aimoré slave woman named Margarida opened a door into the Gê world. Since most of the Gê peoples lived in the central highlands of Brazil, the opening of such doors in the early seventeenth century did not immediately impact them. But through doors such as these, change would come, and when it did, many of the same kinds of go-betweens that had appeared in the sixteenth century would emerge again to transact the relations between the Gê Indian world and the interests of the Portuguese colonists. The story of Margarida thus represents the end and the beginning. By the time we meet her, the go-betweens of the sixteenth century had already arbitrated many of the interactions between the Portuguese and the Indian worlds in favor of the Portuguese. Multiple coastal settlements were firmly in place, and the Portuguese had "won" large tracts of the coast from Tupi-Guarani-speaking peoples. The arbitration by Margarida represents a new phase, one with Gê peoples and with other indigenous groups living within Brazil. Her role repeats patterns of the sixteenth century in this new encounter of the seventeenth century. The agency of many go-betweens, some named but most not, enabled the Portuguese to win their claim to Brazil in the sixteenth century. The Portuguese did, however, pay a price: cultural hegemony. Cultural domination required the methods of the Jesuits, which few colonists by the end of the sixteenth century were willing to accept. Instead, colonists preferred to rely on the more ambiguous bicultural mameluco go-betweens, who delivered economic, but not cultural, domination. Because mamelucos, rather than Jesuit missionary priests, descended the majority of Indians from the sertão to the coast, most became slaves. Mameluco transactional go-betweens did a poor job of acculturating those Indian slaves into Portuguese society. Sugar planters like Fernão Cabral, Gabriel Soares de Sousa, and Álvaro Rodrigues followed the lead of the mamelucos and allowed their slaves to live on their estates in semi-autonomous villages. They did not want the Jesuits to minister to them or to impose rules on them.

The defeat of the Santidade de Jaguaripe did not end resistance to the growing power of the Portuguese colony. Santidades continued to emerge and to challenge the Portuguese colonial authorities with their mix of religious syncretism and resistance to slavery. In 1602, a Jesuit mission deep in the sertão of Bahia encountered a santidade that, like the Santidade de Jaguaripe, imitated many outward Christian practices, including the requirement that the priests of the santidade be celibate. In 1610, the governor of Brazil wrote to the king that in the wilderness was a santidade of Indians and Africans of more than twenty thousand persons, and he requested permission to attack and enslave them. In 1612, Diogo de Campos Moreno, a Portuguese official appointed to study Brazil, uses *"mocambo,"* a term later used to denote "a community of runaway African slaves," and the term *"santidade"* to describe the ills plaguing Brazil. Moreno blames the appearance of "mocambos among slaves, or camps of runaways, which are called santidades," and other problems on the Indians' poor learning of Christian doctrine from their Jesuit tutors. When the Jesuits attempt to punish Indians, however lightly, he states, "the Indians immediately run away to the forest, where they create . . . abominable rituals and behaviors and join the runaway slaves of Guinea, and from this deaths, robberies, scandals, and violence result." In correspondence in 1613 between the king and the governor of Brazil, Gaspar de Sousa, the king writes that he understands that "in two or three places there are groups of Indians and African slaves who had fled their masters and joined together with others, and that they lived in idolatry, and that they called their communities santidades." The king suggests to the governor that he call on Afonso Rodrigues, son of Álvaro Rodrigues, to help him. In another letter later in the same year, the king refers to the same problem, naming a place 14 leagues (approximately 86 kilometers) from Salvador, on the frontier of the wilderness, as a locale where "there have been many uprisings of Indians and deaths of white people and runaways of slaves from the plantations," and that "30 leagues [approximately 185 kilometers] distant is a big village of runaway Indians that they call santidade."[61]

These sources link santidades with the first mocambos and *quilombos* (runaway slave communities), a powerful form of slave resistance in colonial Brazil. In a remote region between Salvador and Pernambuco, the famous quilombo of Palmares formed sometime near the end of the sixteenth century. In 1602, the governor of Pernambuco organized the first expedition against five or six villages of runaway African slaves located in the wilderness between Bahia and Pernambuco. Already known by the name Palmares, these villages would later become Brazil's most famous quilombo. Situated in the present-day state of Alagoas, Palmares was remote enough during the late sixteenth and early seventeenth centuries to be defended by the escaped slaves, yet close enough for slaves to attack roads, plantations, villages, and even the city of Salvador. Recent archaeological excavations of Palmares reveal extensive Indian influence at the site, a fact that reinforces the image of the community as one formed by both Indians and Africans seeking freedom.[62]

These recurring movements of resistance, redemption, and renewal reveal that the colonial enterprise simultaneously created and repressed new multi-ethnic and religious traditions that appealed to Indian and African slaves and to others living on the margins of the Portuguese colony. Because Brazilian colonial society came to be characterized by high economic exploitation with a tolerance of cultural difference, Indian and/or slave leaders had the opportunity to create syncretic religious rituals that rejected Portuguese rule. Violent responses on the part of slave owners and governors often destroyed such movements of resistance when they were deemed too threatening, but they did not lead to a fundamental change in their strategies of domination. For sugar planters and Crown officials continued to rely on transactional go-betweens who lived between worlds and who could deliver economic domination but not cultural conformity. Highly pronounced economic exploitation continued to coexist, therefore, with a degree of cultural tolerance in the colony of Brazil. Such was the legacy of the sixteenth-century mameluco go-betweens who "won" the sertão for the Portuguese colony. Their complex personalities and cunning strategies created modes of domination that would persist long after they themselves had been forgotten.

Notes

In citing works in the notes, short titles have generally been used. Works, archives, or collections frequently cited have been identified by the abbreviations below.

ABBREVIATIONS

ANTT	Arquivo Nacional da Torre do Tombo, Lisbon
APEB	Arquivo Público do Estado da Bahia
ARSI	Archivum Romanum Societatis Iesu, Rome
Bras.	Provincia Brasiliensis et Maragnonensis, in ARSI
CC	Corpo Cronológico, in ANTT
HCPB	*História da colonização portuguesa do Brasil*
IL	Inquisição de Lisboa, in ANTT
Lus.	Lusitania: Assistencia et Provincia, in ARSI
MB	Leite, Serafim, *Monumenta brasiliae*
NIW	Parry and Keith, *New Iberian World*
PV: C-Bahia	*Primeira visitação . . . : Confissões da Bahia 1591–1592* (1935)
PV: D-Bahia	*Primeira visitação . . . : Denunciações da Bahia 1591–1593*
PV: DC-Pernambuco	*Primeira visitação . . . : Denunciações e Confissões de Pernambuco 1593–1595*
VFL	Vatican Film Library, St. Louis

1. GO-BETWEENS

1. Jarric, *Histoire des choses*, 3:467–475. Jarric's account was based on Guerreiro's *Relação anual*, 1:390–391. Accounts of this meeting also appear in Pero Rodrigues' *Vida do Padre José de Anchieta*, and in Salvador, *História do Brasil*, 302–303. Many historians have included it in accounts of Brazil; see Southey, *History of Brazil*, 1:407–408; Hemming, *Red Gold*, 172–173; Campos, *Crónica*, 89–91. I return to this story at the end of this book.

2. Simmel and Wolff, *Sociology of Georg Simmel*, 122–162; quotations from 141, 145.

3. Simmel and Wolff, *Sociology of Georg Simmel*, on mediators and arbitrators, 148–151; on the *tertius gaudens*, 154–162. Robert Paine recognizes similar agents but labels them differently. He argues that when messages are delivered faithfully, "we recognize the role of go-between," whereas when messages are manipulated and processed, "we recognize a broker." Paine, *Patrons and Brokers*, 6.

4. Frances Karttunen discusses the careers of six men and ten women, among them Sacagawea; see *Between Worlds;* see also the collection of essays on intermediaries edited by Margaret Connell Szasz, *Between Indian and White Worlds*. Mary Karasch, "Damiana da Cunha," quotation from 105.

5. Díaz, *Historia verdadera*, 56–57 and passim; quotation from 57. On Cortés being addressed as Malinche, see 120. Bernal Díaz gives credit to the importance of translators, especially Doña Marina, and consistently notes their presence throughout his memoir. Cortés, on the other hand, mentions Doña Marina only

twice in his letters and rarely explains how he can communicate; see Cortés, *Cartas y documentos*, 14–15, 49, 269–270. The classic account of Malinche's legacy to Mexican identity is Octavio Paz' "Los hijos de la Malinche," in *El laberinto de la soledad;* see also Sandra Messinger Cypess' *La Malinche in Mexican Literature*. A recent account of Malinche's role in the conquest is Anna Lanyon's *Malinche's Conquest*.

6. The twelfth book of the *Codex Florentino* has several images of Doña Marina, all showing her "in between" serving as a translator; Sahagún, *História general*. Another important visual source that similarly records Doña Marina's role in the conquest from an Indian point of view is Alfredo Chavero's *El lienzo de Tlaxcala*.

7. Diamond, *Guns, Germs, and Steel*, 68.

8. Lockhart, *Men of Cajamarca*, 450; Pizarro, *Relación*, 5, 6, 37, 40. See also Lockhart's discussion of the interpreter Martinillo, later known as Don Martín Pizarro, and his rise in social status following the conquest; in *Spanish Peru*, 213–215, and in *Men of Cajamarca*, 450.

9. According to Rolena Adorno, the positioning of the Spaniards can be read by understanding the symbolic value of Andean pictorial space, in which the upper position is more highly valued than the lower, and the right more than the left. According to Adorno, the Spaniards "are ranked on a scale of descending value, from Almagro to Pizarro to Fray Vicente de Valverde to Felipillo the interpreter" (*Guaman Poma*, 95). The underlying Andean iconography in Guaman Poma's depiction of this historical moment, according to Adorno, underscores Guaman Poma's own interpretation: that Almagro had the

highest status among the Spaniards. This is due to the fact that Almagro would later oppose Pizarro after he sentenced Atahualpa to death. Guaman Poma had little respect for Felipillo; Adorno writes that he was "by far the most despicable" (*Guaman Poma*, 95, 164 n. 15) because he betrayed his race; see *Guaman Poma*, 89—93.

10. Guaman Poma, *El primer nueva corónica y buen gobierno*, complete digitized edition available online at the Royal Library, Copenhagen. A text edition, *El primer nueva corónica y buen gobierno*, is edited by John Murra and Rolena Adorno. On his life and writings, see Adorno, "Images of *Indios Ladinos* in Early Colonial Peru," and "Don Felipe Guaman Poma de Ayala."

11. Hagedorn, "'A Friend to Go between Them'"; Amado, "La séduction de l'autre"; Coates, *Convicts and Orphans;* Queija, "El papel de mediadores"; Richter, "Cultural Brokers"; and "Iroquois versus Iroquois." For an overview of cultural brokers in American history, see Hinderaker, "Translation and Cultural Brokerage."

12. White, *Middle Ground*, x—xi.

13. Merrell, "'Customes,'" 125.

14. Merrell, *Into the American Woods*, especially 28—41.

15. Greenblatt, *Marvelous Possessions*, 7, 119, 143—145.

16. Hagedorn, "A Friend to Go between Them"; Kellog, *Law and the Transformation of Aztec Culture*, 13—24.

17. Adorno, "Don Felipe Guaman Poma de Ayala"; Mundy, *Mapping of New Spain;* Boone, *Stories in Red and Black;* Oettinger and Horcasitas, *The Lienzo of Petlacala;* Graham, *Performing Dreams;* Albert and Ramos, *Pacificando o branco.*

18. Hermann, *No reino do desejado*, 23—176.

19. Anonymous Portolan Atlas, known as the Vallard Atlas.

2. ENCOUNTER

1. Cabral commanded thirteen ships, but one was lost off the Cape Verde Islands, leaving the twelve that arrived in Brazil. Pero Vaz de Caminha and a physician, cosmographer, astronomer, and astrologer with the armada, known simply as Mestre (Master) João, wrote directly to the king on 1 May 1500. Each referenced other letters that were written to the king of Portugal (by Cabral as well as by the other ships' captains). All of these letters were dispatched directly to Portugal on the same ship, the supply ship that returned with the news of the discovery, while the rest of the fleet (now eleven ships) sailed on to India. None of these letters, save those of Caminha and Mestre João, are known to historians today. The third account is from a diary known as the "Relação do piloto anônimo," which included a description of Brazil as part of a report on the whole of Cabral's expedition. There are minor discrepancies in the accounts: Caminha says that they landed on the 23rd of April; Mestre João and the anonymous Portuguese cite the date as the 24th. The Caminha letter was first published only in 1817. See the modern edition of the letter in Amado and Figueiredo, *Brasil 1500*, 73—122. William B. Greenlee published an English translation of the letter in the 1930s; see *Voyage of Pedro Alvares Cabral.* For Mestre João's letter, see the modern edition, "Carta do Mestre João 1° de Maio de 1500," in Amado and Figueiredo, *Brasil 1500*, 123—130; for the anonymous account, see the

excerpt pertaining to Brazil in "Relação
do português anônimo, 1500," in Amado
and Figueiredo, *Brasil 1500*, 131–141; and
for the full account, which includes what
happened after the fleet left Brazil, as of
this writing, there is an online version at
Folha Online: http://www1.uol.com.br/
fol/brasil500/histdescob4.htm.

2. Mestre João describes how he went
ashore with two pilots to shoot the sun
at midday with the astrolabe. He judged
that they were seventeen degrees south of
the equator. See "Carta do Mestre João"
in Amado and Figueiredo, *Brasil 1500*,
123–124. Patricia Seed explores how the
Portuguese used their navigational exper-
tise in just this way to claim dominion
over new lands; see *Ceremonies of Possession*, 100–148.

3. Greenblatt, *Marvelous Possessions*,
139.

4. Pinzón commanded the *Niña*, the
small caravel, on Columbus' first voyage.
Pinzón outfitted four ships in 1499 and set
his course farther south than had Columbus; he sailed first to the Canary Islands,
then to the Cape Verde Islands before
seeking winds to carry him across the
Atlantic. He passed below the equator,
losing sight of the North Star, during the
crossing. It is thought that Pinzón landed
first at 5° S, at present-day Cabo de São
Roque, before turning northwest. The two
encounters described here therefore took
place between Cabo de São Roque and the
Amazon River, which Pinzón is credited
with discovering; see Manzano Manzano,
Los Pinzones. The Anghiera text is known
as *Libretto de tutta la navigatione de re de
Spagna de le isole et terreni novamente trovati*, and this account appears in chapter
29. The relevant portion of Anghiera's
account may also be found as "El primer

viaje de Vicente Yáñez al Brasil (1499–
1500) en las *Décadas del Nuevo Mundo
del milanés Pedro Mártir de Anglería*,"
in Manzano Manzano, *Los Pinzones*,
3:39–44. The quoted phrases are taken
from the English translation by Theodore Cachey of Anghiera's *Libretto* . . . ,
51–52, available at the John Carter
Brown Library (hereafter cited as JCB).

5. Known today as the "Relação do
piloto anônimo" or as the "Relação do
português anônimo," this account was a
log written during Cabral's voyage and
was first published in Venice in 1507 from
a now lost original. Fracanzano (or Fran-
canzano) da Montalboddo included it in
Paesi nuovamente retrovati, books 2 and
3. For a modern edition, see "Relação do
português anônimo, 1500," in Amado and
Figueiredo, *Brasil 1500*, 131–141. Modern
scholars are uncertain if its author was in
fact a pilot; see Amado and Figueiredo,
Brasil 1500, 131 n. 1.

6. "Carta de Pero Vaz de Caminha,"
in Amado and Figueiredo, *Brasil 1500*,
quotes from pages 96, 98, 110. Diogo
Dias was knowledgeable in the arts of
seafaring and contact with new peoples,
since he had accompanied Vasco da Gama
to India as a scribe. He was therefore a
man of status and experience in Cabral's
fleet. His brother, Bartolomeu Dias, was
the first Portuguese to round the Cape
of Good Hope, and he commanded one
of the ships in Cabral's fleet. On this trip,
however, his ship went down rounding
the Cape of Good Hope. Diogo, pilot
of another ship, did survive the voyage.
See Amado and Figueiredo, *Brazil 1500*,
520–521.

7. See Barros, *Asia* . . . , *Primeira
Decada*, book 5, chap. 2, ff. 55v–56. Barros uses the term *"negro,"* which could

also mean that the sailor was a slave; he states that the interpreter tried to communicate in the "language of Guinea."

8. "Carta de Pero Vaz de Caminha," in Amado and Figueiredo, *Brasil 1500,* quotation from 94. Amado cites twenty-one degredados that Cabral had with him to use as needed; see "La séduction de l'autre," 242. Coates gives the English equivalent of *degredados* as "male criminal exiles" in *Convicts and Orphans,* xviii. The anonymous Portuguese writes that the two degredados had been condemned to death in Portugal and that they had been brought on the armada for just such a contingency; see "Relação do português anônimo," in Amado and Figueiredo, *Brasil 1500,* 137. Pero Vaz de Caminha names one of the men as Afonso Ribeiro, a servant of Dom João Telo; see "Carta de Pero Vaz de Caminha," in Amado and Figueiredo, *Brasil 1500,* 105. Caminha suggests that past experience had taught the captains to be suspicious of the information given by persons taken by force; see "Carta de Pero Vaz de Caminha," in Amado and Figueiredo, *Brasil 1500,* 94.

9. O'Callaghan, *Reconquest and Crusade,* 41−44, 214−215; Hanson, *Atlantic Emporium,* 18; Russell, *Prince Henry,* 33−34; António Dias Farinha, "Norte de África."

10. Brooks, *Landlords and Strangers,* 49−119; Bovill, *Golden Trade.* Vogt, *Portuguese Rule,* 1−6, quotation from 1 (the term "Maghrib" refers to north and northwest Africa between the Atlantic Ocean and Egypt). Dunn, *Adventures of Ibn Battuta,* 3.

11. On the secret planning of the attack, the actual assault, and the significance of the fall of Ceuta, see Russell, *Prince Henry,* 31−58, as well as Farinha, "Norte

de África," in Bethencourt and Chaudhuri, *História da expansão portuguesa,* 1:119−123. The attack against Tangier in 1437, led by Prince Henry and his brother Fernando, was a complete failure. The Portuguese were beaten by Sala ben Sala, the Muslim governor of Ceuta during the 1415 Portuguese attack. The Portuguese lost many men, and Prince Fernando was taken prisoner. The Muslims demanded Ceuta for Prince Fernando's freedom, but Prince Henry and his brothers were unwilling to concede the city. Fernando eventually died in prison. See Russell, *Prince Henry,* 167−194; Farinha, "Norte de África," 1:123−124; and Hanson, *Atlantic Emporium,* 103−104.

12. Bethencourt, "O contacto," 1:93; Amado, "La séduction de l'autre." See also Elkiss, "On Service," 44−53; Couto, "Contribuição dos 'lançados,'" 31−34; Hein, "Portuguese Communication," 41−51; and Brooks, *Landlords and Strangers.*

13. This is the central theme of Russell's *Prince Henry.*

14. There is a wealth of literature on Portuguese shipbuilding; a useful introduction in English is Unger, "Portuguese Shipbuilding," 229−249. The Order of Christ emerged after the suppression of the Templars and inherited all of its properties. The appointment of Prince Henry as administrator general represented the Portuguese Crown's desire to assert royal control over this powerful religious military order. See Russell, *Prince Henry* 77−80.

15. Riley, "Ilhas atlânticas," 1:145−159.

16. Of the Atlantic islands, only the Canaries, claimed by Spain, were inhabited. On the Portuguese colonization of the Atlantic islands, see Rodney, *History,* 71−75, and Brooks, *Landlords and*

Strangers, 143–166. On the use of degre-dados, see Coates, *Convicts and Orphans*, 22–23, 35–37, 60–64, and Pieroni, *Excluídos do reino*, 24–31.

17. Brooks, *Landlords and Strangers*, 143–166; Riley, "Ilhas atlânticas," 1:157; Tenreiro, *Ilha de São Tomé*, 59–63; Gar-field, *History of São Tomé Island*. The Jew-ish children came from refugee families expelled from Spain in 1492; the children were baptized and given to the captain and governor of São Tomé; see "Jews Trans-ported to the Island of São Thomé, 1493," in Blake, *Europeans in West Africa*, 1:86–87. The descendants of many of these orphans, according to Garfield, founded some of the wealthiest families on the island of São Tomé.

18. On how the Portuguese maritime trade established a competing route to the trans-Saharan trade, see Herbert, "Portuguese Adaptations," 411–423; Lovejoy, *Transformations in Slavery*, 35; Vogt, *Portuguese Rule*, 1–20; and Brooks, *Landlords and Strangers*, 59–142. On the key importance of translators, interme-diaries, and cultural brokers, see Barreto, *História da Guiné*, 24–28; Curto, "A lín-gua," 1:414–433, especially 417–421; Hein, "Portuguese Communication"; and Brooks, *Landlords and Strangers*, 135–140, quotation from 135.

19. Zurara, *Crónica*, chapter 10, 1:55.

20. Zurara, *Crónica*, chapters 12–13 and 16–17, 1:61–69, 79, 82. The ran-som for Adahu was negotiated by Prince Henry's intermediary, Martim Fernandes, who spoke "Moorish" (i.e., Arabic). Antão Gonçalves also received a ransom of ten slaves and some gold dust for two other captives that he returned. In addi-tion to Zurara's account, cited above, see also Barreto, *História da Guiné*, 18; Hein,

"Portuguese Communication," 42; Rus-sell, *Prince Henry*, 130–134.

21. Barros, *Asia de Joam de Barros*, book 1, chapter 6, ff. 9. Barros follows Zurara's account, describing the actions of Antão Gonçalves and Nuno Tristão and the "ransoming" of several captives by their kin, who paid for their release in "slaves of different lands and a good quantity of gold dust," Barros, *Asia de Joam de Barros*, book 1, chapter 6, ff. 9v; book 1, chapter 7, ff. 11. See Hein's discussion of the impor-tance of these exchanges in "Portuguese Communication," 42–43.

22. Words of the Venetian Cadamosto, also known as Alvise da Mosto, who sailed past the Senegal River on a Portuguese expedition in 1455 and 1456, quoted in "Viagens de Cadamosto e Pedro de Sin-tra: Primeira viagem de Cadamosto (22-3-1455)," in Brásio, *Monumenta missionaria*, 1:314. See also Riley, "Ilhas atlânticas," 156, and Brooks, *Landlords and Strangers*, 126.

23. This story is related in Zurara, *Crónica*, chapter 27, 1:115–118, and Bar-ros, *Asia de Joam de Barros*, book 1, chap-ter 9, ff. 12v. The language spoken by the interpreter is given in the sources as Azenegue, a Berber dialect; see Barreto, *História da Guiné*, 24–25. Zurara drew seven lessons from Sintra's death, among them that captains should never deviate from the instructions given by their lords, that captains should listen to the counsel of their men, and that men who did not know how to swim should not cross water on enemy lands without being sure of a safe retreat. Sintra, according to Zurara, did not know how to swim. See Zurara, *Crónica*, chapter 28, 1:120–121.

24. According to Zurara (chapter 29, 1:122), João Fernandes was one of the

escudeiros, which historian Carl Hanson translates as "small nobility," or "pages," who were "typically inexperienced youths who would later become *caveleiros* [middle nobility] themselves"; see *Atlantic Emporium*, 85. One can speculate that João Fernandes was a young man who desired to serve the prince and receive a favor in return. His story is related in Zurara, *Crónica*, chapters 29, 32, 34, and 35, 1:122–143; Barros, *Asia de Joam de Barros*, book 1, chapters 9 & 10, ff. 12v–14v; and Barreto, *História da Guiné*, 24–28. Jeanne Hein makes the claim that Fernandes negotiated with Berber merchants the opening of a trading route that would connect the Portuguese ships with the inland trans-Saharan trade. His return to Portugal, and especially the unloading of the African trading goods—gold and slaves—she argues, "created a sensation and inspired immediately the launching of a vast enterprise of direct commercial trade with Africa"; see "Portuguese Communication," 43.

25. Curto, "A língua," 419; Hein, "Portuguese Communication," 44. For Cadamosto's accounts, see "Primeira viagem de Cadamosto (22-3-1455)" and "Segunda viagem de Cadamosto (Março—1456)," in Brásio, *Monumenta missionaria*, 1:287–366, passim, especially 365–366; Barreto, *História da Guiné*, 48. According to Peter Russell, Cadamosto's presence reveals that Prince Henry had no intention of barring Italian merchants from the African trade so long as they gave a portion of the profits of their voyages to him; see *Prince Henry*, 292–296. Cadamosto, known in Italian as Alvise da Mosto, remained in Portugal for a decade before returning to Venice, where he was renowned as a navigator and served as a

commander of fleets and fortresses as well as a senator; see Lane, *Venice*, 277–278. On Usodimare, see "Carta de Antoniotto Usodimare," in Brásio, *Monumenta missionaria*, 1:381–383.

26. "Carta de Antoniotto Usodimare," in Brásio, *Monumenta missionaria*, 1:381–383. Usodimare claims that the king of Portugal tried to suborn the emissary of the African chief, but the emissary convinced him that he would only return to Africa with Usodimare.

27. Barreto, *História de Guiné*, 58; Rui de Pina, *Crónicas*, chapter 57, 993; see also Bethencourt, "O contacto," 90; observations of Jerome Münzer, as quoted by Boxer in *Church Militant*, 3.

28. Barros, *Asia de Joam de Barros*, book 3, chapter 5; Couto, "Pêro da Covilhã," 185–192; Hein, "Portuguese Communication," 46–47. Covilhã never returned to Portugal; he was found in Ethiopia by a subsequent diplomatic mission from Portugal in 1520, for which he served as interpreter; see Couto, "Pêro da Covilhã." Russell-Wood, *A World on the Move*, 12–15, quotation from 14 and 15.

29. The journal is commonly attributed to Álvaro Velho; quotations are from the English translation by E. G. Ravenstein, *Journal of the First Voyage*, 6–12; 16–24.

30. [Velho], *Journal of the First Voyage*, 23–24. In an appendix, Ravenstein cites da Gama's interpreters as Martim Afonso, who had lived in the Kongo; Fernão Martins, an African slave who spoke Arabic; and João Nunes (or João Martins), a New Christian *degredado* who knew some Arabic and Hebrew; see "Muster-Roll of Vasco da Gama's Fleet," in [Velho], *Journal of the First Voyage*, 176–179. Barros includes the roles of the interpreters in these events; see *Asia de Joam de Barros*,

book 4, chapters 4–11, ff. 43v–53v. See also Hein, "Portuguese Communication," 41–50, and Prestholdt, "Portuguese Conceptual Categories," 383–407.

31. These English translations of *Os Lusíadas* are from Landeg White (Oxford: Oxford University Press, 1997). Other details on these meetings are from [Velho], *Journal of the First Voyage*, 37.

32. Da Gama's pilot from Malindi (in present-day Kenya) to Calicut was a great Muslim navigator, Ibn Majid; see Pearson, *The Portuguese in India*, 32, and [Velho], *Descobrimento das Índias*, 150–152.

33. [Velho], *Journal of the First Voyage*, 48–49.

34. Camões, *Lusíads*, translation of Landeg White, 143–144. Monsayeed is also known as Monçaide, Bontaibo, "the Moor of Tunis," and "the Castilian"; see "Muster-Roll," in [Velho], *Journal of the First Voyage*, 180–181, and *Descobrimento das Índias*, 153.

35. [Velho], *Journal of the First Voyage*, 60–63. Robert S. Wolff describes da Gama as "blundering" into India and uses this lack of an appropriate gift as evidence; see "Da Gama's Blundering," 306–309. On the importance of the exchange of letters, see Curto, "A língua," 422; Amado, "La séduction de l'autre," 242.

36. Gaspar da Gama reveals the complexities of a life as a go-between. According to the journal attributed to Álvaro Velho, Gaspar da Gama claimed to be a Christian who was forced to convert to Islam. Girolamo Sernigi, a Florentine merchant living in Lisbon, refers to him in his second letter written to Florence shortly after da Gama's return as a "pilot whom they [da Gama and his men] took by force" and a Jew. And King Manuel describes him as a Jewish merchant who converted to Chris-

tianity. See [Velho], *Journal of the First Voyage*, 84–86; "Girolamo Sernigi's Second Letter to a Gentleman of Florence," in [Velho], *Journal of the First Voyage*, 137; "King Manuel to the Cardinal Protector," in [Velho], *Journal of the First Voyage*, 115; and "Muster-Roll," in [Velho], *Journal of the First Voyage*, 179.

37. Girolamo Sernigi, a Florentine merchant living in Lisbon, wrote two letters to an unnamed person in Florence following Vasco da Gama's return to Portugal. Sernigi gives the size of da Gama's crew as 118 men, of whom 55 died on the journey; see "Girolamo Sernigi's First Letter to a Gentleman at Florence," in [Velho], *Journal of the First Voyage*, 123–124.

38. Paraphrased from Barros, *Asia de Joam de Barros*, book 5, chapter 1, ff. 55. A modernized version of this same text is found as "João de Barros, Décadas da Ásia (1552)," in Amado and Figueiredo, *Brasil 1500*, 419–420.

39. On board were experienced mariners such as Bartolomeu Dias (who discovered the Cape of Good Hope), Nicolau Coelho (captain of one of da Gama's ships), Pero Escolar (a pilot on da Gama's expedition), Diogo Dias (a clerk on da Gama's expedition and brother of Bartolomeu Dias), and João de Sá (a clerk on da Gama's expedition); see "Muster-Roll," in [Velho], *Journal of the First Voyage*, 175–178. The degredados were, according to a letter attributed to King Manuel, twenty men condemned to death to leave where Cabral best saw fit; King Manuel to King Ferdinand of Aragon, "Carta Besicken, 23 outubro de 1503," in Amado and Figueiredo, *Brasil 1500*, 367–368; Couto, "Achamento."

40. "Carta de D. Manuel aos Reis Católicos, 29 de Julho de 1501," and "Carta

Besicken," both in Amado and Figueiredo, *Brasil 1500*, 222–225, 370–371. King Manuel's letter to the zamorin is reproduced as "Carta de D. Manuel ao Samorim de Calicut, 11 de Março de 1500," in Amado and Figueiredo, *Brasil 1500*, 63–72.

41. "Carta de Pero Vaz de Caminha," in Amado and Figueiredo, *Brasil 1500*, 94, 114; "Relação do português anônimo," in Amado and Figueiredo, *Brasil 1500*, 137.

42. "Carta de D. Manuel aos Reis Católicos" and "Carta Besicken," both in Amado and Figueiredo, *Brasil 1500*, 222–225, 370–371; "Relação do piloto anônimo"; Prestholdt, "Portuguese Conceptual Categories," 393.

43. In *The Portuguese in India*, M. N. Pearson argues that the Portuguese never intended to trade peacefully, for had they wished to do so, they would have been welcomed as "merely another group of foreign merchants come to trade and so increase their customs receipts. . . . For the Portuguese, peaceful trade alongside Muslims on a basis of equality was impossible, for the crusade element was inherent in their presence in the Indian Ocean" (74). Pearson contends that the Portuguese did have clear superiority at sea, which they used as the means to control what had once been *mare librum;* 38 and 36–60 passim. See also Robert S. Wolff, "Da Gama's Blundering," especially 309.

44. "Carta de Cantino a Hércules D'Este [Ercole d'Este], 17 October 1501," in Amado and Figueiredo, *Brasil 1500*, 249–250.

45. "Amerigo Vespucci to Piero Soderini (in Florence), Lisbon, 1504 [the *Lettera*]," in Vespucci, *Letters from a New World*, 57–97; see Luciano Formisano's description of this letter, known as the *Lettera*, xxii–xxv, xxviii–xxxv.

46. Pereira, *A navegação*, 188–195.

47. "Vespucci to Soderini, 1504 [the *Lettera*]," in Vespucci, *Letters from a New World*, 87–89.

48. Vespucci may have been the first to describe cannibalism in Brazil, for none of the documents from the 1500 expedition describe it. Vespucci mentions cannibalism in all three of his letters that describe his two voyages to Brazil, but only in one letter, his last, does he relate the killing and eating of a crew member. This last letter is considered by scholars to be the most prone to "slipping into the fictional devices of an adventure yarn." See Formisano, "Introduction," in Vespucci, *Letters from a New World*, xxiv.

49. "Déclaration du vegage," 104–105.

50. "Vespucci to Soderini, 1504 [the *Lettera*]," in Vespucci, *Letters from a New World*, 89, 89–95.

51. I thank my colleague Colin Wells for this insight. Wells believes that in the ancient world the presence of interpreters was so common that it did not need to be explained to readers. He cites, for example, the communication between Jesus of Nazareth and Pontius Pilate, which was likely made possible by an interpreter, who remains unnamed and unmentioned in early Christian texts.

52. "Vespucci to Lorenzo di Pierfrancesco de' Medici, n.d. [*Mundus novus*]," and "Vespucci to Lorenzo di Pierfrancesco de' Medici (in Florence), Lisbon, 1502," both in Vespucci, *Letters from a New World*, 47–48 and 31–33, respectively.

53. The king's notary was Valentim Fernandes, and the document is the "Certidão de Valentim Fernandes, 20 Maio de 1503," in Amado and Figueiredo, *Brasil 1500*, 300–302. The letter from the king

of Portugal to the king of Castile is known as the Besicken Letter and is not thought to be an actual copy of a letter, but rather a distillation of knowledge acquired in Italy about the Portuguese discoveries, particularly in India. See "Carta Besicken," in Amado and Figueiredo, *Brasil 1500*, 365–395; see also *Copy of a Letter*, quotation from the facsimile reproduction of page one. Barros, *Asia de Joam de Barros*, book 5, chapter 2, ff. 56.

54. "Carta de Pero Vaz de Caminha," in Amado and Figueiredo, *Brasil 1500*, 116–117.

55. "Vespucci to Lorenzo di Pierfrancesco de' Medici (in Florence), Seville, 18 July 1500"; "Vespucci to Lorenzo di Pierfrancesco de' Medici (in Florence), Cape Verde, 4 June 1501"; and "Vespucci to de' Medici, 1502," all in Vespucci, *Letters from a New World*, 3, 19–27, and 29–35, respectively.

56. The first letter is "Carta de João de Affaitadi [Giovanni Francesco di Agostini Affaitadi] a Domingos Pisani [Domenico Pisani de Giovanni], 26 de Junho de 1501," in Amado and Figueiredo, *Brasil 1500*, 163–174. This letter eventually made its way into the voluminous diary of Marino Sanuto, a Venetian who loved to keep track of facts; see "Copia et sumario di una letera di sier Domenego Pixani, el cavalier, orator nostro in Spagna, a la Signoria," in Sanuto, *I diarii*, 4:99–102. The second letter is "Carta de João Matteo Crético [Giovanni Matteo Camerino to the Doge of Venice], 27 junho de 1501," in Amado and Figueiredo, *Brasil 1500*, 177–178. On the quickness of Venetians to respond to these new developments, see Burke, "Early Modern Venice," 392.

57. The Florentine merchant's letter is "2a Carta de Bartolomeu Marchionni

fins de julho de 1501," in Amado and Figueiredo, *Brasil 1500*, 193–199. The Priuli diary may be found as "Diário de Jerônimo Priuli [Girolamo Priuli] agosto e setembro de 1501," in Amado and Figueiredo, *Brasil 1500*, 209–218. Also of interest is "Crônica de Daniele Barbado, 1501," in Amado and Figueiredo, *Brasil 1500*, 259–261. See Lane's discussion of Priuli's fears, which Lane sees as unwarranted, in *Venice*, 285–292.

58. Perrone-Moisés, *Vinte luas*.

59. It continues to be a mystery why there are few Portuguese maps from the fifteen and early sixteenth centuries, leading to the hypothesis of secrecy. See A. Cortesão, *Cartografia portuguesa antigua*, 171–173; Guedes, "A cartografia portuguesa antiga," 19; Couto, *Construção do Brasil*, 190. Lane writes in *Venice* that the Portuguese became the leaders in cartography in the fifteenth century but "either wore out their own charts or destroyed them for the sake of secrecy" (276).

60. Cortesão and Teixeira da Mota, *Portugaliae monumenta cartographica*, 1: xiii, xxxi, xxxiv, xlv, quotation from xxxi. Lane writes that the Fra Mauro map was in fact commissioned for Prince Henry by his brother. It was delivered in 1459, just before Prince Henry died; see Lane, *Venice*, 277.

61. "Vespucci to de' Medici, 1502," and "Vespucci to de' Medici [*Mundus novus*]," both in Vespucci, *Letters from a New World*, 30 and 55, respectively. Scholars who doubt the policy of secrecy include Maria Fernanda Alegria, João Carlos Garcia, and Francesc Relaño; see their article, "Cartografia e viagens," in Bethencourt and Chaudhuri, *História da expansão portuguesa*, 1:38–39.

62. On the back of the map is written, "Carta da navigar per le Isole nou-
vam tr[ovate] in le parte de l'India: dono
Alberto Cantino al S. Duca Hercole"
(Nautical chart for the Islands newly
found in the region of India: Gift of
Alberto Cantino to his Lordship the Duke
Ercole). Cortesão and Teixeira da Mota,
Portugaliae monumenta cartographica, 1:7.
Alegria, Garcia, and Relaño agree that
the Cantino map was likely copied from
the padrão real; see "Cartografia e viagens," 1:41. On the Spanish *padrón real,*
see Sandman, "Mirroring the World,"
83—108. The Venetian gold ducat was
the standard trading coin of the Mediterranean at the end of the fifteenth century,
and it became the basis for the Portuguese
cruzado; see Spufford, *Money,* 320—321.
Twelve gold ducats would have been a
handsome sum, equivalent to one-third of
the annual wages of an English craftsman
in the building trades at the time. I thank
my colleague John J. McCusker for this
insight.

63. Albuquerque and Tavares, "Algumas observações."

64. Cortesão and Teixeira da Mota,
Portugaliae monumenta cartographica,
1:7. The seam of the pasted correction is
clearly visible to the naked eye.

65. Cortesão and Teixeira da Mota, *Portugaliae monumenta cartographica,* 1:12.

66. Ibid.

67. Ibid., 1:11.

68. Formisano, "Introduction," in Vespucci, *Letters from a New World,* xx—xxii.
In private correspondence, the term "New
World" had already been used; hence Vespucci was not the first to coin the phrase, as
the letters of Giovanni Matteo Camerino,
Bartolomeu Marchionni, an unknown
young man (*o jovem*), and even King Man-

uel make clear; see "Carta de João Matteo
Crético [Giovanni Matteo Camerino to
the Doge of Venice], 27 Junho de 1501,"
"2a Carta de Bartolomeu Marchionni, fins
de julho de 1501," "Carta do jovem das
caravelas, 29 August 1501," and "Carta de
D. Manuel aos Reis Católicos, 29 Julho
de 1501"—all in Amado and Figueiredo,
Brasil 1500, 177—178, 195, 241, 221.

69. "Vespucci to de' Medici [*Mundus
novus*]," in Vespucci, *Letters from a New
World,* 45. Anthony Grafton explores
how the realities of the Americas challenged the European vision of the world
and the authority of the classical texts in
New Worlds, Ancient Texts.

70. Bartolomé de Las Casas believed
Vespucci's fourth letter to Soderini, the
Lettera, to be a fake, and that Vespucci
was "usurping the glory owed to the
Admiral [Columbus], its true artificer";
see Formisano's "Introduction," in Vespucci, *Letters from a New World,* xxx.

71. "Vespucci to de' Medici, 1502," in
Vespucci, *Letters from a New World,* 32—
33, and "Vespucci to de' Medici [*Mundus
novus*]," in Vespucci, *Letters from a New
World,* 50. Vespucci's description clearly
condemns the Indians for their eating of
human flesh because it is easier to get than
other meats. Similarly, the transposing
of European cultural norms of food production, that is, the smoking and salting
of pork, onto the cannibalism ceremony
serves to further underscore the barba-
rism of the Indians in Vespucci's letter.

72. The broadsheet appeared in the
1505 Augsburg edition of the *Mundus
novus* letter; see Hans Wolff, *America,* 29.
Translation courtesy of my colleague Eve
Duffy.

73. Kupčík, *Münchner Portolankarten;*
Hans Wolff, "The Munich Portolan

Charts," 134–135; Colin, "Woodcutters and Cannibals," 176; Sturtevant, "First Visual Images," 1:420.

74. Colin, "Woodcutters and Cannibals," 180–181. Colin argues that the lavishly illustrated manuscript maps, which depicted more complex representations of Brazil, were owned by wealthy individuals, but that printed maps, which invariably contained a depiction of cannibalism, were aimed at a general audience. Lestringant traces the degrading of the "other" in the changing portrayal of cannibals in the writings from the Renaissance to the Romantic period in *Cannibals*.

75. All of the Indians taken by Columbus arrived safely in Spain, but several died after becoming sick with smallpox; at least one returned to Hispaniola with Columbus in 1493; see Cook, "Sickness, Starvation, and Death," 363–366. On the Indians taken by Pinzón, see "El primer viaje de Vicente Yáñez al Brasil," in Manzano Manzano, *Los Pinzones*, 3:41. Oveido states that there were thirty-six captured; see "Versión que del descubrimiento del Amazonas, por Vicente Yáñez Pinzón, nos da el cronista Gonzalo Fernández de Oveido," in Manzano Manzano, *Los Pinzones*, 3:46. That these Indians became slaves once they arrived in Spain is clearly evident in another document reproduced by Manzano Manzano: "R.C. al corregidor de Palos para que Diego Prieto restituya a los Pinzones un esclavo que éstos habían traído del Brasil," Granada, 20 de junio de 1501, in *Los Pinzones*, 3:36. "Vespucci to Soderini, 1504 [the *Lettera*]," in Vespucci, *Letters from a New World*, 90; "Déclaration du vegage," 101.

76. "Carta de Cantino a Hércules D'Este [Ercole d'Este]," in Amado and Figueiredo, *Brasil 1500*, 247; see also "Pietro

Pasqualigo to brothers in Lisbon, 19 October 1502," in Fracanzano da Montalboddo, *Paesi nuovamente retrovati*, book 6. "Déclaration du vegage," 106; Perrone-Moisés, *Vinte luas*, 27. The French league (*lieüe*) was 2.4 nautical miles, or 4,445 meters; therefore, the approximate distance swum was 13 kilometers.

77. Sturtevant, "First Visual Images," 1:423, 447 n. 17. Not all agree that this man is meant to represent a Tupinambá Indian; see Hinrich Sieveking's introduction to *Das Gebetbuch Kaiser Maximilians*, xxiii.

3. POSSESSION

1. Cortesão and Teixeira da Mota, *Portugaliae monumenta cartographica*, 1:58. The map is part of "L'Atlas Miller," Bibliothèque Nationale, Paris, and the cartographers are thought to be Lopo Homen, Pedro Reinel, and Jorge Reinel, as well as the miniaturist Gregorio Lopes; see Hans Wolff, *America*, 48, 177.

2. Cortesão and Teixeira da Mota, *Portugaliae monumenta cartographica*, 1:58. According to Suzi Colin, the depiction of Indians in the Reinel map shows that the miniaturist was familiar with the physical appearance of the Indians, with their use of feathers (perhaps even painting them from ones he had seen in Europe), and with their weapons; "Woodcutters and Cannibals," 176–178.

3. Armstrong, "Logwood and Brazilwood," 38–43; Dean, *With Broadax and Firebrand*, 45–50.

4. Rodney, *History*, 74; Couto, "Contribuição dos 'lançados,'" 31–34.

5. Rodney, *History*, 77–94; Brooks, *Landlords and Strangers*, 135–140. Zeron

emphasizes the marginal social status of the lançados and suggests that many were expatriated Jews in addition to degredados; see "Pombeiros e tangosmaos."

6. Rodney, *History*, 203. According to an eighteenth-century French observer, there were 15,000 Afro-Portuguese living on the upper Guinea coast in 1784; see Rodney, *History*, 200.

7. Coates, "Exiles and Orphans," 158–159. In *Convicts and Orphans*, 86–87, Coates argues that the Portuguese Crown initially deliberately created intermediaries, but later, when it found that it was unable to control them, developed a more controlled policy of using degredados.

8. Isaacman and Isaacman, "Prazeros as Transfrontiersmen," 1–39.

9. King João III reaffirmed that brazilwood was a royal monopoly when he granted hereditary captaincies in the 1530s. In the donation of Pernambuco to Duarte Coelho, the contract states that "the brazilwood of the said captaincy [Pernambuco] . . . belongs to me [i.e., the king] and will always be mine and my successors' . . . neither the said captain [Duarte Coelho] nor anyone else may trade . . . nor sell . . . nor extract . . . with the penalty that he who goes against this will lose all his property to the Crown and will be exiled (degredado) forever to the island of São Tomé" ("Foral de Duarte Coelho," 24 September 1534, in *HCPB*, 3:312). On the Brazil contract, see Johnson, "Portuguese Settlement," 7–9. The first brazilwood contracts resemble the monopoly over the Guinea trade given to Fernão Gomes, a Lisbon merchant, in 1469. In addition to paying an annual fee in return for exclusive rights, Gomes also had to explore 100 leagues (approximately 600 kilometers) of the African coast south of Sierra

Leone every year. See Barreto, *História da Guiné*, 59–60, and Luís Adão da Fonseca, *O essencial*, 44–45. Pedro Rondinelli's letter describes the return of seven ships to Lisbon, four belonging to João da Nova, who had gone to India, and three that had arrived from Brazil; "Rondinelli to an unknown Italian, Seville, 3 October 1502," in Amado and Figueiredo, *Brasil 1500*, 270. Scholars generally believe the trading place described by Vespucci to be Cabo Frio, just east of Rio de Janeiro, and the southernmost limit of the brazilwood stands; "Amerigo Vespucci to Piero di Tommaso Soderini, 1504 [the *Lettera*]," in Vespucci, *Letters from a New World*, 96. The Venetian source is "Relação de Leonardo da Cá Maser [Leonardo Masari; Lunardo Masser], 23 de outubro de 1505," in Amado and Figueiredo, *Brasil 1500*, 401. This is the agent that the government of Venice sent to Portugal to gather information on the new Portuguese discoveries; see Burke, "Early Modern Venice," 392. For the value of the quintal, see Rowlett, "How Many?" and "Quintal, kintal, kentle," *Oxford English Dictionary Online*. Three ducats would have been the rough equivalent of twenty-six days of wages for an English craftsman in the building trades at the time; thus Noronha made the equivalent of almost nine days' wages from each hundredweight. I thank my colleague John J. McCusker for this approximation.

10. "Déclaration du vegage," 103–106; Perrone-Moisés, *Vinte luas*, 25–26, 63–65.

11. "Carta de doação da capitania de Pernambuco a Duarte Coelho, 5 September 1534," in *HCPB*, 3:309; "Livro da náoo bertoa que vay pera a Terra do Brazyll," in *HCPB*, 2:343–347; quotations from "1511.

The log and captain's instructions of the ship *Bretoa* off Brazil," in *NIW*, 5:30.

12. The details concerning the trading post emerge in the suit brought by the French baron and commander of the French Navy of the Mediterranean, Bertrand d'Ornesam, Baron of Saint Blanchard, against Dom Martinho, the archbishop of Funchal [Portugal], and Antonio Correa, Bartholomeu Ferraz, Gonçalo Leite, Gaspar Palha, and Pero Lopes de Sousa. Documents from the suit are transcribed in P. L. de Sousa, *Diário da navegação*, 2:19–43. The French post was destroyed by Pero Lopes de Sousa, brother of Martim Afonso de Sousa, the nobleman sent by the king to establish the first colony in Brazil; ibid., 2:19–43. See also Marchant, *From Barter to Slavery*, 39 n. 55. Alonso de Santa Cruz, who sailed with Sebastian Cabot to the Río de la Plata from 1525 to 1527, later wrote that the Portuguese had an "asiento" at Pernambuco, which they called a "factoria"; see *Islario general*, 1:543.

13. Pigafetta, *Magellan's Voyage*, 1:43–44; on the pilot Carvalho and his son, see 1:152 n. 8. List of sailors, "Livro da náoo bertoa que vay pera a Terra do Brazyll," in *HCPB*, 2:345.

14. *A nova gazeta*; P. L. de Sousa, *Diário da navegação*. Pero Lopes de Sousa sailed with his brother, Martim Afonso de Sousa, who was charged with exploring the southern coast of Brazil, particularly the Río de la Plata area, founding the first colony in Brazil (São Vicente, 1532), and ridding the coast of French brazilwood traders. Interpreters are often mentioned in P. L. de Sousa's diary; see *Diário da navegação*, 1:197–198, 209, 305.

15. Rogoziński, "Phillips (Phellyppes), John (I)," in *Pirates!* 254; Marsden, "Voy-age of the 'Barbara,'" 97–100; "Voyage of the Barbara to Brazil, Anno 1540," in Burns, *Documentary History*, 51. Richard Hakluyt describes a second English voyage to Brazil in 1540, funded by several "substantial and wealthy" merchants of Southampton, as well as a voyage to Bahia in 1542; see Hakluyt, *Principal Navigations*, 8:15.

16. Marsden, "Voyage of the 'Barbara,'" 97–100; Rogoziński, *Pirates!* 254; quotations from "Voyage of the Barbara," in Burns, *Documentary History*, 51–55; I have modernized the archaic English. On their location, still in doubt, see Rogoziński, *Pirates!* 254. The desertion occurred after "a Portugal and a Frenchman and certain of the same country with them [i.e., Indians]" approached by land and "commanded us in his king's name for to avoid the country," but the captain and crew refused (Burns, *Documentary History*, 52). The Portuguese man then ordered the Frenchman to cut the anchor line of the *Barbara*, but due to the careful watch kept by the men on the *Barbara*, he was apprehended instead. He escaped, and three nights later the speechman and all the other Frenchmen deserted, taking with them the coxswain and all the trading goods. Such bitter fighting ensued that the English dared not land again, and sailed on to Haiti.

17. "A brief relation of two sundry voyages made by the worshipful M. William Hawkins of Plimmouth . . . in the yeere 1530 and 1532," in Hakluyt, *Principal Navigations*, 8:14–15. According to Alden T. Vaughan, however, the systematic use of indigenous interpreters by the English began later, with Sir Walter Raleigh, who deliberately brought Indians to England to learn English and to train as future

intermediaries in his exploration and colonization projects; see Vaughan, "Sir Walter Ralegh's Indian Interpreters," 341–376.

18. Staden, who hailed from Hesse, first went in 1547 to Portugal, where he signed on as a gunner on a ship bound for Brazil. This voyage took him to Pernambuco on a brazilwood run; after returning to Portugal, he enlisted with a Spanish expedition headed for the Río de la Plata. But after being shipwrecked off São Vicente, he found employment as a gunner at the fortress of Bertioga. While working in São Vicente, he was taken captive. After his captivity by the Tupinambá, Staden returned to Germany, where he wrote an account of his adventures published first as *Warhaftige Historia* (1557) and then as *Warachtige historie* (1558). The English translation, from which all subsequent quotes are drawn, is *Hans Staden: The True History of His Captivity, 1557* (hereafter cited as *True History*). On the value of Staden's account, see Forsyth, "Three Cheers for Hans Staden," 17–36, and Whitehead, "Hans Staden," 722–751. The German historians Annerose Menninger, Michaela Schmölz-Häberlein, and Mark Häberlein, however, doubt the veracity of Staden's account. Schmölz-Häberlein and Häberlein cite the importance of the work of Annerose Menninger, who argues that Staden's book became a best seller because "Staden treated his readers to extensive encounters with cannibalistic practices." In her view, works that featured cannibalism "dominated the market" in sixteenth-century Germany; see Menninger, Schmölz-Häberlein, and Häberlein, "Hans Staden, Neil L. Whitehead, and the Cultural Politics of Scholarly Publishing," 748. As is apparent

below, I do accept Staden as a physical and transactional go-between, as well as a representational go-between.

19. It is impossible to know how the Tupinikin and the Tupinambá interacted before the arrival of Europeans, but the overlay of competing European powers on the groups did nothing to allay the hostilities that existed between them. See Monteiro, "Crises and Transformations," 3:981–990.

20. Staden, *True History*, quotations from 71–76.

21. Ibid., quotations from 76–77. Karwattuware was a collector for the French ship *Maria Bellete*, which hailed from Dieppe; ibid., 117, 123.

22. Ibid., 90.

23. Ibid., 90, 101, 103.

24. Ibid., 119. The captain gave Abbati Bossange "some five ducats' worth in knives, axes, looking-glasses, and combs" (120); the *Maria Bellete*, bound for Dieppe, Normandy, was presumed lost at sea; ibid., 123–124.

25. Thevet, *Les singularitez* (1558); all subsequent quotations are from the following modern edition by Frank Lestringant: Thevet, *Le Brésil* (1997). Jean de Léry, *Histoire d'un voyage fait* (1578); see the modern edition, also edited by Lestringant: Jean de Léry, *Histoire d'un voyage faict* (1994). All subsequent quotations, unless otherwise noted, are from the English translation by Janet Whatley: Jean de Léry, *History of a Voyage* (1992).

26. Thevet, *Le Brésil*, 8, 125, 147; see also Lestringant, *Mapping the Renaissance World*, 9.

27. Léry, *History of a Voyage*, 43, 161.

28. Ibid., 101, 171.

29. Ibid., 101, 169–171.

30. Nicolas Durand de Villegagnon, who led the French colony in Guanabara Bay (Rio de Janeiro), also saw this pattern as repulsive and feared abuse of Indian women by the men in his party. According to Léry, Villegagnon "forbade on pain of death that any man bearing the name of Christian live with the savages' women"; Léry, *History of a Voyage*, 43. Thevet makes the same observation; see *Le Brésil*, 168.

31. Vespucci could not fathom "why they make war upon one another," for he observed that "they do not have private property, or command empires or kingdoms, and have no notion of greed, that is, greed either for things or for power, which seems to me to be the cause of wars and all acts of disorder." Vespucci reported that the only reason that he could discover for these violent and cruel wars was that their origin lay deep in the past and that the Indians "wish to avenge the death of their ancestors." See "Vespucci to Lorenzo di Pierfrancesco de' Medici, Lisbon 1502," in Vespucci, *Letters from a New World*, 33—34. The report of the Gonneville expedition, which reached southern Brazil in 1504, for example, states that the chief with whom Gonneville lived for six months wished his son Essomericq to return to France with Gonneville to learn about European arms, "which they desired in order to dominate their enemies"; see "Déclaration du veg- age," 102.

32. Léry, *History of a Voyage*, 120.

33. There is an important literature on cannibalism in Brazil, much of it based on the accounts of Staden, Thevet, Léry, and the letters of the Jesuits (see Chapter 4 herein). Although William Arens doubts the existence of cannibalism in *The Man-Eating Myth*, arguing that accounts of cannibalism are exaggerated and that the same accounts are repeated over and over by Europeans claiming to be eyewitnesses, there are too many accounts of cannibalism from too many different sources to dismiss the practice. Moreover, modern anthropologists have documented the practice in the living memories of some indigenous groups. For an introduction into the complexity of this issue, see Conklin, *Consuming Grief*, xxiv—xxxi, 3—15.

34. Staden, *True History*, 112; Léry, *History of a Voyage*, 73—75.

35. Staden, *True History*, 148; Léry, *History of a Voyage*, 127; Schmidel, *Relatos de la conquista*, 104. See Frank Lestringant's analysis of Léry's reporting of cannibalism in *Cannibals*, 68—80, and Janet Whatley's introduction to Léry, *History of a Voyage*, xv—xxxviii.

36. Léry, *History of a Voyage*, 162—163, 128.

37. Staden, *True History*, 162, 148; Léry, *History of a Voyage*, 128.

38. Léry, *History of a Voyage*, 128.

39. Marchant, *From Barter to Slavery*, 70—71.

40. Salisbury, *Manitou and Providence*, 9.

41. "King João III to Martim Afonso de Sousa, Lisbon, 28 September," in P. L. de Sousa, *Diário da navegação*, 1:415—418. Alonso de Santa Cruz' atlas of islands has a description of São Vicente; see his *Islario general*, as quoted in P. L. de Sousa, *Diário da navegação*, 1:408.

42. I use the Portuguese league (6,174 meters) for my approximate translations; however, the Portuguese league was longer than the Spanish league (5,556 meters), which caused great difficulty in applying the treaty to concrete situations. For the

original documents in Latin and Spanish, with an English translation, see "The Bull *Inter Caetera* (Alexander VI). May 4, 1493," in Davenport, *European Treaties*, 71–78, and "Treaty between Spain and Portugal concluded at Tordesillas, June 7, 1494. Ratification by Spain, July 2, 1494. [Ratification by Portugal, September 5, 1494]," in Davenport, *European Treaties*, 84–100; quotation from 95. On the impact of the treaty on Portuguese and Spanish claims and on cartography, see Marcos, "La cartografía del segundo viaje de Colón y su decisiva influencia en el Tratado de Tordesillas," in *Tratado*, 85–108; Analola Borges, "El Tratado de Tordesillas y la conquista del Río de la Plata," in *Tratado de Tordesillas*, 1:345–356; as well as Couto, *Construção do Brasil*, 122–160. Some scholars have long argued that the Portuguese king delayed the "official" discovery of Brazil until after this treaty with Spain had been signed. The hypothesis is—for no conclusive documentation has ever been found—that Bartolomeu Dias made experimental voyages to the South Atlantic and that Duarte Pacheco Pereira sailed along the coast of Brazil in 1498 to see where the future line of Tordesillas would bisect Brazil. See J. Cortesão, *Descobrimentos*, 4:1002–1012; Couto, *Construção do Brasil*, 151–160. The letter written from Brazil in 1500 by Mestre João makes reference to a map that the king should consult that would show the location of Brazil. The map was in the possession of Pero Vaz Bisagudo [Pero Vaz da Cunha], a captain who had sailed to the Senegal River in 1490 with the objective of constructing a trading post there. See "Carta do Mestre João, 1° de maio de 1500," in Amado and Figueiredo, *Brasil 1500*, 125, 520. The map has never been found.

43. The Spaniard Alonso de Santa Cruz writes in his sixteenth-century atlas of the islands of the world that the line of demarcation fell north of São Vicente, near São Sebastião, just south of Rio de Janeiro (*Islario general*, 1:547–548), whereas the Portuguese maps by Reinel and Teixeira both show all of Brazil to the Río de la Plata estuary within the line of demarcation; see Maps 3.1 and 3.2 herein.

44. "Bachelor" in this context referred to the fact that he was educated, or very well spoken; see Prado, *Primeiros povoadores*, 62 n. 27. Jaime Cortesão hypothesizes that the "bacharel" was the same man as a degredado in São Tomé, also known as "bacharel," who left São Tomé with Bartolomeu Dias and went to Brazil in 1498 on a secret voyage to reconnoiter the southern Atlantic; see his *Descobrimentos*, 4:1002–1012. Other references to "O bacharel" are in P. L. de Sousa, *Diário da navegação*, 2:209–212, 412.

45. "1530. Luis Ramírez to his father, on his experiences in the Río de la Plata," in *NIW*, 5:249.

46. P. L. de Sousa, *Diário da navegação*, 1:350–352.

47. See the letter from King João III to Martim Afonso de Sousa, Lisbon, 28 September 1532, in *HCPB*, 3:160–161.

48. Although undated and unsigned, the map is attributed to Luís Teixeira, who had visited Brazil in the 1570s; it was probably drawn in the 1580s; [Teixeira], *Roteiro de todos os sinais*.

49. On the donatários, see Johnson, "Portuguese Settlement," 13–19, and Couto, *Construção do Brasil*, 219–230. On the model provided by the Atlantic islands for early sugar cultivation in Brazil, see Schwartz, *Sugar Plantations*,

7–15. Guanche (the indigenous peoples from the Canary Islands), Africans, and mulattoes labored as slaves on Madeira and Canary Island plantations, while Africans from Benin, Angola, and Senegambia worked as slaves in São Tomé; ibid., 9–14.

50. Monteiro, "Crises and Transformations," 3.1:991.

51. "Luís de Góis to King João III, Santos [São Vicente], 12 May 1548," in *HCPB*, 3:259; Menezes, *Aconteceu no velho São Paulo;* Couto, *Construção do Brasil,* 227; Monteiro, "Crises and Transformations," 992.

52. Staden, *True History,* 43–44, quotation from 58.

53. Ibid., 106–116.

54. P. L. de Sousa, *Diário da navegação,* 1:155; Calmon, *História do Brasil,* 1:148–150; Tavares, *História da Bahia,* 67–68; Carneiro, *Cidade do Salvador,* 29. The surname Correia is often added to Diogo Álvares' name, but as Janaína Amado points out, none of the sixteenth-century sources use it; see "Mythic Origins," 783–811. The name "Caramuru" refers to an eel found in Brazil; see Cardim, "Do clima e terra do Brasil . . .," in *Tratados da terra,* 139, and the beautiful drawing of a *caramuru* in Lisboa, *História dos animaes,* 82–85.

55. "Pero do Campo Tourinho to King João III, Porto Seguro, 28 July 1546," in Accioli de Cerqueira e Silva, *Memorias históricas,* 1:199, and "Duarte Coelho to King João III, Olinda, Pernambuco, 20 December 1546," in *HCPB,* 3:314–316. See also Tavares, *História da Bahia,* 90–91. The sixteenth-century chronicler is Gabriel Soares de Sousa, in *Tratado descritivo;* quotation from 74.

56. Duarte Coelho and his wife were from prominent families in Portugal; they were accompanied by Beatriz' brother, Jerônimo de Albuquerque; see Prado, *Pernambuco,* 163–171.

57. "Duarte Coelho to King João III, Olinda, 27 April 1542," in *HCPB,* 1:313–314, and "Duarte Coelho to King João III, Olinda, 24 November 1550," in *Cartas de Duarte Coelho a El Rei,* 104.

58. "Duarte Coelho to King João III, Olinda, 27 April 1542," in *HCPB,* 1:314, and "Duarte Coelho to King João III, Olinda, 20 December 1546," in *HCPB,* 1:314–316.

59. The interpreter received "14 mil reis" (14,000 reis), whereas the overseer received "10 mil reis" (10,000 reis); "Pero de Góis to Martin Ferreira, Rainha [Paraíba do Sul], 18 August 1545," in *HCPB,* 3:262–263. Pero de Góis' problems emerge in his letter to King João III, Rainha [Paraíba do Sul], 29 April 1546, in *HCPB,* 3:263. According to G. S. de Sousa, Pero de Góis returned to Lisbon a "broken" man, having spent all of his own assets, as well as thousands of cruzados (one cruzado = 480 reis) of his partner Martim Ferreira's, in his endeavor to colonize his grant; *Tratado descritivo,* 94–95.

60. "Pero do Campo Tourinho to King João III, Porto Seguro, 28 July 1546," in *HCPB,* 2:266–267. A transcript of the trial is available in *HCPB,* 3:271–283. Many years later, a resident of Salvador denounced Tourinho's imprisonment as a plot hatched by his own son, with the support of Franciscan friars. According to Gaspar Dias Barbosa, the whole thing was done so that André do Campo could govern in place of his father; see "Denunciation of Gaspar Dias Barbosa, 16 August 1591," in *PV:D-Bahia,* 340. On Tourinho and his captaincy, see Moreira, *Mareantes,* 254–258, and R. G. Brito, *Saga.*

Many but not all of the confessions and denunciations can be found in the books of denunciations and confessions that were first published as *Primeira visitação do Santo Ofício às partes do Brasil pelo Licenciado Heitor Furtado de Mendonça: Confissões da Bahia 1591–1592* (Rio de Janeiro: F. Briguiet, 1935; cited as *PV: C-Bahia*) and *Primeira visitação do Santo Ofício às partes do Brasil pelo Licenciado Heitor Furtado de Mendonça: Denunciações da Bahia 1591–1593* (São Paulo: Paulo Prado, 1925; cited as *PV: D-Bahia*). For the convenience of the interested reader, wherever possible, I have cited confessions and denunciations from these first two publications. Ronaldo Vainfas has produced a new edition of the confessions; see *Primeira visitação . . . Confissões da Bahia 1591–1592* (São Paulo: Companhia das Letras, 1997), which modernizes the names of the individuals, as I have also done. Sandra Lauderdale Graham has published an English translation of several confessions, including Nobre's, in "Confessing to the Holy Office of the Inquisition, Bahia, Brazil (1592, 1618)," 234–245. The full trial records, which contain all the confessions, denunciations, interrogations, sentences, and other documents, are to be found in the Inquisição de Lisboa collection (cited as IL) of the Arquivo Nacional da Torre do Tombo (cited as ANTT).

61. The heirs of Coutinho sued the Crown for their loss of property and were compensated in 1576 with 400 mil reis (400,000 reis) in gold from a tax on everything produced by the captaincy; see Tavares, *História da Bahia*, 90–91. On the arrival of Tomé de Sousa, see Calmon, *História da fundação*, 129–145. The royal instructions carried by Sousa are tran-

scribed in "Regimento de Tomé de Sousa, 17 December 1548," in *HCPB*, 1:345–350.

62. "King João III to Diogo Álvares, 19 November 1548," in "Cartas Regias sobre Tomé de Sousa, 1548–1551," in APEB: Cópias 627; Carneiro, *Cidade do Salvador*, 25.

63. "Regimento de Tomé de Sousa, 17 December 1548," in *HCPB*, 1:345–350; "Manoel da Nóbrega to Simão Rodrigues (in Lisbon), Bahia, 10? April 1549," in *MB*, 1:110–112. Timothy Coates thinks that this high number of degredados, commonly cited by historians, is not feasible; see *Convicts and Orphans*, 78–79.

64. This was the origin of the town known as Santo André da Borda do Campo. "Tomé de Sousa to the king, 1 June 1553," in *HCPB*, 3:365. The German traveler was Ulrich Schmidel; see his *Relatos de la conquista*, 106.

65. Léry, *History of a Voyage*, 7.

66. "Letter of Nicholas Barré, from Antarctic France [Rio de Janeiro], 25 May 1556," as it appears in Lescarbot, *Histoire de la Novvelle-France*, 1:303. See also Frank Lestringant's introduction to Thevet, *Le Brésil*, 18.

67. "Letter of Nicholas Barré, from Antarctic France [Rio de Janeiro], 25 May 1556," in Lescarbot, *Histoire de la Novvelle-France*, 1:304. Villegagnon also wrote of the plot; see his letter to Jean Calvin, 31 March 1557, as it appears in Léry, *History of a Voyage*, xlix–lii. Thevet writes about the plot in his *La cosmographie universelle* [1575]; see Léry's discussion of Thevet's reference in *History of a Voyage*, lii–liii.

68. Calmon, *História da fundação*, 49–50 n. 5, and "Igreja recebe certidão de batismo de índia," *O Estado de S. Paulo*, Saturday, 6 January 2001, http://www.estado. estadao.com.br/editorias/2001/01/06/

ger712.html. "Manoel da Nóbrega to Simão Rodrigues (in Lisbon), Bahia, end of July 1552," in *MB*, 1:369. See Fernandes, *De cunhã*, for an examination of the roles of Indian women in the sixteenth-century colonization of Brazil.

69. "Pero Correia to Simão Rodrigues (in Lisbon), São Vicente, 10 March 1553," in *MB*, 1:435–436; "Manoel da Nóbrega to Luís Gonçalves da Câmara (in Lisbon), São Vicente, 31 August 1553," in *MB*, 1:524–527; "Tomé de Sousa to King João III, 1 June 1553," in *HCPB*, 3:365; Luis, "Testamento," 563–569. For a fascinating historiographical essay on how Ramalho came to be seen as the "patriarch of the Paulistas [residents of São Paulo]," see Ferretti and Capelato, "João Ramalho," 67–87.

70. Jaboatão, *Catalogo genealogico.* Gonzalo Fernández de Oviedo y Valdés, *Historia general y natural de las Indias* [1535], as quoted in notes to P. L. de Sousa, *Diário da navegação*, 1:153–155.

71. Fonseca, *Nobiliarchia pernambucana*, 2:349–350.

4. CONVERSION

1. One of the few historians to study the Jesuits as intermediaries is Maria Cândida D. M. Barros, "The Office of *Lingua*," 110–140. Dauril Alden also characterizes the Jesuits in Brazil as mediators, writing, "Though the Jesuits seldom adopted an unpopular position, they continually sought to protect the Amerindians against settler abuses and, along with other religious, were assigned by the crown responsibilities for *mediating between employers and Indian laborers*" (see *Making of an Enterprise*, 658, emphasis

mine). William B. Taylor similarly characterizes the clergy of eighteenth-century Mexico as "sacred instruments expected to mediate between Christians and God" and as positioned to mediate "between members of a divided colonial society" (*Magistrates of the Sacred*, 12–13).

There is a voluminous literature on the sixteenth-century Jesuits in Brazil, much of it consisting of published collections of letters, sermons, and evangelical tools. The major source for this chapter is the comprehensive collection of Jesuit letters edited by Serafim Leite, *Monumenta brasiliae* (*MB*), which transcribes the Jesuit letters in the major Jesuit archives from 1549 to 1568. Leite's history, *História da Companhia de Jesus no Brasil*, also remains fundamental. An important new work on the late sixteenth and early seventeenth century is that by Charlotte de Castelnau-L'Estoile, *Les ouvriers d'une vigne stérile*. In English, see the first chapter of Thomas M. Cohen's *Fire of Tongues*, the relevant chapters in John Hemming's *Red Gold*, and the dated but comprehensive biography of José de Anchieta by Helen Dominian titled *Apostle of Brazil*.

2. O'Malley, *The First Jesuits*, 365; Alden, *Making of an Enterprise*, 14.

3. O'Malley, *The First Jesuits*, 93.

4. Ibid., 300, 76.

5. "Manoel da Nóbrega to Simão Rodrigues (in Lisbon), Bahia, 10? April 1549," in *MB*, 1:110; "Regimento de Tomé de Sousa, 17 December 1548," in *HCPB*, 1:347; "Nóbrega to Simão Rodrigues, Bahia, 10? April 1549," in *MB*, 1:112; "Nóbrega to Simão Rodrigues, Bahia, 9 August 1549," in *MB*, 1:129; "Nóbrega to Simão Rodrigues, Porto Seguro, 6 January 1549," in *MB*, 1:160–161; "Nóbrega to Simão Rodrigues, Porto Seguro, 6

January 1549," in *MB*, 1:161; "António Pires to fathers and brothers of Coimbra, Pernambuco, 2 August 1551," in *MB*, 1:252; "Afonso Brás to the fathers and brothers of Coimbra, Espírito Santo, 24 August 1551," in *MB*, 1:274.

6. See, for example, the letter of Enrique Enríquez to Ignatius de Loyola, Simão Rodrigues, and others, Vembar, India, 31 October 1548, in Wicki, *Monumenta histórica*, 1:276–300.

7. "Nóbrega to Simão Rodrigues, Bahia, 10? April 1549," in *MB*, 1:112; Nóbrega, "Informação das terras do Brasil," in *MB*, 1:153; Nóbrega, "Informação das terras do Brasil," in *MB* 1:153.

8. For the Jesuit use of indigenous languages in India, see, for example, the letter of Enrique Enríquez to Ignatius de Loyola, Simão Rodrigues, and others, Vembar, India, 31 October 1548, in Wicki, *Monumenta histórica*, 1:276–300. For the first use of indigenous languages in Brazil, see "Nóbrega to Simão Rodrigues, Salvador, 6 January 1550," in *MB*, 1:159; "João de Azpilcueta [Juan de Azpilcueta Navarro] to the fathers and brothers of Coimbra, Bahia, 28 March 1550," in *MB*, 1:180; "Azpilcueta to the fathers and brothers of Coimbra, Salvador, August 1551," in *MB*, 1:279.

9. "Azpilcueta to the fathers and brothers of Coimbra, Salvador, August 1551," in *MB*, 1:279. António Pires refers to these same meetings between Azpilcueta and the translators in Puerto Seguro in his letter to the fathers and brothers of Coimbra, Pernambuco, 1 August 1551, in *MB*, 1:252. "Azpilcueta [Navarro] to the fathers and brothers of Coimbra, Porto Seguro, 19 September 1553," in *MB*, 2:9.

10. Barros notes that under Nóbrega, the Society actively cultivated vocations

from Portuguese colonists as a means to develop their mission; see "The Office of Lingua," 118. On Correia, see "José de Anchieta to Inácio de Loyola (in Rome), São Vicente, end of March 1555," in *MB*, 2:205; "A brother in Brazil to the brothers in Portugal, São Vicente, 10 March 1553," in *MB*, 1:431–432; "Nóbrega to Simão Rodrigues, São Vicente, March 1553," in *MB*, 1:457; "A brother in Brazil to the brothers of Portugal, São Vicente, 10 March 1553," in *MB*, 1:427.

11. "Nóbrega to Simão Rodrigues, São Vicente, 10? April 1549," in *MB*, 1:112–113.

12. "Orphan children, written by Francisco Pires to Pero Doménech (in Lisbon), Bahia, 5 August 1552," in *MB*, 1:379.

13. "Nóbrega to Simão Rodrigues, São Vicente, 12 February 1553," in *MB*, 1:420–421; "Orphan children to Doménech, Bahia, 5 August 1552," in *MB*, 1:383; "António Pires to fathers and brothers of Coimbra, Pernambuco, 4 June 1552," in *MB*, 1:324; "Pero Correia to Brás Lourenço (in Espírito Santo), São Vicente, 18 July 1554," in *MB*, 2:70; "Anchieta to Loyola, Piratininga, 1 September 1554," in *MB*, 2:110; "Francisco Pires to fathers and brothers of Coimbra, Bahia, 7 August 1552," in *MB*, 1:400.

14. "Nóbrega to Simão Rodrigues, Bahia, 10? April 1549," in *MB*, 1:110–111; "Nóbrega to Dr. Martín Azpilcueta Navarro (in Coimbra), Salvador, 10 August 1549," in *MB*, 1:139–140; "Nóbrega to Dr. Martín Azpilcueta Navarro (in Coimbra), Salvador, 10 August 1549," in *MB*, 1:139–140.

15. "Pero Doménch to Inácio de Loyola (in Rome), Almeirim, Portugal, 12 February 1551," in *MB*, 1:214–215; "Nóbrega to Simão Rodrigues, Salva-

dor, end of August 1552," in *MB*, 1:402; "Francisco Pires to the fathers and brothers of Coimbra, Bahia, 7 August 1552," in *MB*, 1:390–400; "Nóbrega to Simão Rodrigues, Salvador, 6 January 1550," in *MB*, 1:370; Lukács, *Monumenta paedagogica*, 1:546; O'Malley, *The First Jesuits*, 102; Barros, "The Office of *Lingua*," 118.

16. The term derives from the Arabic word "*mamluk*," meaning "slave," but in the Muslim world, beginning as early as the ninth century, "mamluk" or "mameluke" came to mean a slave soldier. The mamelukes originally were Caucasian slaves; later the term came to encompass any slave in the Muslim world who served in an army. Mamluks became powerful; the Mamluk dynasty, for example, ruled Egypt and Syria from 1250 to 1517. After 1517, the Ottoman Turks destroyed the power of the Mamluks as independent rulers, but Mamluks continued to constitute a class of people in Egypt and rose to power again in the seventeenth century; see "Mameluke," *Oxford English Dictionary Online*.

17. "Leonardo Nunes to the fathers and brothers of Coimbra, São Vicente, 20 June 1551," in *MB*, 1:236; "Nóbrega to Simão Rodrigues, Pernambuco, 11 August 1551," in *MB*, 1:269; and "Nóbrega to fathers and brothers of Coimbra, Pernambuco, 13 September 1551," in *MB*, 1:285.

18. "Nóbrega to fathers and brothers of Coimbra, Pernambuco, 13 September 1551," in *MB*, 1:285.

19. "António Pires to the fathers and brothers of Coimbra, Pernambuco 2 August 1551," in *MB*, 1:258; "Anchieta to Loyola, Piratininga, July 1554," in *MB*, 2:77.

20. "Nóbrega to Diego Laínez (in Rome), Bahia, 30 June 1559," in *MB*, 3:117; "Nóbrega to Loyola, São Vicente, 25 March 1555," in *MB*, 2:169, and to Miguel de Tor-

res (in Lisbon), São Vicente, 14 April 1561, in *MB*, 3:339; "Luís da Grã to Ignatius de Loyola (in Rome), Bahia, 27 December 1554," in *MB*, 2:136, and another letter written in Piratininga to Loyola, 8 June 1556, in *MB*, 2:288. Anchieta also had misgivings about accepting mamelucos into the Society; see his letter to Loyola from Piritininga, July 1554, in *MB*, 2:77, as well as his reservations discussed below. Of the mamelucos prepared, only one, Cipriano, was sent to Portugal; see Serafim Leite, "Cipriano de Brasil," 473, and Barros, "The Office of *Lingua*," 117–120.

21. "Anchieta to Loyola, São Vicente, end of March 1555," in *MB*, 2:194–195.

22. "Catalgo de los padres y hermanos de la provincia del Brasil, en el año de 1574," in ARSI: Bras. 5; "Everard Mercurian to Ignacio Tolosa, Rome, 12 December 1574," in ARSI: Bras. 2:44; "Algumas coisas que da provincia do Brasil se propõem ao nosso padre general este año de 1579 e respostas a elas," in ARSI: Bras. 2:28v–30v. The suitability of the Brazilian-born of Portuguese parentage apparently continued to be discussed in Brazil. When the Jesuit visitor Cristovão de Gouveia arrived in Brazil a few years after Mercurian's death, he wrote to the new father general, Claudio Aquaviva, that the Brazilian-born did most of the work of evangelism because of their facility with the Indian language. They had greater authority with Indians than did those from Portugal, who rarely learned the Indian language well. See "Gouveia to Aquaviva, 1 November 1584," in ARSI: Lus. 68:410–411v; also in Serafim Leite, *História da Companhia de Jesus no Brasil*, 2:432–433.

23. "Nóbrega to Simão Rodrigues, Bahia, 6 January 1550," in *MB*, 1:158; "Anchieta to Loyola, Piratininga, São

Vicente, 1 September 1554," in *MB*, 2:109; "Pero Correia to Simão Rodrigues (in Lisbon), São Vicente, 10 March 1553," in *MB*, 1:438; "António Pires to the fathers and brothers of Coimbra, Pernambuco, 2 August 1551," in *MB*, 1:263; "Nóbrega to the fathers and brothers of Coimbra, Pernambuco, 13 September 1551," in *MB*, 1:286; "Pero Correia to Belchior Nunes (in Coimbra), São Vicente, 8 June 1551," in *MB*, 1:222. Susan Sleeper-Smith has found that the Jesuits in North America similarly paid attention to Indian women, who in turn became important mediators and cultural brokers; see *Indian Women and French Men*.

24. "António Pires to the fathers and brothers of Coimbra, Pernambuco, 4 June 1552," in *MB*, 1:326.

25. "António de Quadros to Juan de Polanco (in Rome), Lisbon, 17 March 1554," in *MB*, 2:34; "António Pires to the fathers and brothers of Coimbra, Pernambuco, 4 June 1552," in *MB*, 1:325.

26. The Jesuits frequently cited the fact that one language was universally understood along the coast of Brazil, from Maranhão to Paraguay. This was the *língua geral*, or "universal language," that they believed greatly aided their initial evangelization. On the língua geral, see Freire and Rosa, *Línguas gerais*, and Castelnau-L'Estoile, *Les ouvriers d'une vigne stérile*, 141–169. José de Anchieta's grammar, catechism and confessional manual, dialogue of faith, and dictionary are published today as Anchieta, *Arte de gramática da língua mais usada na costa do Brasil, Doutrina Cristã, Diálogo da fé*, and *Vocabulário na língua brasílica*.

27. Anchieta, *Diálogo da fé;* see Shapiro, "From Tupã to the Land without Evil," 126–130, and Métraux, *A religião*, 40–55.

28. "Leonardo Nunes to the fathers and brothers of Coimbra, São Vicente, 20 June 1551," in *MB*, 1:233; "Vicente Rodrigues to the fathers and brothers of Coimbra, Bahia, 17 September 1552," in *MB*, 1:410–411; "Pero Correia to Brás Lourenço (in Espírito Santo), São Vicente, 18 July 1554," in *MB*, 2:70.

29. "Gaspar Barzaeus to fathers and brothers in India and Europe, Hormuz, 1 December 1549," in Wicki, *Monumenta histórica*, 1:595–638; the debate in the synagogue is transcribed in ibid., 1: 698–725.

30. "Orphan children to Doménech, Bahia, 5 August 1552," in *MB*, 1:383–384; "Azpilcueta to the fathers and brothers of Coimbra, Bahia, 28 March 1550," in *MB*, 1:180; "Orphan children to Doménech, Bahia, 5 August 1552," in *MB*, 1:386; "Nóbrega to Simão Rodrigues, Bahia, end of August 1552," in *MB*, 1:408.

31. "Nóbrega to Simão Rodrigues, Bahia, end of August 1552," in *MB*, 1:408. See also Barros' discussion of this strategy in "The Office of *Língua*," 124.

32. "Pero Correia to Simão Rodrigues (in Lisbon), São Vicente, June 1551," in *MB*, 1:230, and "Pero Correia to Belchior Nunes Barreto (in Coimbra), São Vicente, 8 June 1551," in *MB*, 1:220.

33. These are not the exact words, but they are very similar to what was said, based on a description of the preaching given in the letter written for the orphan children by Francisco Pires to Pero Doménech, Bahia, 5 August 1552, in *MB*, 1:378.

34. "Orphan children to Doménech, Bahia, 5 August 1552," in *MB*, 1:386–387.

35. "Nóbrega to Dr. Martín de Azpilcueta Navarro (in Coimbra), Salvador, 10 August 1549," in *MB*, 1:144.

36. "António Pires to the fathers and brothers of Coimbra, Pernambuco, 2

August 1551," in *MB*, 1:253; "Leonardo Nunes to the fathers and brothers of Coimbra, São Vicente, 20 June 1551," in *MB*, 1:233.

37. "Nóbrega to fathers and brothers of Coimbra, Pernambuco, 13 September 1551," in *MB*, 1:288; "António Pires to the fathers and brothers of Coimbra, Pernambuco, 2 August 1551," in *MB*, 1:253.

38. "Bishop Pedro Fernandes Sardinha to Simão Rodrigues (in Lisbon), Bahia, July 1552," *MB*, 1:358–360. See Sandra Lauderdale Graham's translation of this letter in "The Jesuit and the Bishop."

39. "Bishop Pedro Fernandes Sardinha to Simão Rodrigues (in Lisbon), Bahia, July 1552," *MB*, 1:361–362. Barros also notes the importance of this conflict between Nóbrega and the bishop in "The Office of *Língua*," 115–116.

40. "Nóbrega to Simão Rodrigues, Bahia, end of July 1552," in *MB*, 1:369–370, 373–374.

41. "Nóbrega to King João III, São Vicente, October 1553," in *MB*, 2:15–17.

42. "Leonardo Nunes to the fathers and brothers of Coimbra, São Vicente, November 1550," in *MB*, 1:204–206; "Pero Correia to João Nunes Barreto (in Africa), São Vicente, 20 June 1551," in *MB*, 1:226; "Leonardo Nunes to the fathers and brothers of Coimbra, São Vicente, 20 June 1551," in *MB*, 1:233.

43. "A brother in Brazil to brothers in Portugal, São Vicente, 10 March 1553," in *MB*, 1:430.

44. "Nóbrega to Simão Rodrigues, São Vicente, 12 February 1553," in *MB*, 1:420–423; "Nóbrega to Simão Rodrigues, São Vicente, March 1553," in *MB*, 1:457; "Nóbrega to Luís Gonçalves da Câmara (in Lisbon), São Vicente, 15 June 1553," in *MB*, 1:492.

45. "Governor Tomé de Sousa to King João III, [São Vicente], 1 June 1553," in *HCPB*, 3:366; "Nóbrega to Luís Gonçalves da Câmara (in Lisbon), São Vicente, 15 June 1553," in *MB*, 1:492; "King João III to Duarte da Costa, Governor of Brazil, Lisbon, 23 July 1554," in *MB*, 2:73. The distant outpost was the residence of Maniçoba, alluded to by Pero Correia in his letter to Brás Lourenço (in Espírito Santo), São Vicente, 18 July 1554, in *MB*, 2:71.

46. "Leonardo Nunes to the fathers and brothers of Coimbra, São Vicente, November? 1550," in *MB*, 1:207–208; "Tomé de Sousa to King João III, 1 June 1553," in *HCPB*, 3:365; "Diogo Jácome to the fathers and brothers of Coimbra, São Vicente, 20 June 1551," in *MB*, 1:243–244.

47. "Nóbrega to Luís Gonçalves da Câmara (in Lisbon), São Vicente, 15 June 1553," in *MB*, 1:498–499. Nóbrega uses the metaphor "petra scandali" to describe Ramalho, which is evocative of the verse in the *Biblia Sacra Vulgata* (Jerome's fifth-century translation of the Greek and Hebrew scriptures, which was recognized as authoritative during the Council of Trent in 1546, and therefore well known to Jesuits): "et lapis offensionis et petra scandali qui offendunt verbo nec credunt in quod et positi sunt" (1 Peter 2:7–9), translated in the *New International Version* as "A stone that causes men to stumble and a rock that makes them fall," see http://bible.gospelcom.net/bible?

48. "Nóbrega to Luís Gonçalves da Câmara (in Lisbon), wilderness of São Vicente, 31 August 1553," in *MB*, 1:524–527.

49. Leme, *Genealogia paulistana*, 1:30; "Pero Correia to Simão Rodrigues (in Lisbon), São Vicente, 10 March 1553," in *MB*, 1:435–436.

50. "Nóbrega to Luís Gonçalves da Câmara (in Lisbon), wilderness of São Vicente, 31 August 1553," in *MB*, 1:524–527. Apparently, Ramalho was still married, for nothing came of Nóbrega's plan to regularize his common-law marriage in Brazil.

51. "Nóbrega to King João III, São Vicente, October 1553," in *MB*, 2:16; "Anchieta to Loyola, São Paulo de Piratininga, 1 September 1554," in *MB*, 2:115.

52. "Anchieta to Loyola, São Paulo de Piratininga, 1 September 1554," in *MB*, 2:115.

53. "Anchieta to Loyola, São Paulo de Piratininga, 1 September 1554," in *MB*, 2:116.

54. "Missionarii S.I. Piscariae, Punicale, 19 June 1549," in Wicki, *Monumenta histórica*, 1:484–489, 481–484; "José de Anchieta to Ignatius de Loyola (in Rome), Piratininga, 1 September 1554," in *MB*, 2:117; "José de Anchieta to Ignatius de Loyola (in Rome), São Vicente, end of March 1555," in *MB*, 2:200–201.

55. "Anchieta to Loyola, São Vicente, end of March 1555," in *MB*, 2:203–205.

56. "Ignatius de Loyola to Pedro de Ribadeneira (in Brussels), Rome, 3 March 1556," in *MB*, 2:265.

57. "Nóbrega to Miguel de Torres (in Lisbon), Rio Vermelho, Bahia, August 1557," in *MB*, 2:401; "Nóbrega to Miguel de Torres (in Lisbon), Salvador, 8 May 1558," in *MB*, 2:445–459.

58. "[António Pires?] to the provincial of Portugal, Salvador, 12 September 1558," in *MB*, 2:475.

59. "Informação dos primeiros aldeamentos na Bahia," in Anchieta, *Cartas: Informações*, 358–359.

60. Anchieta, *De gestis Mendi de Saa*. The title of the poem in English would be "Concerning the Deeds of Mem de Sá"; "António Blázquez to Diego Laínez, Salvador, 30 April 1558," in *MB*, 2:439; "[António Pires?] to the provincial of Portugal, Salvador, 12 September 1558," *MB*, 2:469–473.

61. Castelnau-L'Estoile reflects on the pessimistic tone that the Jesuits felt later, at the end of the sixteenth century, when a common metaphor for their mission in Brazil was "a sterile vine," *Les ouvriers d'une vigne stérile*.

62. The play, with commentary and notes, is found in Anchieta, *Teatro de Anchieta*, 115–140; Armando Cardoso, S.J., "O primeiro auto: A pregação universal," in ibid., 59–67.

63. Cardoso, "O primeiro auto," in ibid., 59–67, and "Na festa do natal ou pregação universal," in ibid., 115–116.

64. "Manoel da Nóbrega to Dom Henrique, São Vicente, 1 June 1560," in *MB*, 3:245. After the death of King João III in 1557, his grandson Sebastião became the direct heir to the throne. But as he was only three years old at the time, his grandmother Catarina de Áustria (Catherine of Austria, sister of the Spanish king Charles V) and his great-uncle Dom Henrique (known in English as Cardinal Prince Henry) fought over who should serve as regent. At the time when Nóbrega wrote this letter, Dom Henrique was regent; see Hermann, *No reino do desejado*, 73–85.

65. "José de Anchieta to Diego Laínez (in Rome), São Vicente, 8 January 1565," in *MB*, 4:123.

66. "Anchieta to Laínez (in Rome), São Vicente, 8 January 1565," in *MB*, 4:120–181, 126.

67. Ibid., 4:129–139.

68. Ibid., 4:133.

69. Ibid., 4:134. Staden mentions José Adorno in *True History*, 62 and 176–177 n. 41. According to genealogists, there were four Adorno brothers who came to Brazil, one of whom married a daughter of Diogo Álvares "Caramuru" in Bahia; see Doria, "Adornos e Dorias em S. Paulo," and Jaboatão, *Catalogo genealogico*, 115.

70. "Anchieta to Laínez (in Rome), São Vicente, 8 January 1565," in *MB*, 4:169–171.

71. Ibid., 4:171.

72. Ibid., 4:176–177.

5. BIOLOGY

1. "Anchieta to Laínez (in Rome), São Vicente, 8 January 1565," in *MB*, 4:134.

2. Crosby, *Columbian Exchange*. For a reprinting of many of the "classic" articles on the biological side of what Crosby coined the "Columbian Exchange," see Kiple and Beck, *Biological Consequences of European Expansion, 1450–1800*.

3. Here I follow Alchon, *A Pest in the Land*, 3–5, 145.

4. For the history of disease in sixteenth-century Brazil, see the brief summaries by Russell-Wood in *A World on the Move*, 119–122, and by Alchon in *A Pest in the Land*, 84–90. On the population decline, see the pioneering efforts of Dean, "Indigenous Populations," 9–11; Hemming, *Red Gold*, 139–160; Monteiro, "A dança dos números," 17–18; Alden and Miller, "Out of Africa"; and Alencastro, *O trato dos viventes*, 127–138. Studies on the ecological changes afoot in sixteenth-century Brazil are still few in number. Russell-Wood provides a global perspective on the Portuguese role in the exchange of plants in the Portuguese maritime world in *A World on the Move*, 148–182. The place of the sixteenth-century ecological changes in the destruction of the Atlantic forest is brilliantly analyzed in Dean's *With Broadax and Firebrand*, 41–90; and S. W. Miller documents in *Fruitless Trees* the destructive policies of the Crown's timber monopoly.

5. See, for example, the possibilities uncovered by Graham in *Performing Dreams*, and by the anthropologists in Albert and Ramos' *Pacificando o branco*.

6. Ann Ramenofsky argues that a minimum of eleven, and potentially as many as fourteen, diseases diffused to the Americas; see "Diseases of the Americas," in Kiple, *Cambridge World History*, 323–324. Ramenofsky leaves out tuberculosis and venereal syphilis because of the extensive controversy over whether these diseases existed in the Americas prior to 1492. Through their movements and interactions, humans directly spread influenza, measles, mumps, rubella, smallpox, pneumonia, scarlet fever, and pertussis, whereas yellow fever, anthrax, bubonic plague, typhus, and malaria were introduced through insect and animal vectors.

7. "Endemic" is defined in the *Oxford English Dictionary Online* as "habitually prevalent in a certain country, and due to permanent local causes," and "epidemic" is defined as "prevalent among a people or a community at a special time, and produced by some special causes not generally present in the affected locality."

8. The demographic collapse of the indigenous American Indian population is well documented for Spanish America; for an introduction to the field and its literature, see Cook, *Born to Die* and *Demographic Collapse;* Cook and Lovell, *Secret*

Judgments of God; Denevan, *Native Population;* Whitmore, *Disease and Death;* Lovell, *Conquest and Survival.*

9. Crosby, *Columbian Exchange,* 74-121; Crosby develops his idea of the domestic animal as an ally of the European imperialist in *Ecological Imperialism.*

10. McNeil, *Plagues and Peoples,* 54-93, quotations from 73, 74, 93; Alchon, *A Pest in the Land,* 6-31.

11. McNeil, *Plagues and Peoples,* 210-211. Frank C. Innes maintains that the North American population was a "healthy population adjusted to its environment" before 1492; see "Disease Ecologies of North America," 520-523, 522; Mary Karasch argues that before 1492 the peoples of South America had a limited number of diseases; see "Disease Ecologies of South America," 537-539.

12. Alchon, *A Pest in the Land,* 32-59, quotation from 59.

13. Denevan, "The Pristine Myth," 369-385; Dean, *With Broadax and Firebrand,* 20-40.

14. Kiple, "Disease Ecologies of the Caribbean," 498-499; the population data for Hispaniola is in Cook, *Born to Die,* 21-24, 60-64, 85-88. A detailed description of the first epidemic on Hispaniola is Cook's, "Sickness, Starvation, and Death," 349-386; see Sauer's classic *Early Spanish Main,* 156-157, 204, for the transformation of the landscape; quotation from 156.

15. Dean believes that coastal Tupi populations had already begun to decline from epidemic infectious disease before 1550; see his "Indigenous Populations," 9-12.

16. Dean's number of ships may be found in "Indigenous Populations," 10;

Pearson's numbers are in *The Portuguese in India,* 62; Cook cites the numbers of Pierre and Huguette Chanu in *Born to Die,* 53.

17. Cook, "Sickness, Starvation, and Death," passim; Sauer, *Early Spanish Main,* passim.

18. "Carta de Pero Vaz de Caminha, 1º de Maio de 1500," in Amado and Figueiredo, *Brasil 1500,* 74-75; "Relação do piloto anônimo." See Vespucci's fifth and sixth letters, "Vespucci to Lorenzo di Pierfrancesco de' Medici [*Mundus novus*]," in Vespucci, *Letters from a New World,* 45-56, quotation from 46; and "Vespucci to Piero Soderini, Lisbon, 4 September 1504," in ibid., 85-97.

19. "Carta de Pero Vaz de Caminha," in Amado and Figueiredo, *Brasil 1500,* 99-100; "Relação do português anônimo," in ibid., 134—the author uses the phrase "*bem dispostas*"; "Vespucci to de' Medici, 1502," in Vespucci, *Letters from a New World,* 34, 33; "Vespucci to de' Medici [*Mundus novus*]," in ibid., 47-48, 51.

20. "Vespucci to Lorenzo di Pierfrancesco de' Medici, Lisbon, 1502," in ibid., 34, 31; "Vespucci to de' Medici [*Mundus novus*]," in ibid., 47; "Vespucci to Piero Soderini, Lisbon, 4 September 1504," in ibid., 85-97.

21. Perrone-Moisés, *Vinte luas,* 19-20, 56. The "illness of the sea" might have been fevers or scurvy. The term "apoplexy" generally means stroke; see Poirier and Derouesné, "Apoplexy and Stroke," 584.

22. The ship left Santa Catarina on 3 July 1504, and Essomericq was baptized on the brink of death on 14 September 1504; see Perrone-Moisés, *Vinte luas,* 25.

23. Ships carry organisms in their ballast water, which may explain why the

men, both French and Guarani, who were apparently healthy on shore, became sick once they re-embarked. See Mary E. Wilson, "Travel and the Emergence of Infectious Diseases," 39–46. Outbreaks of influenza on luxury ships make it clear that the threat posed by ships as a disease environment continues; see "Preliminary Guidelines for the Prevention and Control of Influenza-like Illness among Passengers and Crew Members on Cruise Ships," Atlanta, Georgia: Division of Quarantine, National Center for Infectious Diseases, Centers for Disease Control and Prevention, August 1999. http://www.cdc.gov/travel/CDCguideflufnl.pdf.

24. Pigafetta, *Magellan's Voyage*, 1: 37–57.

25. "Relación escrita y presentada al Emperador por Andres de Urdaneta de los sucesos de la armada del Comendador Loaisa, desde 24 de julio de 1525 hasta el año 1535," in Navarrete, *Colección de los viages*, 5:367, and "Relación que dío Juan de Areizaga de la navegación de la armada de Loaisa hasta desembocar el estrecho . . . ," in ibid., 5:204. "Luis Ramírez to his father, on his experiences in the Río de la Plata," in *NIW*, 5:249. Cabot had three ships and a caravel; see "Testimony of Sebastian Cabot concerning his voyage to the Río de la Plata," in *NIW*, 5:252. For the trading log kept by Enrique Montes, see "Relatório de escambo."

26. Schmidel, *Derrotero y viaje*, 18, 76, and 136–144 passim.

27. Carta de Pero Vaz de Caminha, in Amado and Figueiredo, *Brasil 1500*, 84; "De la habilitación que tuvo y viage que hizo la Armada del Emperador Carlos V, de que era Capitán general Fernando Magallanes . . . ," in Navarrete, *Colección de los viages*, 4:11; see also "Relación

de los bastimentos que lleva la Armada de Magallanes," in ibid., 4:167; "Luis Ramírez to his father, on his experiences in the Río de la Plata," in *NIW*, 5:250; Pigafetta, *Magellan's Voyage*, 1:57.

28. See the petition of Mem de Sá, 2, and the testimony of the king's surgeon, Mestre Afonso, 37, both in "Instrumento dos serviços de Mem de Sá [1560]"; "Relatório de escambo," http://www.historiadobrasil.com.br/viagem/docs01.htm; Santa Cruz, *Islario general*, 1:547.

29. P. L. de Sousa, *Diário da navegação*, 1:135–136, 197; Oviedo, *Historia general*, 2:369.

30. "1545. Pero de Góis to his partner Martin Ferreira," in *NIW*, 5:54.

31. Garcia d'Avila, who first arrived in Brazil with Tomé de Sousa in 1549, is traditionally credited with distributing the first cattle in Brazil, cattle that had come from the Cape Verde Islands. But it is more likely that cattle were established well before the royal governor arrived. For Dean's thesis that cattle arrived with Martim Afonso, see *With Broadax and Firebrand*, 75. The citations of cattle and other domestic animals are to be found in the following reports and letters: Nóbrega, "Informação das terras do Brasil, Bahia," in *MB*, 1:148; "Afonso Brás to the fathers and brothers of Coimbra, Espírito Santo, 24 August 1551," in *MB*, 1:275; and "Luís da Grã to Inácio de Loyola (in Rome), Bahia, 27 December 1554," in *MB*, 2:131.

32. Thevet, *Le Brésil*, 175; Léry, *History of a Voyage*, 59; "Vicente Rodrigues to fathers and brothers of Coimbra, Bahia, 17 May? 1552," in *MB*, 1:305; "Manoel da Nóbrega to Tomé de Sousa (in Lisbon), Bahia, 5 July 1559," in *MB*, 3:96.

33. On wheat, see "Luís da Grã to Inácio de Loyola (in Rome), Bahia, 27

December 1554," in *MB*, 2:131. Only in Pernambuco, the richest settlement in Brazil, was wheat bread available; see "Rui Pereira to fathers and brothers of Portugal, Pernambuco, 6 April 1561," in *MB*, 3:335; on fruits, see "A brother in Brazil to brothers in Portugal, São Vicente, 10 March 1553," in *MB*, 1:427. Nóbrega drank orange juice as a treat in São Vicente; see "Ambrósio Pires to Diego Mirón (in Lisbon), Porto Seguro, first months of 1555," in *MB*, 2:150. Fernão Cardim has a discussion of European fruits, grains, and vegetables in "Do Clima e terra do Brasil e de algumas cousas notáveis que se acham na terra como no mar," in Cardim, *Tratados da terra*, 160−161. The reference to peas and grasses comes from Brandão, *Dialogues*, 202; see especially 228 nn. 45 and 46. Brandão questioned whether the Guinea squash was in fact from Africa. In his dialogues he writes: "Now there is something that looks like what in the Kingdom [Portugal] they call the Guinea squash; but I think, rather, it is indigenous" (*Dialogues*, 202). Nóbrega ate "abobras de Guiné" (Guinea squash) cooked in water in São Vicente; see "Ambrósio Pires to Diego Mirón (in Lisbon), Porto Seguro, first months of 1555," in *MB*, 2:150.

34. When genealogists in the eighteenth and nineteenth centuries began to reconstruct the marriages of mameluco children of prominent Portuguese colonists, they were able to follow the marriages of women more easily than those of men. With the exception of Jerônimo d'Albuquerque's mameluco sons, whose marriages to Portuguese women are recorded, the mameluca daughters of João Ramalho and Diogo Álvares were far more likely to marry Europeans and to have their marriages recorded in par-

ish and probate registers than were their mameluco brothers. Of Correa's sixteen known children, twelve were women, and all twelve women married European men. In contrast, only one son married. Less is known about the marriages of Ramalho's mameluco children, but what we do know reflects the same pattern: mameluca daughters married Portuguese men, whereas the marriages of mameluco sons did not occur or are unknown. On Jerônimo d'Albuquerque's descendants, see Fonseca, *Nobiliarchia pernambucana*, 2:349−350. On Álvares' descendants, see Jaboatão, *Catalogo genealogico*, 69−119; Tavares, *História da Bahia*, 41; Couto, *Construção do Brasil*, 312, and Calmon, *História da fundação*, 30. For Ramalho's offspring, see Luis, "O testamento de João Ramalho," and especially Leme, *Genealogia paulistana*, 1:1−48.

35. "Nóbrega to Simão Rodrigues (in Lisbon), Bahia, 6 January 1550," in *MB*, 1:165.

36. "Tomé de Sousa to King João III, Salvador, 1551," in *HCPB*, 3:362.

37. See the letters of Vicente Rodrigues to fathers and brothers of Coimbra, Bahia, 17 May? 1552, in *MB*, 1:303−305, 306−314; "Vicente Rodrigues to Simão Rodrigues (Lisbon), Salvador, May 1552," in *MB*, 1:316−321; "Francisco Pires to fathers and brothers of Coimbra, Bahia, 7 August 1552," in *MB*, 1:395−396; "Orphan children, written by Francisco Pires, to Pero Doménech (Lisbon), Salvador, 5 August 1552," in *MB*, 1:379, 387.

38. The armada was in São Vicente by February 1553; see Nóbrega's first letter from São Vicente, dated 12 February 1553, in *MB*, 1:419−424; "Pero Correia to Brás Lourenco (in Espírito Santo), São Vicente, 18 July 1554," in *MB*, 2:70−71; "A

brother in Brazil (São Vicente) to brothers in Portugal, São Vicente, 10 March 1553," in *MB*, 1:425–433.

39. "Pero Correia to Brás Lourenço (in Espírito Santo), São Vicente, 18 July 1554," in *MB*, 2:70–71; "José de Anchieta to Inácio de Loyola (in Rome), Piratininga, 1 September 1554," in *MB*, 2:108; "José de Anchieta to Inácio de Loyola (in Rome), São Vicente, end of March 1555," in *MB*, 2:209; the outlying mission was Maniçoba.

40. Staden, *True History*, 98–100.

41. The disease is similar to Creutzfeldt-Jakob disease (popularly known as mad cow disease) and is thought to be caused by the ingestion of human brain tissue. See "Cannibalism's Clues to CJD," BBC News Online, Friday, 23 March 2001, http://news.bbc.co.uk/1/low/uk/1235525.stm. Elizabeth Pennisi argues that similar diseases, spread through cannibalism, may have been common in the past; see "Cannibalism and Prion Disease May Have Been Rampant in Ancient Humans," 227–229, and "Ancient Cannibals Spread Disease?" *Science Now*, 10 April 2003, 1.

42. Although we have no information about the health of the sailors on this particular ship, the year before, sometime after August 1553, Captain Pero de Góis, who was looking for French ships to attack near Rio de Janeiro, described the difficulties he had in a letter to the king; among them were that many of his sailors were "sick." See "Letter of Pero de Góis to King João III, Salvador, 29 April 1554," in Accioli de Cerqueira e Silva, *Memorias históricas*, 1:317–318.

43. Staden, *True History*, 84–88.

44. The Indian chief Cuñambeba is possibly Koniam-Bebe in Staden's

account; see Serafim Leite's discussion in *MB*, 4:145 n. 45. Some scholars identify Pindahousou, whom Thevet met, as Pindobuçu, whom Anchieta met in Ubatuba; Thevet, *Le Brésil*, 150; *MB*, 4:132 n. 24.

45. See Nóbrega's letter to Miguel de Torres (in Lisbon) written from Rio Vermelho, Bahia, August 1557, before Mem de Sá arrived, in *MB*, 2:402, as well as his letter to Miguel de Torres (in Lisbon) written from Salvador, 8 May 1558, after Mem de Sá had arrived, in *MB*, 2:445–459.

46. Thevet, *Le Brésil*, 80, 95. "Letter of Nicholas Barré [the pilot], from Antarctic France [Rio de Janeiro], [1555]," as it appears in Lescarbot, *Histoire de la Novvelle-France*, 1:299–300. Thevet was in Brazil for ten weeks between 10 November 1555 and 31 January 1556, and he appeared to have been sick for most of that time; see Thevet, *Le Brésil*, 150, 167, 19–20.

47. Thevet, *Le Brésil*, 150. Some scholars identify this chief as the same one whom Anchieta met in Ubatuba: Pindobuçu; see *MB*, 4:132 n. 24.

48. "Letter of Barré," in Lescarbot, *Histoire de la Novvelle-France*, 1:304.

49. Dean, "Indigenous Populations," 7; Staden, *True History*, 131–133.

50. Petition of Mem de Sá in "Instrumento dos serviços de Mem de Sá [1560]," 2, and testimonies of João d'Araujo, Heitor Antunes, Francisco de Moraes, Master Afonso, and Bras Alcoforado in "Instrumento dos serviços de Mem de Sá [1560]," 9, 16–17, 25, 37, 58.

51. Cook, *Born to Die*, 52.

52. Crosby recognizes the importance of ships and sailors, seeing both as essential for the exchange of plants, animals, and disease; see *Ecological Imperialism*,

104–131. The role played by ships and boats in the transmission of disease has been well documented by historians; see Hopkins, *Princes and Peasants*, and a new edition titled *The Greatest Killer*, passim; McNeil, *Plagues and Peoples*, passim; and Watts, *Epidemics and History*, passim. On the black death and its transmission, see Park, "Black Death," 612. Samuel K. Cohn, Jr., argues that the black death was not the same as the bubonic plague and that it was not carried by fleas on rats; see "The Black Death," 703–738.

53. "Antonio de Heredia to Luis Gonçalves da Camara (in Lisbon), Cochim, 25 November 1552," in Wicki, *Monumenta histórica*, 2:409; "Manuel Teixeira to fathers and brothers of Coimbra, Goa, 15 November 1551," in ibid., 2:202; "Manuel Álvares to fathers and brothers of Coimbra, Bahia, 4 September 1560," in *MB*, 3:274, 303; "Rui Pereira to fathers and brothers of Portugal, Bahia, 15 September 1560," in *MB*, 3:303–304.

54. "António de Sá to fathers and brothers of Bahia, Espírito Santo, February 1559," in *MB*, 3:18–22. Sá uses the words *"prioris," "câmaras de sangue,"* and *"peste"* to describe the epidemic. He does not specify if the French ship was loading before or after the disease broke out. "António de Sá to fathers and brothers of Bahia, Espírito Santo, 13 June 1559," in *MB*, 3:38–39; "José de Anchieta to Diego Laínez (in Rome), São Vicente, 30 July 1561," in *MB*, 3:380; "Anchieta to Diego Laínez (in Rome), São Vicente, 16 April 1563," in *MB*, 3:555.

55. "José de Anchieta to Diego Laínez (in Rome), São Vicente, 1 June 1560," in *MB*, 3:267; "José de Anchieta to Diego Laínez (in Rome), São Vicente, 30 July 1561," in *MB*, 3:380.

56. "José de Anchieta to Diego Laínez (in Rome), São Vicente, 1 June 1560," in *MB*, 3:252–252.

57. "António Blázquez to the provincial of Portugal, Bahia, June 1557," in *MB*, 2:394; "Manoel da Nóbrega to Miguel de Torres and the fathers and brothers of Portugal, Bahia, 5 July 1559," in *MB*, 3:60–61; "Ambrósio Pires to fathers and brothers of Coimbra, Porto Seguro, 5 May 1554," in *MB*, 2:51. Brother Gregorio later contracted smallpox.

58. "Luís da Grã to Diego Mirón (in Lisbon), Espírito Santo, 24 April 1555," in *MB*, 2:225; "António Blázquez to Diego Laínez (in Rome), Bahia, 1 September 1561," in *MB*, 3:397, 410; "Pedro da Costa to fathers and brothers of São Roque (in Lisbon), Espírito Santo, 27 July 1565," in *MB*, 4:270–271; "Inácio de Azevedo to Francisco de Borja (in Rome), Bahia, 19 November 1566," in *MB*, 4:373.

59. *Plasmodium vivax* causes benign tertian malaria, *Plasmodium falciparum* causes malignant tertian malaria, and *Plasmodium malariae* causes quartan malaria; F. L. Dunn, "Malaria," 855–862.

60. Mary Karasch believes that the "fevers" described by the Jesuits were malaria; see "Disease Ecologies of South America," 539–540. Brandão, *Diálogos*, 146. *"Maleita"* is defined as "malaria" in Antônio Houaiss, *Dicionário electrônico Houaiss da língua portuguesa* (Rio de Janeiro: Editora Objectiva, 2001), and in Aurélio Buarque de Holanda Ferreira, *Novo dicionário da língua portuguesa*, 1st ed. (Rio de Janeiro: Nova Fronteira, 1975); the etymology given in Holanda Ferreira is from the Latin *febris maledicta*. The etymology of malaria comes from the Italian *mal aire;* see "malaria," *Oxford English Dictionary Online*.

61. The protozoal parasites that cause malaria (*Plasmodium falciparum, Plasmodium vivax, Plasmodium ovale,* and *Plasmodium malariae*) have a life cycle that is split between a vertebrate host (humans) and an insect vector (the mosquito). In the transmission of malaria, the mosquito is always an anopheline mosquito, and 60 of the 380 species of anopheline mosquito can transmit malaria. Only female mosquitoes are involved, as the males do not feed on blood; see Bradley and Dept. of Microbiology and Immunology, University of Leicester, "Biology of Plasmodium Parasites and Anopheles Mosquitos," and F. L. Dunn, "Malaria," 855–862. On the first outbreak of malaria in the Caribbean, see Cook, "Sickness, Starvation, and Death," 375.

62. "Anchieta to Diego Laínez (in Rome), São Vicente, 30 July 1561," in *MB*, 3:380.

63. Yellow fever is a severe infectious disease caused by an arbovirus (*Flaviviridae*). Mosquitoes are the primary disease vector in transmission of the disease from forest monkeys to man and from man to man. Several types of mosquitoes are involved, the *Aedes aegypti* being one of the most important. Those who have been vaccinated or who recover from the disease possess immunity; see "Yellow Fever," World Health Organization, http://www.who.int/mediacentre/factsheets/fs100/en/, and Cooper and Kiple, "Yellow Fever," 1100–1107. On Aleixo de Abreu, yellow fever, and the *doença do bicho, mal do bicho, bicha,* or *os males,* see the editor's note to Brandão's description of it in *Dialogues,* 126 n. 65, and Karasch, "Disease Ecologies of South America," 540.

64. On Nóbrega's illness, see "Nóbrega to Miguel de Torres (in Lisbon), Rio

Vermelho, Bahia, August 1557," in *MB*, 2:404; "Francisco Henriques to Miguel de Torres (in Rome), Lisbon, 3 April 1558," in *MB*, 2:424; "Miguel de Torres to Diego Laínez (in Rome), Lisbon, 16 May 1559," in *MB*, 3:35. The Jesuit report is attributed to Fernão Cardim and is titled "Enformacion de la provincia del Brasil para Nuestro Padre," 155.

65. On the transmission of yellow fever to the Americas in the water casks of ships, see McNeil, *Plagues and Peoples,* 222; on the first outbreaks in the Caribbean, see Kiple and Higgins, "Yellow Fever," 237–248.

66. Cooper and Kiple, "Yellow Fever," 1101–1107, F. L. Dunn, "Malaria," 858; J. C. Miller, "Significance of Drought," 23–24; and Karasch, "Disease Ecologies of South America," 540. On the immunity versus innate resistance of Africans to yellow fever, see the debate between Sheldon Watts ("Yellow Fever Immunities," 955–968) and Kenneth F. Kiple ("Response to Sheldon Watts," 955). Much of the history of the slave trade and disease focuses on the seventeenth, eighteenth, and nineteenth centuries, when slave ships, for example, are known to have introduced many epidemics of smallpox into the Americas; see Dobyns, "Disease Transfer at Contact," 282–283; Alden and Miller, "Out of Africa," 195–224.

67. "Nóbrega to Simão Rodrigues (Lisbon), Bahia, 10 July 1552," in *MB*, 1:351; "Manoel da Nóbrega to Tomé de Sousa (in Lisbon), Bahia, 5 July 1559," in *MB*, 3:101; "[José de Anchieta] to Claudio Aquaviva (in Rome), Carta Ânua da Província do Brasil, de 1581, Bahia, 1 January 1582," in Anchieta, *Cartas: Correspondência,* 308–312. Elephantiasis, an extreme swelling of the legs, scrotum, labia, or arms, was

another disease that was likely introduced through the slave trade. It was endemic in Africa, and the filarial worm adapted its life cycle to mosquito vectors; see Savitt, "Filariasis," 724–730. Two examples of what may have been elephantiasis come from the last decade of the sixteenth century. In 1591, a slave denounced in the Inquisition visit was described as a slave from Guinea with a "very swollen leg," denunciation of Mathias Moreira, 21 August 1591, in *PV:D-Bahia*, 406; and in 1599, Anthony Knivet, an English pirate in Brazil, describes his own swollen leg, saying that it was "common and very dangerous"; see "Anthony Knivet's adventures in Brazil," in *NIW*, 5:136.

68. J. C. Miller, "Central Africa," 27, 38, and "Significance of Drought," 24, 28, 30.

69. "Leonardo do Vale to F. Gonçalo Vaz de Melo, Bahia, 12 May 1563," in *MB*, 4:9–22. Alden and Miller believe that this initial outbreak of smallpox came from Portugal, not Africa; see "Out of Africa," 199.

70. "António Blázquez to Diego Mirón (in Lisbon), 31 May 1564," in *MB*, 4:55–56.

71. Anchieta (and later Brandão; see n. 78 below) is referring to a shark, probably the *Squalus acanthias*, which is known today as *cazón* (Spanish) or *cação-de-espinho* (Portuguese) or spiny dogfish (English). The shark has irregular white spots on the top or sides of the body. The dried skin of the shark was used as sandpaper.

72. "Anchieta to Laínez (in Rome), São Vicente, 8 January 1565," in *MB*, 4: 178–179.

73. "Pedro da Costa to fathers and brothers of São Roque (in Lisbon),

Espírito Santo, 27 July 1565," in *MB*, 4:267–269, 272.

74. "Leonardo do Vale to F. Gonçalo Vaz de Melo, Bahia, 12 May 1563," in *MB*, 4:9–22.

75. "Informação dos primeiros aldeamentos na Bahia," in Anchieta, *Cartas: Informações*, 364.

76. "Confession of Beatriz Mendes, 10 December 1594, Tamaraca," in *PV:DC-Pernambuco*, 102–104. *Bexigas* is given as a variation of *variola*, commonly translated as "smallpox," in several Portuguese dictionaries; see António de Morais Silva, *Novo dicionário compacto da língua portuguesa*, 10th ed., 5 vols. (Lisbon: Horizonte Confluência, 1961); Holanda Ferreira, *Novo dicionário;* Houaiss, *Dicionário electrônico.*

77. Alden and Miller, "Out of Africa," 216.

78. Brandão, *Dialogues*, 107–108. Like Anchieta, Brandão also describes a particularly virulent form of smallpox that he called *pele de lixa* (dogfish skin) in which the "skin peels off the body as if it had been burned in a fire, leaving all the raw flesh exposed." Brandão also recognized that smallpox was spread through person-to-person contact.

79. "[José de Anchieta] to Claudio Aquaviva (in Rome), Carta Ânua da Província do Brasil, de 1581, Bahia, 1 January 1582," in Anchieta, *Cartas: Correspondência*, 308–312. *Sarampão* is defined in several Portuguese dictionaries as a more serious form of *sarampo*, "rubella," "measles," or "German measles"; see Houaiss, *Dicionário electrônico;* Holanda Ferreira, *Novo dicionário;* and Morais Silva, *Novo dicionário compacto.* For the outbreak in Rio de Janeiro that might have been measles, see "Anthony Knivet's adventures in

Brazil," in *NIW*, 5:136; I have modernized the archaic English.

80. "Melchior Nunes Barreto to brothers of Coimbra, Bazaino [Bassein], 7 December 1552," in Wicki, *Monumenta histórica*, 2:501; "Gill Barreto to Ignatius de Loyola (in Rome), Bazaino [Bassein], 16 December 1552," in ibid., 2:543; Brandão, *Dialogues*, 110.

81. "José de Anchieta to Diego Laínez (in Rome), São Vicente, 30 July 1561," in *MB*, 3:376.

82. Ibid., 3:374–375; "José de Anchieta to Diego Laínez (in Rome), São Vicente, 16 April 1563," in *MB*, 3:554–555; "Leonardo do Vale to F. Gonçalo Vaz de Melo, Bahia, 12 May 1563," in *MB*, 4:13–14.

83. "Inventário do engenho de Sergipe por morte de Mem de Sá (1572)," in *Engenho Sergipe do Conde*, 3:37–68; Carta Ânua da Província do Brasil, de 1581, Bahia, 1 January 1582, in Anchieta, *Cartas: Correspondência*, 308.

84. Fernão Cardim reports that Indians in the aldeias lived in large "*ocas*" of up to one hundred persons. Each longhouse was ruled over by a chief; see "Enformacion," 165.

85. "Manoel da Nóbrega to Miguel de Torres and fathers and brothers of Portugal, Bahia, 5 July 1559," in *MB*, 3:60–63. Nóbrega listed the ill Jesuits as Father Francisco Pires, Brother António Rodrigues, and Father António Pires, then wrote, "I will cease from telling of the other illnesses of the brothers and people of this residence, because I would never finish" (*MB*, 3:63).

86. "João de Melo to Gonçalo de Melo (in Lisbon), Bahia, 13 September 1560," in *MB*, 3:281–283; "Antonio Blázquez to Diego Laínez (in Rome), Bahia, 1 September 1561," in *MB*, 3:415–416.

87. "António Rodrigues to fathers and brothers of Bahia, Aldeia do Bom Jesus, Bahia, August 1561," in *MB*, 3:389.

88. "António Pires to fathers and brothers of Portugal, Bahia, 22 October 1560," in *MB*, 3:314; "Leonardo do Vale, commissioned by Luís da Grã, to fathers and brothers of São Roque (in Lisbon), Bahia, 26 June 1562," in *MB*, 3:487.

89. "António Blázquez to Diego Mirón (in Lisbon), Bahia, 31 May 1564," in *MB*, 4:59–63; and "António Blázquez to Diego Mirón (in Lisbon), Bahia, 13 September 1564," in *MB*, 4:72–84.

90. "Rui Pereira to fathers and brothers of Portugal, Bahia, 15 September 1560," in *MB*, 3:291; "Leonardo do Vale to Gonçalo Vaz de Melo (in Lisbon), Bahia, 12 May 1563," in *MB*, 4:12. Gregorio Serrão, who contracted smallpox, was born in Portugal and entered the Society in 1550 as a brother. He sailed for Brazil in 1553 and was in Piratininga in 1554. In September of 1562 he arrived in Salvador to be ordained, and it was here that he became sick. Later he became the rector of the Jesuit college of Bahia; see *MB*, 3:529 n. 11. After the smallpox plague in Espírito Santo, Fr. Diogo Jacome became sick with quartan fevers; see "Pedro da Costa to fathers and brothers of São Roque (in Lisbon), Espírito Santo, 27 July 1565," in *MB*, 4:269–270.

91. "José de Anchieta to the sick brothers of Coimbra, São Vicente, 20 March 1555," in *MB*, 2:155–163; "José de Anchieta to Diego Laínez (in Rome), São Vicente, 30 July 1561," in *MB*, 3:380. In yet another letter to Laínez, Anchieta reiterates the Jesuit belief that "he who gives them illness [i.e., God] also cures them through his mercy"; "José de Anchieta to Diego Laínez (in Rome), Piratininga, March

1562," in *MB*, 3:453. "Ambrósio Pires to fathers and brothers of Coimbra, Porto Seguro, 5 May 1554," in *MB*, 2:51; "Pero Correia to Brás Lourenço (in Espírito Santo), São Vicente, 18 July 1554," in *MB*, 2:66; "Nóbrega to Miguel de Torres (in Lisbon), Rio Vermelho, Bahia, August 1557," in *MB*, 2:404; "Francisco Henriques to Miguel de Torres (in Rome), Lisbon, 3 April 1558," in *MB*, 2:424; "Miguel de Torres to Diego Laínez (in Rome), Lisbon, 16 May 1559," in *MB*, 3:35; "António Blázquez to Diego Laínez (in Rome), Bahia, 1 September 1561," in *MB*, 3: 397; 410.

92. Alchon, *A Pest in the Land*, 9–15.

93. Léry, *History of a Voyage*, 37.

94. "Vicente Rodrigues to fathers and brothers of Coimbra, Bahia, 17 May? 1552," in *MB*, 1:303–305; "Vicente Rodrigues to Simão Rodrigues (Lisbon), Salvador, May 1552," in *MB*, 1:316–321; "Francisco Pires to fathers and brothers of Coimbra, Bahia, 7 August 1552," in *MB*, 1:395–396; "António de Sá to fathers and brothers of Bahia, Espírito Santo, February? 1559," in *MB*, 3:18–19.

95. "Leonardo do Vale to Gonçalo Vaz de Melo (in Lisbon), Bahia, 12 May 1563," in *MB*, 4:9; "José Anchieta to Diego Laínez (in Rome), São Vicente, 8 January 1565," in *MB*, 4:178.

96. "Vicente Rodrigues to fathers and brothers of Coimbra, Bahia, 17 May? 1552," in *MB*, 1:303; "Francisco Pires to fathers and brothers of Coimbra, Bahia, 7 August 1552," in *MB*, 1:396.

97. "Vicente Rodrigues to Simão Rodrigues (in Lisbon), Bahia, May 1552," in *MB*, 1:317.

98. On the measures adopted by Italian towns to limit the spread of plague, see Watts, *Epidemics and History*, 15–25.

On Nóbrega's resistance to the quarantining of the aldeia of Espírito Santo, see "Manoel da Nóbrega to Miguel de Torres and fathers and brothers of Portugal, Bahia, 5 July 1559," in *MB*, 3:63.

99. The land grants are: "Data de sesmaria de Itaparica a D. Antonio de Athaide, Conde de Castanheira por Thomé de Sousa, 1552," in *Anais do Arquivo Público da Bahia* 34 (1957): 87–88, and "Carta Régia de 20 de Novembro de 1565 de transformação de sesmaria em capitania," in Instituto de Açúcar e do Álcool, *Documentos para a história do açúcar*, 1:186. "Testamento de Mem de Sá (1569)," "Inventário do engenho Sergipe por morte de Mem de Sá, (1572)," and "Inventário do engenho Sant'ana por morte de Mem de Sá, (1572)" in Instituto de Açúcar e do Álcool, *Documentos para a história do açúcar*, 3:14, 60–61, 67, 87, 104. Gandavo, *History of the Province of Santa Cruz*, 54.

100. G. S. de Sousa, *Tratado descritivo*, 134–139. A portion of this is available in English as "Description of Bahía and Its District by the Planter Gabriel Soares de Sousa," in *NIW*, 5:99–111.

101. Cardim, "Do clima e terra do Brasil e de algumas cousas notáveis que se acham na terra como no Mar," in Cardim, *Tratados da terra*, 158–159. A jennet (*ginete*) is a Spanish horse, named for a North African Berber tribe known for its horsemanship; see "Jennet," *Oxford English Dictionary Online*.

102. Melville, *A Plague of Sheep*, quotations from 6 and 14. Melville has an ingenious method for tracking environmental change that uses what she calls "throwaway" data, that is, descriptions of the environment that appear in sources "not necessarily written to describe or explain

that environment"; see ibid., 84–85. A similar methodology would work equally well for sixteenth-century Brazil, though I have not attempted it here.

103. Nóbrega argued with Luís de Grã, his successor as provincial, over the desirability of cattle-holding by the Jesuits. Grã wanted to restrict Jesuit property owning, whereas Nóbrega saw the practicality of cattle. Nóbrega's position eventually won out, for not only did the Jesuits become major slaveholders, but they owned substantial herds of cattle as well. On the early Jesuit experience with cattle, see "Manoel da Nóbrega to Simão Rodrigues (in Lisbon), Bahia, 10 July 1552," in *MB*, 1:351; "Manoel da Nóbrega to Francisco Henriques (in Lisbon), São Vicente, 12 June 1561," in *MB*, 3:353, 348–349. On Correia's grant of cows and lands, see "Manoel da Nóbrega to Luís Gonçalves da Câmara (in Lisbon), São Vicente, 15 June 1553," in *MB*, 1:501; "Confirmação das terras doadas pelo Ir. Pero Correia ao Colégio de S. Vicente, São Vicente, 22 March 1553," in *MB*, 1:459–464; and "Luís da Grã to Ignatius de Loyola (in Rome), Piratininga, 8 June 1556," in *MB*, 2:289–290. G. S. de Sousa, *Tratado descritivo*, 136.

104. Cardim, "Do clima e terra," in Cardim, *Tratados da terra*, 158–159; Gandavo, *History of the Province of Santa Cruz*, 54; Brandão, *Dialogues*, 263. In the ungulate irruption model, these populations would have grown dramatically initially, then after peaking, declined until the numbers of animals reached an accommodation with the ability of the land to support them; see Melville, *A Plague of Sheep*, 6–9.

105. G. S. de Sousa, *Tratado descritivo*, 134–136; Melville, *A Plague of Sheep*, 114.

106. Cardim, "Enformacion," 162–164; "Informação dos primeiros aldeamentos na Bahia," in Anchieta, *Cartas: Informações*, 385.

107. Schwartz, *Sugar Plantations*, 28–50.

108. Alchon, *A Pest in the Land*, 3–5, 145.

6. SLAVERY

1. Gandavo wrote "Tratado da terra do Brasil" in 1574 and *Historia da provincia Sãcta Cruz a qu' vulgarme[n]te' chamamos Brasil* in 1576. Although scholars believe that Gandavo wrote to encourage the poor to settle in Brazil, and that his book was a propaganda piece, the book remained virtually unknown until the nineteenth century, a fact that suggests to scholars that the Portuguese Crown suppressed the work. See John Stetson's introduction to Pero de Magalhães Gandavo, *Histories of Brazil*, 1:13–44. Quotations are from "Treatise," 2:149, and *História*, 15v.

2. The lack of a moral debate over slavery in Portugal is discussed by Russell-Wood, "Iberian Expansion," 33, 35–36, and Russell, *Prince Henry*, 246. Anthony Pagden's discussion of the early-sixteenth-century debate over moral questions in Castile suggests a process that may also have characterized Portugal. Pagden describes juntas of intellectuals wherein *pareceres* (opinions or briefs) authored by trained lawyers and theologians were presented to the Crown. Pagden writes that the pareceres often "vanished" unread, particularly if they disagreed with royal will. The purpose of such juntas, Pagden argues, "was to legitimate, not to judge"; see *Fall of Natural Man*, 27–30. Russell describes a similar process in Portugal before the Portuguese took the decision

to attack Tangier. A series of pareceres were presented to King Duarte by members of the royal council in 1432. These pareceres were sophisticated documents that debated such questions as whether or not Christians had the right to wage a just war against non-Christians who did not pose a threat. Their existence suggests that similar kinds of documents may have been produced in Portugal on the legality of the slave trade. The writings of Las Casas are well known; see *Brevissima relación de la destrucción de las Indias* (1552), available in English as *The Devastation of the Indies: A Brief Account*, and Las Casas' *Historia de las Indias*. The classic study of Spain's moral debate over the conquest is that of Lewis Hanke; see the new edition of *The Spanish Struggle for Justice in the Conquest of America* (2002).

3. Blackburn, "Old World Background," 65–102, and *Making of New World Slavery*, 34–64.

4. See Everson, *The Politics*, 5–7.

5. See Dyson, *The City of God*, 942–943.

6. Aquinas, *Summa theologica*, Second part of the Second part q. 57; Supplement q. 52.

7. Russell, *Prince Henry*, 83–87, 241, 246–249, 252; Meyerson, *The Muslims of Valencia*, 71–83.

8. Elbl, "Volume of . . . Slave Trade," 35 n. 6.

9. João de Barros gives an extensive account of the foundation of the fort at Mina in which there is a long negotiation between the African chief of the coast, Caramansa, and the Portuguese captain, Diogo de Azambuja, that took place through an interpreter; see *Asia de Joam de Barros*, book 3, chapters 1 and 2, ff. 24–26v. Hein states that an independent

Portuguese merchant by the name of João Bernardes, who was trading with Caramansa, was important to the negotiations between Caramansa and Diogo de Azambuja; "Portuguese Communication," 45. On the significance of the negotiations, see also Vogt, *Portuguese Rule*, 22–24. Before Portugal lost Mina to the Dutch in 1637, Portuguese sea captains traded cottons, metal hardware, and slaves from Benin, the Kongo, and Angola for African gold.

10. Scholars have noted the importance of royal historians of the fifteenth century such as Gomes Eanes de Zurara and João de Barros. Russell-Wood describes Barros as the "official mouthpiece" of Portuguese expansion and one who served as an "apologist for royal policies and aspirations" in the sixteenth century; see his "Iberian Expansion," 28. See also the analyses of Zurara and Barros by Saunders, *Social History of Black Slaves*, 35–43; Sweet, "Iberian Roots," 143–166; and Costa, "Portuguese-African Slave Trade," 41–61. Saunders emphasizes the importance of the lawyers who wrote the briefs and presented the Portuguese Crown's appeals for papal bulls that legitimized the slave trade; see *Social History of Black Slaves*, 37.

11. Russell, *Prince Henry*, 5.

12. Zurara, *Crónica*, 1:51, 57.

13. Blackburn, "Old World Background," 74, 79; Blackburn, *Making of New World Slavery*, 42–44; Sweet, "Iberian Roots," 149; O'Callaghan, *Reconquest and Crusade*, 148.

14. Zurara, *Crónica*, 1:73–75; Russell, *Prince Henry*, 197–198. This monopoly granted to Henry also entitled him to the royal fifth of whatever was imported from the newly discovered regions; see Russell, *Prince Henry*, 198.

15. Zurara, *Crónica*, 1:77. Note that Zurara draws a distinction between Moors and Black Africans: the Black Africans receive the curse, not the Moors.

16. Goldenberg, *The Curse of Ham*, 1. Extensive literature exists on the Curse of Ham and the origins of European racism; see Braude, "Sons of Noah," 103–142; Evans, "From the Land of Canaan," 27–28, 32–33; Sweet, "Iberian Roots," 148–149; Saunders, *Social History of Black Slaves*, 38–39; and Blackburn, *Making of New World Slavery*, 67–72.

17. Goldenberg, *The Curse of Ham*, 149. The misreading occurred when two different sounds for *h* were represented by one sign.

18. Zurara, *Crónica*, 1:77. Goldenberg, *The Curse of Ham*, 178–182. The Portuguese *Corrigida Fiel* version of 1753 has Caim (Cain) as the son of Adam and Eve, Cão (Ham) as the son of Noah, and Canaã (Cannan) as the son of Ham. I thank my colleague Francisco García Treto for this reference.

19. Goldenberg, *The Curse of Ham*, 197.

20. Zurara, *Crónica*, 1:77; Braude, "Sons of Noah," 134; Saunders, *Social History of Black Slaves*, 38.

21. Goldenberg, *The Curse of Ham*, 131–138; Sweet, "Iberian Roots," 146–147, 159; Evans, "From the Land of Canaan," 26–27, 31–32; Blackburn, "Old World Background," 99, and *Making of New World Slavery*, 79–81.

22. Zurara, *Crónica*, 1:107–108.

23. Prince Henry had been granted the right to collect the fifth, usually claimed by the king, from voyages that he underwrote, as well as exemption from taxes; see "Carta Régia ao Infante D. Henrique (1-6-1439)" and "Carta de Privilégio a D.

Henrique (20-10-1443)" in Brásio, *Monumenta missionaria*, 1:261–262, 266–267; Zurara, *Crónica*, 1:109.

24. Russell-Wood, "Iberian Expansion," 30; Saunders, *Social History of Black Slaves*, 35; Russell, *Prince Henry*, 241.

25. Russell, *Prince Henry*, 245–246; Zurara, *Crónica*, 1:146–147.

26. Sweet, "Iberian Roots," 161; Costa, "Portuguese-African Slave Trade," 47.

27. Zurara, *Crónica*, 1:109, 146–147.

28. Augustine's development of the legal basis of war is summarized by O'Callaghan, *Reconquest and Crusade*, 13. Aquinas, *Summa theologica*, 2:1359–1360.

29. Russell-Wood argues that during the Reconquest "no theologian or sovereign in the Christian kingdoms of the Iberian peninsula doubted that the repeated offensives against the followers of Islam constituted 'just war'" ("Iberian Expansion," 24). On the ex post facto papal declarations and bulls, see Russell-Wood, "Iberian Expansion," 27–28, and Saunders, *Social History of Black Slaves*, 36–38. O'Callaghan, in *Reconquest and Crusade*, provides an overview of the "crusading mentality" found in Iberia during the Reconquest and the ransoming of captives of war. The papal bull "Dum diversas" was granted by Nicholas V in 1452; see "Bula 'Dum Diversas' de Nicolau V (18-6-1452)," in Brásio, *Monumenta missionaria*, 1:2692–271.

30. On the transition from slave raiding to slave trading, see Elbl, "Volume of . . . Slave Trade," 35 n. 6, and Saunders, *Social History of Black Slaves*, 36–38. For the papal bull "Romanus pontifex," see "The Bull Romanus Pontifex (Nicholas V.) January 8, 1455," in Davenport, *European Treaties*, 9–26. The rewards

from the slave trade granted to the Order of Christ are explained in "Doação da vintena dos escravos à Ordem de Cristo (26-12-1457)," in Brásio, *Monumenta missionaria*, 1:391–393. On the baptism of slaves in the *Ordenações manuelinas*, see Saunders, *Social History of Black Slaves*, 40–41; the law is "Que todos os que teverem escravos de Guinee os baptizem," liv. 5, tit. 99, *Ordenações manuelinas Online*, http://www.uc.pt/ihti/proj/manuelinas/ORDEMANU.HTM.

31. Sea captains learned to keep their slave interpreters under their control, but the power of the interpreter was such that it was not uncommon for slave interpreters to obtain their freedom. Saunders states that after four voyages (in theory, at least), a slave interpreter earned his freedom, because for each voyage he gained a slave for his master and the four earned for his master equaled his own price; see *Social History of Black Slaves*, 12; see also Curto, "A língua," 418. Hein suggests that African slave interpreters had the right to trade in Africa, and they were able to use those privileges to their own advantage; see "Portuguese Communication," 45.

32. On the lançados and the slave trade, see Rodney, *History*, 95–121; Brooks, *Landlords and Strangers*, 135–140; Barreto, *História da Guiné*, 68–69; Fage, "Upper and Lower Guinea," 507; Saunders, *Social History of Black Slaves*, 13; and Herbert, "Portuguese Adaptations," 415.

33. Ryder, *Benin and the Europeans*, 44–45; Birmingham, *Trade and Conflict in Angola*, 32; Garfield, *History of São Tomé Island*, passim; Vansina, "Kongo Kingdom," 555, 557; Fage, "Upper and Lower Guinea," 553; Zeron, "Pombeiros e tangosmaos." Monteiro finds a case of

the term "*pombeiro*" used in Brazil in the early seventeenth century to refer to "creolized Indian slaves specialized in the art of enslaving Indians from the independent villages of the interior"; see "From Indian to Slave," 109.

34. *Portrait of a Black Man* may have been executed in Venice in 1506, when Dürer was known to have been there, or possibly later, in Nuremburg c. 1515. *Portrait of Katherina* was clearly made during a year he spent in Antwerp, 1520–1521, when he had extensive contacts with merchants and was fascinated by the things they returned with in their ships. See Massing, "Quest for the Exotic," 115–119, 288–289. The increasing degradation of Africans is noted by Boxer, who quotes a Portuguese duke, brother of the king, telling a Bohemian knight that slaves from Africa are bought and sold like cattle; see *Church Militant*, 5.

35. Russell-Wood, "Iberian Expansion," 18.

36. Elbl, "Volume of . . . Slave Trade," 47.

37. Fernando Oliveira led an eventful life that crossed the boundaries set by powerful institutions in sixteenth-century Europe. Born in 1507 in Aveiro, Portugal, he was educated by the Dominicans at Evora, but left the order after becoming a priest. In 1536, he wrote a grammar of the Portuguese language. He became tutor to the children of the famous chronicler of Portuguese expansion, João de Barros. In 1545, having left the household of Barros, and after having made a trip to Rome, he joined up with a French ship. But because the French were at war with the English, after an encounter with an English ship, he found himself a prisoner of the English. In England, he became a retainer of King

Henry VIII. He returned to Portugal in 1547 and was denounced to the Inquisition, tried, and sentenced to prison. Freed in 1550, two years later, he signed on to a ship as priest and sailed to Morocco. There he fell into the hands of pirates and was taken to Argel. In 1552, after having a ransom paid for his freedom, he returned to Portugal and began writing *Arte da guerra do mar*. In 1554, before the publication of the book, the king of Portugal ordered him imprisoned; after the publication of the book, the Inquisition imprisoned him again. He later wrote two books on shipbuilding. He died in the 1580s. See "Comentário preliminar" by Quirino da Fonseca to Fernando Oliveira, in Oliveira, *Arte da guerra do mar*, and Boxer, *Church Militant*, 32–33.

38. In his introduction, Oliveira recognized that he must conform to the "customs" and "pleasures" of those for whom he wrote, and he described himself both as a priest and as an eyewitness. Quotations are from Oliveira, *Arte da guerra do mar*, 23–24. Scholars who underscore that Oliveira's criticisms apply to the African slave trade are Saunders, *Social History of Black Slaves*, 43; Boxer, *Church Militant*, 32; and Costa, "Portuguese-African Slave Trade," 56.

39. Oliveira, *Arta da guerra do mar*, 24–24.

40. Fr. Tomás de Mercado, O.P., and Fr. Bartolomé de Albornoz, O.P., both denounced the Portuguese slave trade; Mercado's book *Suma de tratos y contratos* went through four editions in the sixteenth century, but Albornoz' book, which was more critical of the slave trade, was almost unknown. The archbishop of Mexico, Alonso de Montufar, did draw an explicit connection between the illegality of the

Indian slave trade and the illegality of the African slave trade, but in a private letter to King Philip II; see Boxer, *Church Militant*, 32–34. Saunders cites other Spanish and Portuguese clergy who also expressed misgivings about the slave trade; see *Social History of Black Slaves*, 44.

41. Las Casas, *Historia de las Indias*, 1:126–132. See Russell-Wood's discussion of Las Casas in "Iberian Expansion," 29.

42. The long-term ramifications of this conflict are discussed by Alden, *Making of an Enterprise*, 474–501, and Cohen, *Fire of Tongues*, 13–93.

43. The first references to the slave trade in Brazil are "Pedro Rondinelli to an unknown Italian, Seville, 3 October 1502," in Amado and Figueiredo, *Brasil 1500*, 267–272; "Llyuro da náoo bertoa que vay pera a Terra do brazyll de que som armadores bertolameu marchone e benadyto morelle e fernã de lloronha e francisco miz que partio deste porto de Lix.a a xxij de feureiro de 511," in *HCPB*, 2:343–347; *A nova gazeta*, 40; and "Fernando Magallanes va al descubrimiento de un estrecho para pasar del Océano atlántico meridional al otro mar Occidental de América," in Navarrete, *Colección de los viages*, 4:31.

44. On the slave trade from Cananéia, see "Memoria de Diego García" (García led an expedition to the Río de la Plata in 1526 and was in São Vicente in 1527), as quoted in P. L. de Sousa, *Diário da navegação*, 1:502. On the slave trade from Pernambuco, see "Carta de doação da capitania de Pernambuco ao Duarte Coelho, 5 September 1534," in *HCPB*, 3:310. Figures for the size of the African slave trade are from Elbl, "Volume of . . . Slave Trade," 74. Brandão contrasts the mortality of native Brazilians in Portugal to that of

Africans—from Guiné or São Tomé—and to Southeast Asians from India, "who do very well"; see *Dialogues*, 105.

45. On the slaves in São Vicente, see "Luís de Góis to King João III, Santos [São Vicente], 12 May 1548," in *HCPB*, 3:259, and Stols, "Um dos primeiros documentos," 415-419. For the slaves in Pernambuco and Paraíba do Sul, see "Duarte Coelho to King João III, Olinda, 27 April 1542," in *HCPB*, 3:314; "Pero de Góis to Martim Ferreira, Rainha [Paraíba do Sul], 18 August 1545," in *HCPB*, 3:262; and Staden, *True History*, 39.

46. See Chapter 2, "Encounter," in this work for a discussion of an African interpreter traveling with Cabral in 1500. That an African slave was present on Magellan's expedition is known because waves swept the man overboard, where he drowned; see "Fernando Magallanes va al descubrimiento de un estrecho para pasar del Océano atlántico meridional al otro mar Occidental de América," and "Relación escrita por Maximiliano Transilvano de cómo y por quién y en qué tiempo fueron descubiertas y halladas las islas Molucas," both in Navarrete, *Colección de los viages*, 4:38, 240. References to African slaves sent by the king appear in "Antônio Cardoso de Barros to King João III, Salvador, 30 April 1551," in "Notícias antigas do Brasil," 19.

47. "Nóbrega to Simão Rodrigues (in Lisbon), Bahia, 6 January 1550," in *MB*, 1:166; "António Pires to fathers and brothers of Coimbra, Pernambuco, 4 June 1552," in *MB*, 1:325-326; "Francisco Pires to fathers and brothers of Coimbra, Bahia, 7 August 1552," in *MB*, 1:395. Many other letters describe the Jesuit mission to the Indian slaves in the 1550s and 1560s; see *MB*, Vols. 1-3, passim. On Staden's

slave, see Staden, *True History*, 62. The petition of the town council of Salvador is "Câmara of Salvador to the king, 18 December 1556," in Bertha Leite, "Dom Pedro Fernandes Sardinha," 543.

48. Schmidel, *Derrotero y viaje*, 44, 138-139, 162-164, 176-177, 181, 206. Rodrigues was on the same expedition as Schmidel. See his long letter to the fathers and brothers of Coimbra, São Vicente, 31 May 1553, in *MB*, 1:468-481; the reference to Guarani slaves sold in São Vicente comes from 479.

49. "Nóbrega to Simão Rodrigues (in Lisbon), Bahia, 9 August 1549," in *MB*, 1:121-122; "Pero de Góis to King João III, Rainha [Paraíba do Sul], 29 April 1546," in *HCPB*, 3:263. Gabriel Soares de Sousa makes a reference to an Henrique Luis, possibly the same man, noting only that the sugar mills of Henrique Luis in Ilhéus "now have few people," that is, slaves; G. S. de Sousa, *Tratado descritivo*, 78, 94-95. "Duarte Coelho to King João III, Olinda, 20 December 1546," in *Cartas de Duarte Coelho a El Rei*, 92.

50. "Nóbrega to Simão Rodrigues (in Lisbon), Bahia, 9 August 1549," in *MB*, 1:122-125, and "Nóbrega to Tomé de Sousa (in Lisbon), Bahia, 5 July 1559," in *MB*, 3:80-81.

51. "Regimento of Tomé de Sousa, 17 December 1548," in *HCPB*, 3:348; "Pero Borges [Ouvidor Geral do Brasil] to King João III, Porto Seguro, 7 February 1550," in *MB*, 1:174-175. "Leonardo Nunes to the fathers and brothers of Coimbra, São Vicente, November 1550," in *MB*, 1:202, and "Leonardo Nunes to the fathers and brothers of Coimbra, São Vicente, 20 June 1551," in *MB*, 1:233-234. Nunes also suggests that one of the reasons slave raiding had stopped was that

the Indians had obtained arms due to the unscrupulous trading practices of some Portuguese and thus were able to defend themselves.

52. Léry, *History of a Voyage*, 121. On resgate, see Thomas, *Política indigenista*, 48–49.

53. Léry, *History of a Voyage*, 121. "Rui Pereira to fathers and brothers of Portugal, Pernambuco, 6 April 1561," in *MB*, 3:334; "[Brás Lourenço] to Miguel de Torres (in Lisbon), Espírito Santo, 10 June 1562," in *MB*, 3:468; "Nóbrega to Simão Rodrigues (in Lisbon), Bahia, 6 January 1550," in *MB*, 1:166; and "Nóbrega to Tomé de Sousa (in Lisbon), Bahia, 5 July 1559," in *MB*, 3:79–80.

54. "Regimento of Tomé de Sousa, 17 December 1548," in *HCPB*, 3:345.

55. A Jesuit history of the mission villages records the declaration of a just war by the governor; see "Informação dos primeiros aldeamentos na Bahia," in Anchieta, *Cartas: Informações*, 363–364. For other primary sources on the shipwreck, see the collection of documents published by Bertha Leite in *Instituto Histórico e Geográfico Brasileiro, IV Congresso de História Nacional*, 437–605. Nóbrega's reaction is in his letter to Tomé de Sousa (in Lisbon), Bahia, 5 July 1559, in *MB*, 3:82. See also Calmon, *História do Brasil*, 1:265–266.

56. Jesuit reservations about the effects of this war are in the history of the mission villages, "Informação dos primeiros aldeamentos na Bahia," in Anchieta, *Cartas: Informações*, 363–364.

57. "João Gonçalves to fathers and brothers of Coimbra, Bahia, 12 June 1555," in *MB*, 2:241–242; "Nóbrega to Tomé de Sousa (in Lisbon), Bahia, 5 July 1559," in *MB*, 3:80; "Nóbrega to Simão Rodrigues (in Lisbon), Salvador, 9 August 1549," in

MB, 1:126; Nóbrega's request for more slaves is in his letter to Miguel de Torres (in Lisbon), Bahia, 8 May 1558, in *MB*, 2:455

58. On the first slaves owned by the Society of Jesus in Brazil, see "Nóbrega to Simão Rodrigues (in Lisbon), Bahia, 10 July 1552," in *MB*, 1:351 and 351 n. 10; "Nóbrega to Simão Rodrigues (in Lisbon), Bahia, end of August 1552," in *MB*, 1:403; and "Luís da Grã to Diego Mirón (in Lisbon), Bahia, 27 December 1554," in *MB*, 2:145. The ruling on slavery from the father general of the Society is in the letter of Diego Laínez to Nóbrega, Trent, 16 December 1562, in *MB*, 3:514. Luís da Grã, who became the second provincial of Brazil, disagreed with Nóbrega over the Society's acquisition of property. He wanted to teach through the example of poverty and did not favor the Society acquiring either cattle or slaves; see "Nóbrega to Diego Laínez (in Rome), São Vicente, 12 June 1561," in *MB*, 3:364. Two decades later, the Jesuit Miguel García argued so vehemently against the immorality of Indian and African slavery in Brazil that he was sent back to Portugal; see "Cristovão de Gouveia to Claudio Aquaviva (in Rome), Bahia, 15 July 1583," in ARSI: Lus. 68:337; "Miguel García to Claudio Aquaviva (in Rome), Bahia, 26 January 1583," in ARSI: Lus. 68:335–336v. See also the recent work of Zeron, "Les jésuites," and Alden, *Making of an Enterprise*, 507–527.

59. Gandavo, "Treatise," 2:165; "Lei de 20 de Março de 1570 sobre a liberdade dos gentios," in Thomas, *Política indigenista*, 221–222.

60. G. S. de Sousa describes the well-populated Rio de São Francisco in *Tratado descritivo*, 63; Cardim, "Enformacion," 162.

61. Alencastro, *O trato dos viventes*, 389 n. 130; "Carta ânua da província do Brasil, 1581," in Anchieta, *Cartas: Correspondência*, 312; Cardim, "Enformacion," in ARSI: Bras. 15.

62. "Lei de 20 de Março de 1570 sobre a liberdade dos gentios," in Thomas, *Política indigenista*, 221–222. On the Jesuit opposition to Indian slavery in Brazil from this period through the seventeenth century, see Alden, *Making of an Enterprise*, 474–501.

63. "Informação dos primeiros aldeamentos na Bahia," in Anchieta, *Cartas: Informações*, 374–378. See also Gandavo's account in *Historia da provincia Sãcta Cruz*, 45v–46.

64. "Everard Mercurian to José de Anchieta, Rome, 15 January 1579," in ARSI: Bras. 2:46. Mercurian wanted the annual letters to be shorter, to be less offensive, and to avoid criticizing the soldiers and the greed of the Portuguese colonists. On the Mercurian period in Brazil, see my "Jesuits in Brazil," 787–814.

65. Mem de Sá led a fleet against the French fort in Guanabara Bay in 1560 and routed the French. North of Rio de Janeiro, however, the French still engaged in the dyewood trade with Indian allies. The continued presence of the French undoubtedly added to the governor's desire to destroy the Indian chiefs of the region. For a brief time, there were two governors, one for the north and one for the south. The governor of the south, António Salema, led this expedition. On these events, see Reis, *O indígena do vale do Paraíba*, 55–56, and Hemming, *Red Gold*, 119–136.

66. "Ânua de Tolosa, 1576," in ARSI: Bras. 15-2:284–286; see also Serafim Leite, *História da Companhia de Jesus no Brasil*, 1:426–431.

67. Gandavo, "Treatise," 2:175, and *Historia da provincia Sãcta Cruz*, 46.

68. "Articles touching the dutie of the Kings Majestie our Lord, and to the common good of all the estate of Brazill," in Purchas, *Hakluytus Posthumus*, 16:507. This text is attributed to Fernão Cardim, whose manuscripts were seized by the English pirate Francis Cook in 1601. Cook took Cardim to England. Several of Cardim's manuscripts were later published by Samuel Purchas, who claimed that he bought the manuscripts for twenty shillings and thought them to be by "a Portugal Friar (or Jesuit) which had lived thirty years in those parts." See Ana Maria de Azevedo's introduction to Cardim, *Tratados da terra*, 12–14, 21–22.

69. There are few studies of the mamelucos involved in this trade; see Raminelli, "Da vila ao sertão," 209–219; Metcalf, "Álvaro Rodrigues," 37–45; and Hemming, *Red Gold*, 151–160.

70. Álvaro Rodrigues declared before the inquisitor that he was the son of Afonso Rodrigues, whom he defined as a "white man," and his wife, Luzia Álvares, a mameluca daughter of Diogo Álvares by an unnamed Indian woman. See "Trial of Álvaro Rodrigues," in ANTT: IL 16,897. Domingos Fernandes Nobre declared before the inquisitor that he was born in Pernambuco, the mameluco son of Miguel Fernandes, a white man, and Joana, "a black woman of the people of this land"; see "Trial of Domingos Fernandes Nobre, 'o Tomacaúna,'" in ANTT: IL 10,776.

71. G. S. de Sousa describes the entrada of Antônio Dias Adorno, as well as the well-populated Rio de São Francisco and trading for slaves there, in *Tratado descritivo*, 63–64, 81, 86, 89–90. For the accounts of Nobre and Rodrigues, see the

confession of Nobre in the trial of Domingos Fernandes Nobre, in ANTT: IL 10,776, and the first interrogation (*sessão*) of Álvaro Rodrigues, in the trial of Alvaro Rodrigues, in ANTT: IL 16,897.

72. "Confession, Domingos Fernandes Nobre," and "Confession, Francisco Afonso Capara," in "Trial of Nobre," in ANTT: IL 10,776.

73. Pires was the son of a Portuguese farmer and his Indian slave, Catarina. At the time of his confession in 1592, he was a farmer on the Sergipe do Conde plantation in Bahia; see "Confession of Francisco Pires," in "Trial of Francisco Pires, 1592," in ANTT: IL 17,809.

74. "Confession, Domingos Fernandes Nobre," in "Trial of Nobre," in ANTT: IL 10,776. "Confession of Sebastião Madeira," in "Trial of Sebastião Madeira," in ANTT: IL 11,212; "Denunciations of Marçal de Aragão and Sebastião Madeira," in "Trial of Lázaro da Cunha," in ANTT: IL 11,068.

75. "Tobaca," "Tovaca," and "Tova cuçu" are defined as the "antbird" in Houaiss, *Dicionário electrônico*, and Holanda Ferreira, *Novo dicionário*. Other names are easier to translate because clues appear in the text. "Aratuam" is defined as "Arara" and explained to mean "a large colored bird." "Arara" is a word of Tupi origin that is a common designator of Latin American parrots (*Psittacidae*), including the Ara (Houaiss, *Dicionário electrônico*); "Pinasamoquu" is defined in the deposition as "linha comprida"—literally "Long Line"—and in the seventeenth-century Jesuit *Vocabulario na língua brasilica*, ed. Plinio Ayrosa (São Paulo: Departamento de Cultura, 1938), one of the various definitions of "Linha" ("Linha assi grossa do alto") is "Pĩdaçamuçû." "Jocorutu/

Jucurutu" is defined as "*curuja*," that is, *coruja*, "owl." "Jabotim" is defined in the text as "*cágado*"; the *Vocabulario* gives the translation of "Cagado da terra" as "*jaboti*," which translates as "land turtle." The names appear in "Confession of Pedro Bastardo," in *PV:DC-Pernambuco*, 28. "Denunciation of Adão Vaz, 14 January 1592," in "Trial of Domingos Fernandes Nobre," in ANTT: IL 10.777; "Ratificação of Francisco Pires, 17 January 1593," in "Trial of Lázaro da Cunha," in ANTT: IL 11,068; "Confession of Sebastião Madeira, 9 March 1592," in "Trial of Sebastião Madeira," in ANTT: Il 11,212; "Confession of Gonçalo Álvares," in "Trial of Francisco Pires," in ANTT: IL 17,809.

76. "Confession of Domingos Fernandes Nobre," in "Trial of Domingos Fernandes Nobre," in ANTT: IL 10,776.

77. Many in Bahia denounced Domingos Fernandes for his tatoos, including his wife; see "Trial of Domingos Fernandes Nobre," in ANTT: IL 10,776. For descriptions of tattooing, see "Confession of Domingos Fernandes Nobre," in "Trial of Domingos Fernandes Nobre," in ANTT: IL 10,776; "Confession of Francisco Afonso Capara," in "Trial of Francisco Afonso Capara," in ANTT: IL 17, 813; "Confession of João Gonçalves," in "Trial of João Gonçalves," in ANTT: IL 13,098; "Confession of Sebastião Madeira," in "Trial of Sebastião Madeira," in ANTT: IL 11,212; "Denunciation of Marçal de Aragão," in "Trial of Lázaro da Cunha," in ANTT: IL 11,068; "Confession of Thomas Ferreira," in "Trial of Thomas Ferreira," in ANTT: IL 11,635; "Confession and first interrogation of Manoel Branco," in "Trial of Manoel Branco," in ANTT: IL 11,072; "Confession of Gonçalo Álvares," in "Trial of Francisco Pires," in ANTT: IL 17,809.

78. [Cardim], "Articles," in Purchas, *Hakluytus Posthumus*, 16:505–506.

79. On the Tupi-Guarani tradition of migration, the concept of a "land without evil," and messianism, see Nimuendajú-Unkel, *Los mitos de creación;* Métraux, "Migrations historiques," 1–47, *La religion des Tupinamba*, 201–252, and "Messiahs of South America," 53–60; Schaden, *Aculturação e messianismo;* and Clastres, *Land-without-Evil*. Within the literature there is disagreement over whether the prophetic movements existed before colonization or emerged as a result of it; see Fausto's discussion in "Fragmentos de história e cultura Tupinambá," 385–387.

80. Giving arms to Indians hostile to the Portuguese was expressly forbidden by the Crown; see the "Regimento of Tomé de Sousa, 17 December 1548," in *HCPB*, 3:348.

81. "Confession of Francisco Pires," in "Trial of Francisco Pires," in ANTT: IL 17,809.

82. "Confession of Pedro Bastardo," in *PV: DC-Pernambuco*, 28; "Confession of Sebastião Madeira," in "Trial of Sebastião Madeira," in ANTT: IL 11,212; "Denunciation of Tristão Rodrigues" and "Confession of Lázaro da Cunha," in "Trial of Lázaro da Cunha," in ANTT: IL 11,068.

83. "Informação dos primeiros aldeamentos na Bahia," in Anchieta, *Cartas: Informações*, 385–386.

84. "Carta ânua da província do Brasil, de 1581, Bahia, 1 January 1582," in Anchieta, *Cartas: Correspondência*, 311; "John Vincent to Richard Gibbon, in Madrid, 1592," summarized in United Kingdom, Public Record Office, *Calendar of State Papers*, 245:354; "First interrogation of Francisco Pires," in "Trial of

Francisco Pires, 13 March 1592," in ANTT: IL 17,809.

85. [Cardim], "Articles," in Purchas, *Hakluytus Posthumus*, 16:505–506.

86. "Inventário do engenho de Sergipe por morte de Mem de Sá (1572)," in Instituto de Açúcar e do Álcool, *Documentos para a história do açúcar*, 3:37–68.

87. Cardim, "Enformacion," 143. See also the annual letters of José de Anchieta, "Carta ânua da província do Brasil, de 1583," and "Carta ânua de 1584," both in Anchieta, *Cartas: Correspondência*, 344–361 and 368–386, respectively. The Jesuit visitor to the missions, Cristovão de Gouveia, also comments repeatedly about the mission of Jesuits to slaves; see "Cristovão de Gouveia to Claudio Aquaviva, 1 November 1584," in ARSI: Lus. 68:407–409, and Gouveia's report of his visit to Brazil, "Visitas dos padres," in ARSI: Bras. 2:139–149.

88. Gouveia, "Visitas dos padres," in ARSI: Bras. 2:139–149.

89. "Informação dos primeiros aldeamentos na Bahia," in Anchieta, *Cartas: Informações*, 386.

90. [Cardim], "Articles," in Purchas, *Hakluytus Posthumus*, 16:505–506.

91. "Manoel Teles Barreto to King Philip, Bahia, 25 February 1584," in ANTT: Corpo Cronológico, III maço 20, doc. 54.

92. In his first letter from Brazil, Gouveia describes excellent relations with Barreto on the voyage out and explains the general aversion held by the colonists for the Jesuits. In addition to the Jesuit position on Indian slavery, the limits Jesuits placed on the amount of service that colonists could demand from mission Indians and the Jesuits' several pending land disputes with colonists were two

other reasons why the colonists increasingly complained about the Society. See "Gouveia to Claudio Aquaviva, Bahia, 25 July 1583," in ARSI: Lus. 68:337. Luís da Fonseca describes Governor Barreto as being adverse to the Jesuits in Portugal, and even more so once he arrived in Brazil, when "he had the knife in the cheese"; "Fonseca to Claudio Aquaviva, Bahia, 28 August 1584," in ARSI: Lus. 68:398–399v. In his final report, Gouveia makes clear that no Jesuit father may confess a person who participates in the practice of bringing Indians from the sertão in "the customary, but illicit manner," because the priest could not give absolution unless the individual had truly given up such practices and had restored to the Indians that which the law required; see "Visita do Padre Cristovão de Gouveia," in "Visitas dos padres visitadores," in ARSI: Bras. 2: 253–274 or 2:139–149v. The uprising in Porto Seguro, which led to conflict in the town council and which involved the bishop, occurred before 1579; see "Everard Mercurian to José de Anchieta, Rome, 15 January 1579," in ARSI: Bras. 2:45–46v.

93. Cardim, "Enformacion," 164; "Memoriale Visitationis Brasiliae," 1584, in ARSI: Lus. 68: 414–418.

94. "Lei que S. M. passou sobre os Indios do Brasil que não podem ser captivos e declara o que o podem ser," in Thomas, Política indigenista, 222–224.

95. Ibid.

96. "Confession of Gonçalo Álvares," in "Trial of Francisco Pires," in ANTT: IL 17,809. The second entrada is described in the "Confession of Bastião Madeira," in "Trial of Sebastião Madiera," in ANTT: IL 11,212, and in the "Denunciation of Marçal de Aragão," the "Denunciation

of Baltazar Camelo," the "Denunciation of Adão Vaz," and the "Denunciation of Simão Dias"—all in "Trial of Domingos Fernandes Nobre," in ANTT: IL 10,776.

97. Gandavo, "Treatise," 2:149.

7. RESISTANCE

1. The epidemic is described in "Carta ânua da província do Brasil de 1581, Bahia, 1 January 1582," in Anchieta, Cartas: Correspondência, 308. The descriptions of the Santidade de Jaguaripe are from the denunciation of Álvaro Rodrigues in "Trial of Domingos Fernandes Nobre," in ANTT: IL 10,776, and the confession of Gonçalo Fernandes in his trial, in ANTT: IL 17,762.

2. The most complete study of the Santidade de Jaguaripe is Vainfas' A heresia dos índios, in which he also argues that it was an example of resistance to Portuguese colonialism. An earlier account may be found in Calasans' Fernão Cabral de Ataíde e a santidade de Jaguaripe. I explore the millenarianism of the movement as a form of slave resistance in "AHR Forum," 1531–1559. Two well-researched descriptions of the movement are Siqueira, "A elaboração da espiritualidade do Brasil colônia," 207–228, and Schwartz, Sugar Plantations, 47–50. Other historians who have analyzed the movement include Queiroz, Messianismo no Brasil, 146–148; Ribeiro, "Brazilian Messianic Movements," 55–69; and Bastide, African Religions of Brazil, 173–174.

3. Anghiera, "Libretto de tutta la navigatione"; "Vespucci to Piero Soderini (in Florence), Lisbon, 4 September 1504, [the Lettera]," in Vespucci, Letters from a New World, 87–89; "Déclaration du vegage," 105–106.

4. "Carta de Pero Vaz de Caminha 1° de Maio de 1500," in Amado and Figueiredo, *Brasil 1500*, 73–122.

5. The place was thought to be Cabo Frio; see "Vespucci to Soderini, Lisbon, 4 September 1504," in Vespucci, *Letters from a New World*, 95–96, and Santa Cruz, *Islario general*, 1:546.

6. "Vespucci to Lorenzo di Pierfrancesco de' Medici, Lisbon, 1502," in Vespucci, *Letters from a New World*, 33; "Déclaration du vegage," 98–100; P. L. de Sousa, *Diário da navegação*, 1:157–159.

7. "Pero de Góis to King João III, Rainha [Paraíba do Sul], 29 April 1546," in *HCPB*, 3:263; quoted passage is the translation published in *NIW*, 5:52.

8. Staden, *True History*, 39.

9. "Jerónimo de Albuquerque to King João III, Olinda, 28 August 1555," in *HCPB*, 3:381; "Duarte da Costa to King João III, Salvador, 10 June 1555," in *HCPB*, 3:377–379; "Instrumento dos serviços de Mem de Sá [1560]," 4–5; "Mem de Sá to King Sebastião, Salvador, 1 June 1558," in *Documentos relativos a Mem de Sá*, 97–98; "António Blázquez to Diego Laínez (in Rome), Bahia, 10 September 1559," in *MB*, 3:139.

10. Staden, *True History*, 105–111; Léry, *History of a Voyage*, 118.

11. Léry, *History of a Voyage*, 113; Staden, *True History*, 105.

12. Staden, *True History*, 64; Thevet, *Le Brésil*, 206. Several scholars note the similarity between Staden's Koyan Bebe and Thevet's Quoniambec and suggest that they were the same chief; see Lestringant's comment in Thevet, *Le Brésil*, 376 n. 4, and Serafim Leite, *MB*, 4:145 n. 45.

13. Fragment of a letter from Pero Correia to Simão Rodrigues (in Lisbon),

São Vicente, June 1551, in *MB*, 1:230, and "Copia de uma carta de Pero Correia," in *Cartas avulsas*, 120–122; "Nóbrega to King João III, Pernambuco, 14 September 1551," in *MB*, 1:291; "José de Anchieta to Ignatius de Loyola (in Rome), Piratininga, 1 September 1554," in *MB*, 2:117; "José de Anchieta to Ignatius de Loyola (in Rome), São Vicente, end of March 1555," in *MB*, 2:200–201.

14. "José de Anchieta to Diego Laínez (in Rome), São Vicente, 8 January 1565," in *MB*, 4:137.

15. Nóbrega, "Informação das terras do Brasil," in *MB*, 1:152.

16. On the differences between pajés and caraíbas, see Fausto, "Fragmentos de história e cultura Tupinambá," 385–388, Lestringant's comment in Thevet, *Le Brésil*, 355 n. 1, and Lestringant's note in his Paris 1994 edition of Léry, *Histoire d'un voyage faict*, 396. Jesuit letters and reports that describe the healing roles of the hechiceros and feiticeiros include "Nóbrega to Dr. Martín de Azpilcueta Navarro (in Coimbra), Salvador, 10 August 1549," in *MB*, 1:144; Nóbrega, "Informação das terras do Brasil," in *MB*, 1:152; and "José de Anchieta to Inácio de Loyola (in Rome), Piratininga, 1 September 1554," in *MB*, 2:109–110. Cardim's definition of "*caraíba*" is in "Do princípio e origem dos índios do Brasil," in *Tratados da terra*, 166–167. "*Feiticeiro*" and "*santa coisa*" are defined in Ayrosa, *Vocabulário na língua brasílica*. Anchieta's linking of *caraíba* to European man is in "Informação do Brasil," in Anchieta, *Cartas: Informações*, 340.

17. Staden, *True History*, 148–149; Thevet, *Le Brésil*, 144; and Lestringant's Paris 1994 edition of Léry, *Histoire d'un voyage faict*, 468, 396.

18. "António Pires to the fathers and brothers of Coimbra, Pernambuco, 2 August 1551," in *MB*, 1:255–256; "Luís da Grã to Inácio de Loyola (in Rome), Bahia, 27 December 1554," in *MB*, 2:134; Nóbrega, "Informação das terras do Brasil," in *MB*, 1:152.

19. "António Pires to the fathers and brothers of Coimbra, Pernambuco, 2 August 1551," in *MB*, 1:256. Luís da Grã did not see the shamans as agents of the devil; rather, he saw them as simple liars and deceivers; see his letter to Inácio de Loyola (in Rome), Bahia, 27 December 1554, in *MB*, 2:134. "João de Azpilcueta to the fathers and brothers of Coimbra, Bahia, 28 March 1550," in *MB*, 1:181.

20. Nóbrega, "Informação das terras do Brasil," in *MB*, 1:150–152.

21. As quoted in Gaspar da Madre de Deus, *Memórias para a história*, 91.

22. "Pero Correia to João Nunes Bareto (in Africa), São Vicente, 20 June 1551," in *MB*, 1:225.

23. "Diogo Jácome to the fathers and brothers of Coimbra, São Vicente, 20 June 1551," in *MB*, 1:242; "António Pires to fathers and brothers of Coimbra, Pernambuco, 4 June 1552," in *MB*, 1:324; and "Luís da Grã to Ignatius de Loyola (in Rome), Piratininga, 8 June 1556," in *MB*, 2:292.

24. "João de Azpilcueta, also known as Juan de Azpilcueta Navarro, to fathers and brothers of Coimbra, 24 June 1555," in *MB*, 2:246. The expedition was ordered by Tomé de Sousa and consisted of twelve colonists, Azpilcueta, and many Indians. The men were instructed to explore the interior and look for gold and other precious minerals.

25. Ibid.

26. Léry, *Histoire d'un faict* (Paris 1994), 397–405; quotations from Léry, *History of a Voyage*, 140–144.

27. Staden, *True History*, 148–150.

28. Léry, *History of a Voyage*, 108–109; Thevet, *Le Brésil*, 136.

29. "Informação do Brasil e de suas capitanias (1584)," in Anchieta, *Cartas: Informações*, 339.

30. When Mem de Sá was recruiting men in São Vicente to join in the war against the French in Rio de Janeiro, the Indians were scandalized that only a few mamelucos were willing to go. They "now make fun of the Christians, saying that they are weak," the town council of São Paulo wrote to Queen Catherine, 20 May 1561, in *MB*, 3:341–347.

31. "Duarte da Costa to King João III, Salvador, 10 June 1555," in *HCPB*, 3: 337–379.

32. "António Blázquez to Diego Laínez (in Rome), Bahia, 10 September 1559," in *MB*, 3:139.

33. "Instrumento dos serviços de Mem de Sá [1560]"; "Mem de Sá to King Sebastião, Salvador, 1 June 1558," in *Documentos relativos a Mem de Sá*, 97–98; "António Blázquez to Diego Laínez (in Rome), Bahia, 10 September 1559," in *MB*, 3:139; on the decline of Espírito Santo, see "Nóbrega to Dom Henrique, São Vicente, 1 June 1560," in *MB*, 3:242, and a letter comissioned by Brás Lourenço to Miguel de Torres (in Lisbon), Espírito Santo, 10 June 1562, in *MB*, 3:462. On the war in Paraguaçu, see "Nóbrega to Tomé de Sousa (in Lisbon), Bahia, 5 July 1559," in *MB*, 3:95–96, and "António Rodrigues to Manoel da Nóbrega (in Espírito Santo Aldeia), Paraguaçu, 28 September 1599," in *MB*, 3:155–158. Mem de Sá's son was Fernão de Sá; his nephew was Baltazar de Sá.

34. "Informação do Brasil e de suas capitanias," in Anchieta, *Cartas: Informações*, 311.

35. Gandavo, "Treatise," 2:165; Clastres, *Land-without-Evil*, passim; Métraux, "Migrations historiques," passim; the reference to the Indian slave uprising during Holy Week 1568 is in "Informação dos primeiros aldeamentos na Bahia," in Anchieta, *Cartas: Informações*, 381.

36. "José de Anchieta to fathers and brothers of Portugal, Piratininga, end of April 1557," in *MB*, 2:366–367.

37. "Manoel da Nóbrega to Miguel de Torres and fathers and brothers of Portugal, Bahia, 5 July 1559," in *MB*, 3:54.

38. "Leonardo do Vale to Gonçalo Vaz de Melo (in Lisbon), Bahia, 12 May 1563," in *MB*, 4:9–22. On the Jesuit mission to Tinharé, see the letters of António Blázquez to Diego Laínez (in Rome), Bahia, 1 September 1561, in *MB*, 3:394–434, and Luís da Grã to Miguel de Torres (in Lisbon), Bahia, 22 September 1561, in *MB*, 3:428–432, 435–451. The Jesuit history of the aldeias (1584) is "Informaçao dos primeiros aldeamentos na Bahia," in Anchieta, *Cartas: Informações*, 365.

39. "Confession of Luísa Barbosa, 23 August 1591," in *PV:C-Bahia*, 83–85.

40. "Informação dos primeiros aldeamentos na Bahia," in Ancheita, *Cartas: Informações*, 381.

41. Jesuit annual letter, 1585, in *Annuae litterae Societatis Iesu*, 129–141. I thank my colleague Colin Wells for his help in translating this letter. The author of the 1585 annual letter was either José de Anchieta, who was the provincial until 1585 or 1586, or Marçal de Beliarte, who replaced him.

42. Ibid.

43. Ibid.

44. Ibid.

45. Ibid.

46. The visiting inquisitor initiated six trials that deal directly with the Santidade de Jaguaripe: Domingos Fernandes Nobre, IL 10,776; Fernão Cabral de Taíde, IL 17,065; Gonçalo Fernandes, IL 17,762; Iria Álvarez, IL 1,335; Cristovão de Bulhões, IL 7,950; and Pantalião Ribeiro, IL 11,036—all in ANTT. The trial of Marcos Tavares, in ANTT: IL 11,080, makes reference to his belief in Santidade, as does the incomplete trial of Heitor Antunes, in ANTT: IL 4,309.

47. G. S. de Sousa, *Tratado descritivo*, 140, 134; Cardim, "Narrativa epistolar de uma viagem," in *Tratados da terra*, 217; [Luis Teixeira], *Roteiro de todos os sinais*, 7.

48. "Denunciation of Domingos de Almeida, 30 June 1591," in *PV:D-Bahia*, 251–253; "Denunciation of Domingos de Oliveira, 2 August 1591," in *PV:D-Bahia*, 264–266; "Certificate of Manoel Teles Barreto, governor of Brazil, 8 August 1586," and "First Interrogation of Cabral, 23 September 1591," both in "Trial of Fernão Cabral de Taíde," in ANTT: IL 17,065; "Confession of Domingos Fernandes Nobre, 11 February 1592," in *PV: C-Bahia*, 219–227.

49. "First Interrogation of Cristovão de Bulhões, 20 November 1592," in "Trial of Bulhões," in ANTT: IL 7,950. Cristovão de Bulhões was born in São Vicente; his father was a Christian mulatto from Mina, Africa, and his mother was a baptized Indian slave; see his confession and the second interrogation.

50. "Confession of Gonçalo Fernandes, 13 January 1592," in *PV:C-Bahia*, 111–114. Fernão Cabral gave Gonçalo letters for Nobre and some manioc flour for the trek,

but Gonçalo and his slave returned after two days out, fearing attacks by Indians in the sertão.

51. "Confession of Bras Dias, 25 January 1592," in *PV:C-Bahia*, 159–160; "Confession of Paulos Dias, 3 March 1592," in "Trial of Domingos Fernandes Nobre," in ANTT: IL 10,776; "Confession of Cristovão de Bulhões, 20 January 1592," in *PV:C-Bahia*, 135–139.

52. "Confession of Domingos Fernandes Nobre, 11 February 1592," in *PV: C-Bahia*, 219–227.

53. "Confession of Domingos Fernandes Nobre, 11 February 1592," in *PV:C-Bahia*, 219–227; "Confession of Cristovão de Bulhões, 20 January 1592," in *PV:C-Bahia*, 135–139; and "Confession of Pantalião Ribeiro, 6 September 1591," in "Trial of Pantalião Ribeiro," in ANTT: IL 11,036.

54. "First Interrogation of Fernão Cabral de Taíde, 23 September 1591," in "Trial of Cabral," in ANTT: IL 17,065; "Confession of Pantalião Ribeiro, 6 September 1591," in "Trial of Ribeiro," in ANTT: IL 11,036.

55. Confession of Domingos Fernandes Nobre, 11 February 1592, *PV:C-Bahia*, 219–227; and confession of Paulos Dias, 3 March 1592, in trial of Nobre, in ANTT: IL 10,776.

56. "First Interrogation of Fernão Cabral de Taíde, 23 September 1591," in "Trial of Cabral," in ANTT: IL 17,065; "Denunciation of Belchior da Fonseca, 6 August 1591," in *PV:D-Bahia*, 276–277; "Denunciation of Francisco de Abreu, 13 August 1591," in *PV:D-Bahia*, 315–316; "Denunciation of António da Fonseca, 17 August 1591," in *PV:D-Bahia*, 346–347; "Denunciation of Domingos de Oliveira, 2 August 1591," in *PV:D-Bahia*, 264–265; "Denunciation of Bernaldino Ribeiro

da Grã, 21 August 1591," in *PV:D-Bahia*, 381–382; "Denunciation of Domingos de Almeida, 30 June 1591," in *PV:D-Bahia*, 251–253. In his first interrogation, 23 September 1591, Cabral refers to the husband of "Mother of God" as a second pope; see "Trial of Fernão Cabral de Taíde," in ANTT: IL 17,065. "Confession of Dona Margarida da Costa, 30 October 1591," in *PV:C-Bahia*, 101–102; "Denunciation of Antônio da Fonseca, 17 August 1591," in *PV:D-Bahia*, 346–347; "Denunciation of Maria da Fonseca, 17 August 1591," in *PV:D-Bahia*, 352–353; and "Confession of Cristovão de Bulhões, 20 January 1592," in *PV:C-Bahia*, 135–139. See "-picu, pocu, pucu," from the Tupi *pu'ku*, meaning "long," in Houaiss, *Dicionário electrônico;* the Portuguese *"Longa cousa"* is defined in Ayrosa, *Vocabulário na língua brasílica,* as "Mucû, Pukû," and *"Comprida coisa ou compridão"* is defined as "Puku." As Vainfas points out, the Indian slave's original name, Cão Grande, was already a Portuguese version of an Indian name; see Vainfas, *A heresia dos índios,* 127.

57. "Confession of Dona Margarida da Costa, 30 October 1591," in *PV:C-Bahia*, 101–102; "Confession, 2 August 1591"; "First Interrogation, 23 September 1591"; "Third Interrogation, 14 August 1592"; and "Fourth Admonition [*admoestação*], 18 August 1592"—all of Fernão Cabral in "Trial of Fernão Cabral de Taíde," in ANTT: IL 17,065; "Denunciation of Francisco de Abreu, 13 August 1591," in *PV:D-Bahia*, 315–316; "Denunciation of Álvaro Rodrigues, 27 January 1592," in "Trial of Domingos Fernandes Nobre," in ANTT: IL 10,776. Most of those who denounced Cabral said that it was "common knowledge" that Cabral entered the church, but Cristovão de Bulhões said that he "saw"

Cabral "revere and bow his head" to the idol in the church; see "Confession of Cristovão de Bulhões, 20 January 1592," in *PV:C-Bahia*, 135–139. See "Caraíba" in Houaiss, *Dicionário electrónico*, and "Homen Branco" in Ayrosa, *Vocabulário na língua brasílica*. Vainfas believes that Cabral was manipulating the meaning of the Tupi words to deceive the inquisitor; see Vainfas, *A heresia dos índios*, 193.

58. "Denunciation of Fernão Cardim, 14 August 1591," in *PV:D-Bahia*, 327–329.

59. "Denunciation of Belchior da Fonseca, 6 August 1591," in *PV:D-Bahia*, 276–277; "Denunciation of João Bras, 17 August 1591," in *PV:D-Bahia*, 350–351; "Denunciation of Álvaro Rodrigues, 27 January 1592," in "Trial of Domingos Fernandes Nobre," in ANTT: IL 10,776.

60. "Confession of Gonçalo Fernandes, 13 January 1592," in *PV:C-Bahia*, 111–114; "Denunciation of Paulo Adorno, 11 February 1592," in "Trial of Fernão Cabral de Taíde," in ANTT: IL 17,065; "Denunciation of Maria Antunes, 22 August 1591," in *PV:D-Bahia*, 410–412; "Denunciation of Pero de Moura, 30 October 1592," in *PV:D-Bahia*, 567–568; Jesuit annual letter, 1585, in *Annuae litterae Societatis Iesu*, 129–141. The governor named the mission village Santo Antonio; see "Certificate of Manoel Teles Barreto, 8 August 1586," in "Trial of Fernão Cabral de Taíde," in ANTT: IL 17,065.

61. "Confession of Gonçalo Fernandes, 13 January 1592," in *PV:C-Bahia*, 111–114, and "Third Interrogation of Gonçalo Fernandes, 2 December 1592," in "Trial of Gonçalo Fernandes," in ANTT: IL 17,762. "Denunciation of João Ribeiro, 22 August 1591," in *PV:D-Bahia*, 423–424.

62. "Second Interrogation of Marcos Tavares, 20 June 1593," in "Trial of Marcos Tavares," in ANTT: IL 11,080; "Second and Third Interrogations of Iria Álvares, 14 and 15 June 1595," in "Trial of Iria Álvares," in ANTT: IL 1,335; Jesuit annual letter, 1585, in *Annuae litterae Societatis Iesu*, 129–141; "Denunciation of Mecia Barbosa, 25 August 1591," in *PV:D-Bahia*, 453–455, and "Denunciation of João da Rocha Vicente (Mecia Barbosa's husband), 24 August 1591," in *PV:D-Bahia*, 444–447.

63. "Denunciation of Álvaro Rodrigues, 27 January 1592," in "Trial of Domingos Fernandes Nobre," in ANTT: IL 10,776; "Certificate of Manoel Teles Barreto, 8 August 1586," in "Trial of Fernão Cabral," in ANTT: IL 17,065.

64. "Leonardo do Vale on behalf of Luís da Grã to Diego Laínez (in Rome), Bahia, 23 September 1561," in *MB*, 3:441. Bras Dias stated that Antônio had been raised in the "*aldeias da conversão*" (mission villages) of the Jesuits and that he had invented the movement; see *PV: C-Bahia*, 160. On the Jesuit mission to Tinharé, see "António Blázquez to Diego Laínez, 1 September 1561," in *MB*, 3:424–427; "Luís da Grã to Miguel de Torres (in Lisbon), Bahia, 22 September 1561," in *MB*, 3:428–432, 435–451; "Leonardo do Vale on behalf of Luís da Grã to Diego Laínez (in Rome), Bahia, 23 September 1561," in *MB*, 3:441; "Leonardo do Vale to Gonçalo Vaz de Melo (in Lisbon), Bahia, 12 May 1563," in *MB*, 4:9–22; and "Informação dos primeiros aldeamentos na Bahia," in Anchieta, *Cartas: Informações*, 362.

65. "Confession of Domingos Fernandes Nobre, 10 February 1592," in *PV: C-Bahia*, 219–227. Vainfas comes to much the same conclusion on the youth of Antônio; see Vainfas, *A heresia dos índios*, 113–114.

66. Vainfas, *A heresia dos índios*, 116; "Fourth Admonition of Fernão Cabral de Taíde, 18 August 1592," in "Trial of Fernão Cabral," in ANTT: IL 17,065.

67. "Sentence of Fernão Cabral," in his trial, in ANTT: IL 17,065; "Confession of Paulos Dias, 3 March 1592," in "Trial of Domingos Fernandes Nobre," in ANTT: IL 10,776; "Denunciation of Belchior da Fonseca, 6 August 1591," in *PV:D-Bahia*, 276–278. On the significance of the flood in Tupi mythology, see Edgard Leite, *Homens vindos do céu*, 131–135, and Métraux, *A religião dos Tupinambás*, 31–33, where Métraux summarizes the myth recorded by Thevet. Cardim describes the myth in "Do princípio e origem dos índios do Brazil," in *Tratados da terra*, 165; see Vainfas' interpretation of the ambiguity and hybridity of these beliefs in *A heresia dos índios*, 112–114.

68. "Confession of Gonçalo Fernandes, 13 January 1592," in *PV:C-Bahia*, 111–114; Cardim, *Tratados da terra*, 175, 123–124.

69. "Confession of Bras Dias, 25 January 1592," in *PV:C-Bahia*, 159–160; "Confession of Domingos Fernandes Nobre, 11 February 1592," in *PV:C-Bahia*, 219–227; "Denunciation of Diogo Dias, 26 August 1591," in *PV:D-Bahia*, 473–476. The roots of the word "*abusão*" lie in the Latin noun "*abusio*," meaning "a false use of tropes," and the verb "*abutor*," "to make full use of, to use fully" (per *Cassell's Latin Dictionary*), and in the Spanish and Portuguese verb "*abusar*," "to abuse." In Portuguese, the word "*abusão*" was common in the sixteenth century, whereas in old English, the word "abusion," now obsolete, is defined by the *Oxford English Dictionary Online* as "perversion of the truth; deceit, deception, imposture; also an instance of such perversion or deception."

70. On the Tupi-Guarani tradition of migration, the concept of a "land without evil," and messianism, see Nimuendajú-Unkel, *Los mitos de creación;* Métraux, "Migrations historiques," 201–252, and "Messiahs of South America"; Schaden, *Aculturação e messianismo;* and Clastres, *Land-without-Evil*. There is disagreement over whether the prophetic movements existed before colonization or if they emerged as a response to it; see Fausto, "Fragmentos de história e cultura Tupinambá," 385–387.

71. Quotations from Lanternari, *Religions of the Oppressed*, xii, and Daniels, *Millennialism*, xxv. See also Trompf, "Introduction," in Trompf, *Cargo Cults and Millenarian Movements*, 1–23. There are numerous historical examples of conflict between millenarians and government authorities in Brazilian history; the most famous is that between Antônio Conselheiro and the Brazilian national government at Canudos, described by Euclides da Cunha in *Os sertões*, trans. by Samuel Putnam as *Rebellion in the Backlands;* but see also the regional civil war in Santa Catarina, Brazil, in Diacon, *Millenarian Vision*.

72. "Confession of Luísa Rodrigues, 6 February 1592," in *PV:C-Bahia*, 206; "Third Interrogation of Iria Álvares, 15 June 1595," in "Trial of Iria Álvares," in ANTT: IL 1,335; "Confession of Gonçalo Fernandes, 13 January 1592," in *PV:C-Bahia*, 111–114.

73. "Denunciation of Álvaro Rodrigues, 27 January 1592," in "Trial of Domingos Fernandes Nobre," in ANTT: IL 10,776.

74. See Norman Cohn, *Pursuit of the Millennium*, 7–10.

75. "Orphan children, signed by Diego Tompinambá Peribira Mongetá Quatiá,

written by Francisco Pires, to Pero Doménech (in Lisbon), Bahia, 5 August 1552," in *MB*, 1:386–387, and "Pero Correia to Brás Lourenço (in Espírito Santo), São Vicente, 18 July 1554," in *MB*, 2:70.

76. Anchieta, *Doutrina Cristã*, 1:172–175, and "Anchieta to Diego Laínez (in Rome), São Vicente, 16 April 1563," in *MB*, 3:561–562.

77. "António Blázquez for Manoel da Nóbrega to Diego Laínez (in Rome), Bahia, 10 September 1559," in *MB*, 3:143. Carole Myscofski, "Messianic Themes," 77–94. Were the Jesuits themselves millenarian in their thinking? Marjorie Reeves believes so; she describes the Jesuits as the order that inherited the millenarian outlook of Joachimism in the sixteenth century, arguing that they saw themselves charged with evangelizing the world and fulfilling prophecies that heralded the second coming of Christ; see *Influence of Prophecy*, 274–290. The millenarian beliefs of António Vieira, the influential seventeenth-century Jesuit in Brazil and Portugal, are well known; see Cohen, *Fire of Tongues*. But John W. O'Malley, who has written an influential book on the early Jesuits, does not characterize them as millenarian; rather, he sees them as practical in their thinking and not apocalyptic in their outlook; see *The First Jesuits*, 262, 269, 322, and 372.

78. "Denunciation of Álvaro Rodrigues," in "Trial of Domingos Fernandes Nobre," in ANTT: IL 10,776; "Denunciation of Maria Carvalha, 30 October 1591," in *PV:D-Bahia*, 550; "First Interrogation of Cristovão de Bulhões, 20 November 1592," in "Trial of Bulhões," in ANTT: IL 7,950; and "Confession of Brás Dias, 25 January 1592," in *PV:C-Bahia*, 159.

79. Sweet, *Recreating Africa*, 119–160, quotation from 119; Souza, *The Devil and the Land*, 98–111.

80. MacGaffey, *Religion and Society*, 43; Sweet, *Recreating Africa*, 104; and Marina de Souza, *Reis negros*, 62–71.

81. "Confession of Cristovão de Bulhões, 20 January 1592," in *PV:C-Bahia*, 135–139; "Confession of Domingos Fernandes Nobre, 10 February 1592," in *PV:C-Bahia*, 219–227; "Confession of Fernal Cabral de Taíde, 2 August 1591," in *PV:C-Bahia*, 35–37. One denunciation stated that the statue was of wood and that it looked like an Indian; "Denunciation of Diogo Dias, 26 August 1591," in *PV:D-Bahia*, 473–476. Gaspar Dias Barbosa gave its dimensions as 1 *covado* and stated that it had "*uma veste*," or some sort of "dress"; "Denunciation of Gaspar Dias Barbosa, 16 August 1591," in *PV:D-Bahia*, 340–342. The description of crosses in piles with marks on the ground comes from the "Confession of Bras Dias, 25 January 1592," in *PV:C-Bahia*, 159–160. On the cross in Central Africa, see MacGaffey, *Religion and Society*, 44–47, 116.

82. Sweet, *Recreating Africa*, 161–174; Laura de Mello e Souza, *The Devil and the Land*, 93–175, 257.

83. "Carta ânua da província do Brasil, 1581," in Anchieta, *Cartas: Correspondência*, 312; Cardim, "Narrativa epistolar," in Cardim, *Tratados da terra*, 244, 250. Gouveia recognized the need for more interpreters and wanted to send two Jesuit brothers to Angola so they could learn the language properly; "Cristovão de Gouveia to Aquaviva, 25 July 1583," in ARSI: Lus. 68:337. On Christianity in Africa, and especially in the Kongo kingdom, see Thornton, "Development of an African Catholic Church," 147–167; on

millenarian movements in Africa in the eighteenth century, see Thornton, *The Kongolese Saint Anthony*.

84. Jesuit annual letter, 1585, in *Annuae litterae Societatis Iesu*, 129–141.

85. The Jesuit annual letter was often used by Jesuit historians who wrote about the Santidade de Jaguaripe; see Vainfas, *A heresia dos índios*, 201–211, and Laura de Melo e Souza, *Inferno atlântico*, 58–88. The Jesuit annual letter of 1585 suggests that the leader captured and hanged was Antônio, but as of August 1586, the governor believed that the "pope" had fled and that there was no further news of him. See "Certificate of Manoel Teles Barreto, 8 August 1586," in "Trial of Fernão Cabral de Taíde," in ANTT: IL 17,065.

8. POWER

1. Brazil never did have a permanent, resident office of the Inquisition, unlike Mexico or Peru, both of which had permanent offices. The Lisbon Inquisition, under whose purview Brazil fell, therefore relied on temporary tribunals, such as Mendonça set up during his visit, and civil and religious authorities in Brazil; see Wadsworth, "In the Name of the Inquisition," 19–54. On the Inquisition in Mexico, see Alberro, *Inquisición y sociedad en México*, and in Peru, see Castañeda Delgado, Hernández Aparicio, and Millar Carvacho, *La Inquisición de Lima*. As a physical go-between, Mendonça arrived sick from his sea voyage, as did many of the others who crossed the Atlantic with him; Garcia, introduction to *PV:DC-Pernambuco*, vii. On the inquisitor as mediator, see Menchi, "Inquisizione come repressione o inquisizione come mediazi-

one?" 53–77. On the representation of Brazil as sinful, a purgatory, and the realm of the devil, drawn from the corpus of trials compiled by Mendonça (as representational go-between), see Laura de Mello e Souza, *O diabo e a terra de Santa Cruz*, and Vainfas, *Trópico dos pecados*.

2. The data on Bahia are from G. S. de Sousa, *Tratado descritivo*, 162, and Schwartz, *Sugar Plantations*, 82. The data on Pernambuco are from Cardim, "Narrativa epistolar de uma viagem," in Cardim, *Tratados da terra*, 255. One arroba is generally accepted to be 32 pounds. The numbers of Jesuits is given in "Catálogo de los padres y hermanos de la provincia del Brasil, ano de 1586," in ARSI: Bras. 15-1:28, also published in Anchieta, *Textos históricos*, 107–113. The size of the *aldeias* is given in the 1589 catalog, "Catálogo de los padres y hermanos de la provincia del Brasil, ano de 1589," in ARSI: Bras. 15-1:32. On the alliances between Jesuits and local elites, see Alden, *Making of an Enterprise*, 474.

3. "Publication of the Edicts of Faith, 28 July 1591," in *PV:C-Bahia*, 11–13.

4. "Confession of Frutuoso Álvarez, 20 July 1591," in *PV:C-Bahia*, 23–27; "Confession of Baltazar Martins, 31 July 1591," in *PV:C-Bahia*, 30–33; "Confession of Fernão Cabral de Taíde, 2 August 1591," in *PV:C-Bahia*, 35–37; "Confession of Maria Lopez, 3 August 1591," in *PV:C-Bahia*, 39–42; "Confession of Brianda Fernandes, 20 August 1591," in *PV:C-Bahia*, 57–58.

5. Robert Rowland graciously allowed me to consult the unpublished Gulbenkian Inquisition Database (1987). A second useful list of trials from Mendonça's visit to Brazil has been compiled by Sonia Siqueira, *A Inquisição portuguesa e a sociedade colonial*, 361–397. Combining the

two indices gives 168 known trials for six-teenth-century Brazil. Surprisingly, there were only 16 trials of New Christians who were accused of practicing rituals or customs labeled as Jewish. This was 10 percent of the total, a small percentage, given the Portuguese Inquisition's tendency to pursue New Christians and the rumor that many New Christians fled Portugal for the more tolerant environment of Brazil. The sexual crimes investigated by the inquisitor have been well studied by Brazilian historians. See the work of Vainfas, *Trópico dos pecados;* Mott, *Escravidão, homossexualidade e demonologia;* and Bellini, *A coisa obscura.*

6. Although the Society of Jesus never had particularly close ties to the Inquisition, the Jesuits of the college in Salvador were expressly asked to sit on the inquisitorial mesa; see Serafim Leite, *História da Companhia de Jesus no Brasil,* 2 : 389. Francisco de Lemos, a Jesuit interpreter, provided the translation when Fernão Ribeiro, an Indian from the aldeia of São João, did not speak Portuguese; see "Confession of Fernão Ribeiro, 12 August 1591," in *PV: C-Bahia,* 47–48. Denunciations made by Jesuits include those by Fernão Cardim, Simão Pinto, Baltazar de Miranda, Marçal Beliarte, Luís da Grã, and João Vicente; see *PV: D-Bahia,* 327–329, 339, 349–350, 371, and 329–331; the denunciation of João Vicente is in the trial of Dominges Fernandes Nobre, in ANTT: IL 10,776.

7. "Confession of Fernão Cabral, 2 August 1591," in his trial, in ANTT: IL 17,065, and published in *PV: C-Bahia,* 35–37.

8. "Confession of Fernão Cabral, 2 August 1591," in *PV: C-Bahia,* 35–37; see Higgins, "Pica," 927–928, and also Sweet, *Recreating Africa,* 61–62.

9. "Trial of Fernão Cabral de Taíde," in ANTT: IL 17,065. The two Jesuits who denounced Cabral were Fernão Cardim, 14 August 1591, in *PV: D-Bahia,* 327–328, and Simão Pinto, 16 August 1591, in *PV: D-Bahia,* 339. "Denunciation of Nuno Pereira de Carvalho, 9 August 1591," in *PV: D-Bahia,* 297–298, and "Denunciation of Beatiz Gomes, 27 August 1591," in *PV: D-Bahia,* 481–482.

10. "Denunciation of Luísa de Almeida, 18 August 1591," in *PV: D-Bahia,* 365–366; Cabral was the godfather of Luísa de Almeida's son. "Denunciation of Simão Pinto, 16 August 1591," in *PV: D-Bahia,* 339.

11. "Petition of Father António Pires, provincial of Brazil, 9 September 1571," in "Informação dos primeiros aldeamentos na Bahia," in Anchieta, *Cartas: Informações,* 371–373. Cabral was forced to return the six Indians.

12. "Denunciation of Fernão Cardil [*sic*], 14 August 1591," in *PV: D-Bahia,* 327–328.

13. G. S. de Sousa, *Tratado descritivo,* 136.

14. Serafim Leite, "Os 'Capítulos' de Gabriel Soares de Sousa," 218–220; Alden, *Making of an Enterprise,* 481.

15. "Capítulos que Gabriel de Sousa deu em Madrid ao S. Dom Christovão de Moura contra os padres da Companhia . . . ," in ARSI: Bras. 15:383–389. Transcribed in Serafim Leite, "Os 'Capítulos' de Gabriel Soares de Sousa," 217–247.

16. Alden, *Making of an Enterprise,* 91.

17. The six Jesuits were Marçal Beliarte, Ignacio Tolosa, Rodrigo de Freitas, Luís da Fonseca, Quiricio Caxa, and Fernão Cardim. Three of the six served with the inquisitor (Beliarte, Fonseca, and Cardim). Their responses to G. S. de

Sousa may be found as "Huas breves respostas dos mesmos padres q' deles forão
avisados por hum seu parente quem os
elle mostrou," in "Capítulos que Gabriel
de Sousa deu em Madrid . . .," in ARSI:
Bras. 15:383–389. Transcribed in Serafim
Leite, "Os 'Capítulos' de Gabriel Soares
de Sousa," 217–247.

18. "Denunciation of Isabel Beliaga,
21 January 1592," in "Trial of Domingos
Fernandes Nobre," in ANTT: IL 10,776;
"Confession of Domingos Fernandes
Nobre, 11 February 1592," in PV:C-Bahia,
220–227.

19. "Confession of Domingos Fernandes Nobre, 11 February 1592," PV:C-
Bahia, 220–227.

20. Fernão Cardim, "Enformacion,"
163. Although signed by Cristovão de
Gouveia and dated 31 December 1583, this
document is attributed to Fernão Cardim.

21. "Denunciation of João Vicente, 11
February 1592," in "Trial of Domingos
Fernandes Nobre," in ANTT: IL 10,776.
João Vicente was an English Jesuit in Bra-
zil; his given name was John Yates.

22. Jesuit annual letter from Brazil,
1581, "Carta ânua da província do Brasil de 1581," Bahia, 1 January 1582, in
Anchieta, Cartas: Correspondência, 302–
322.

23. "John Vincent to Richard Gibbon
(in Madrid), 1592," summarized in United
Kingdom, Public Record Office, Calendar
of State Papers, 245:353–355.

24. "First Interrogation of Francisco
Pires, 25 August 1592," in his trial, in
ANTT: IL 17,809.

25. "First Interrogation of Lázaro da
Cunha, 29 October 1592," in "Trial of
Lázaro da Cunha," in ANTT: IL 11,068.
The two men denounced by Vicente were
Afonso Pereira, known as "Marigui" in

the Indian language, who was a resident
of Sergipe o Novo, and Mateus Antunes,
a resident of Pernambuco. "Denunciation
of João Vicente, 11 February 1592," in
"Trial of Domingos Fernandes Nobre,"
in ANTT: IL 10,776.

26. "Confession of Gonçalo Álvares,
3 March 1592," in "Trial of Francisco
Pires," in ANTT: IL 17,809.

27. "Informação dos primeiros aldeamentos na Bahia," in Anchieta, Cartas:
Informações, 379. Serafim Leite, História
da Companhia de Jesus no Brasil, 1:446 n.
4. Gaspar Lourenço died in 1581. In the
annual letter of 1582, José de Anchieta
describes him as not only a rare example
of virtue, but a brilliant linguist who suffered more than any other for the conversion of Indians, undertaking many missions, facing grave dangers, and gaining
great fame among the Indians. See "Carta
ânua da província do Brasil de 1581,"
Bahia, 1 January 1582, in Anchieta, Cartas: Correspondência, 305.

28. "Informação dos primeiros aldeamentos na Bahia," in Anchieta, Cartas:
Informações, 380–381; Serafim Leite,
História da Companhia de Jesus no Brasil,
1:441–442. In Tratado descritivo, G. S.
de Sousa states that Garcia d'Avila was
the captain selected by the governor (68).
Serafim Leite, however, suggests that
Garcia d'Avila was sent by the governor
after the events described here; História da
Companhia de Jesus no Brasil, 1:440 n. 2.

29. Serafim Leite, História da Companhia de Jesus no Brasil, 1:441–442.

30. "Informação dos primeiros aldeamentos na Bahia," in Anchieta, Cartas:
Informações, 383.

31. Ibid., 382–385; Jesuit annual letter from 1576, "Ânua de Ignacio Tolosa,
1576," in ARSI: Bras. 15-2:284–286; much

of this letter appears in Serafim Leite, *História da Companhia de Jesus no Brasil* 1:445.

32. "Informação dos primeiros aldeamentos na Bahia," in Anchieta, *Cartas: Informações*, 385.

33. Points 4, 13, 14, 40, and 41 in Serafim Leite, "Os 'Capítulos' de Gabriel Soares de Sousa."

34. "Confession of Domingos Fernandes Nobre," in *PV: C-Bahia*, 219–227.

35. The proverb can be found in many collections; see, for example, Casanovas, *Provérbios e frases proverbiais do século XVI*, 98. I thank many colleagues for helping me to decipher this proverb, especially Richard Woods, Florence Weinberg, and Arturo Madrid.

36. "Confession of Pantalião Ribeiro, 6 September 1591," in "Trial of Pantalião Ribeiro," in ANTT: IL 11,036. *La Celestina*, first published in 1499 and attributed to Fernando de Rojas, is a novel in dialogue; see Rojas, *The Celestina: A Novel in Dialogue*. The *Comédia Eufrosina* appeared in Lisbon in 1555 and later appeared on the list of books banned by the Inquisition. The proverb appears in the beginning of act 1, scene 3; see Jorge Ferreira de Vasconcellos, *Comédia Eufrosina*, 39. A copy of the play existed in Salvador; see the confession of Nuno Fernandes, 1 February 1592, in *PV: C-Bahia*, 189. On the go-between in Spanish literature, see Ruggerio, *Evolution of the Go-Between*.

37. On the availability of wine in Brazil during Nobre's lifetime, see G. S. de Sousa, *Tratado descritivo*, 139; "Letter commissioned by Brás Lourenço to Miguel de Torres (in Lisbon), Espírito Santo, 10 June 1562," in *MB*, 3:460–468; and [Belchior Cordeiro, S.J.], "Emformação dalgumas cousas do Brasil [1577]," 193–194.

38. Jesuit annual letter, 1585, in *Annuae litterae Societatis Iesu*, 129–141.

39. Points 5 and 42 in Serafim Leite, "Os 'Capítulos' de Gabriel Soares de Sousa." G. S. de Sousa describes himself as having begun a sugar mill and as owning "a village of slaves" managed by an overseer on his estate in Jaguaripe; see *Tratado descritivo*, 159–160. The information on Rodrigues' estate comes from the trial of Álvaro Rodrigues, in ANTT: IL 16,897.

40. "Second Denunciation of Pero Novais, 10 February 1592," in "Trial of Fernão Cabral de Taíde," in ANTT: IL 17,065. Novais calls Antonio Lopes Ilhoa a "New Christian merchant who now lives in Lisbon," but according to Gabriel Soares de Sousa, he owned a sugar mill in Paraguaçu in the mid-1580s; see G. S. de Sousa, *Tratado descritivo*, 154. "First Interrogation of Fernão Cabral, 23 September 1591," in "Trial of Fernão Cabral de Taíde," in ANTT: IL 17,065; "Confession of Cristovão de Bulhões, 20 January 1592," in *PV: C-Bahia*, 135–139.

41. "Denunciation of Francisco d'Abreu, 13 August 1591," in *PV: D-Bahia*, 315–316.

42. "Denunciation of Bernaldino Ribeiro da Grã, 21 August 1591," in *PV: D-Bahia*, 381–382.

43. "Denunciation of Álvaro Rodrigues, 27 January 1592," in "Trial of Domingos Fernandes Nobre," in ANTT: IL 10,776. Rodrigues claimed he had this letter, but if he presented it to the inquisitor, it never made it into either Cabral's or Nobre's trials.

44. "Denunciation of Álvaro Rodrigues, 27 January 1592," in "Trial of Domingos Fernandes Nobre," in ANTT: IL 10,776. Rodrigues says that he ordered blows to

the head given with swords ("*mandou dar golpes com espadas nas cabeças dos feiticeiros*"), which suggests that the leaders were killed in the Indian style: with war clubs, which the Portuguese called "wooden swords."

45. "Conclusion and Sentence, 20 August 1592," in "Trial of Fernão Cabral," in ANTT: IL 17,065. The priest who denounced Cabral, Gaspar de Palma, replied, when asked by the inquisitor, that Cabral was a rich man with an estate worth more than 20,000 cruzados; see *PV: D-Bahia*, 322.

46. "Anchieta to Captain Miguel de Azeredo (in Espírito Santo), Bahia, 1 September 1592," in Anchieta, *Cartas: Correspondência*, 405–406. See also Vainfas, *A heresia dos índios*, 214–215.

47. "Sentence of Domingos Fernandes Nobre, 29 March 1592," in "Trial of Domingos Fernandes Nobre," in ANTT: IL 10,776; "Sentence of Pantalião Ribeiro, 29 March 1593," in "Trial of Pantalião Ribeiro," in ANTT: IL 11,036; "Sentence of Cristovão de Bulhões, 19 December 1592," in "Trial of Cristovão de Bulhões," in ANTT: IL 7,956; "Sentence of Lázaro da Cunha, 13 March 1593," in "Trial of Lázaro da Cunha," in ANTT: IL 11,068.

48. "Sentence of Francisco Pires, 9 September 1592," in "Trial of Francisco Pires," in ANTT: IL 17,809.

49. "Sentence of Álvaro Rodrigues, 19 December 1592," in "Trial of Álvaro Rodrigues," in ANTT: IL 16,897. Rodrigues was also accused of holding stolen property that belonged to his cousin's widow, of living with more than one woman, and of living under a decree of excommunication.

50. "Cardinal Archduke to Heitor Furtado de Mendonça, 13 January 1592,"

in Baião, "Correspondência inédita," 543–544; "Inquisitors António de Mendonça, Diogo de Souza, and Marcos Teixeira to Heitor Furtado de Mendonça, 24 October 1592," in ibid., 545–546; "Bishop of Elvas, Diogo de Sousa, and Marcos Teixeira to Heitor Furtado de Mendonça, 1 April 1593," in ibid., 547–548; "Diogo Soares and Marcos Teixeira to Heitor Furtado de Mendonça, 27 March 1594," in ibid., 549–550; "Bishop of Elvas, Diogo de Sousa, and Marcos Teixeira to Heitor Furtado de Mendonça, 17 December 1594," in ibid., 550–551. The first two prisoners sent to Lisbon by Mendonça were Salvador da Maia, denounced for disrespecting the crucifix, and Luís Álvares, denounced for fleeing from the Inquisition. The second two were Gaspar Afonso Castanho, the master of a slave ship who was accused of a heretical statement, and João Nunes, the holder of the brazilwood contract who was accused of keeping a crucifix in or near a chamber pot. Castanho was sent to Lisbon, where the tribunal there set him free; Nunes was jailed in Salvador until the order to free him arrived from Lisbon.

51. A sheet appended to the last page of Cabral's trial reveals that in April 1593, Cabral petitioned Mendonça for a transcript of his trial; see "Trial of Fernão Cabral," in ANTT: IL 17,065. Moreover, various inserts bound into the trial of Diogo de Morrim, in ANTT: IL 6345, reveal that both men were challenging their sentences. See also Vainfas, *A heresia dos índios*, 215.

52. "Decisions [Determinacões]," in *PV: C-Bahia*, xxxvii–xxxviii; Vainfas, *A heresia dos índios*, 213.

53. "Lei sobre se não poderem captivar os gentios das partes do Brasil, e

viverem em sua liberdade, salvo no caso declarado na dita lei," 11 November 1591, in Thomas, *Política indigenista,* 224–225.

54. "Lei de 26 de Julho de 1596 sobre a liberdade dos índios," 26 July 1596, in Thomas, *Política indigenista,* 225–226.

55. "Relação de Pero Rodrigues, 1597," in VFL: Bras. 15, reel 159.

56. Monteiro, *Negros da terra,* passim, and Thomas, *Política indigenista,* passim; Cohen, *Fire of Tongues,* 54–66.

57. Guerreiro, *Relação anual,* 1:390–391; Jarric, *Histoire des choses,* 3:467–475; Pero Rodrigues, *Vida do Padre José de Anchieta,* 23.

58. Salvador, *História do Brasil,* 303; see also Hemming, *Red Gold,* 172–173.

59. Salvador, *História do Brasil,* 303; Guerreiro, *Relação anual,* 1:390–391; Jarric, *Histoire des choses,* 3:467–475.

60. Guerreiro, *Relação anual,* 1:390–391; Jarric, *Histoire des choses,* 3:467–475.

61. Guerreiro, *Relação anual,* 1:380–382; Jarric, *Histoire des choses,* 3:475–480; "Diogo de Meneses to the king, 1 September 1610," in ANTT: Fragmentos, caixa I, maço I, doc. 6. Stuart Schwartz believes that Meneses' numbers are inflated to convince the Crown of the need for military action; see *Sugar Plantations,* 49. Moreno, *Livro que dá razão,* 110–113. "King Philip III (Filipe II) to Gaspar de Sousa, 19 January 1613 and 24 May 1613," both in *Cartas d'el Rey.*

62. Alves Filho, *Memorial dos Palmares,* 10–11; Vainfas, "Deus contra Palmares," 60–62. Costa, *Anais Pernambucanos,* 2:195–199; Freitas, *Palmares,* 41; Funari, "A arqueologia de Palmares," 26–51. See also "Correspondencia de Diogo Botelho," 1–258, and Metcalf, "*AHR Forum,*" 1531–1559.

Bibliography

ARCHIVES AND LIBRARIES

Arquivo Nacional da Torre do Tombo, Lisbon (cited as ANTT)
    Corpo Cronológico (cited as CC)
    Fragmentos
    Inquisição de Lisboa (cited as IL)
Arquivo Público do Estado da Bahia (cited as APEB)
    Cópias
Archivum Romanum Societatis Iesu, Rome (cited as ARSI)
    Provincia Brasiliensis et Maragnonensis (cited as Bras.)
    Lusitania: Assistencia et Provincia (cited as Lus.)
Biblioteca da Ajuda, Lisbon
Vatican Film Library, St. Louis (cited as VFL)
    Fondo Gesuitico

PUBLISHED PRIMARY SOURCES

Abbeville, Claude d'. *L'Arrivee des peres capucins, et la conversion des sauvages à nostre saincte foi.* Paris, 1613.
———. *Histoire de la mission des peres capucins en l'Isle de Maragnan et terres circonvoisines.* Paris, 1614.
Amado, Janaína, and Luiz Carlos Figueiredo. *Brasil 1500: Quarenta documentos.* Brasilia: Editora Universidade de Brasília, São Paulo: Imprensa Oficial, 2001.
Anchieta, José de. *Arte de gramática da língua mais usada na costa do Brasil.* 1595. Facsimile ed. Rio de Janeiro: Biblioteca Nacional, 1933.
———. *Cartas: Correspondência ativa e passiva.* São Paulo: Edições Loyola, 1984.

————. *Cartas: Informações, fragmentos históricos e sermões.* Rio de Janeiro: Civilização Brasileira, 1933. Reprint, Belo Horizonte: Editora Itatiaia; São Paulo: Editora da Universidade de São Paulo, 1988.

————. *De gestis Mendi de Saa.* Trans. Armando Cardoso. Rio de Janeiro: Arquivo Nacional, 1958.

————. *Diálogo da fé: Texto tupi e português.* 2 vols. São Paulo: Edições Loyola, 1988.

————. *Doutrina Cristã.* 2 vols. São Paulo: Edições Loyola, 1993.

————. *Lírica portuguesa e tupi.* São Paulo: Edições Loyola, 1984.

————. *Sermões.* São Paulo: Edições Loyola, 1987.

————. *Teatro de Anchieta.* São Paulo: Edições Loyola, 1977.

————. *Textos históricos.* São Paulo: Edições Loyola, 1989.

————. *Vocabulário na língua brasílica.* São Paulo: Departamento de Cultura, 1938.

Anghiera, Pietro Martire d'. *Libretto de tutta la navigatione de re Spagna de le isole et terreni novamente trovati.* Venice, 1504.

————. "Libretto de tutta la navigatione de re Spagna de le isole et terreni novamente trovati." Transcription with notes by Luciano Formisano. Translated into English by Theodore J. Cachey, Jr. Typescript.

————. *Questa e una opera necessaria a tutti li navigate chi hano in diverse parte del mondo.* Venice, 1490.

————. *Questa e una opera necessaria a tutti li naviga[n]ti (1490) Alvise Cà da Mosto. Together with Libretto de tutta la navigatione de Re de Spagna (1504).* Facsimile ed. Introduction by Felipe Fernández-Armesto. Delmar, NY: John Carter Brown Library and Scholars' Facsimiles and Reprints, 1992.

Annuae litterae Societatis Iesu anni MDLXXXI ad patres et fratres eiusdem societatis. Rome, 1583.

Annuae litterae Societatis Iesu anni MDLXXXIII ad patres et fratres eiusdem societatis. Rome, 1585.

Annuae litterae Societatis Iesu anni MDLXXXIV ad patres et fratres eiusdem societatis. Rome, 1586.

Annuae litterae Societatis Iesu anni MDLXXXV ad patres et fratres eiusdem societatis. Rome, 1587.

Anonymous Portolan Atlas known as the "Vallard Atlas." Dieppe, 1547. Digital Scriptorium Database, The Huntington Library. http://sunsite.berkeley.edu/Scriptorium/hehweb/HM29.html.

A nova gazeta da terra do Brasil (New zeutung ausz presillandt 1515). Trans. Clemente Brandenburger. São Paulo: Livraria Edanee, 1922.

Aquinas, St. Thomas. *The summa theologica.* Trans. Fathers of the English Dominican Province. New York: Benziger Brothers, 1947.

Avezac, M. d', ed. *Campagne du navire l'Espoir de Honfleur 1503–1505: Relation authentique du voyage du capitaine de Gonneville ès nouvelles terres des Indes.* Paris: Challamel Aîne, Libraire-Éditeur, 1869.

Ayrosa, Plinio, ed. *Vocabulário na língua brasílica* [1622]. São Paulo: Departamento de Cultura, 1938.

Baião, António. "Correspondência inédita do Inquisidor Geral e Conselho Geral do Santo Ofício para o primeiro visitador da inquisição no Brasil." *Brasília* (Coimbra) 1 (1942): 543–551.

Barros, João de. *Asia de Joam de Barros dos fectos que os portugueses fizeram no descobrimento e conquista dos mares e terras do oriente.* Lisbon, 1552.

———. *Asia de Joam de Barros dos fectos que os portugueses fizeram no descobrimento e conquista dos mares e terras do oriente. Segunda Decada.* Lisbon, 1553.

Blake, John William, ed. *Europeans in West Africa, 1450–1560.* 2 vols. London: The Hakluyt Society, 1942.

Brandão, Ambrósio Fernandes. *Diálogos das grandezas do Brasil.* Rio de Janeiro: Coroa, Edições de Ouro, 1968.

———. *Dialogues of the Great Things of Brazil.* Trans. Frederick Holden Hall, William F. Harrison, and Dorothy Winters Welker. Albuquerque: University of New Mexico Press, 1986.

Brásio, António. *Monumenta missionaria africana: África ocidental (1342–1499).* Lisbon: Agência Geral do Ultramar, 1958.

Brito, Bernardo Gomes de. *História trágico-marítima em que se escrevem chronologicamente os naufragios que tiverão as naos de Portugal.* 3 vols. Lisbon, 1735–1750.

———. *História trágico-marítima.* [1735]. Rio de Janeiro: Lacerda Editores / Contraponto Editora, 1998.

Burns, E. Bradford. *A Documentary History of Brazil.* New York: Alfred A. Knopf, 1966.

Camões, Luís Vaz de. *The Lusíads.* Trans. Landeg White. Oxford: Oxford University Press, 1997.

Cardim, Fernão. "Enformacion de la provincia del Brasil para Nuestro Padre." In Mauro, *Le Brésil au XVIIe siècle: Documents inédits relatifs à l'Atlantique portugais,* 133–166.

———. *Tratados da terra e gente do Brasil.* Ed. Ana Maria de Azevedo. Lisbon: Comissão Nacional para as Comemorações dos Descobrimentos Portugueses, 1977.

Cartas avulsas, 1550–1568. Azpilcueta Navarro e outros. Rio de Janeiro: Oficina Industrial Graphica, 1931. Reprint, Belo Horizonte: Editora Itatiaia; São Paulo: Editora da Universidade de São Paulo, 1988.

Cartas de Duarte Coelho a El Rei. Facsimile and transcribed ed. Ed. José Antonio Gonsalves de Mello and Cleonir Xavier de Albuquerque. Recife: Imprensa Universitária, 1967.

Cartas d'el Rey escriptas aos s[enho]res Álvaro de Sousa e Gaspar de Sousa. Transcr. Deoclecio Leite de Macedo. Rio de Janeiro: Biblioteca Itamarati, 1989.

Chavero, Alfredo. *El lienzo de Tlaxcala.* Mexico City: Editorial Cosmos, 1979.

Copia der newen Zeytung aus Presillg Landt. Nuremberg: Hieronymus Holtzel, 1514.

Copy of a Letter of the King of Portugal Sent to the King of Castile Concerning the Voyage and Success of India. [Besicken Letter 1505]. Trans. Sergio J. Pacifici. Minneapolis: University of Minnesota Press, 1955.

[Cordeiro, Belchior, S.J.]. "Emformação dalgumas cousas do Brasil [Por Belchior Cordeiro, 1577]." Ed. and transcr. Serafim Leite. Academia Portuguesa da História, *Annais: II Série* 15 (1965): 176–201.

"Correspondencia de Diogo Botelho (Governador do estado do Brasil, 1602–1608)." *Revista do Instituto Histórico e Geográfico Brasileiro* 73, part 1 (1910): 1–258.

Cortés, Hernán. *Cartas y documentos*. Mexico City: Editorial Porrúa, 1963.

Cortesão, Armando. *Cartografia portuguesa antiga*. Lisbon: Comissão Executiva das Comemorações do Quinto Centenário da Morte do Infante D. Henrique, 1960.

Cortesão, Armando, and Avelino Teixeira da Mota. *Portugaliae monumenta cartographica*. 6 vols. Lisbon: Comissão Executiva das Comemorações do Quinto Centenário da Morte do Infante D. Henrique, 1960.

Cortesão, Jaime. *Os descobrimentos portugueses*. 5 vols. Lisbon: Livros Horizonte, 1975.

Costa, F. A. Pereira da. *Anais Pernambucanos*. Vol. 1, *1493–1590*. Recife: Arquivo Público Estadual, 1952.

Cunha, Euclides da. *Rebellion in the Backlands*. Trans. Samuel Putnam. Chicago: University of Chicago Press, 1944.

———. *Os sertões: Campanha de Canudos*. Rio de Janeiro: Laemmert, 1902.

"Data de sesmaria de Itaparica a D. Antonio de Athaide, Conde de Castanheira por Thomé de Sousa, 1552." *Anais do Arquivo Público da Bahia* 34 (1957): 87–88.

Davenport, Frances Gardiner. *European Treaties Bearing on the History of the United States and Its Dependencies to 1648*. Washington, D.C.: Carnegie Institution of Washington, 1917.

De Bry. Theodor. *Americae tertia pars*. Frankfurt, 1592.

"Déclaration du vegage du capitaine Gonneville et ses compagnons ès Indes." In Avezac, *Campagne du navire l'Espoir de Honfleur*, 87–110.

Díaz del Castillo, Bernal. *Historia verdadera de la conquista de la Nueva España*. 4th ed. Mexico City: Editorial Porrúa, 1966.

Documentos relativos a Mem de Sá, Governador Geral do Brasil. Rio de Janeiro: Biblioteca Nacional, 1906.

Everson, Stephen, ed. *The Politics/Aristotle*. Cambridge: Cambridge University Press, 1988.

Fonseca, Antonio José Victoriano Borges da. *Nobiliarchia pernambucana*. 2 vols. *Annaes da Bibliotheca Nacional do Rio de Janeiro* 47 (1925) and 48 (1926).

Fracanzano da Montalboddo. *Paesi nuovamente retrovati. Et novo mondo da Alberico Vesputio Florentino intitulato*. Venice, 1507.

Gandavo, Pero de Magalhães. *Historia da provincia Sãcta Cruᶻ a qu' vulgarme[n]te' chamamos Brasil*. Lisbon, 1576.

———. *História da província Santa Cruᶻ a que vulgarmente chamamos Brasil*. Facsimile ed. Lisbon: Biblioteca Nacional, 1984.

————. *The Histories of Brazil*. Trans. John B. Stetson. New York: The Cortés Society, 1922. Reprint, New York: Kraus Reprint, 1969.

————. *History of the Province of Santa Cruz*. Trans. John B. Stetson. In *The Histories of Brazil*. New York: The Cortés Society, 1922. Reprint, New York: Kraus Reprint, 1969.

————. "Treatise on the Land of Brazil." [*Tratado da terra do Brazil* (1574)]. Trans. John B. Stetson. In *The Histories of Brazil*. New York: The Cortés Society, 1922. Reprint, New York: Kraus Reprint, 1969.

Gaspar da Madre de Deus, Frei. *Memórias para a história da capitania de São Vicente*. [1797]. São Paulo: Editora da Universidade de São Paulo and Livraria Itatiaia, 1975.

Das Gebetbuch Kaiser Maximilians. Introduction by Hinrich Sieveking. Munich: Prestel, 1987.

Gonsalves de Mello, José Antonio, and Cleonir Xavier de Albuquerque. *Cartas de Duarte Coelho a El Rei*. Recife: Imprensa Universitária, 1967.

Greenlee, William Brooks. *The Voyage of Pedro Alvares Cabral to Brazil and India, from contemporary documents and narratives*. London: Printed for the Hakluyt Society, 1938.

Guaman Poma [de Ayala]. *El primer nueva corónica y buen gobierno*. [1615]. Royal Library of Denmark online facsimile edition. http://www.kb.dk/elib/mss/poma.

————. *El primer nueva corónica y buen gobierno*. Ed. John V. Murra and Rolena Adorno. Mexico City: Siglo Veintiuno, 1980.

Guerreiro, Fernão. *Relação anual das coisas que fizeram os padres da Companhia de Jesus nas suas missões* . . . . [1603–1611]. 3 vols. Coimbra: Imprensa da Universidade, 1930–1942.

Hakluyt, Richard. *The Principal Navigations: Voyages Traffiques and Discoveries of the English Nation . . . of these 1600 years*. 10 vols. London: J. M. Dent and Sons, 1927–1928.

História da colonização portuguesa do Brasil. Edição monumental comemorativa do primeiro centenário da independência do Brasil. 3 vols. Ed. Carlos Malheiro Dias, Ernesto de Vasconcelos, Roque Gameiro. Porto: Litografia Nacional, 1921–1924.

Instituto de Açúcar e do Álcool. *Documentos para a história do açúcar*. Vol. 1, *Legislação, 1534–1596*. Rio de Janeiro: Serviço Especial de Documentação Histórica, 1954.

————. *Documentos para a história do açúcar*. Vol. 3, *Engenho Sergipe do Conde, espólio de Mem de Sá, 1569–1579*. Rio de Janeiro: Serviço Especial de Documentação Histórica, 1963.

"Instrumento dos serviços de Mem de Sá [1560]." In *Documentos relativos a Mem de Sá*, 1–90.

Jaboatão, Fr. Antonio de S. Maria. *Catalogo genealogico das principais famílias que procederam de Albuquerques e Cavalcantes em Pernambuco e Caramurús na Bahia*.

[1768]. Rio de Janeiro, 1889. Reprint, Salvador: Imprensa Oficial da Bahia, 1950.

Jarric, Pierre du. *Histoire des choses plus memorables advenues tant eʒ Indes Orientales, que autre païs de la descouverte des Portugais.* 3 vols. Bordeau, 1608–1614.

Kupčík, Ivan. *Münchner Portolankarten "Kunstmann I–XIII" und ʒehn weitere Portolankarten.* Munich and Berlin: Deutscher Kunstverlag, 2000.

Laborie, Claude. *La mission jésuite du Brésil: Lettres et autres documents (1549–1570).* Paris: Éditions Chandeigne, 1998.

Las Casas, Bartolomé de. *Brevíssima relación de la destrucción de las Indias.* [1552]. Mexico City: Secretaría de Educación Pública, 1945.

———. *The Devastation of the Indies: A Brief Account.* Trans. Herma Briffault. Baltimore: Johns Hopkins University Press, 1992.

———. *Historia de las Indias.* 3 vols. Mexico City: Fondo de Cultura Económica, 1951.

Lauderdale Graham, Sandra. "Confessing to the Holy Office of the Inquisition, Bahia, Brazil (1592, 1618)." In Mills, Taylor, and Lauderdale Graham, *Colonial Latin America,* 234–245.

———. "The Jesuit and the Bishop, Bahia, Brazil (1552–1553)." In Mills, Taylor, and Lauderdale Graham, *Colonial Latin America,* 93–103.

Leite, Bertha. "Dom Pedro Fernandes Sardinha." *Instituto Histórico e Geográfico Brasileiro, IV Congresso de História Nacional, Anais* 7 (1949): 543.

Leite, Serafim, S.J. *Monumenta brasiliae.* 5 vols. Rome: Monumenta Historica Societatis Iesu, 1956.

Leme, Luiz Gonzaga da Silva. *Genealogia paulistana.* 9 vols. São Paulo: Duprat, 1903–1905.

Léry, Jean de. *Histoire d'un voyage fait en la terre du Bresil, autrement dite Amerique.* La Rochelle, 1578.

———. *Histoire d'un voyage faict en la terre du Brésil, autrement dite Amerique.* Geneva, 1594.

———. *Histoire d'un voyage faict en la terre du Brésil (1578).* 2nd ed., 1580. Ed. Frank Lestringant. Paris: Librairie Générale Française, 1994.

———. *History of a Voyage to the Land of Braʒil, otherwise called America.* Trans. Janet Whatley. Berkeley: University of California Press, 1992.

Lescarbot, Marc. *Histoire de la Novvelle-France.* Paris: Adrian Perier, 1618. Reprint, Marc Lescarbot. *The History of New France.* 3 vols; 1: 210–331. Toronto: The Champlain Society, 1907.

Ley, Charles David. *Portuguese Voyages: 1498–1663.* London: J. M. Dent, 1947.

Lisboa, Frei Cristovão de. *História dos animaes e árvores do Maranhão.* [1627]. Ed. Jaime Walter et al. Lisbon: Comissão Nacional para as Comemorações dos Descobrimentos Portugueses, 2000.

Lukács, Ladislaus, ed. *Monumenta paedagogica Societatis Iesu.* Vol. 105. Rome: Monumenta Historica Societatis Iesu, 1965.

Manzano Manzano, Juan. *Los Pinzones y el descubrimiento de América.* Vol. 3, *Apéndice documental.* Madrid: Ediciones de Cultura Hispánica, 1988.

Mauro, Frédéric, ed. *Le Brésil au XVIIe siècle: Documents inédits relatifs à l'Atlantique portugais.* Coimbra, 1961.

Mills, Kenneth, William B. Taylor, and Sandra Lauderdale Graham, eds. *Colonial Latin America: A Documentary History.* Wilmington, Del.: Scholarly Resources, 2002.

Moreno, Diogo de Campos. *Livro que dá razão do estado do Brasil.* [1612]. Recife: Arquivo Público Estadual, 1955.

Navarrete, Martín Fernández de. *Colección de los viages y descubrimientos que hicieron por mar los españoles . . ..* [1825–1837]. 5 vols. Buenos Aires: Editorial Guaranía, 1946.

Nóbrega, Manoel da. *Cartas do Brasil, 1549–1560.* Rio de Janeiro, 1931. Reprint, Belo Horizonte: Editora Itatiaia; São Paulo: Editora da Universidade de São Paulo, 1988.

———. "Informação das terras do Brasil." [1549]. In Leite, *Monumenta brasiliae,* 1:145–154.

"Notícias antigas do Brasil, 1531–1551." *Anais da Biblioteca Nacional do Rio de Janeiro* 58 (1935): 9–28.

Oliveira, Fernando. *Arte da guerra do mar.* [1555]. Lisbon: Arquivo Histórico da Marinha, 1937.

Ordenações Manuelinas. Online edition. http://www.uc.pt/ihti/proj/manuelinas/ORDEMANU.htm.

Oviedo y Valdés, Gonzalo Fernández de. *Historia general y natural de las Indias.* [1535]. Biblioteca de Autores Españoles. 4 vols. Madrid: Ediciones Atlas, 1959.

Parry, J. H., and Robert G. Keith, eds. *New Iberian World.* 5 vols. New York: Times Books, 1984.

Pereira, Paulo Roberto. *Os três únicos testemunhos do descobrimento do Brasil: Carta de Pero Vaz de Caminha, carta de Mestre João Faras, relação do piloto anônimo.* 2nd ed. Rio de Janeiro: Lacerda Editores, 1999.

Pigafetta, Antonio. *Magellan's Voyage: A Narrative Account of the First Circumnavigation.* 2 vols. Vol. 1, ed. and trans. R. A. Skelton. New Haven: Yale University Press, 1969.

———. *Navegation et descouvrement de la Inde Superieure et isles de Malucques.* [1519]. Vol. 2, facsimile ed. New Haven: Yale University Press, 1969.

Pina, Rui de. *Crónicas de Rui de Pina.* Ed. M. Lopes de Almeida. Porto: Lello & Irmão, 1977.

Pizarro, Pedro. *Relación del descubrimiento y conquista de los reinos del Perú.* [1561]. 2nd ed. Ed. Guillermo Lohmann Villena. Lima: Pontificia Universidad Católica del Perú, 1986.

Primeira visitação do Santo Ofício às partes do Brasil pelo Licenciado Heitor Furtado de Mendonça: Confissões da Bahia 1591–1592. Prefácio de Capistrano de Abreu. Rio de Janeiro: F. Briguiet, 1935.

Primeira visitação do Santo Ofício às partes do Brasil pelo Licenciado Heitor Furtado de Mendonça: Confissões da Bahia 1591–1592. Ed. Ronaldo Vainfas. São Paulo: Companhia das Letras, 1997.

Primeira visitação do Santo Ofício às partes do Brasil pelo Licenciado Heitor Furtado de Mendonça: Denunciações da Bahia 1591–1593. Introdução de Capistrano de Abreu. São Paulo: Paulo Prado, 1925.

Primeira visitação do Santo Ofício às Partes do Brasil: Denunciações e Confissões de Pernambuco 1593–1595. Estudo introductório de José Antônio Gonsalves de Mello. Recife: FUNDARPE, 1984.

Ptolemaeus, Claudius. *Geographia.* Strassburg, 1513.

Purchas, Samuel. *Hakluytus Posthumus or Purchas His Pilgrimes.* Vol. 16. Glasgow: James MacLehose and Sons, 1906.

"Relação do piloto anônimo." Ed. Jean Marcel C. Franca. Folha Online—Brasil 500, http://wwwl.uol.com.br/fol/brasil500/histdescobl.htm.

"Relatório de escambo." [Relación de lo recebido y pagado por Enrique Montes en la isla de Santa Catarina, de 1527]. Trans. Jean François Cleaver. http://www.historiadobrasil.com.br/viagem/docso1.htm.

Rodrigues, Pero. *Vida do Padre José de Anchieta da Companhia de Jesus.* [1617]. 3rd ed. São Paulo: Edições Loyola, 1981.

Rojas, Fernando de. *The Celestina: A Novel in Dialogue.* Trans. Lesley Byrd Simpson. Berkeley: University of California Press, 1955.

———. *Celestina: Tragicomedia de Calisto y Melibea.* 2 vols. Ed. Miguel Marciales. Urbana: University of Illinois Press, 1985.

[Rotz, Jean]. *The Maps and Text of the Bokeof Idrography Presented by Jean Rotz to Henry VIII.* Facsimile ed. Ed. Helen Wallis. Oxford: Oxford University Press, 1981; printed for presentation to the members of the Roxburghe Club.

Rumeu de Armas, Antonio. "Una carta inédita del Apostol del Brasil, Beato José de Anchieta al Rey Felipe II: La expedición de Diego Flores de Valdes al Magallanes." *Hispania* 45, no. 159 (1985): 5–32.

Sahagún, Bernardino de. *História general de las cosas de Nueva España Códice florentino.* [*Codex Florentino*]. Facsimile ed. 3 vols. Mexico City: Secretaría de Gobernacíon, 1979.

Salvador, Frei Vicente do. *História do Brasil: 1500–1627.* [1627]. 4th ed. Ed. Capistrano de Abreu and Rodolfo Garcia. São Paulo: Edições Melhoramentos, 1954.

Santa Cruz, Alonso de. *Islario general de todas las islas del mundo.* 2 vols. Ed. Antonio Blázquez. Madrid: Imprenta del Patronato de Huérfanos de Intendencia e Intervención Militares, 1918.

Sanuto, Marino. *I diarii di Marino Sanuto.* Vol. 4, Venice, 1879–1903. Reprint, Bologna: Forni Editore, 1969–1970.

Schmidel, Ulrich. *Derrotero y viaje al Río de la Plata y Paraguay.* [1567]. Ed. Roberto Quevedo. Asunción: Biblioteca Paraguaya, 1983.

————. *Relatos de la conquista del Río de la Plata y Paraguay, 1534–1554.* Madrid: Alianza Editorial, 1986.

————. *Wahrhafftige historien einer wunderbaren Schiffart.* Graz, Austria: Akademische Druck- u. Verlagsanstalt, 1962.

Schubert, Guilherme. "Os autos de Anchieta." *Revista do Instituto Histórico e Geográfico Brasileiro* 147, no. 351 (1986): 371–390.

Segunda visitação do Santo Ofício às partes do Brasil: Denunciações da Bahia (1618). Introdução de Rodolfo Garcia. *Anais da Biblioteca National do Rio de Janeiro* 49 (1927).

Segunda visitação do Santo Ofício às partes do Brasil pelo inquisidor e visitador o licenciado Marcos Teixeira: Livro das Confissões e Ratificações da Bahia 1618–1620. Anais do Museu Paulista 17 (1963).

Sousa, Gabriel Soares de. *Tratado descritivo do Brasil em 1587.* 4th ed. São Paulo: Companhia Editora Nacional, 1971.

Sousa, Pero Lopes de. *Diário da navegação de Pero Lopes de Sousa 1530–1532.* 2 vols. Rio de Janeiro: Commissão Brasileira dos Centenários Portugueses, 1940.

Staden, Hans. *Hans Staden: The True History of His Captivity, 1557.* Trans. Malcolm Letts. New York: Robert M. McBride, 1929.

————. *Warachtige historie ende beschrivinge eens lants in America ghelegen.* Antwerp, 1558.

————. *Warhaftige Historia und Beschreibung eyner Landtschafft der wilden nacketen grimmigen Menschenfresser Leuthen in der Newenwelt America gelegen.* Marburg, 1557.

Tanner, Mathias. *Societatis Jesu. Americana.* Prague: Typis Universitatis Carolo-Ferdinandeae, 1675.

[Teixeira, Luís]. *Roteiro de todos os sinais, conhecimentos, fundos, baixos, alturas e derrotas que há na costa do Brasil desde o cabo de Santo Agostinho até ao estreito de Fernão de Magalhães.* [1582–1585]. Facsimile ed. Ed. Melba Ferreira da Costa. Lisbon: Tagol, 1988.

Thevet, F. André. *Le Brésil d'André Thevet: Les singularités de la France Antarctique (1557).* Ed. Frank Lestringant. Paris: Éditions Chandeigne, 1997.

————. *The New Found World, or Antarctike.* Trans. Thomas Hacket. London, 1568.

————. *Les singularitez de la France Antarctique, autrement nommée Amerique.* Paris, 1558.

El Tratado de Tordesillas y su proyección. 2 vols. Valladolid: Seminario de Historia de America, Universidad de Valladolid, 1973.

United Kingdom. Public Record Office. *Calendar of State Papers, Domestic Series, of the Reigns of Edward VI, Mary, Elizabeth* (1547–[1625]). London: Longman, Brown, Green, Longmans & Roberts, 1856–1872.

[Vallard, Nicholas]. *Atlas.* Dieppe, 1547.

Vasconcellos, Jorge Ferreira de. *Comédia Eufrosina.* [1561]. Lisbon: Imprensa Nacional de Lisboa, 1919.

Vasconcellos, Simão de. *Chronica da Companhia de Jesu do estado do Brasil.* Vol. 1, *Da entrada da Companhia de Jesu nas partes do Brasil.* Lisbon, 1663.

————. *Vida do Veneravel Padre Joseph de Anchieta da Companhia de Jesu.* Lisbon, 1672.

[Velho, Álvaro]. *O descobrimento das Índias: O diário da viagem de Vasco da Gama.* Ed. Eduardo Bueno. Rio de Janeiro: Objectiva, 1998.

————. *A Journal of the First Voyage of Vasco da Gama, 1497–1499.* Trans. E. G. Ravenstein. London: Hakluyt Society, 1898.

————. *Roteiro da viagem que em descobrimento da India pelo cabo da boa esperança feʒ Dom Vasco da Gama em 1497.* Ed. Diogo Kopke and Antonio da Costa Paiva. Porto: Typographia Commercial Portuense, 1838.

Vespucci, Amerigo. *Letters from a New World: Amerigo Vespucci's Discovery of America.* Ed. and trans. Luciano Formisano. New York: Marsilio, 1992.

————. *Mundus novus.* Rome, 1504.

————. *Mundus novus.* Venice, 1504.

————. *Van der nieuwer werelt oft landtscap nieuwelicx gheou[n]den.* [*Mundus novus*]. Antwerp, 1507 or 1508.

————. *Von der neü gefunden Region.* [*Mundus novus*]. Basel, 1505.

Waldseemüller, Martim. *Cosmographiae introductio cum quibusdam geometriae ac astronomiae principiis ad eam rem necessariis: Insuper Quatuor Americi Vespucii navigationes.* St. Die, 1507.

————. *Orbis typus universalis iuxta hydrographorum traditionem.* Nuremburg, circa 1513.

Wicki, Josef, S.J., ed. *Monumenta histórica Societatis Iesu: Documenta indica.* Vol. 1 (1540–1549); Vol. 2 (1550–1553). Rome: Monumenta Historica Societatis Iesu, 1948–1950.

Zurara, Eanes Gomes de. *Crónica dos feitos notáveis que se passaram na conquista da Guiné por mandado do Infante D. Henrique.* [1453]. 2 vols. Lisbon: Academia Portuguesa da História, 1978–1981.

SECONDARY SOURCES

Accioli de Cerqueira e Silva, Ignacio de. *Memorias históricas e políticas da província da Bahia.* [1835–1852]. 6 vols. Annotated by Braz do Amaral. Bahia: Impresa Oficial do Estado, 1919.

Adorno, Rolena. "Don Felipe Guaman Poma de Ayala: Author and Prince." In Adorno et al., *Guaman Poma de Ayala,* 32–45.

————. *Guaman Poma: Writing and Resistance in Colonial Peru.* Austin: University of Texas Press, 1986.

————. "Images of *Indios Ladinos* in Early Colonial Peru." In Andrien and Adorno, *Transatlantic Encounters*, 232–270.

Adorno, Rolena, et al., eds. *Guaman Poma de Ayala: The Colonial Art of an Andean Author.* New York: Americas Society/Art Gallery, 1992.

Alberro, Solange. *Inquisición y sociedad en México, 1571–1700.* Mexico City: Fondo de Cultura Económica, 1988.

Albert, Bruce, and Alcida Rita Ramos, eds. *Pacificando o branco: Cosmologias do contato no Norte-Amazônico.* São Paulo: Editora UNESP and Imprensa Oficial do Estado, 2002.

Albuquerque, Luís de, and J. Lopes Tavares. "Algumas observações sobre o planisfério 'Cantino' (1502)." In *Agrupamento de Estudos de Cartografia Antiga XXI Secção de Coimbra.* Coimbra: Junta de Investigações do Ultramar, 1967. (*Separata da Revista do Centro de Estudos Geográficos* 3, no. 22–23).

Alchon, Suzanne Austin. *A Pest in the Land: New World Epidemics in a Global Perspective.* Albuquerque: University of New Mexico Press, 2003.

Alden, Dauril. "Changing Jesuit Perceptions of the Brasis during the Sixteenth Century." *Journal of World History* 3 (1992): 205–218.

————. *The Making of an Enterprise: The Society of Jesus in Portugal, Its Empire, and Beyond: 1540–1750.* Stanford: Stanford University Press, 1996.

————. "Serafim Leite, S.J., Premier Historian of Colonial Brazil: An Overdue Appreciation." In *Jesuit Encounters in the New World: Jesuit Chroniclers, Geographers, Educators and Missionaries in the Americas, 1549–1767,* ed. Joseph A. Gagliano and Charles E. Ronan, 21–35. Rome: Institutum Historicum S.I., 1997.

Alden, Dauril, and Joseph C. Miller. "Out of Africa: The Slave Trade and the Transmission of Smallpox to Brazil, 1560–1831." *Journal of Interdisciplinary History* 18 (1987): 195–224.

Alegria, Maria Fernanda, João Carlos Garcia, and Francesc Relaño. "Cartografia e viagens." In Bethencourt and Chaudhuri, *História da expansão portuguesa,* 1: 38–39.

Alencastro, Luiz Felipe de. *O trato dos viventes: Formação do Brasil no Atlântico Sul.* São Paulo: Companhia das Letras, 2000.

Alves Filho, Ivan. *Memorial dos Palmares.* Rio de Janeiro: Xenon Editora, 1982.

Amado, Janaína. "Mythic Origins: Caramuru and the Founding of Brazil." *Hispanic American Historical Review* 80 (2000): 783–811.

————. "La séduction de l'autre: Premiers intermédiares de l'empire portugais." In *Naissance du Brésil modern, 1500–1800,* ed. Katia de Queiros Mattoso et al., 237–248. Paris: Presses de l'Université de Paris-Sorbonne, 1988.

Andrien, Kenneth J., and Rolena Adorno, eds. *Transatlantic Encounters: Europeans and Andeans in the Sixteenth Century.* Berkeley: University of California Press, 1991.

Araújo, Alexandre Herculano de Carvalho e. *History of the Origin and Establishment of the Inquisition in Portugal.* Trans. John C. Branner. Stanford, 1926. Reprint, New York: Ktav Publishing House, 1972.

Arens, William. *The Man-Eating Myth: Anthropology and Anthropophagy.* New York: Oxford University Press, 1979.

Armstrong, Wayne P. "Logwood and Brazilwood: Trees That Spawned 2 Nations." *Pacific Horticulture* 53 (1992): 38–43.

Aufderheide, Patricia. "True Confessions: The Inquisition and Social Attitudes in Brazil at the Turn of the Seventeenth Century." *Luso Brazilian Review* 10 (1972): 208–240.

Axtell, James. *Imagining the Other: First Encounters in North America.* Essays on the Columbian Encounter, series ed. Carla Rahn Phillips and David J. Weber. Washington, D.C.: American Historical Association, 1991.

Baptista, José Luiz. *Historia das entradas: Determinação das áreas que exploraram.* Rio de Janeiro: Livraria J. Leite, n.d.

Barreto, João Franco. *História da Guiné, 1418–1918.* Lisbon: J. Barreto, 1938.

Barros, Maria Cândida D. M. "The Office of *Lingua*: A Portrait of the Religious Tupi Interpreter in Brazil in the Sixteenth Century." *Itinerario: European Journal of Overseas History* [Leiden] 25, no. 2 (2001): 110–140.

Bastide, Roger. *The African Religions of Brazil: Toward a Sociology of the Interpenetration of Civilizations.* Trans. Helen Sebba. Baltimore: Johns Hopkins University Press, 1978.

Bellini, Lígia. *A coisa obscura: Mulher, sodomia e inquisição no Brasil colonial.* São Paulo: Brasiliense, 1989.

Bellotto, Heloísa Liberalli. "Política indigenista no Brasil colonial (1570–1757)." *Revista do Instituto de Estudos Brasileiros* 29 (1988): 49–60.

Bennassar, Bartolomé, and Richard Marin. *Histoire du Brésil, 1500–2000.* Paris: Fayard, 2000.

Bethell, Leslie, ed. *Colonial Brazil.* Cambridge: Cambridge University Press, 1987.

Bethencourt, Francisco. "O contacto entre povos e civilizações." In Bethencourt and Chaudhuri, *História da expansão portuguesa,* 1:88–115.

———. *O imaginario da magia: Feiticeiras, saludadores e nigromantes no século XVI.* Lisbon: Centro de Estudos de História e Cultura Portuguesa, 1987.

———. "Portugal: A Scrupulous Inquisition." In *Early Modern European Witchcraft: Centres and Peripheries,* ed. Bengt Ankarloo and Gustav Henningsen, 403–422. Oxford: Clarendon Press, 1990.

Bethencourt, Francisco, and Kirti Chaudhuri, eds. *História da expansão portuguesa.* Vol. 1, *A formação do império (1415–1570).* Lisbon: Círculo de Leitores, 1998.

Birmingham, David. *Trade and Conflict in Angola: The Mbundu and Their Neighbours under the Influence of the Portuguese, 1483–1790.* Oxford: Clarendon Press, 1966.

Black, John W. *West Africa: Quest for God and Gold, 1454–1578.* London: Curzon Press; Totowa, N.J.: Rowman and Littlefield, 1977.

Blackburn, Robin. *The Making of New World Slavery: From the Baroque to the Modern, 1492–1800.* London: Verso, 1997.

———. "The Old World Background to European Colonial Slavery." *The William and Mary Quarterly,* 3rd ser., 54 (1997): 65–102.

Boone, Elizabeth Hill. *Stories in Red and Black: Pictorial Histories of the Aztec and Mixtec.* Austin: University of Texas Press, 2000.

Boschi, Caio Cesar. "As visitas diocesanas e a Inquisição na colonia." *Revista Brasileira de História* 14, no. 7 (1987): 151–184.

Bovill, Edward William. *The Golden Trade of the Moors: West African Kingdoms in the Fourteenth Century.* 2nd ed. Princeton: Markus Wiener Publishers, 1995.

Boxer, Charles Ralph. *The Church Militant and Iberian Expansion, 1440–1770.* Baltimore: Johns Hopkins University Press, 1978.

———. *João de Barros: Portuguese Humanist and Historian of Asia.* New Delhi: Concept Publishing, 1981.

Bradley, Titus, and Department of Microbiology and Immuniology, University of Leicester. "Biology of Plasmodium Parasites and Anopheles Mosquitos." 1996. http://www-micro.msb.le.ac.uk/224/Bradley/Biology.html.

Braude, Benjamin. "The Sons of Noah and the Construction of Ethnic and Geographical Identities in the Medieval and Early Modern Periods." *The William and Mary Quarterly*, 3rd ser., 54 (1997): 103–142.

Brito, Rossana G. *A saga de Pero do Campo Tourinho.* Petropolis, Rio de Janeiro: Vozes, 2000.

Brooks, George E. *Landlords and Strangers: Ecology, Society, and Trade in Western Africa, 1000–1630.* Boulder: Westview Press, 1993.

Burke, Peter. "Early Modern Venice as a Center of Information and Communication." In *Venice Reconsidered: The History and Civilization of an Italian City-State, 1297–1797*, ed. John Martin and Dennis Romano, 389–419. Baltimore: Johns Hopkins University Press, 2000.

Calasans, José. *Fernão Cabral de Ataíde e a santidade de Jaguaripe.* Bahia: S. A. Artes Gráficas, 1952.

———. *A Santidade de Jaguaripe.* Bahia, 1952.

Calmon, Pedro. *Historia da fundação da Bahia.* Bahia: Secretaria de Educação e Saúde, 1949.

———. *História do Brasil.* Vol. 1, *Século XVI: As origens.* Rio de Janeiro: Livraria José Olympio Editora, 1959.

Campos, João da Silva. *Crônica da capitania de São Jorge dos Ilhéus.* Rio de Janeiro: Ministério da Educação e Cultura, Conselho Federal de Cultura, 1981.

Carneiro, Edison. *A cidade do Salvador (1549): Uma reconstituição histórica.* 2nd ed. Rio de Janeiro: Civilização Brasileira, 1980.

Casanovas, C. F. de Freitas. *Provérbios e frases proverbiais do século XVI.* Brasília: Ministério da Educação e Cultura, Instituto Nacional do Livro, 1973.

Castañeda Delgado, Paulino, Pilar Hernández Aparicio, and René Millar Carvacho. *La Inquisición de Lima.* 3 vols. Madrid: Deimos, 1989–1998.

Castelnau-L'Estoile, Charlotte de. *Les ouvriers d'une vigne stérile: Les jésuites et la conversion des Indiens au Brésil, 1580–1620.* Lisbon and Paris: Fundação Calouste Gulbenkian and Commission Nationale pour les Commémorations des Découvertes Portugaises, 2000.

Céard, Jean, and Jean-Claude Margolin. *Voyager à la Renaissance*. Paris: Éditions Maisonneuve et Larose, 1987.

Chiappelli, Fredi, ed. *First Images of America: The Impact of the New World on the Old*. 2 vols. Berkeley: University of California Press, 1976.

Clastres, Hélène. *The Land-without-Evil: Tupí-Guaraní Prophetism*. Trans. Jacqueline Grenez Brovender. Urbana: University of Illinois Press, 1995.

Coates, Timothy Joel. *Convicts and Orphans: Forced and State-Sponsored Colonizers in the Portuguese Empire, 1550–1755*. Stanford: Stanford University Press, 2001.

———. "Exiles and Orphans: Forced and State-Sponsored Colonizers in the Portuguese Empire, 1550–1720." Ph.D. diss., University of Minnesota, 1993.

Cohen, Thomas M. *The Fire of Tongues: António Vieira and the Missionary Church in Brazil and Portugal*. Stanford: Stanford University Press, 1998.

Cohn, Norman. *The Pursuit of the Millennium: Revolutionary Millenarians and Mystical Anarchists of the Middle Ages*. 2nd ed. Oxford: Oxford University Press, 1970.

Cohn, Samuel K., Jr. "The Black Death: End of a Paradigm." *American Historical Review* 107 (2002): 703–738.

Colin, Suzi. "Woodcutters and Cannibals: Brazilian Indians as Seen on Early Maps." In Wolff, *America: Early Maps of the New World*, 175–181.

Conklin, Beth A. *Consuming Grief: Compassionate Cannibalism in an Amazonian Society*. Austin: University of Texas Press, 2001.

Cook, Noble David. *Born to Die: Disease and New World Conquest, 1492–1650*. Cambridge: Cambridge University Press, 1998.

———. *Demographic Collapse: Indian Peru, 1520–1620*. Cambridge: Cambridge University Press, 1981.

———. "Sickness, Starvation, and Death in Early Hispaniola." *Journal of Interdisciplinary History* 32 (2002): 349–386.

Cook, Noble David, and W. George Lovell, eds. *Secret Judgments of God: Old World Disease in Colonial Spanish America*. Norman: University of Oklahoma Press, 1991.

Cooper, Donald B., and Kenneth F. Kiple. "Yellow Fever." In Kiple, *The Cambridge World History of Human Disease*, 1100–1107.

Costa, Emilia Viotti da. "The Portuguese-African Slave Trade: A Lesson in Colonialism." *Latin American Perspectives* 12 (1985): 41–61.

Couto, Jorge. "O achamento da terra de Vera Cruz." *Camões: Revista de Letras e Culturas Lusófonas* 8 (January–March 2000). http://www.instituto-camoes.pt/revista/revista8.htm.

———. *A construção do Brasil*. Lisbon: Cosmos, 1997.

———. "A contribuição dos 'lançados' para os descobrimentos." *Vértice* 2, no. 9 (1988): 31–34.

———. "Pêro da Covilhã." In Medina, *Os descobrimentos*, 185–192.

Crosby, Alfred W. *The Columbian Exchange: Biological and Cultural Consequences of 1492*. Westport, Conn.: Greenwood Press, 1972.

———. *Ecological Imperialism: The Biological Expansion of Europe, 900–1900*. Cambridge: Cambridge University Press, 1986.

Cunha, Manuela Carneiro da. *História dos índios no Brasil*. São Paulo: Companhia das Letras, 1992.

Cunha, Manuela Carneiro da, and Eduardo B. Viveiros de Castro. "Vingança e temporalidade: Os Tupinamba." *Journal de la Société des Américanistes* 171 (1985): 191–208.

Curto, Diogo Ramada. "A língua e o império." In Bethencourt and Chaudhuri, *História da expansão portuguesa*, 1:414–433.

Cypess, Sandra Messinger. *La Malinche in Mexican Literature: From History to Myth*. Austin: University of Texas Press, 1991.

Daniels, Ted. *Millennialism: An International Bibliography*. New York: Garland Publishers, 1992.

Dean, Warren. "Indigenous Populations of the São Paulo–Rio de Janeiro Coast: Trade, Aldeamento, Slavery and Extinction." *Revista de História* 117 (1984): 3–26.

———. *With Broadax and Firebrand: The Destruction of the Brazilian Atlantic Forest*. Berkeley: University of California Press, 1995.

Dedieu, Jean Pierre. *L'Inquisition*. Paris: Cerf/Fides, 1987.

Delaforce, Angela, and James Yorke. *Portugal's Silver Service: A Victory Gift to the Duke of Wellington*. London: Victoria and Albert Museum, 1992.

Denevan, William M. *The Native Population of the Americas in 1492*. 2nd ed. Madison: University of Wisconsin Press, 1992.

———. "The Pristine Myth: The Landscape of the Americas in 1492." *Annals of the Association of American Geographers* 82, no. 3: (1992): 369–385.

Deswarte, Sylvie. *Il "Perfetto Cortegiano" Dom Miguel da Silva*. Rome: Bulzoni, Editore, 1989.

Diacon, Todd A. *Millenarian Vision, Capitalist Reality: Brazil's Contestado Rebellion, 1912–1916*. Durham: Duke University Press, 1991.

———. "Peasants, Prophets, and the Power of a Millenarian Vision in Twentieth-Century Brazil." *Comparative Studies in Society and History* 32 (1990): 488–514.

Diamond, Jared. *Guns, Germs, and Steel: The Fates of Human Societies*. New York: W. W. Norton, 1997.

Dobyns, Henry F. "Disease Transfer at Contact." *Annual Review of Anthropology* 22 (1993): 282–283.

Dominian, Helen G. *Apostle of Brazil: The Biography of Padre José de Anchieta, S.J. (1534–1597)*. New York: Exposition Press, 1958.

Doria, Francisco Antônio. "Adornos e Dorias em S. Paulo." Brazil-L Archives. Posted 12 April 2000. http://archiver.rootsweb.com/th/read/BRAZIL/2000-04.

Dunn, Frederick L. "Malaria." In Kiple, *The Cambridge World History of Human Disease*, 855–862.

Dunn, Ross E. *The Adventures of Ibn Battuta: A Muslim Traveler of the Fourteenth Century*. Berkeley: University of California Press, 1986.

Dyson, R. W., ed. and trans. *The City of God against the Pagans*. Cambridge: Cambridge University Press, 1998.

Elbl, Ivana. "The Volume of the Early Atlantic Slave Trade, 1450–1521." *The Journal of African History* 38 (1997): 31–75.

Elkiss, T. H. "On Service to the Crown—Portuguese Overseas Expansion: A Neglected Aspect." *Journal of the American Portuguese Society* 10 (1976): 44–53.

Evans, William McKee. "From the Land of Canaan to the Land of Guinea: The Strange Odyssey of the 'Sons of Ham.'" *American Historical Review* 85 (1980): 27–28.

Fage, J. D. "Upper and Lower Guinea." In *The Cambridge History of Africa*, Vol. 3, *From c. 1050 to c. 1600*, ed. Roland Oliver, 463–503 Cambridge: Cambridge University Press, 1977.

Farinha, António Dias. "Norte de África." In Bethencourt and Chaudhuri, *História da expansão portuguesa*, 1:118–136.

Fausto, Carlos. "Fragmentos de história e cultura Tupinambá: Da etnologia como instrumento crítico de conhecimento etno-histórico." In Cunha, *História dos índios no Brasil*, 383–396.

Fernandes, João Azevedo. *De cunhã a mameluca: A mulher tupinambá e o nascimento do Brasil.* João Pessoa: Editora Universitária, 2003.

Ferretti, Danilo J. Zioni, and Maria Helena Rolim Capelato. "João Ramalho e as origens da nação: Os paulistas na comemoração do IV centenário da descoberta do Brasil." *Tempo* (Rio de Janeiro) 8 (1999): 67–87.

Figueiredo, Ariosvaldo. *O negro e a violência do branco: O negro em Sergipe.* Rio de Janeiro: José Álvaro, 1977.

Flores, Moacyr. "Os autos-de-fe na Inquisição portuguesa." *Veritas* 22, no. 87 (1977): 272–278.

Fonseca, Luís Adão da. *O essencial sobre Bartolomeu Dias.* Lisbon: Imprensa Nacional–Casa da Moeda, 1987.

Forsyth, Donald W. "Three Cheers for Hans Staden: The Case for Brazilian Cannibalism." *Ethnohistory* 32 (1985): 17–36.

Freire, José Bessa Ribamar, and Maria Carlota Rosa, eds. *Línguas gerais: Política lingüística e catequese na América do Sul no período colonial.* Rio de Janeiro: Eduerj, 2003.

Freitas, Décio. *Palmares: A guerra dos escravos.* 4th ed. Rio de Janeiro: Edições Graal, 1982.

Funari, Pedro Paulo de Abreu. "A arqueologia de Palmares—sua contribuição para o conhecimento da história da cultura afro-americana." In Reis and Gomes, *Liberdade por um fio*, 26–51.

Furtado, Jorge, and Guel Arraes. *A invenção do Brasil.* Rio de Janeiro: Editora Objetiva, 2000.

Garfield, Robert. *A History of São Tomé Island, 1470–1655: The Key to Guinea.* San Francisco: Mellen Research University Press, 1992.

Goldenberg, David M. *The Curse of Ham: Race and Slavery in Early Judaism, Christianity, and Islam.* Princeton: Princeton University Press, 2003.

Grafton, Anthony. *New Worlds, Ancient Texts: The Power of Tradition and the Shock of Discovery*. Cambridge: Harvard University Press, 1992.

Graham, Laura. *Performing Dreams: Discourses of Immortality among the Xavante of Central Brazil*. Austin: University of Texas Press, 1995.

Greenblatt, Stephen. *Marvelous Possessions: The Wonder of the New World*. Chicago: University of Chicago Press, 1991.

————, ed. *New World Encounters*. Berkeley: University of California Press, 1993.

Guedes, Max Justo. "A cartografia portuguesa antiga." In *Tesouros da cartografia portuguesa*. Lisbon: Commisão Nacional para as Comemorações dos Descobrimentos Portugueses, 1997.

Guerra, Alvaro. *José de Anchieta (sua vida e suas obras)*. 2nd ed. São Paulo: Melhoramentos de São Paulo, 1922.

Hagedorn, Nancy L. "'A Friend to Go between Them': The Interpreter as Cultural Broker during Anglo-Iroquois Councils, 1740–1770." *Ethnohistory* 35 (1988): 60–80.

Hanke, Lewis. *The Spanish Struggle for Justice in the Conquest of America*. Dallas: Southern Methodist University Press, 2002.

Hanson, Carl A. *Atlantic Emporium: Portugal and the Wider World, 1147–1497*. New Orleans: University Press of the South, 2001.

————. *Economy and Society in Baroque Portugal, 1668–1703*. Minneapolis: University of Minnesota Press, 1981.

Hein, Jeanne. "Portuguese Communication with Africa on the Searoute to India." *Terrae Incognitae* 25 (1993): 41–51.

Hemming, John. *Red Gold: The Conquest of the Brazilian Indians*. Cambridge: Harvard University Press, 1978.

Henningsen, Gustav, John Tedeschi, and Charles Amiel, eds. *The Inquisition in Early Modern Europe: Studies on Sources and Methods*. Dekalb: Northern Illinois University Press, 1986.

Herbert, Eugenia W. "Portuguese Adaptations to Trade Patterns: Guinea to Angola (1443–1640)." *African Studies Review* 17 (1974): 411–423.

Hermann, Jacqueline. *No reino do desejado: A construção do sebastianismo em Portugal séculos XVI e XVII*. São Paulo: Companhia das Letras, 1998.

Heywood, Linda M., ed. *Central Africans and Cultural Transformations in the American Diaspora*. Cambridge: Cambridge University Press, 2002.

Higgins, Brian T. "Pica." In Kiple, *The Cambridge World History of Human Disease*, 927–931.

Hilbert, Klaus. "A descoberta a partir da 'Nova gazeta da terra do Brasil.'" *Estudos Ibero-Americanos* (Rio Grande do Sul, Brazil) Edição Especial no. 1 (2000): 39–56.

Hinderaker, Eric. "Translation and Cultural Brokerage." In *A Companion to American Indian History*, ed. Philip J. Deloria and Neal Salisbury, 357–375. Malden, Mass.: Blackwell Publishers, 2002.

Hopkins, Donald R. *Princes and Peasants: Smallpox in History.* Chicago: University of Chicago Press, 1983. New edition titled *The Greatest Killer: Smallpox in History.* Chicago: University of Chicago Press, 2002.

Innes, Frank C. "Disease Ecologies of North America." In Kiple, *The Cambridge World History of Human Disease,* 519–535.

Isaacman, Allen, and Barbara Isaacman. "The Prazeros as Transfrontiersmen: A Study in Social and Cultural Change." *The International Journal of African Historical Studies* 8 (1975): 1–39.

Johnson, H. B. "Portuguese Settlement, 1500–1580." In Bethell, *Colonial Brazil,* 1–38.

Jourdin, Michel Mollat du, and Monique de La Roncière. *Sea Charts of the Early Explorers, Thirteenth to Seventeenth Century.* Trans. L. le R. Dethan. New York: Thames and Hudson, 1984.

Kamen, Henry. *Inquisition and Society in Spain in the Sixteenth and Seventeenth Centuries.* London: Weidenfeld and Nicolson, 1985.

Karasch, Mary. "Damiana da Cunha: Catechist and *sertanista.*" In *Struggle and Survival in Colonial America,* ed. David G. Sweet and Gary B. Nash, 102–120. Berkeley: University of California Press, 1981.

———. "Disease Ecologies of South America." In Kiple, *The Cambridge World History of Human Disease,* 535–543.

Karttunen, Frances. *Between Worlds: Interpreters, Guides, and Survivors.* New Brunswick: Rutgers University Press, 1994.

Kellog, Susan. *Law and the Transformation of Aztec Culture: 1500–1700.* Norman: University of Oklahoma Press, 1995.

Kiple, Kenneth F., ed. *The African Exchange: Toward a Biological History of Black People.* Durham: Duke University Press, 1988.

———, ed. *The Cambridge World History of Human Disease.* Cambridge: Cambridge University Press, 1993.

———. "Disease Ecologies of the Caribbean." In Kiple, *The Cambridge World History of Human Disease,* 497–504.

———. "Response to Sheldon Watts, 'Yellow Fever Immunities in West Africa and the Americas in the Age of Slavery and Beyond.'" *Journal of Social History* 34 (2001): 955.

Kiple, Kenneth F., and Stephen V. Beck. *Biological Consequences of European Expansion, 1450–1800.* Vol. 26, *An Expanding World: The European Impact on World History 1450–1800.* Aldershot, Hampshire: Variorum, Ashgate Publishing, 1997.

Kiple, Kenneth F., and Brian T. Higgins. "Yellow Fever and the Africanization of the Caribbean." In *Disease and Demography in the Americas,* ed. John W. Verano and Douglas H. Ubelaker, 237–248. Washington, D.C.: Smithsonian Institution Press, 1992.

Lamalle, Edmond, S.J. "L'Archivio generale di un grande ordine religioso: Quello della compagnia di Gesú." *Archiva Ecclesiae: Bollettino dell'Associazione Archivistica Ecclesiastica* 24−25 (1981−1982): 89−120.

Lane, Frederic Chapin. *Venice: A Maritime Republic.* Baltimore: Johns Hopkins University Press, 1973.

Lanternari, Vittorio. *The Religions of the Oppressed: A Study of Modern Messianic Cults.* Trans. Lisa Sergio. New York: Alfred A. Knopf, 1963.

Lanyon, Anna. *Malinche's Conquest.* St. Leonards, NSW, Australia: Allen and Unwin, 1999.

Leite, Edgard. *Homens vindos do céu: Contatos religiosos no litoral da América portuguesa, séculos XVI e XVII.* Rio de Janeiro: Papéis e Cópias, 1997.

Leite, Serafim, S.J. "Os 'Capítulos' de Gabriel Soares de Sousa." *Ethnos: Revista do Instituto Portuguêsa de Arqueologia, História e Ethnografia* 2 (1942): 217−248.

———. *Os 'Capítulos' de Gabriel Soares de Sousa.* Rio de Janeiro: Imprensa Nacional, 1945.

———. "Cipriano de Brasil, primeiro Jesuita filho de América (1540−1563)." *Verbum* [Rio de Janeiro] 9 (1952): 469−476.

———. *História da Companhia de Jesus no Brasil.* Vols. 1−3. Rio de Janeiro: Civilização Brasileiro, 1938.

Leite, Solidonio. *Os Judeus no Brasil.* Rio de Janeiro: J. Leite e Cia., 1923.

Lestringant, Frank. *Cannibals: The Discovery and Representation of the Cannibal from Columbus to Jules Verne.* Trans. Rosemary Morris. Berkeley: University of California Press, 1997.

———. *Mapping the Renaissance World: The Geographical Imagination in the Age of Discovery.* Trans. David Fausett. Berkeley: University of California Press, 1994.

———. "The Philosopher's Breviary: Jean de Léry in the Enlightenment." *Representations* 33 (1991): 200−211.

Levenson, Jay A., ed. *Circa 1492: Art in the Age of Exploration.* Washington, D.C.: National Gallery of Art; New Haven: Yale University Press, 1991.

Levine, Robert M. *Vale of Tears: Revisiting the Canudos Massacre in Northeastern Brazil, 1893−1897.* Berkeley: University of California Press, 1992.

Lipiner, Elias. *Os judaizantes nas capitanias de cima.* São Paulo: Editôra Brasiliense, 1969.

Lockhart, James. *The Men of Cajamarca: A Social and Biographical Study of the First Conquerors of Peru.* Austin: University of Texas Press, 1972.

———. *Spanish Peru, 1532−1560: A Colonial Society.* Madison: University of Wisconsin Press, 1968.

Lovejoy, Paul E. *Transformations in Slavery: A History of Slavery in Africa.* Cambridge: Cambridge University Press, 1983.

Lovell, George. *Conquest and Survival in Colonial Guatemala: A Historical Geography of the Cuchumatán Highlands, 1500−1821.* Rev. ed. Montreal and Kingston: McGill-Queen's University Press, 1992.

Luis, Washington. "O testamento de João Ramalho." *Revista do Instituto Histórico e Geográfico de São Paulo* 9 (1904): 563−569.

MacCormack, Sabine. *Religion in the Andes: Vision and Imagination in Early Colonial Peru*. Princeton: Princeton University Press, 1991.

MacGaffey, Wyatt. *Religion and Society in Central Africa: The BaKongo of Lower Zaire*. Chicago: The University of Chicago Press, 1986.

Manzano Manzano, Juan. *Los Pinzones y el descubrimiento de América*. 3 vols. Madrid: Ediciones de Cultura Hispánica, 1988.

Marchant, Alexander. *From Barter to Slavery: The Economic Relations of Portuguese and Indians in the Settlement of Brazil, 1500–1580*. Baltimore: Johns Hopkins University Press, 1942. Reprint, Gloucester, Mass.: Peter Smith, 1966.

Marcos, Jesús Varela, ed. *El Tratado de Tordesillas en la cartografía histórica*. Valladolid: Junta de Castilla y León, 1994.

Marques, Alfredo Pinheiro. "L'Atlas Miller: Un problème résolu. L'Art dans la cartographie portugaise." *Revue de la Bibliothèque Nationale de France* 4 (Winter 1994): 53–56.

———. *Portugal and the European Discovery of America: Christopher Columbus and the Portuguese*. Lisbon: Casa da Moeda, 1992.

Marsden, R. G. "Voyage of the 'Barbara' of London to Brazil in 1540." *English Historical Review* 24 (1909): 96–100.

Martin, A. Lynn. *The Jesuit Mind: The Mentality of an Elite in Early Modern France*. Ithaca and London: Cornell University Press, 1988.

Massing, Jean Michel. "The Quest for the Exotic: Albrecht Dürer in the Netherlands." In *Circa 1492: Art in the Age of Exploration*, ed. Jay A. Levenson, 115–119. Washington, D.C.: National Gallery of Art; New Haven: Yale University Press, 1991.

Mathew, K. S. *Indo-Portuguese Trade and the Fuggers of Germany: Sixteenth Century*. New Delhi: Manohar, 1997.

Matta, Roberto da. "Religion and Modernity: Three Studies of Brazilian Religiosity." *Journal of Social History* 25 (1991): 389–406.

Mattoso, Kátia M. de Queirós. "Bahia opulenta: Uma capital portuguêsa no novo mundo (1549–1763)." *Revista de História* 114 (1983): 5–20.

Mattoso, Kátia M. de Queirós, et al., eds. *Naissance du Brésil moderne, 1500–1808*. Paris: Presses de l'Université de Paris-Sorbonne, 1988.

McCoog, Thomas M., ed. *The Mercurian Project: Forming Jesuit Culture, 1573–1580*. Rome: Institutum Historicum Societatis Iesu; St. Louis: The Institute of Jesuit Sources, 2004.

McGeagh, Robert. "Thomas Fields and the Precursors of the Guaraní *Reducciones*." *Colonial Latin American Historical Review* 2 (1993): 35–56.

McNeil, William H. *Plagues and Peoples*. New York: Anchor Books, 1998.

Medina, João, ed. *Os descobrimentos*. Vol. 4, *História de Portugal dos tempos pré-históricos aos nossos dias*. Amadora, Portugal: Ediclube, 1995.

Medina, José Toribio. *El veneciano Sebastián Caboto al servicio de España*. Santiago, Chile: Imprenta y Encuadernación Universitaria, 1908.

Melville, Elinor G. K. *A Plague of Sheep: Environmental Consequences of the Conquest of Mexico*. Cambridge: Cambridge University Press, 1994.

Menchi, Silvana Seidel. "Inquisizione come repressione o inquisizione come mediazione?" *Annuario dell'Instituto Storico Italiano per l'età moderna e contemporanea* 35–36 (1983–1984): 53–77.

Mendonça, José Lourenço D. de, and Antonio Joaquim Moreira. *História dos principais actos e procedimentos da inquisição em Portugal.* Lisbon: Imprensa Nacional, Casa da Moeda, 1980.

Menezes, Raimundo de. *Aconteceu no velho São Paulo.* Coleção Saraiva. São Paulo, 1954.

Menninger, Annerose, Michaela Schmölz-Häberlein, and Mark Häberlein. "Hans Staden, Neil L. Whitehead, and the Cultural Politics of Scholarly Publishing." *Hispanic American Historical Review* 81 (2001): 748.

Merrell, James H. "'The Customes of Our Countrey': Indians and Colonists in Early America." In *Strangers within the Realm: Cultural Margins of the First British Empire,* ed. Bernard Bailyn and Philip D. Morgan, 117–156. Chapel Hill: Institute of Early American History and Culture and University of North Carolina Press, 1991.

———. *Into the American Woods: Negotiators on the Pennsylvania Frontier.* New York: W. W. Norton, 1999.

Metcalf, Alida C. "*AHR Forum:* Millenarian Slaves? The Santidade de Jaguaripe and Slave Resistance in the Americas." *American Historical Review* 104 (1999): 1531–1559.

———. "Álvaro Rodrigues: Um intermediário no mundo português." In *Sexualidade, família e religião na colonização do Brasil,* ed. Maria Beatriz Nizza da Silva, 37–45. Lisbon: Livros Horizonte, 2001.

———. "Domingos Fernandes Nobre: 'Tomacauna,' a Go-Between in Sixteenth-Century Brazil." In *The Human Tradition in Colonial Latin America,* ed. Kenneth J. Andrien, 51–63. Wilmington, Del.: Scholarly Resources, 2002.

———. "Escravos milenários? Messiânismo e resistência à escradivão no Brasil seiscentista." In *Brasil: Colonização e escravidão,* ed. Maria Beatriz Nizza da Silva, 311–323. Rio de Janeiro: Nova Fronteira, 2000.

———. "Intermediários no mundo português: Lançados, pombeiros, e mamelucos do século XVI." *Annais da Sociedade Brasileira de Pesquisa Histórica* 13 (1997): 3–13.

———. "O Jesuita como intermediário na Baía nos fins do século XVI." In *De Cabral a Pedro I: Aspectos da colonização portuguesa no Brasil,* ed. Maria Beatriz Nizza da Silva, 79–88. Porto: Universidade Portucalense Infante D. Henrique, 2001.

———. "Jesuits in Brazil: Defining the Vision." In *The Mercurian Project: Forming Jesuit Culture, 1573–1580,* ed. Thomas M. McCoog, S.J., 787–814. Rome: Institutum Historicum Societatis Iesu; St. Louis: The Institute of Jesuit Sources, 2004.

———. "Os limites da troca cultural: O culto da Santidade no Brasil colonial." In *Cultura portuguesa na terra de Santa Cruz,* ed. Maria Beatriz Nizza da Silva, 35–52. Lisbon: Editorial Estampa, 1995.

Métraux, Alfred. "Messiahs of South America." *The Interamerican Quarterly* 3, no. 2 (1941): 53–60.

————. "Migrations historiques des Tupi-Guarani." *Journal de la Société des Américanistes de Paris* 19 (1931): 1–47.

————. *A religião dos Tupinambás e suas relações com a das demais tribos Tupi-Guaranis.* 2nd. ed. Trans. Estêvão Pinto. São Paulo: Companhia Editora Nacional, 1979.

————. *La religion des Tupinamba et ses rapports avec celle des autres tribus Tupi-Guarani.* Paris: Librairie Ernest Leroux, 1928.

Meyerson, Mark D. *The Muslims of Valencia: In the Age of Fernando and Isabel, between Coexistence and Crusade.* Berkeley: University of California Press, 1991.

Miller, Joseph C. "Central Africa during the Era of the Slave Trade." In Heywood, *Central Africans and Cultural Transformations in the American Diaspora,* 21–69.

————. "The Significance of Drought, Disease, and Famine in the Agriculturally Marginal Zones of West-Central Africa." *The Journal of African History* 23 (1982): 23–24.

Miller, Shawn William. *Fruitless Trees: Portuguese Conservation and Brazil's Colonial Timber.* Stanford: Stanford University Press, 2000.

Monteiro, John Manuel. "The Crises and Transformations of Invaded Societies: Coastal Brazil in the Sixteenth Century." In *The Cambridge History of Native Peoples of the Americas,* ed. Frank Salomon and Stuart Schwartz, Vol. 3, *South America, Part One,* 981–990. Cambridge: Cambridge University Press, 1999.

————. "A dança dos números: A população indígena no Brasil desde 1500." *Tempo e Presença* 16, no. 273 (1994): 17–18.

————. "From Indian to Slave: Forced Native Labour and Colonial Society in São Paulo during the Seventeenth Century." *Slavery and Abolition* 9 (1988): 105–127.

————. "The Heathen Castes of Sixteenth-Century Portuguese America: Unity, Diversity, and the Invention of the Brazilian Indians." *Hispanic American Historical Review* 80 (2000): 697–719.

————. *Negros da terra: Índios e bandeirantes nas origens de São Paulo.* São Paulo: Editora Schwarcz, 1994.

Monter, William. *Frontiers of Heresy: The Spanish Inquisition from the Basque Lands to Sicily.* Cambridge: Cambridge University Press, 1990.

Moreira, Manuel Antonio Fernandes. *Os mareantes de Viana e a construção da Atlantidade.* Viana do Castelo, Portugal: Câmara Municipal, 1994.

Mota, A. Teixeira da. *Novos documentos sobre uma expedição de Gonçalo Coelho ao Brasil, entre 1503 e 1505.* Lisbon: Junta de Investigações do Ultramar, 1969.

Mott, Luiz R. B. "Acotunda: Raízes setecentistas do sincretismo religioso afro-brasileiro." *Revista do Museu Paulista* 31 (1986): 124–147.

————. *Escravidão, homossexualidade e demonologia.* São Paulo: Ícone Editora, 1988.

Mundy, Barbara E. *The Mapping of New Spain: Indigenous Cartography and the Maps of the Relaciones Geográficas.* Chicago: University of Chicago Press, 2000.

Murase, Miyeko, ed. *Turning Point: Oribe and the Arts of Sixteenth-Century Japan.* New York and New Haven: Metropolitan Musuem of Art and Yale University Press, 2003.

Myscofski, Carole. "Messianic Themes in Portuguese and Brazilian Literature in the Sixteenth and Seventeenth Centuries." *Luso Brazilian Review* 28 (1991): 77–94.

Nascimento Raposo, José do. "Social Characteristics of Those Accused before the Coimbra Inquisition, 1541–1820." *Revue des Etudes Juives* 141 (1982): 201–217.

Nimuendajú-Unkel, Curt. *Los mitos de creación y de destrucción del mundo como fundamentos de la religión de los apapokuva-guaraní.* [1914]. Ed. Jürgen Riester. Lima: Centro Amazónico de Antropología y Aplicación Práctica, 1978.

Novinsky, Anita. *Cristãos-novos na Bahia, 1624–1654.* São Paulo: Editora Perspectiva, 1972.

O'Callaghan, Joseph F. *Reconquest and Crusade in Medieval Spain.* Philadelphia: University of Pennsylvania Press, 2003.

Oettinger, Marion, and Fernando Horcasitas. *The Lienzo of Petlacala: A Pictorial Document from Guerrero, Mexico.* Philadelphia: American Philosophical Society, 1982.

Oliver, Roland, ed. *The Cambridge History of Africa.* Vol. 3, *From c. 1050 to c. 1600.* Cambridge: Cambridge University Press, 1977.

O'Malley, John W. *The First Jesuits.* Cambridge, Mass.: Harvard University Press, 1993.

Pagden, Anthony. *The Fall of Natural Man: The American Indian and the Origins of Comparative Ethnology.* Cambridge: Cambridge University Press, 1982.

Paine, Robert, ed. *Patrons and Brokers in the East Arctic.* Newfoundland Social and Economic Papers no. 2. Newfoundland: Institute of Social and Economic Research, Memorial University of Newfoundland, 1971.

Park, Katharine. "Black Death." In Kiple, *The Cambridge World History of Human Disease,* 612–616.

Paz, Octavio. *El laberinto de la soledad.* Mexico City: Fondo de Cultura Económica, 1959.

Pearson, M. N. *The Portuguese in India.* Cambridge: Cambridge University Press, 1987.

Pennisi, Elizabeth. "Cannibalism and Prion Disease May Have Been Rampant in Ancient Humans." *Science* 300, no. 5617 (2003): 227–229.

Pereira, Moacyr Soares. *A navegação de 1501 ao Brasil e Américo Vespúcio.* Rio de Janeiro: ASA Artes Gráficas, 1984.

Perrone-Moisés, Leyla. *Vinte luas: Viagem de Paulmier de Gonneville ao Brasil, 1503–1505.* São Paulo: Companhia das Letras, 1992.

Perry, Mary Elizabeth, and Anne J. Cruz. *Cultural Encounters: The Impact of the Inquisition in Spain and the New World.* Berkeley: University of California Press, 1991.

Pessar, Patricia R. *From Fanatics to Folk: Brazilian Millenarianism and Popular Culture.* Durham: Duke University Press, 2004.

————. "Three Moments in Brazilian Millenarianism: The Interrelationship between Politics and Religion." *Luso Brazilian Review* 28 (1991): 95–116.

Pieroni, Geraldo. *Os excluídos do reino: A Inquisição portuguesa e o degredo para o Brasil colônia.* Brasília: Editora Universidade de Brasília, 2000; São Paulo: Imprensa Oficial do Estado, 2000.

Pinto, Maria do Carmo Teixeira, and Lucilia Maria Ferreira. "Inquisição de Evora: Dez anos de funcionamento (1541–1550)." *Revista de História Económica e Social* 22 (1988): 51–76.

Poirier, Jacques, and Christian Derouesné. "Apoplexy and Stroke." In Kiple, *The Cambridge World History of Human Disease,* 584–587.

Porto, José da Costa. *Nos tempos do visitador: Subsídio ao estudo da vida colonial pernambucana, nos fins do século XVI.* Recife: Universidade Federal de Pernambuco, 1968.

Prado, J. F. de Almeida. *Pernambuco e as capitanias do norte do Brasil.* São Paulo: Compania Editora Nacional, 1939.

————. *Primeiros povoadores do Brasil, 1500–1530.* São Paulo: Companhia Editora Nacional, 1939.

Prestholdt, Jeremy. "Portuguese Conceptual Categories and the 'Other' Encounter on the Swahili Coast." *Journal of Asian and African Studies* 36 (2001): 383–407.

Queija, Berta Ares. "El papel de mediadores y la construcción de un discurso sobre la identidad de los mestizos peruanos (siglo XVI)." In Queija and Gruzinski, *Entre dos mundos,* 37–38.

Queija, Berta Ares, and Serge Gruzinski, eds. *Entre dos mundos: Fronteras culturales y agentes mediadores.* Seville: Escuela de Estudios Hispano-Americanos, 1997.

Queiroz, Maria Isaura Pereira de. *O messianismo no Brasil e no mundo.* São Paulo: Dominus Editora, 1965.

Quirino, Tarcízio Rêgo. *Os habitantes do Brazil no fim do século XVI.* Recife: Instituto de Ciencia do Homen, 1966.

Ramenofsky, Ann. "Diseases of the Americas, 1492–1700." In Kiple, The Cambridge World History of Human Disease, 317–328.

Raminelli, Ronald. "Da vila ao sertão: Os mamelucos como agentes da colonização." *Revista de História* 58 (1993/1994): 209–219.

————. "Eva Tupinamba." In *História das mulheres no Brasil,* ed. Mary del Priore and Carla Bassanezi, 11–44. São Paulo: Editora Contexto, 1997.

Reeves, Marjorie. *The Influence of Prophecy in the Later Middle Ages: A Study in Joachimism.* Notre Dame: University of Notre Dame Press, 1993.

Reis, João José, and Flávio dos Santos Gomes, eds. *Liberdade por um fio: História dos quilombos no Brasil.* São Paulo: Companhia das Letras, 1996.

Reis, Paulo Pereira dos. *O indígena do vale do Paraíba.* São Paulo: Governo do Estado de São Paulo, 1979.

Ribeiro, René. "Brazilian Messianic Movements." In Thrupp, *Millennial Dreams in Action: Studies in Revolutionary Religious Movements,* 55–69.

————. "Messianic Movements in Brazil." *Luso Brazilian Review* 29 (1992): 71–81.

Ricard, Robert. "Algunas enseñanzas de los documentos inquisitoriales del Brasil (1591–1595)." *Anuario de Estudios Americanos* (Seville) 5 (1948): 705–715.

Richter, Daniel K. "Cultural Brokers and Intercultural Politics: New York-Iroquois Relations, 1664–1701." *The Journal of American History* 75 (1988): 40–67.

————. "Iroquois versus Iroquois: Jesuit Missions and Christianity in Village Politics, 1642–1686." *Ethnohistory* 32 (1985): 1–16.

Riley, Carlos. "Ilhas atlânticas e costa africana." In Bethencourt and Chaudhuri, *História da expansão portuguesa*, 1 : 137–162.

Rodney, Walter. *A History of the Upper Guinea Coast: 1545–1800.* New York and London: Monthly Review Press, 1970.

Rodrigues, Francisco. *História da Companhia de Jesus na assistencia de Portugal.* 4 vols. Porto: Apostolado da Imprensa, 1931–1950.

Rogoziński, Jan. *Pirates! Brigands, Buccaneers, and Privateers in Fact, Fiction, and Legend.* New York: Da Capo Press, 1996.

Rowlett, Russ. "How Many? A Dictionary of Units of Measurement." http://www.unc .edu/~rowlett/units/index.html.

Ruggerio, Michael J. *The Evolution of the Go-Between in Spanish Literature through the Sixteenth Century.* Berkeley: University of California Press, 1966.

Russell, Peter. *Prince Henry "the Navigator": A Life.* New Haven: Yale University Press, 2000.

Russell-Wood, A. J. R. "Iberian Expansion and the Issue of Black Slavery: Changing Portuguese Attitudes, 1440–1770." *The American Historical Review* 83 (1978): 16–42.

————. *A World on the Move: The Portuguese in Africa, Asia, and America, 1415–1808.* New York: St. Martin's Press, 1992.

Ryder, A. F. C. *Benin and the Europeans, 1485–1897.* New York: Humanities Press, 1969.

Salisbury, Neal. *Manitou and Providence: Indians, Europeans, and the Making of New England, 1500–1643.* New York and Oxford: Oxford University Press, 1982.

Salvador, José Gonçalves. *Cristãos-novos, jesuítas e Inquisição.* São Paulo: Livraria Pioneira Editora, 1969.

Sandman, Alison. "Mirroring the World: Sea Charts, Navigation, and Territorial Claims in Sixteenth-Century Spain." In *Merchants and Marvels: Commerce, Science, and Art in Early Modern Europe,* ed. Pamela H. Smith and Paula Findlen, 83–108. New York: Routledge, 2002.

Saraiva, António José. *Inquisição e cristãos-novos.* Porto: Editorial Inova, 1969.

Sauer, Carl O. *The Early Spanish Main.* Berkeley: University of California Press, 1966.

Saunders, A. C. de C. M. *A Social History of Black Slaves and Freedmen in Portugal, 1441–1555.* Cambridge: Cambridge University Press, 1982.

Savitt, Todd L. "Filariasis." In Kiple, *The Cambridge World History of Human Disease,* 724–730.

Schaden, Egon. *Aculturação e messianismo entre índios brasileiros*. São Paulo: Escola de Communicações e Artes da Universidade de São Paulo, 1972.

Schwartz, Stuart B. *Sugar Plantations in the Formation of Brazilian Society: Bahia, 1550–1835*. Cambridge: Cambridge University Press, 1985.

Seed, Patricia. *Ceremonies of Possession in Europe's Conquest of the New World, 1492–1640*. Cambridge: Cambridge University Press, 1995.

Shapiro, Judith. "From Tupã to the Land without Evil: The Christianization of Tupi-Guarani Cosmology." *American Ethnologist* 14 (1987): 126–139.

Shirley, Rodney W. *The Mapping of the World: Early Printed World Maps, 1472–1700*. Holland Press Cartographica, 9. London: Holland Press, 1984.

Silva, Maria Beatriz Nizza da, ed. *Brasil: Colonização e escravidão*. Rio de Janeiro: Nova Fronteira, 1999.

———. *Cultura portuguesa na terra de Santa Cruz*. Lisbon: Editorial Estampa, 1995.

———. *De Cabral a Pedro I: Aspectos da colonização portuguesa no Brasil*. Porto: Universidade Portucalense Infante D. Henrique, 2001.

———. *Sexualidade, família e religião na colonização do Brasil*. Lisbon: Livros Horizonte, 2001.

Simmel, Georg. *The Sociology of Georg Simmel*. Trans. Kurt H. Wolff. New York: Free Press, 1950.

Siqueira, Sonia A. "A elaboração da espiritualidade do Brasil colônia: O problema do sincretismo." *Anais do Museu Paulista* 36 (1975): 207–228.

———. *A Inquisição portuguesa e a sociedade colonial*. São Paulo: Editora Ática, 1978.

Sleeper-Smith, Susan. *Indian Women and French Men: Rethinking Cultural Encounter in the Western Great Lakes*. Amherst: University of Massachusetts Press, 2001.

Southey, Robert. *History of Brazil*. 2nd ed. 3 vols. London, 1822. Reprint, New York: Greenwood Press, 1969.

Souza, Laura de Mello e. *The Devil and the Land of the Holy Cross: Witchcraft, Slavery, and Popular Religion in Colonial Brazil*. Trans. Diane Grosklaus Whitty. Austin: University of Texas Press, 2003.

———. *O diabo e a terra de Santa Cruz: Feitiçaria e religiosidade popular no Brasil colonial*. São Paulo: Companhia das Letras, 1986.

———. *Inferno atlântico: Demonologia e colonização, séculos XVI–XVIII*. São Paulo: Companhia das Letras, 1993.

Souza, Marina de. *Reis negros no Brasil escravista: História da festa de coroação de Rei Congo*. Belo Horizonte: Editora UFMA, 2002.

Spufford, Peter. *Money and Its Use in Medieval Europe*. Cambridge: Cambridge University Press, 1988.

Stols, Eddy. "Um dos primeiros documentos sôbre o engenho dos Schetz em São Vicente." *Revista de História* 37 (1968): 415–419.

Sturtevant, William C. "First Visual Images of Native America." In Chiappelli, *First Images of America: The Impact of the New World on the Old*, 1:417–454.

Sweet, James H. "The Iberian Roots of American Racist Thought." *The William and Mary Quarterly*, 3rd ser., 54 (1997): 143–166.

————. *Recreating Africa: Culture, Kinship, and Religion in the African-Portuguese World, 1441–1770*. Chapel Hill: University of North Carolina Press, 2003.

Szasz, Margaret Connell. *Between Indian and White Worlds: The Cultural Broker*. Norman: University of Oklahoma Press, 1994.

Tachot, Louise Bénat, and Serge Gruzinski, eds. *Passeurs culturels: Mécanismes de métissage*. Paris: Presses universitaires de Marne-la-Vallée; Éditions de la Maison des sciences de l'homme, 2001.

Tavares, Luís Henrique Dias. *História da Bahia*. 10th ed. São Paulo: Editora UNESP; Salvador: EDUFBA, 2001.

Taylor, William B. *Magistrates of the Sacred: Priests and Parishioners in Eighteenth-Century Mexico*. Stanford: Stanford University Press, 1996.

Tedeschi, John A. *The Prosecution of Heresy: Collected Studies on the Inquisition in Early Modern Italy*. Binghamton, N.Y.: Medieval and Renaissance Texts and Studies, 1991.

Tenreiro, Francisco. *A Ilha de São Tomé*. Lisbon: Junta de Investigações do Ultramar, 1961.

Thomas, Georg. *Política indigenista dos portugueses no Brasil, 1540–1640*. Trans. Jesus Hortal. São Paulo: Edições Loyola, 1982.

Thornton, John. "The Development of an African Catholic Church in the Kingdom of Kongo, 1491–1750." *Journal of African History* 25 (1984): 147–167.

————. *The Kongolese Saint Anthony: Dona Beatriz Kimpa Vita and the Antonian Movement, 1684–1706*. Cambridge: Cambridge University Press, 1998.

Thrupp, Sylvia L., ed. *Millenial Dreams in Action: Studies in Revolutionary Religious Movements*. New York: Schocken Books, 1970.

Trompf, G. W., ed. *Cargo Cults and Millenarian Movements: Transoceanic Comparisons of New Religious Movements*. Berlin: Mouton de Gruyter, 1990.

Unger, Richard W. "Portuguese Shipbuilding and the Early Voyages to the Guinea Coast." In *Vice-Almirante A. Teixeira da Mota in memoriam I*, 229–249. Lisbon: Academia da Marinha e Instituto de Investigação Científica Tropical, 1987. Reprinted in *The European Opportunity*, ed. Felipe Ferández-Armesto, 2: 43–63. Aldershot, UK: Variorum/Ashgate, 1995.

Vainfas, Ronaldo. "Deus contra Palmares: Representações senhoriais e idéias jesuíticas." In Reis and Gomes, *Liberdade por um fio*, 60–62.

————. *A heresia dos índios: Catolicismo e rebeldia no Brasil colonial*. São Paulo: Companhia das Letras, 1995.

————. "A heresia do trópico: Santidades ameríndias no Brasil colonial." Professor Titular Thesis, Universidade Federal Fluminense, 1993.

————. *História e sexualidade no Brasil*. Rio de Janeiro: Edições Graal, 1986.

————. *Trópico dos pecados: Moral, sexualidade e Inquisição no Brasil*. Rio de Janeiro: Editora Campus, 1989.

Vansina, Jan. "The Kongo Kingdom and Its Neighbors." In *General History of Africa*, Vol. 5, ed. B. A. Ogot., 547–587. London: UNESCO, 1992.

Vaughan, Alden T. "Sir Walter Ralegh's Indian Interpreters, 1584–1618." *The William and Mary Quarterly* 59 (2002): 341–376.

Viotti, Pe. Hélio Abranches, S.J., and Pe. Murillo Moutinho, S.J. *Anchieta nas artes*. 2nd ed. São Paulo: Edições Loyola, 1991.

———. *Anchieta o apóstolo do Brasil*. São Paulo: Edições Loyola, 1966.

Viveiros de Castro, Eduardo. *A inconstância da alma selvagem—e outros ensaios de antropologia*. São Paulo: Cosac & Naify, 2002.

Vogt, John. *Portuguese Rule on the Gold Coast, 1469–1682*. Athens: University of Georgia Press, 1979.

Wadsworth, James E. "In the Name of the Inquisition: The Portuguese Inquisition and Delegated Authority in Colonial Pernambuco, Brazil." *The Americas* 61 (2004): 19–54.

Watts, Sheldon. *Epidemics and History: Disease, Power and Imperialism*. New Haven: Yale University Press, 1997.

———. "Yellow Fever Immunities in West Africa and the Americas in the Age of Slavery and Beyond: A Reappraisal." *Journal of Social History* 34 (2001): 955–968.

White, Richard. *The Middle Ground: Indians, Empires, and Republics in the Great Lakes Region, 1650–1815*. Cambridge: Cambridge University Press, 1991.

Whitehead, Neil L. "Hans Staden and the Cultural Politics of Cannibalism." *Hispanic American Historical Review* 80 (2000) 722–751.

Whitmore, Thomas M. *Disease and Death in Early Colonial Mexico: Simulating Amerindian Depopulation*. Boulder: Westview Press, 1992.

Wilson, Bryan. *Magic and the Millennium*. St. Albans, Herts, U.K.: Paladin, 1975.

Wilson, Mary E. "Travel and the Emergence of Infectious Diseases." *Emerging Infectious Diseases* 1, no. 2 (1995): 39–46.

Wiznitzer, Arnold. *Jews in Colonial Brazil*. New York: Columbia University Press, 1960.

Wolff, Hans, ed. *America: Early Maps of the New World*. Münich: Prestel, 1992.

———. "The Munich Portolan Charts: Past and Present." In Wolff, *America: Early Maps of the New World*, 134–135.

Wolff, Robert S. "Da Gama's Blundering: Trade Encounters in Africa and Asia during the European 'Age of Discovery,' 1450–1520." *The History Teacher* 31 (1998): 306–309.

Zeron, Carlos Alberto. "Les jésuites et le commerce d'esclaves entre le Brésil et l'Angola à la fin du XVIe siècle." http://www.fflch.usp.br/dh/ceveh/public_html/biblioteca/artigas/.

———. "Pombeiros e tangosmaos, intermediários do tráfico de escravos na África (século XVI)." *http://www.fflch.usp.br/dh/ceveh/public_html/biblioteca/artigas/*.

Index

CPSIA information can be obtained
at www.ICGtesting.com
Printed in the USA
FFOW01n0057010515
13063FF